THE AUTOBOOK SERIES OF WORKSHOP MANUALS

Alfa Romeo Giulia 1600, 1750, 2000 1962 on
Aston Martin 1921-58
Auto Union Audi 70, 80, Super 90, 1966-72
Audi 100 1969 on
Austin, Morris etc. 1100 Mk. 1 1962-67
Austin, Morris etc. 1100 Mk. 2, 3, 1300 Mk. 1, 2, 3 America 1968 on
Austin A30, A35, A40 Farina 1951-67
Austin A55 Mk. 2, A60 1958-69
Austin A99, A110 1959-68
Austin J4 1960 on
Austin Maxi 1969 on
Austin, Morris 1800 1964 on
Austin, Morris 2200 1972 on
Austin Kimberley, Tasman 1970 on
Austin, Morris 1300, 1500 Nomad 1969 on
BMC 3 (Austin A50, A55 Mk. 1, Morris Oxford 2, 3 1954-59)
Austin Healey 100/6, 3000 1956-68
Austin Healey, MG Sprite, Midget 1958 on
Bedford CA Mk. 2 1964-69
Bedford CF Vans 1969 on
Bedford Beagle HA Vans 1964 on
BMW 1600 1966 on
BMW 1800 1964-71
BMW 2000, 2002 1966 on
Chevrolet Corvair 1960-69
Chevrolet Corvette V8 1957-65
Chevrolet Corvette V8 1965 on
Chevrolet Vega 2300 1970 on
Chrysler Valiant V8 1965 on
Chrysler Valiant Straight Six 1963 on
Citroen DS 19, ID 19 1955-66
Citroen ID 19, DS 19, 20, 21 1966 on
Citroen Dyane Ami 1964 on
Daf 31, 32, 33, 44, 55 1961 on
Datsun Bluebird 610 series 1972 on
Datsun Cherry 100A, 120A 1971 on
Datsun 1000, 1200 1968 on
Datsun 1300, 1400, 1600 1968 on
Datsun 240C 1971 on
Datsun 240Z Sport 1970 on
Fiat 124 1966 on
Fiat 124 Sport 1966 on
Fiat 125 1967-72
Fiat 127 1971 on
Fiat 128 1969 on
Fiat 500 1957 on
Fiat 600, 600D 1955-69
Fiat 850 1964 on
Fiat 1100 1957-69
Fiat 1300, 1500 1961-67
Ford Anglia Prefect 100E 1953-62
Ford Anglia 105E, Prefect 107E 1959-67
Ford Capri 1300, 1600 OHV 1968 on
Ford Capri 1300, 1600, 200 OHC 1972 on
Ford Capri 2000 V4, 3000 V6 1969 on
Ford Classic, Capri 1961-64
Ford Consul, Zephyr, Zodiac, 1, 2 1950-62
Ford Corsair Straight Four 1963-65
Ford Corsair V4 1965-68
Ford Corsair V4 2000 1969-70
Ford Cortina 1962-66
Ford Cortina 1967-68
Ford Cortina 1969-70
Ford Cortina Mk. 3 1970 on
Ford Escort 1967 on
Ford Falcon 6 1964-70
Ford Falcon XK, XL 1960-63
Ford Falcon 6 XR/XA 1966 on
Ford Falcon V8 (U.S.A.) 1965-71
Ford Falcon V8 (Aust.) 1966 on
Ford Pinto 1970 on
Ford Maverick 6 1969 on
Ford Maverick V8 1970 on
Ford Mustang 6 1965 on
Ford Mustang V8 1965 on
Ford Thames 10, 12, 15 cwt 1957-65
Ford Transit V4 1965 on
Ford Zephyr Zodiac Mk. 3 1962-66
Ford Zephyr Zodiac V4, V6, Mk. 4 1966-72
Ford Consul, Granada 1972 on
Hillman Avenger 1970 on
Hillman Hunter 1966 on
Hillman Imp 1963-68
Hillman Imp 1969 on
Hillman Minx 1 to 5 1956-65
Hillman Minx 1965-67
Hillman Minx 1966-70
Hillman Super Minx 1961-65
Jaguar XK120, 140, 150, Mk. 7, 8, 9 1948-61
Jaguar 2.4, 3.4, 3.8 Mk. 1, 2 1955-69
Jaguar 'E' Type 1961-72
Jaguar 'S' Type 420 1963-68
Jaguar XJ6 1968 on
Jowett Javelin Jupiter 1947-53
Landrover 1, 2 1948-61
Landrover 2, 2a, 3 1959 on
Mazda 616 1970 on
Mazda 808, 818 1972 on
Mazda 1200, 1300 1969 on
Mazda 1500, 1800 1967 on
Mazda RX-2 1971 on
Mazda R100, RX-3 1970 on
Mercedes-Benz 190b, 190c, 200 1959-68
Mercedes-Benz 220 1959-65
Mercedes-Benz 220/8 1968 on
Mercedes-Benz 230 1963-68
Mercedes-Benz 250 1965-67
Mercedes-Benz 250 1968 on
Mercedes-Benz 280 1968 on
MG TA to TF 1936-55
MGA MGB 1955-68
MGB 1969 on
Mini 1959 on
Mini Cooper 1961-72
Morgan Four 1936-72
Morris Marina 1971 on
Morris (Aust) Marina 1972 on
Morris Minor 2, 1000 1952-71
Morris Oxford 5, 6 1959-71
NSU 1000 1963-72
NSU Prinz 1 to 4 1957-72
Opel Ascona, Manta 1970 on
Opel GT 1900 1968 on
Opel Kadett, Olympia 993 cc 1078 cc 1962 on
Opel Kadett, Olympia 1492, 1698, 1897 cc 1967 on
Opel Rekord C 1966-72
Peugeot 204 1965 on
Peugeot 304 1970 on
Peugeot 404 1960 on
Peugeot 504 1968 on
Porsche 356A, B, C 1957-65
Porsche 911 1964-69
Porsche 912 1965-69
Porsche 914 S 1969 on
Reliant Regal 1952-73
Renault R4, R4L, 4 1961 on
Renault 5 1972 on
Renault 6 1968 on
Renault 8, 10, 1100 1962-71
Renault 12, 1969 on
Renault 15, 17 1971 on
Renault R16 1965 on
Renault Dauphine Floride 1957-67
Renault Caravelle 1962-68
Rover 60 to 110 1953-64
Rover 2000 1963-73
Rover 3 Litre 1958-67
Rover 3500, 3500S 1968 on
Saab 95, 96, Sport 1960-68
Saab 99 1969 on
Saab V4 1966 on
Simca 1000 1961 on
Simca 1100 1967 on
Simca 1300, 1301, 1500, 1501 1963 on
Skoda One (440, 445, 450) 1955-70
Sunbeam Rapier Alpine 1955-65
Toyota Carina, Celica 1971 on
Toyota Corolla 1100, 1200 1967 on
Toyota Corona 1500 Mk. 1 1965-70
Toyota Corona Mk. 2 1969 on
Triumph TR2, TR3, TR3A 1952-62
Triumph TR4, TR4A 1961-67
Triumph TR5, TR250, TR6 1967 on
Triumph 1300, 1500 1965-73
Triumph 2000 Mk. 1, 2.5 PI Mk. 1 1963-69
Triumph 2000 Mk. 2, 2.5 PI Mk. 2 1969 on
Triumph Dolomite 1972 on
Triumph Herald 1959-68
Triumph Herald 1969-71
Triumph Spitfire, Vitesse 1962-68
Triumph Spitfire Mk. 3, 4 1969 on
Triumph GT6, Vitesse 2 Litre 1969 on
Triumph Stag 1970 on
Triumph Toledo 1970 on
Vauxhall Velox, Cresta 1957-72
Vauxhall Victor 1, 2, FB 1957-64
Vauxhall Victor 101 1964-67
Vauxhall Victor FD 1600, 2000 1967-72
Vauxhall Victor 3300, Ventora 1968-72
Vauxhall Victor FE Ventora 1972 on
Vauxhall Viva HA 1963-66
Vauxhall Viva HB 1966-70
Vauxhall Viva, HC Firenza 1971 on
Volkswagen Beetle 1954-67
Volkswagen Beetle 1968 on
Volkswagen 1500 1961-66
Volkswagen 1600 Fastback 1965-73
Volkswagen Transporter 1954-67
Volkswagen Transporter 1968 on
Volkswagen 411 1968-72
Volvo 120 series 1961-70
Volvo 140 series 1966 on
Volvo 160 series 1968 on
Volvo 1800 1960-73

Hillman Avenger 1970-73 Autobook

By Kenneth Ball
Associate Member, Guild of Motoring Writers
and the Autopress Team of Technical Writers.

Hillman Avenger 1248cc 1970-73
Hillman Avenger 1498cc 1970-73
Hillman Avenger GT 1498cc 1970-73
Sunbeam 1250 1970-73
Sunbeam 1500 1970-73
Plymouth Cricket 1972-73

Damage Recorded

Autobooks

Autopress Ltd. Golden Lane Brighton BN1 2QJ England

The AUTOBOOK series of Workshop Manuals is the largest in the world and covers the majority of British and Continental motor cars, as well as all major Japanese and Australian models. For a full list see the back of this manual.

CONTENTS

ISBN 0 85147 367 9

First Edition 1971
Reprinted 1971
Second Edition, fully revised 1972
Third Edition, fully revised 1973
Reprinted 1973
Reprinted 1974

820

Printed and bound in Brighton England for Autopress Ltd by G Beard & Son Ltd A

ACKNOWLEDGEMENT

My thanks are due to Chrysler (UK) Ltd for their unstinted co-operation and also for supplying data and illustrations.

I am also grateful to a considerable number of owners who have discussed their cars at length and many of whose suggestions have been included in this manual.

Kenneth Ball
Associate Member, Guild of Motoring Writers
Ditchling Sussex England.

INTRODUCTION

This do-it-yourself Workshop Manual has been specially written for the owner who wishes to maintain his car in first class condition and to carry out his own servicing and repairs. Considerable savings on garage charges can be made, and one can drive in safety and confidence knowing the work has been done properly.

Comprehensive step-by-step instructions and illustrations are given on all dismantling, overhauling and assembling operations. Certain assemblies require the use of expensive special tools, the purchase of which would be unjustified. In these cases information is included but the reader is recommended to hand the unit to the agent for attention.

Throughout the Manual hints and tips are included which will be found invaluable, and there is an easy to follow fault diagnosis at the end of each chapter.

Whilst every care has been taken to ensure correctness of information it is obviously not possible to guarantee complete freedom from errors or to accept liability arising from such errors or omissions.

Instructions may refer to the righthand or lefthand sides of the vehicle or the components. These are the same as the righthand or lefthand of an observer standing behind the car and looking forward.

CHAPTER 1

THE ENGINE

1 :1 Description

The Avenger 1250 and 1500 cc engines are four cylinder units with a nominal stroke of 64.3 mm and a nominal bore of 78.6 mm and 86.1 mm respectively. The engine incorporates a cast iron cylinder head giving a compression ratio of 9.2:1—the smaller unit also being available with a compression ratio of 8.1 :1 for areas where only low octane fuels are available—with overhead valves operated by rockers, pushrods and a high lift 3-bearing camshaft, and a 5-bearing crankshaft. Ignition is by battery and coil from a negative earth system charged from a belt driven generator or, in the GT and GLS, which now replaces the GT, a belt driven alternator with integral rectifiers and a transistorized regulator. Vehicles equipped with a heated rear window are also fitted with alternators.

Fuel from the rear tank is supplied to the carburetter(s) by a mechanically operated diaphragm pump, driven from the camshaft and the carburetter installation is a single Stromberg Zenith CDS.150 side-draught carburetter or, on the GT, twin carburetters of the same type. The American version, the Plymouth Cricket, and other export models can be fitted with the Stromberg CDSE carburetter(s) to comply with the requirements of Federal and local regulations for a low hydrocarbon and carbon monoxide content in the exhaust.

The maximum bhp developed by the 1250 cc engine is 53 at 5000 rev/min and for the 1500 cc engine 63 at 5000 rev/min. The latter engine with twin carburetters on the GT model develops 75 bhp at 5400 rev/min. The corresponding maximum torques are 66 lb ft at 3000 rev/min, 80 lb ft at 3000 rev/min and 81 lb ft at 3750 rev/min.

Engine cooling is by a conventional system comprising centrifugal pump and fan, pressurized radiator and thermostat. The system also provides hot water to the air heating radiator in the ventilating system.

The engine, with integral gearbox and clutch or automatic gearbox and torque converter, is mounted in the front of the car under the bonnet on vibration dampers. An exploded view of the working parts is shown in **FIG 1 :1** and of the sump, cylinder block, head and casings in **FIG 1 :2**.

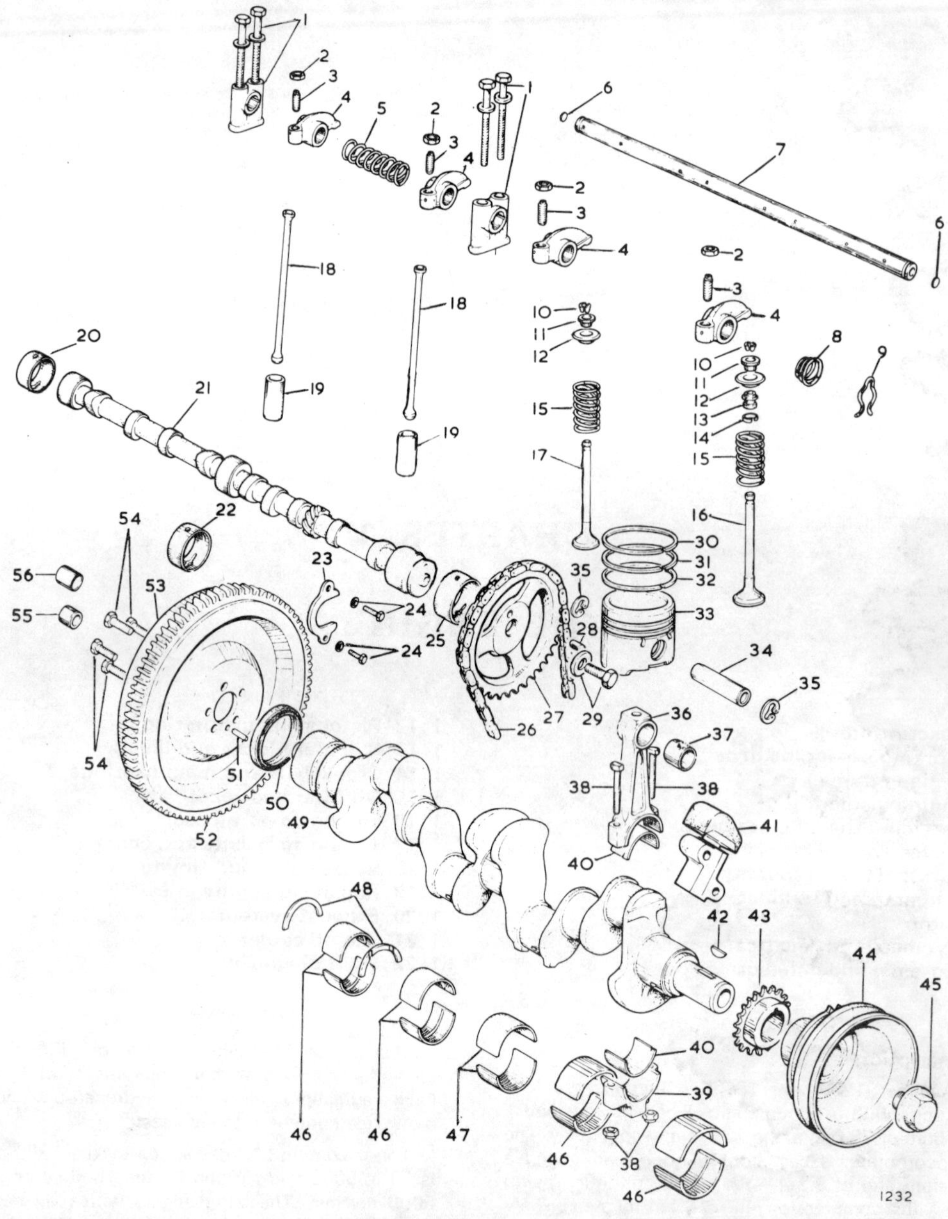

FIG 1:1 Exploded view of working parts of the Avenger engine

Key to Fig 1:1 1 Rocker shaft carrier and fixing bolts 2 Rocker adjustment locknut 3 Rocker adjustment screw 4 Valve rocker 5 Inner spring between rockers 6 Rocker shaft end plugs 7 Rocker shaft 8 Outer spring 9 Outer spring retainer 10 Valve cotters 11 Inner collar 12 Valve spring cap 13 Oil seal (inlet valve only) 14 Oil seal retainer 15 Valve spring 16 Inlet valve 17 Exhaust valve 18 Pushrod 19 Valve lifter tappet 20 Camshaft rear bearing 21 Camshaft 22 Camshaft centre bearing 23 Camshaft thrust plate 24 Thrust plate fixing screws 25 Camshaft front bearing 26 Timing chain 27 Camshaft sprocket 28 Camshaft sprocket dowel 29 Camshaft sprocket fixing screw and washer 30 Top piston ring (chromium plated) 31 Second piston ring (stepped type) 32 Oil scraper ring (slotted type) 33 Piston 34 Gudgeon pin 35 Gudgeon pin circlip retainer 36 Connecting rod 37 Connecting rod small-end bush 38 Big-end bolts and nuts 39 Connecting rod cap 40 Big-end bearing 41 Timing chain automatic tensioner 42 Crankshaft sprocket key 43 Crankshaft sprocket 44 Crankshaft pulley 45 Crankshaft pulley fixing bolt 46 Main bearings No. 1, 2, 4 and 5 47 Main bearing No. 3 48 Thrust washers 49 Crankshaft 50 Crankshaft rear end oil seal 51 Flywheel dowel 52 Flywheel ring gear 53 Flywheel 54 Flywheel fixing bolts 55 Spigot bush (gearbox stemwheel shaft) 56 Spigot bush (converter spigot end)

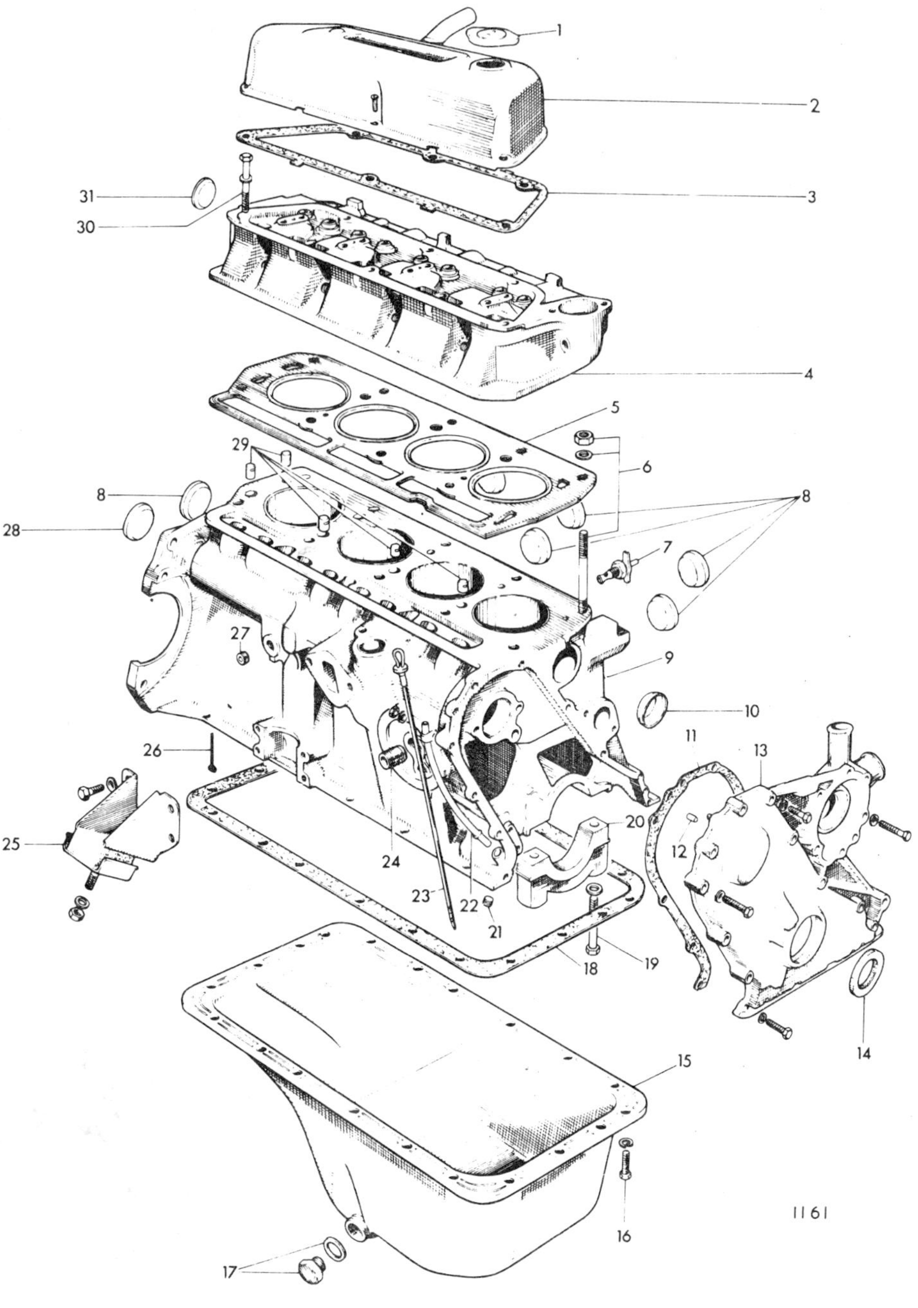

FIG 1:2 Exploded view of cylinder block, head, sump and timing cover

Key to Fig 1:2 1 Oil filler cap 2 Rocker cover 3 Rocker cover gasket 4 Cylinder head 5 Cylinder head gasket 6 Cylinder head stud, nut and washer 7 Cylinder block drain tap 8 Blanking cups (cylinder block) 9 Cylinder block 10 Front blanking cup 11 Timing cover gasket 12 Timing cover dowel 13 Timing cover 14 Oil seal (timing cover) 15 Sump 16 Sump screw and spring washer 17 Sump drain plug and washer 18 Sump gasket 19 Main bearing bolt and washer 20 Front main bearing cap 21 Blanking plug 22 Dipstick tube 23 Dipstick 24 Threaded sleeve (oil filter to cylinder block) 25 Engine rubber mounting assembly 26 Rear main bearing side joint 27 Blanking plug 28 Camshaft rear bearing end blanking cup 29 Water jets 30 Cylinder head bolt and washer 31 Cylinder head rear end blanking cup

Generally speaking, the arrangement of the engine within the compartment allows good accessibility for most servicing necessities. Oil is replenished via the filler cap at the front end of the rocker cover. Carburetter adjustments and air filter element renewals are simply effected and the contacts of the distributor make-and-break and vacuum advance adjustment are accessible on the right of the engine. The starter solenoid is a little awkwardly located to the rear of the battery with the manual button facing to the engine bulkhead.

The fullflow oil filter on the right of the engine is also readily accessible for a change of element. The latter is a throw-away unit which is screwed onto a threaded sleeve in the cylinder block and embodies a bypass valve permitting the flow of unfiltered oil through the engine should the filter become totally blocked.

The introduction of the alternator on certain models in place of the DC generator is being made for a number of reasons. First, it is possible for charging to commence and be maintained at lower engine speeds, secondly, the overall output for the same frame size is increased and, thirdly, the use of silicone diodes in place of the commutator as the rectifying element enables the normal regulator and cut-out to be replaced by a simple and effective transistorized regulator. Strictly speaking, the so-called alternator is no more an AC generating device than the generator. Apart from the fact that the field and armature windings are reversed, the field rotating and the armature, or stator, being stationary, AC is generated in the armature of either machine. In the generator, the rectification is by means of commutator and brushes; in the alternator it is by semiconductor (silicone) diodes. In both machines the output at the terminals is DC the term alternator being a hangover from earlier car installations, mostly on heavier vehicles, in which the rectifier was a separate unit mounted away from the alternator.

1:2 Working on the engine in the car

The arrangement of the engine within the compartment enables an extensive servicing programme to be carried out without the necessity of removing the unit from the car. It is quite possible to raise the front of the car on stands and remove the sump for inspection of big-end and main journal bearings and even the removal of the pistons and connecting rods. Decarbonizing is also commonly done without engine removal.

However, when any of these major operations becomes necessary, it probably is better to undertake a complete overhaul and check the wear and condition of other important components in which case engine removal and transfer to a bench or stand is essential. Then the dismantling procedure, inspection, repair, replacements and ultimate reassembly can be carried out in an ordered sequence so that, on completion, the engine can be returned to the car in virtually a new condition.

1:3 Engine removal

The engine can be removed by unbolting it from the manual gearbox and clutch housing or by removing the complete engine and gearbox assembly as a single unit. On cars with automatic transmission, however, the two must be removed as a complete unit and separation carried out on the garage floor.

The first steps are to disconnect the battery, drain the radiator and disconnect the hoses. Ensure that the heater unit is also drained by placing the control in the 'hot' position. Unbolt the bonnet hinges from the body, remove the bonnet and then protect the side wings and panels by covering them with a fairly thick cloth.

Remove the radiator, loosen the fan belt and remove the fan blades and belt. Disconnect the earth cables on the top fixing bolt of the starter motor and the leads to the starter terminal and alternator or generator. Remove the air cleaner, throttle rod retainer holding the throttle rod in the plastic trunnion on the throttle lever and lift away the throttle rod. Disconnect the choke cable. Each time a cable is disconnected, label it to ensure that it is reconnected to the right point on reassembly. Tie the connections out of the way so that they are not damaged during removal and installation of the engine. Disconnect the LT and HT leads to the distributor and ignition coil and all electrical connections to warning transducers and transmitters.

Disconnect the fuel pipe from the fuel pump and cap the end. Remove the two upper bolts attaching the clutch bellhousing to the gearbox if it is desired to remove the engine without the gearbox, otherwise leave in position for the present.

Raise the car on stands to give adequate working clearance beneath the sump. Attach lifting gear, comprising a bar and two support rods terminating in hooks or eyes linked with matching lugs secured under the cylinder head nuts that normally support the heater hose brackets. Secure to a hoist and take up the slack.

Now, **if it is desired to remove the engine without the gearbox,** support the engine under the sump on a travelling jack, remove the flywheel coverplate bolts, flywheel cover and then remove the starter motor from its seating, with the splashguard. Remove the lower bolts between the clutch bellhousing and gearbox and disconnect the exhaust pipe from the exhaust manifold. Extract the two forward mounting nuts holding the engine mounts to the front crossmember.

Take the weight on the hoist and lift sufficiently to withdraw the front mounting studs from the crossmember, then ease forward to separate the engine from the gearbox, taking care not to jam the gearbox drive shaft splines in those of the clutch driven plate. **As this will leave the front end of the gearbox unsupported, the travelling jack under the engine sump must be transferred to under the gearbox, or other support to the gearbox be provided, before actually separating the two units.**

The engine can now be lifted clear of the compartment and transferred to a bench or stand for dismantling. **FIG 1:3** illustrates removal of the engine with gearbox attached and it will be noticed that the unit needs tilting to the rear to enable the gearbox to clear the underside of the firewall between engine and drivers compartments. When removing the engine alone, the tilt is not so pronounced.

To remove the engine and gearbox as a single unit, first, support the rear axle on stands. Inside the car, remove the three screws holding the gearlever in position and extract the gearlever. Beneath the car, disconnect the propeller shaft from the differential flange, lower the shaft and carefully withdraw it rearwards from the gearbox. Blank off the gearbox opening to prevent loss of oil.

At the gearbox, disconnect the speedometer drive cable, clutch cable and reverse lamp switch leads. Extract the four bolts securing the anti-roll bar to the body frame, take the weight of the gearbox on a travelling jack and remove the rear mounting bolts.

The remainder of the removal sequence is then as for engine removal alone apart from the removal of the bolts attaching the engine to the gearbox and the removal of the starter motor. On account of the length of the combined assembly and the angle at which the unit is suspended—about 45 deg. to the horizontal—care must be taken not to allow it to swing within the compartment and damage other surrounding components.

Removal of units incorporating an automatic gearbox and converter must always be done with the gearbox in position.

1 :4 Engine dismantling

The following procedure relates to an engine already separated from the gearbox. If the engine and gearbox have been removed as a single unit, after the preliminary cleaning of the exterior and draining of the sump, separate the engine and gearbox and then refer to the relevant Chapters and Sections for the detailed servicing of gearbox and clutch.

After cleaning and draining the sump; remove the sump and dipstick tube, unbolt and remove the oil pump, loosen and extract the crankshaft pulley nut and remove the pulley with a suitable extraction tool.

Unbolt and remove the alternator, distributor, and leads to the sparking plugs. Disconnect the fuel line between the fuel pump and carburetter(s) and remove the fuel pump. Unbolt and remove the exhaust manifold and inlet manifold assembly complete with carburetters. Remove the oil filter. Extract the sparking plugs and electrical transmitters and transducers.

From within the bellhousing end of the engine, unbolt and remove the clutch assembly from the flywheel and then unbolt and remove the flywheel (see **Section 1 :5**). Check the oiltightness of the rear bearing cover cap of the camshaft. Remove the rocker cover and unbolt and remove the rocker assembly from the cylinder head. Extract the pushrods, suitably identifying each one so that it can be returned to the same position on reassembly. Remove the cylinder head and gasket.

Unbolt and remove the timing chain case, checking that the locating dowels are tight in the cylinder block. **Note that the timing case bolts are of different lengths and identify each one so that it may be inserted in the correct position on reassembly.**

Loosen the two bolts securing the chain tensioner and remove the tensioner. Extract the bolt and washer securing the camshaft sprocket to the camshaft and ease the sprocket clear of the shaft with a suitable puller. Ease the crankshaft sprocket forward on the crankshaft end and then extract both sprockets with the timing chain. **Recover and preserve the crankshaft sprocket key.** Note that the camshaft sprocket is located on the camshaft by a spigot and dowel.

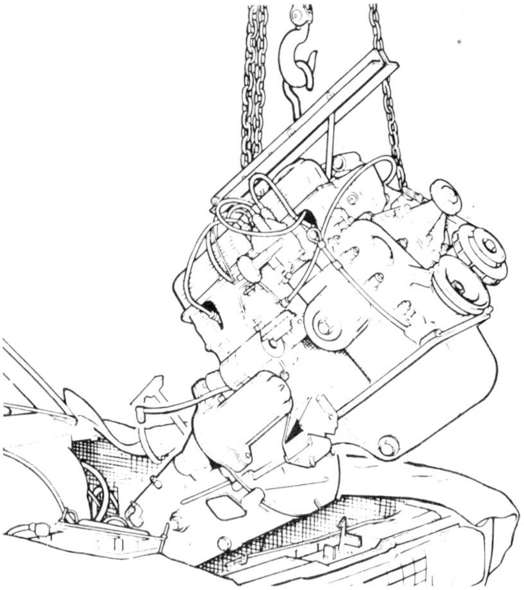

FIG 1 :3 Lifting engine out of front compartment

Withdraw the tappets from their bores in the cylinder block, again identifying them for identical replacement on reassembly. Unbolt and remove the camshaft thrust plate and withdraw the camshaft.

Turn the engine on to its lefthand side. If the dismantling is taking place on a bench and not on a stand, it will be necessary to remove the lefthand engine mounting assembly first. (The lefthand side is the one one which the manifolds are located). Clear any carbon deposits from the upper edge of the cylinder bores, unbolt the big-end bearing caps to each connecting rod and ease the pistons, complete with rings and connecting rod, out of the cylinder bores. Mark each assembly with the cylinder bore number and forward facing position.

Extract the two remaining cylinder head studs—the head is secured to the block by eight bolts and two nuts on studs at diagonally opposite corners—slacken the main bearing journal cap nuts, turn the engine on to its head, remove the caps and bearing shells and, finally, lift the crankshaft out of the cylinder block with the rear oil seal attached. Remove the upper main bearing halfshells and the two thrust washers noting their respective positions.

The engine is now completely dismantled. Thoroughly clean and/or degrease all parts and inspect for excessive wear, corrosion or other defects necessitating replacement of the component. Those which pass inspection, enclose within a plastic bag, mark and store ready for reassembly. Obtain replacements for other parts. Detailed servicing can then be commenced.

It is a sound rule in a complete overhaul to replace all gaskets, oil seals and washers irrespective of the condition of those in the engine before dismantling.

1 : 5 Servicing the cylinder head

The cylinder head of the twin carburetter model has larger inlet valve seats and ports. A letter 'S' is cast on the upper face to help identify it from the single carburetter models. Dual valve springs are fitted and the caps and collets also differ from the other models. A different type valve stem oil seal is incorporated, it is not interchangeable with a valve seal from the single valve spring type.

Using a suitable extraction tool, remove the valve cotters and springs from the cylinder head (see **FIG 1 : 4**). The coil spring is secured in position on the valve stem by a spring cup, sealing ring and split tapered cotter (see **FIG 1 : 5**).

Extract the valves from the cylinder head, noting their positions. The exhaust valve stems and heads are of different diameter to those of the inlet valves (see **Appendix**) and must be kept separate and identified with their cylinder number. Valve springs are the same for both inlet and exhaust valves and need not be identified.

Decarbonize and polish the cylinder head cavities and remove any deposits of carbon from the valve pockets. Blow clear after removal. Next, check the cylinder head lower face for flatness on a faceplate. Local high spots may be reduced by scraping but if the head is warped or seriously out of true, replace it.

Inspect the valve guides for signs of scoring or excessive wear and check that the valve stems are a smooth, close fit in the guides. The clearance when new is .001 inch on the inlet and .0025 inch on the exhaust stems. The corresponding maximum clearances are .0025 and .0045 inch.

Some engines are fitted with .003 inch oversize valve stems and these can be identified by a +3 stamped on the cylinder head in the position shown in FIG 1 : 6. Worn guides—these are machined directly in the metal of the cylinder head—can be reamered out to take valves with oversize stems. Two sizes are available, .015 inch and .030 inch oversize, and when new oversize valves are installed, a mark should be stamped in the position and the old mark, if any, deleted by a chisel cut.

Examine the valve seats and re-grind or re-cut them as necessary. The seats are cut in the metal of the cylinder head and care must be taken when re-cutting not to cut so deep as to bring the edge of the valve head below the surface of the seat surround.

If this should occur, inserts are available for exhaust valves but not for inlet valves. The fitting of these is a specialist task and, if necessary, should be entrusted to a competent Chrysler service garage. Usually, however, it is better to fit a new head. The seat angle is 45 deg. (see **FIG 1 : 6**).

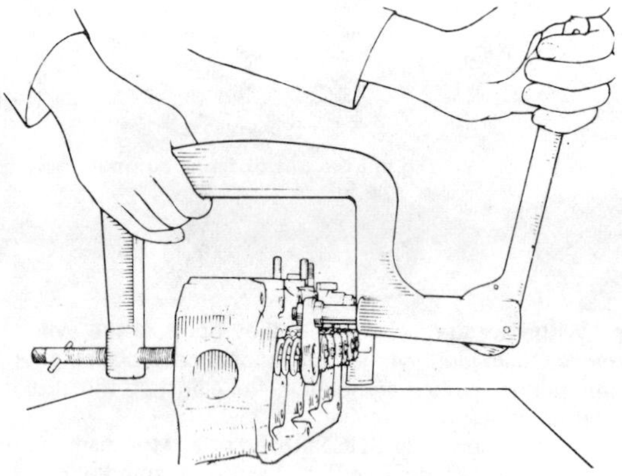

FIG 1 : 4 Removing valves and valve springs from cylinder head

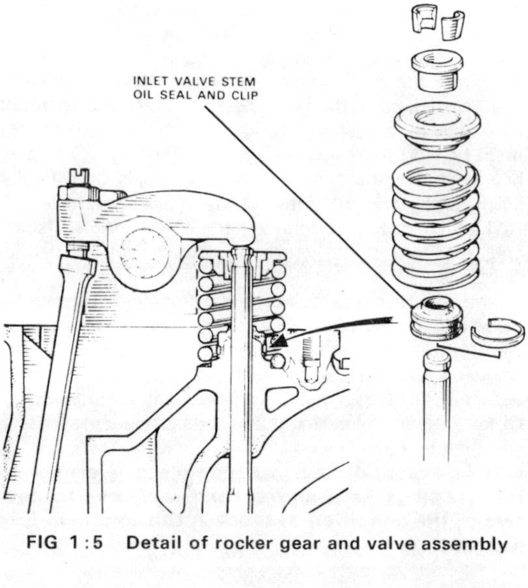

FIG 1 : 5 Detail of rocker gear and valve assembly

1 : 6 Valves and valve rockers

Examine the valves for signs of burnt seatings, bent or scored stems and worn stems. Check the condition of the springs and the load length. This should be 1.505 inch under a load of 70 lb. As a general rule, if one or more springs show evidence of weakness, replace the complete set.

If the valve seats are slightly worn, re-grind them into place with carborundum paste in the usual manner. Badly burned facings may be recut on a suitable machine but not if the degree of re-facing will bring the head of the valve too low as in **FIG 1 : 6**.

Bent or scored stems must be dealt with by replacement. Do not attempt to straighten.

Next examine the rocker shaft assemblies. Remove the spring clips and springs from the end and slide off the components, noting the order and laying each one down in position on a clean sheet of paper. Take each part in turn and examine it, cleaning it free from oil, and replace any which appear to be worn or damaged. Check the springs against each other for equality of length. See that the oil holes and centre duct of the rocker shaft are clear and that the feed hole in the front rocker shaft carrier is also clear.

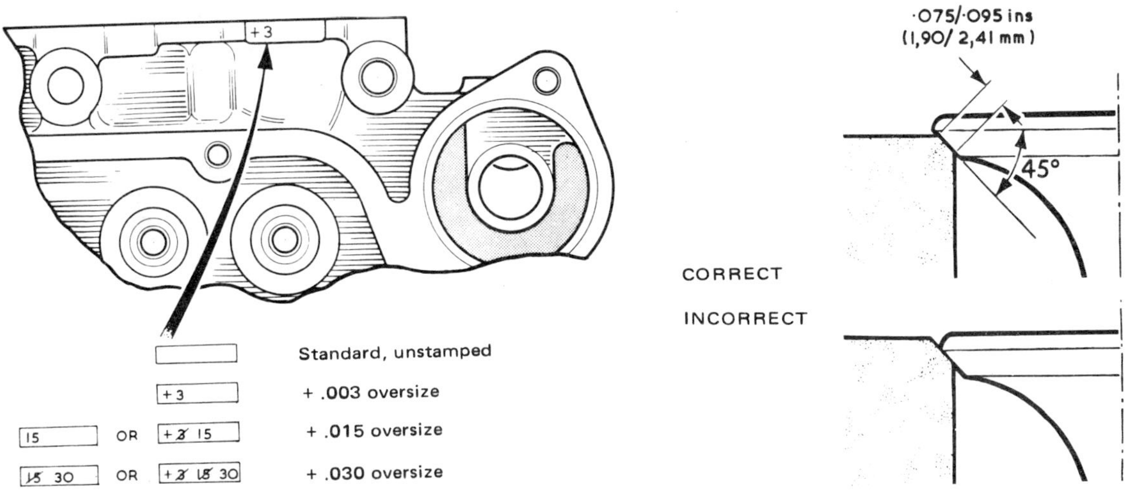

FIG 1:6 Position of valve guide marking and, right, valve seat detail

Check the rocker tips where they bear upon the push-rods and valve stems and, if they are lightly indented, hone out the indentation. If heavily indented or pitted, replace. Reassemble in the reverse order, oiling the shaft and rockers to facilitate assembly, taking particular care to see that the front rocker shaft carrier is the right way round for the oil feed hole to coincide with that in the cylinder head on assembly.

1:7 Camshaft and tappets

A different camshaft is used on the twin carburetter models and it is identified by a band of green paint between the No. 3 and 4 cylinder cams.

Clean the camshaft and examine the surfaces of the cams for signs of wear or corrosion. Slight scoring or pitting can be removed by honing or polishing; otherwise replace the camshaft. Check the condition of the skew gearteeth to the distributor/oil pump drive and the state of the journal bearing surfaces.

Examine the camshaft bearing shells in the crankcase and if they are at all worn or badly scored, withdraw them from their seatings with a suitable tool (see **FIG 1:7**) and, with the same tool, insert the new shells taking care to ensure that the oil hole in each shell is in line with the drilling on the crankcase. Renew the sealing disc at the rear end of the camshaft and ensure that it is oiltight.

The replacement shells are supplied to the correct diameter internally and do not need subsequent reaming.

Clean and examine the tappets for wear on the closed end where they bear on the cam faces and, if there are signs that the case-hardening on the surfaces has deteriorated, renew the tappet. Do not attempt to re-grind the ends as it will only remove the case-hardening and the tappet will then wear badly within a very short period. Unless a new tappet is being fitted, each tappet should be returned to the position from which it was removed in the cylinder block.

Examine the pushrods and replace if bent or if the ends show signs of being hammered.

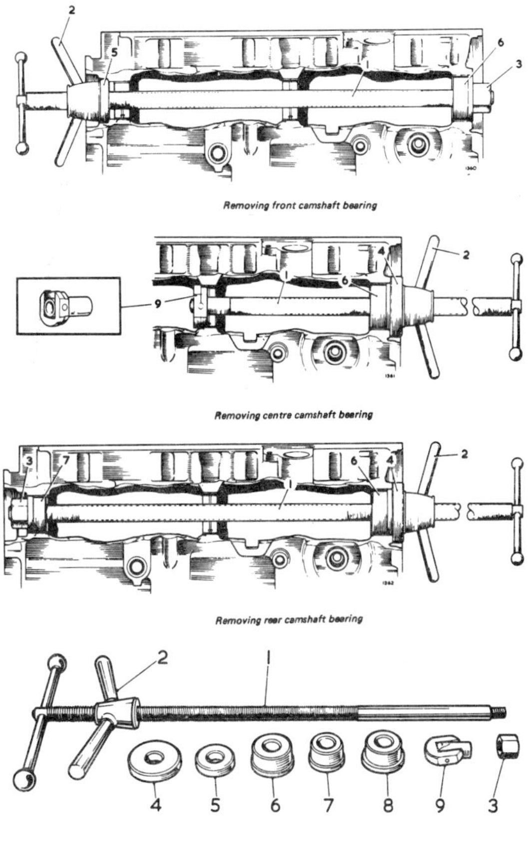

FIG 1:7 Method of removing and reinstalling camshaft bearings using the special tool and accessories below. The numbered bushes each have a particular application as shown in the upper illustrations

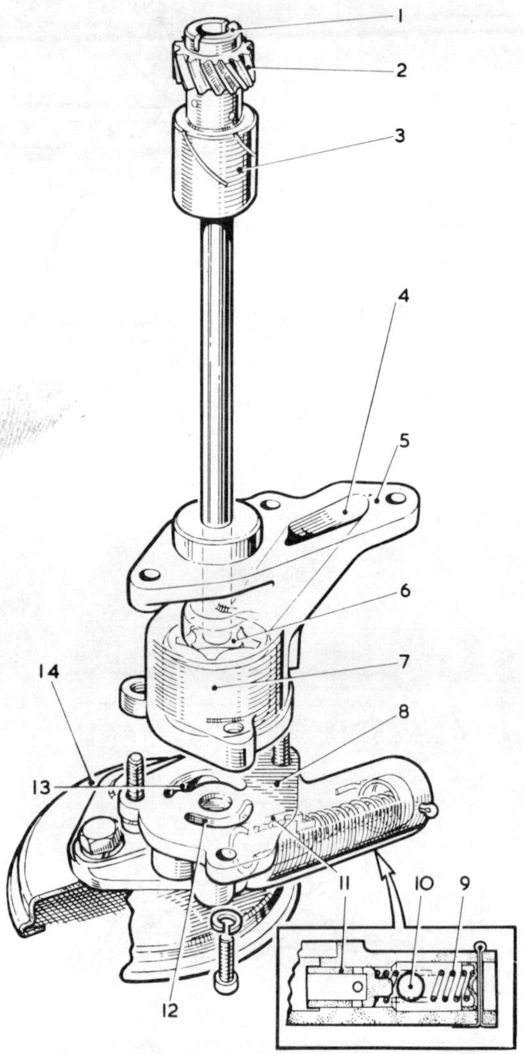

FIG 1:8 Ghosted view through the oil pump and relief valve

Key to Fig 1:8 1 Distributor drive dog 2 Skew gear 3 Oil thrower for skew gear 4 Oil outlet 5 Upper body and flange 6 Rotor 7 Ring 8 Lower body 9 Relief valve spring 10 Ball valve 11 Piston 12 Pump inlet 13 Pump outlet 14 Foot strainer and gauze

1:8 Oil pump and strainer

The oil pump embodies a four-lobe rotor turning within the five lobe centre of a ring free to turn in the pump body, the bore of which bridges the inlet and outlet ports of the pump. A ghosted view of the pump assembly, with drive shaft, relief valve and gauze filter is shown in **FIG 1:8**.

The pumping action is occasioned by the rotor turning the ring with the rotor lobes changing position in the lobe centre with each rotation. In doing this the spaces between the lobes expand while over the entry port and contract while over the exit port, the internal shape of the ring lobe contour being such that the top of the rotor lobes is always in close contact with the ring at all four points.

The clearances, of the order of .001 to .006 inch, are sealed by the oil film and the result is that the cavities draw oil from one side of the body and discharge it through the other with a powerful pump action.

To inspect the pump, which has already been separated from the cylinder block, first unbolt and remove the foot strainer and gauze. The three screws and lockwashers can then be extracted enabling the lower part, with ports and relief valve, to be separated from the upper with the rotor, shaft and drive gear. **When dismantling, take particular care in extracting the five-lobe ring as this is of special sintered material and will break easily if dropped or mishandled.**

Clean all parts in petrol and allow to dry. Replace the ring in the upper body with the chamfered edge towards the upper end of the pump. With suitable feeler gauges check the gaps between the rotor tips and ring lobes and between the ring and body (see **FIG 1:9**). These must be not less than .005 inch nor greater than .008 inch, between ring and body 'B', and not less than .001 nor more than .006 inch between rotor tip and ring 'A'.

Place a straightedge across the centre of the upper body and, again with feeler gauge, check the clearance between the rotor face and straightedge. This must be not less than .001 inch nor more than .003 inch (see **FIG 1:10**).

To clean the relief valve, remove the split cotter pin and extract cap, spring, ball and piston valve. Clean and reassemble.

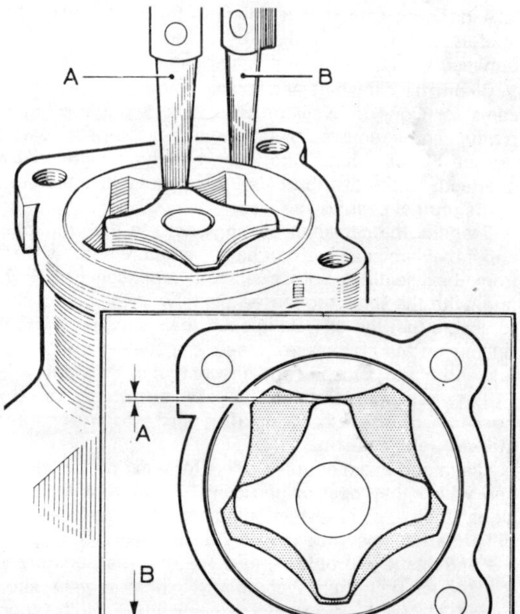

FIG 1:9 Checking rotor clearances with feeler gauges

When reassembling, lightly smear the faces of the contacting surfaces with oil and tighten the three bolts and lockwashers to a torque of 40 lb ft.

Wash the gauze filter in petrol or paraffin and allow to dry, or blow dry with compressed air if available. Do not wipe dry with a linty rag. When clean, refit to the pump intake.

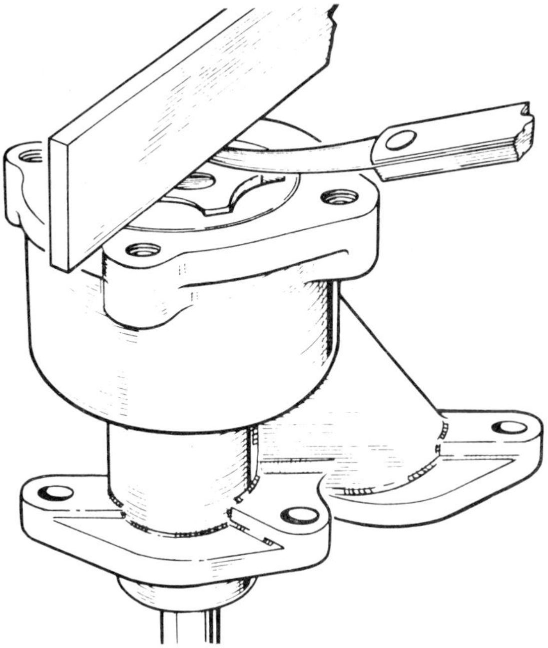

FIG 1:10 Checking rotor end play in body

1:9 Sump

Thoroughly clean the interior and exterior of the sump with paraffin or a proprietary cleaning fluid. Drain and allow to dry. Examine the metal for damage or incipient cracks which might deteriorate into a hole. Check the flat areas around the bolt holes and, if necessary, correct any inclination to 'dishing' by hammering flat on a substantial level surface.

Clean the flange around the area where it is in contact with the cylinder block free from old portions of gasket or sealant and fit a new composition gasket in position, using a jointing compound between sump flange and gasket **but not between gasket and cylinder block when fitting.**

1:10 Flywheel and ring gear

Clean and examine the flywheel and ring gear. Check that the flywheel sits squarely on the end of the crankshaft and that there is no more than .003 inch (.075 mm) runout measured on the surface of the clutch plate facing ring. Check also that the surface is smooth and without scoring. If necessary, the flywheel, mounted on the crankshaft, may be swung between centres in a lathe and the clutch surface refaced providing, however, that the overall thickness at the surface is not reduced by more than .01 inch.

Examine the clutch spigot bearing in the centre of the flywheel and replace if faulty. To remove the old bearing, fill the centre with grease, insert a close-fitting drift or circular bar and apply a sharp hammer blow to its end. Under the impact the grease will enter behind the bush where it sits in the flywheel recess and force it out. The new bush can then be inserted and pressed flush with the rear face of the crankshaft flange. **Always soak a new spigot bush in engine oil for 24 hours before installation.** Vehicles equipped with automatic transmission have a steel bush fitted which supports and centralizes the torque convertor.

Examine the ring gear for signs of damage or burrs on the gear teeth. If they are only slight, clean up with a smooth file but if the wear is extensive or the teeth badly damaged, the ring must be replaced. It is a shrink fit on the flywheel.

To remove the ring, drill two holes, spaced 180 deg. apart, between the tooth root and the edge of the ring deep enough to weaken the ring but not enough to penetrate into the flywheel metal beneath. **Take care not to allow the drill to bite into the side of the flywheel when carrying out this operation.** Apply a sharp chisel to the ring across one of the holes and give it a sharp blow. This should fracture the ring across and fall away from the flywheel. Thoroughly clean the rim of the flywheel and, if possible, insert it in a refrigerating chamber for several hours.

Obtain a new ring and remove any grease or oil from the packing. Place in an oven and raise the temperature to around 220°C. **Do not heat by a flame as the ring is surface hardened and, if the temperature is allowed to rise much above 220°C locally, the casing will be softened and ultimate wear will be rapid.**

When both parts have reached the temperatures of their environments, remove the flywheel and place face downwards on the bench. Remove the ring from the oven and rapidly insert it in position on the flywheel, **chamfered side of the teeth towards the clutch side,** and clamp in position with G-clamps until cool.

The torque loading for the flywheel-to-crankshaft bolts is 40 lb ft.

1:11 Big-ends and connecting rods

The connecting rods are H-section steel forgings with a cylindrical bush at the small-end for insertion of the gudgeon pin and with split big-end bearings housing steel half shells with aluminium-tin or indium-coated copper-lead bearing surfaces. The gudgeon pin is of the floating type retained in position by circlips.

The connecting rods and big-end caps are marked with the respective cylinder number and these identification and location numbers should be on the camshaft side of the engine. If they are not marked stamp or centre-pop each one with its correct number so that when fitted to the engine the marks will be located to the camshaft side. If necessary, lightly stamp the piston crown also with the mating cylinder number.

Clean and examine for signs of damage and for indications of excessive wear on the bearing shells and small-end bush. To remove the piston from the connecting rod, the gudgeon pin circlips must be extracted with circlip pliers, after any carbon deposits have been scraped away, and the gudgeon pin pushed out. At room temperature, the gudgeon pin should be a finger push fit in the piston and only just free to fall out from the small-end bush. Gudgeon pins are available in four grades, each separated from the next by only .0001 inch, identified by colour painting on one end, blue (.9377 to .9378 dia.), white, green and yellow (.9374 to .9375 dia.). If the bush is in good condition and the gudgeon pin is not a just-free fit, use a new pin the next size up or down.

If the bush is scored, drive out with a suitable drift and press, not hammer, in a new bush of the same outer diameter, with a bore to suit the gudgeon pin. Three grades are available, painted to correspond with the gudgeon pin for which they are intended.

When inserting the small-end bush, check that the oil hole coincides with that drilled in the connecting rod (see **FIG 1:1**).

Examine the big-ends and shells and check that the oil holes are clear. At the same time make a preliminary check of the crankshaft big-end journals to see if they are scored or worn. The indium coated bearings are able to carry greater loads than whitemetal bearings but the bearing surfaces are harder and do not yield to abrasive particles which may be carried round in the oil as the softer metal would. Consequently, unless the oil filter has been changed regularly, there is some chance that the crankshaft journals will have been scored by dirt in the oil.

If the scoring is slight and the journals are still perfectly round, the marks may be removed with a fine hone or very fine emerycloth applied circumferentially. Providing that the bearing shells are not damaged or worn, they may be used again. Otherwise, replace them by new shells. Check the wear between the bearings and journals using 'Plastigage' if it is obtainable, if not use internal and external micrometers or calipers. Allow for .0009 to .0024 inch (.022 to .060 mm) running clearance.

When new shells or small-end bushes have been fitted, it is necessary to check that the gudgeon pin and big-end journals will be in proper alignment when assembled. This can be done on a Churchill alignment jig (see **FIG 1:11**) if one is available; alternatively, procure two cylindrical rods about 18 inches long, one the diameter of the gudgeon pin and the other the diameter of the big-end journal.

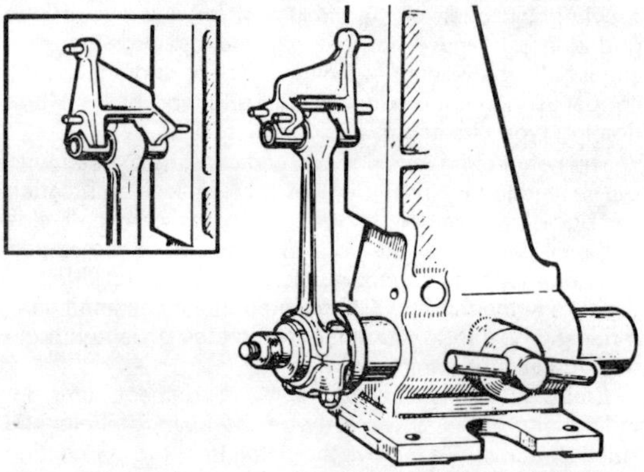

FIG 1:11 Checking alignment of connecting rod bushes

Insert these in the small- and big-ends so that they project equally on either side. To check for parallelism, measure the distance between the two rods with a vernier gauge or micrometer on each side. The distance should be the same measured at the extremities.

To check for 'twist', support the assembly on two knife edges laid side by side on a faceplate, the knife edges being positioned under the extremities of the rods. There should be no rocking about either diagonal.

When reassembling, always check that the oil holes in the bush or bearing shells coincide with those in the connecting rod and are unobstructed.

1:12 Pistons and piston rings

The pistons are of the slotted skirt type and constructed from tin-plated aluminium alloy with a flat crown, the 1500 models have a recessed crown. On the twin carburetter types the piston skirt clearance differs and the grading diameters are smaller. Refer to **Technical Data** for all grading sizes. Three piston rings are fitted, two compression and one scraper.

Generally speaking, the engine is fitted with the standard high compression piston but in certain export engines, for areas where high octane fuels are not readily available, a low compression piston may be used.

After extraction, carefully remove the piston rings, then clean the crown and edges of the ring slots free from carbon deposits, finally polishing the crown with blue-back emerypaper. **This is the only grade of emerypaper which may be used on the soft aluminium heads as other grades bear hard particles of emery which bed into the soft metal.** Wash the skirts free from oil and sludge deposits.

Inspect the piston for cracks or other signs of damage and then mark on the crown by scratches or light pop marks to indicate the cylinder number from which it was taken. If this is done as each piston is taken and cleaned, the chances of subsequent mismatching are small.

The top compression ring is chromium-plated with the word 'Vacrom', etched on one of its side faces. When installed, it may be fitted either way up and it is 'Cargraph' treated to assist bedding in. This treatment leaves it a dull grey and faintly red colour.

The intermediate compression ring is of stepped section and this must be installed with the wider face, marked TOP, uppermost in the groove. The function of this ring is to improve oil consumption as well as to accelerate running-in and incorrect installation may result in a higher oil consumption.

The lower ring is a slotted type scraper ring.

All three rings must be fitted carefully as they are inclined to be brittle and can be broken easily.

If it is necessary to replace the piston, without affecting the cylinder bore, check first the piston diameter grading. This is marked on the crown of the old piston as **A**, **B**, **C** or **D**. A fifth grade **E**, is for service use only and is not likely to be met with in an engine from a car that has been in use. The grades correspond to variations in diameter in steps of .0004 inch, **A** being the smallest diameter (3.2092 to 3.2096 inch) and **D** the largest. These have been fitted in the first place to suit slight production variations in cylinder bore. Choose a new piston of similar grade to that it replaces.

However, after the engine has been in service over a

considerable period, there will be an increase in the cylinder bore diameter due to wear and possibly an ecliptic condition, it is advisable to check the bore before securing a replacement piston as it may be advisable to either renew the block or have the cylinders rebored and obtain new pistons to suit.

A second letter on the piston crown, directly over one end of the gudgeon pin, indicates the gudgeon pin bore diameter, **L, M** or **H**. In some cases, an alternative arrangement of markings may be found.

With a new piston and rings, or when renewing the rings on an existing piston, first check that the clearance of the rings in the grooves is correct, .0015 to .0035 inch (see **FIG 1:13**). Then carefully install the rings after they have been gapped. This involves fitting the ring to the cylinder bore without the piston and checking the gap between the ends when in position. It should be between .014 and .018 inch on the top ring and between .009 and .014 inch on the other two. If it is less, file the ends carefully to increase the gap. If it is greater, select new rings.

When the rings have been installed, turn them in their grooves so that the gaps are 120 deg. apart.

After a period in service, the chromium plated finish of the compression ring will have left a glazed deposit on the cylinder walls. When a new compression ring is fitted, it is necessary first to remove this glaze or the new rings may not bed down properly.

To remove the glaze, construct a wooden plug that will fit snugly in the bore with a sheet of No. 1 grade emery-cloth wrapped around it. By moving this up and down, like a piston, and rotating it at the same time for about three minutes, the glazed surface will be removed. Do not carry on too long or the bore may be enlarged. **If this process is done with the cylinder block in situ on the sump and with the crankshaft in position, block off the lower end to prevent the emery and metal dust falling onto the crankshaft or into the sump.**

Wash down the bores thoroughly, dry and then coat the surface with a thin film of engine oil. The new compression ring can then be fitted and gapped.

The final stage is to fit the piston with rings to the connecting rod, taking care that it is the right way round with the grade mark or its equivalent to the front of the engine (see **FIG 1:12**). Insert the gudgeon pin and secure with the circlips. The first of these can then be encircled by the piston ring clamp which will hold all the gaps closed for easy entrance into the cylinder during the next stage of reassembly.

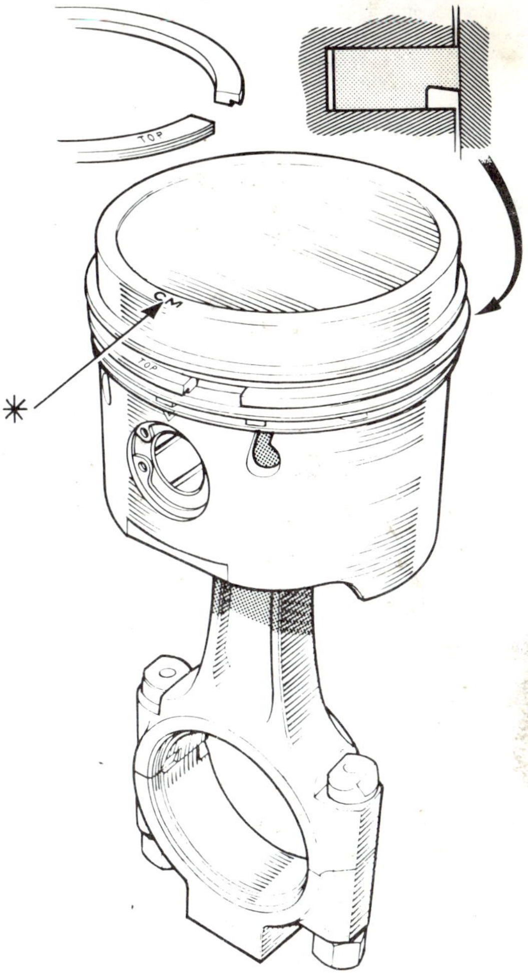

FIG 1:12 Assembly of piston and connecting rod showing the grade marks for piston and gudgeon pin stamped on the piston head. Above detail shows correct insertion of stepped scraper ring

1:13 Cylinder blocks and liners

Cylinder blocks should first be washed to clear them of grease and external dirt not already removed, using a suitable detergent fluid. The waterways must next be swilled through with a high pressure jet to clear the jacket of sludge and rust. The block is then dried and examined for signs of cracks, external corrosion and leakage around the pressed steel core plugs. Examine the bore carefully for scores, check for out-of-round and measure for cylinder wall wear.

Cylinders which are heavily scored or are seriously out-of-round will need a rebore. Reboring is a specialist

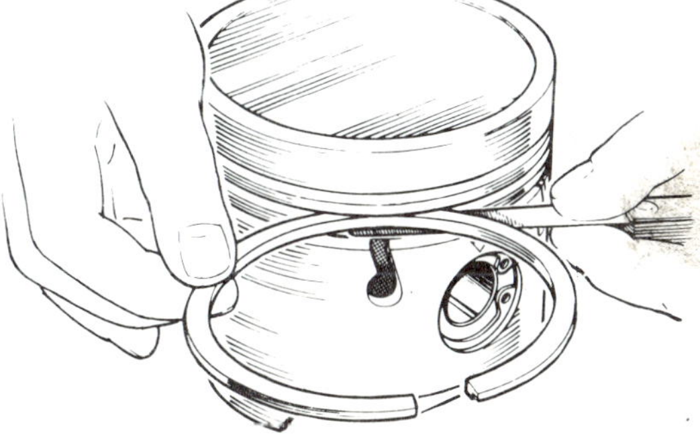

FIG 1:13 Checking ring clearance in slots with a feeler gauge

skill necessitating equipment not usually in the possession of an owner-mechanic. It is, therefore, advisable to put this out to a Chrysler agent equipped to undertake the work or, alternatively, to fit a service replacement block.

In some cases the cylinders may have liners fitted. New liners can be installed after the old ones have been removed but this, again, is a task better delegated to the garage or service agent.

Check all tapped holes and studs for good screw threads and see that the cylinder head surface is clean and flat, free from scores or other marks which will affect gas and water tightness when the head is bolted down on the gasket. Check the mounting faces of the oil filter table, distributor and water pump.

1:14 Crankshaft and main bearings

The 5-bearing, 1.264 inch throw crankshaft revolves in whitemetal lined, steel shells secured in position by the bearing caps. The rear bearing has, in addition to the bearing shell, two semi-circular copper/lead faced thrust washers to control end float. These can be seen in the exploded view of working parts (see **FIG 1:1**).

When the engine is completely dismantled, the removal of the crankshaft is by removal of the bearing caps and half bearing shells. The upper half then comes away from the crankcase portion of the cylinder block.

Lubrication of the big-end journal bearings is via oilways drilled in the crankshaft deriving their supply from the main bearings which, in turn, are fed from an oil duct drilled from end to end in the crankcase and plugged by screw plugs. The transverse ducts from the oilway supply both the main and camshaft bearings, a central tapping, immediately above the lefthand end of the sump gasket in the drawing, accommodating the oil pressure transducer.

After cleaning, the crankshaft must be inspected for the condition of the main and big-end bearing surfaces. If these are scored or are in any degree oval, it is best to completely replace the crankshaft. Regrinding is, in any case, a specialist task which should be entrusted to a service garage or agent.

Check that the oilways are clear and free from oil sludge. Inspect the surfaces of the bearing half-shells and replace if necessary. Examine the condition of the end thrust washers and be prepared to replace them by over size if the end float is found, on assembly, to be excessive.

Crankshafts fitted to new engines may have any one of the following undersize journal diameters and are identified by a letter stamped on the centre webs (see **FIG 1:14**). Standard journal sizes are not stamped with an identifying letter, that is, when both big-end and main journal diameters are a standard size. Where the main journals are —.010 inch (.25 mm) undersize but the big-end journals are standard the crankshaft is stamped with the letter 'M'. When this condition is reversed, that is, with the big-end journals undersized and the main journals standard, it is stamped with the letter 'P'. When both journals are —.010 inch (.25 mm) undersize the crankshaft is identified by the letters 'PM'

Rear oil seal:

A sectional view of the position and location of the rear oil seal is shown in **FIG 1:15**. When renewing the seal the rear main bearing cap must be removed before the seal is extracted. This applies particularly if the renewal is performed with the engine in the car after the flywheel or convertor drive plate has been taken off. Damage may be inflicted on the journal on which the seal operates, or on the taper at the rear end of the crankshaft over which the seal passes as it is removed or fitted. Furthermore, the outer rubber diameter of the new seal may be damaged if the seal is forced into position without releasing the rear main bearing cap bolts.

The seal must be removed without the use of steel tools, such as a screwdriver, as they will scratch the crankshaft seal journal. Use a piece of hardwood to displace the seal from its recess. Rotate the crankshaft slowly with a $1\frac{5}{16}$ inch AF ring spanner and examine the seal journal and the 'lead on' taper at the end of the crankshaft, ensuring they are perfectly clean and free from burrs. Check that the recesses in the cylinder block and the bearing cap are also perfectly clean.

Refer to **FIG 1:16** and fit the two new side seals to the rear main bearing cap. If necessary blunt the sharp edges of the rear bearing location, where the seals make contact, so that they are not cut or damaged as the bearing is refitted. Fit the main bearing cap, tighten the two bolts then release them half a turn. Smear Shell Retinax 'A' grease on the inside of the rear oil seal and on the crankshaft journal. Do not use oil and do not spread the grease to the outside of the seal or seal recesses.

Fit the seal into position with its contracting spring towards the front of the engine as shown in **FIG 1:15**, make sure it is parallel with the flywheel face and press it into position by finger pressure only. Tighten the rear bearing bolts. Check the distance at four equally spaced points around the journal, between the face of the seal and the flywheel mounting face of the crankshaft. All four dimensions must be equal. To correct any misalignment of the seal, slacken the bearing bolts again and relocate the seal with fingers only.

Tighten the bearing bolts to the correct torque figure.

End thrust:

Crankshaft end thrust is taken up by two semi-circular steel washers located at each side of the upper half rear main bearing shell. The thrust faces of the washers are copper/lead faced and have two vertical oil grooves cut across the bearing surface. The bearing surfaces must face outwards to bear against the crankshaft thrust faces. Oversize thrust washers are available as a service item for use with crankshafts which have had the thrust faces reground.

End thrust should be between .002 and .008 inch (.05 and .20 mm). To check, prise the crankshaft forward when all bearings and caps are fitted and measure with feeler gauges between the thrust faces of the washers and crankshaft.

Assembling:

After fitting the main bearing shells and crankshaft, tighten the bolts to 52 lb ft (7 kg m) torque. Check that the crankshaft turns freely and smoothly. Clearance between

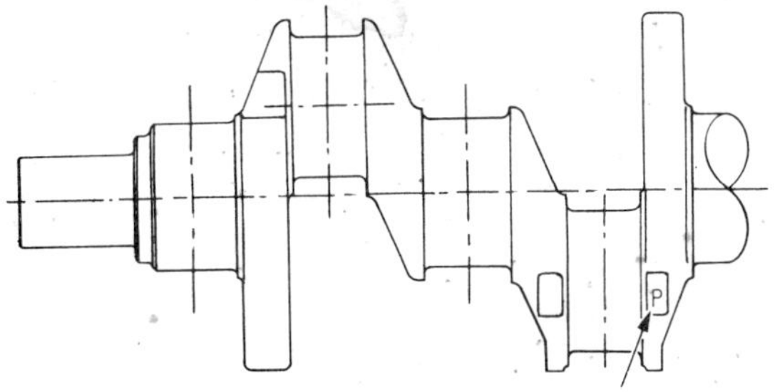

FIG 1:14 Journal diameter identification letters

Key to Fig 1:14
P=Crankpin undersize
M=Main journal undersize
PM=Main journal and crankpin undersize

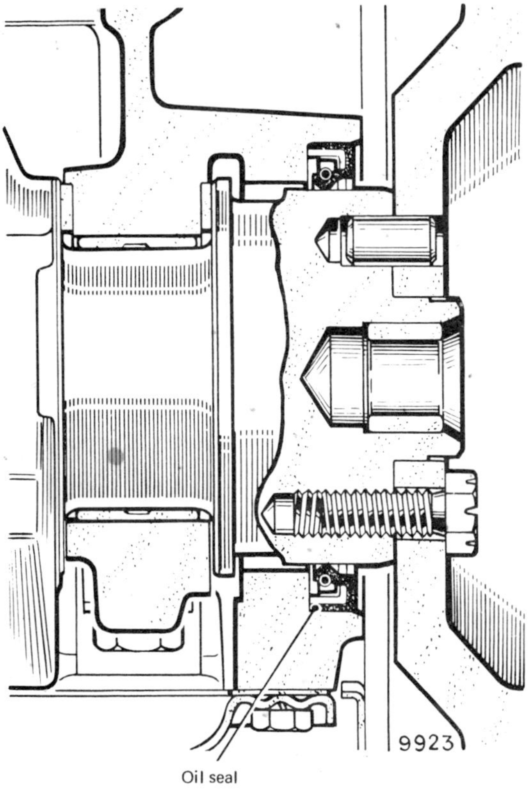

FIG 1:15 Sectional view of the position and location of the crankshaft rear oil seal

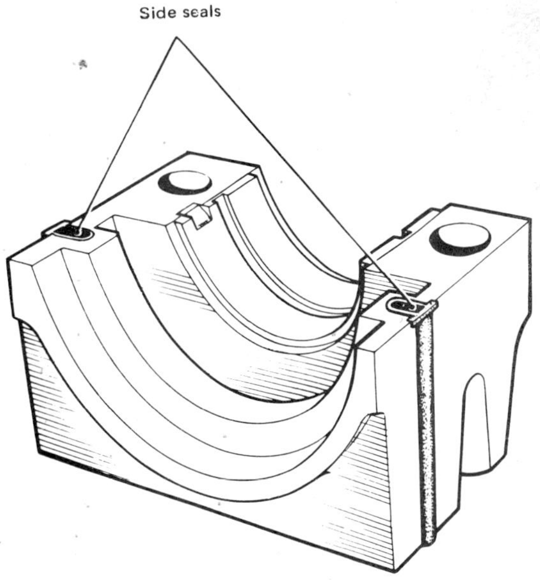

FIG 1:16 Rear main bearing cap with side seals fitted

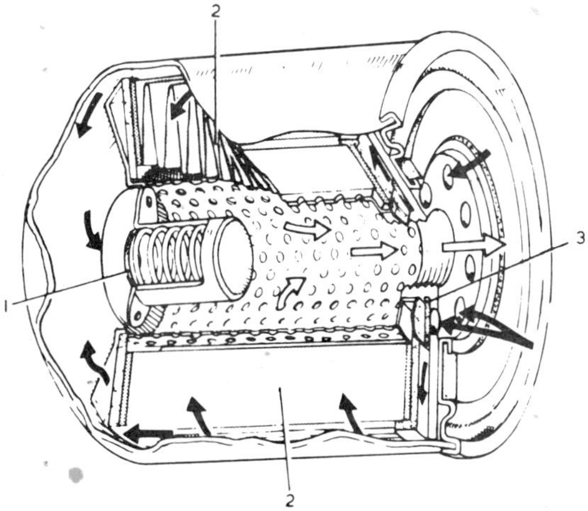

FIG 1:17 View through replaceable oil filter cartridge. The numbers are referred to in the text

the journals and bearings should be between .0005 and .0025 (.012 and .063 mm), this can be checked by using the 'Plastigage' method.

Now insert the first piston into the cylinder, sliding the rings clear of the clamp into the bore, and checking that the grading mark on the crown is facing the front of the engine. Insert the bearing shells, fit the bearing cap and tighten to a torque of 29 lb ft (4 kg m). Repeat with the other three pistons.

1:15 Oil filter and relief valve

The fullflow oil filter is a throw-away unit screwed onto a threaded sleeve inserted into the oilway on the side of the cylinder block (see **FIG 1:17**).

Oil from the engine driven pump enters through the outer peripheral section via an anti-drain valve comprising the two metal plates 3, and through the cartridge filter walls 2, to the central cylindrical duct leading, through the screw spigot, to the main oilways of the

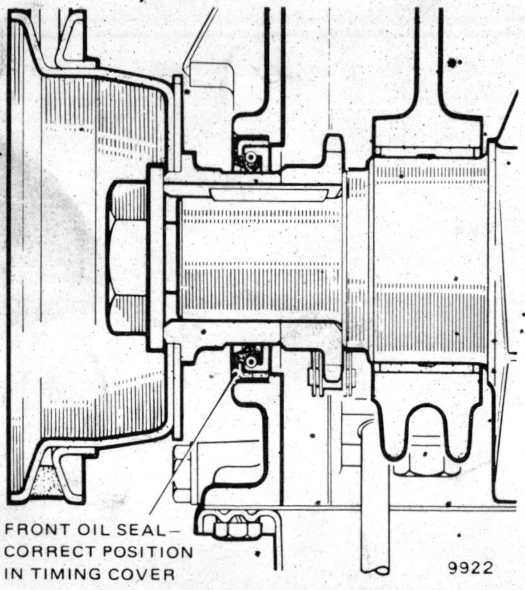

FIG 1:18 Sectional view of the position and location of the timing gear cover oil seal

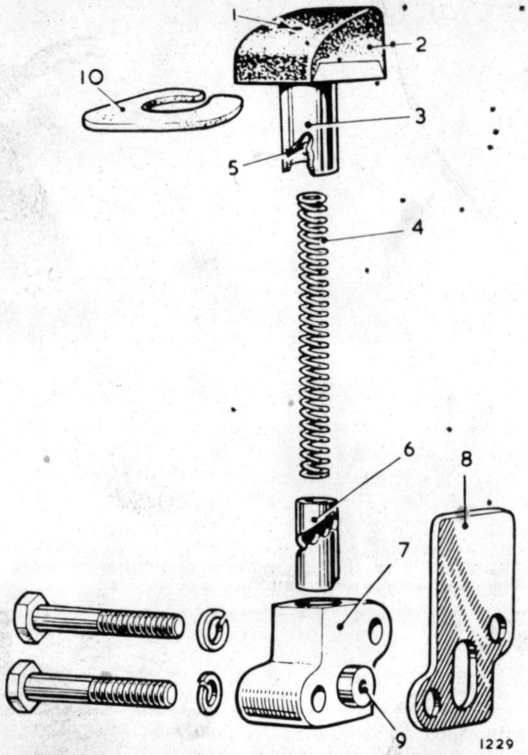

FIG 1:19 Components of the timing chain adjuster mechanism

Key to Fig 1:19 1 Oil feed hole 2 Slipper head 3 Plunger 4 Compression spring 5 Limit peg 6 Restraint cylinder 7 Body 8 Backplate 9 Oil feed hole 10 Cardboard packer

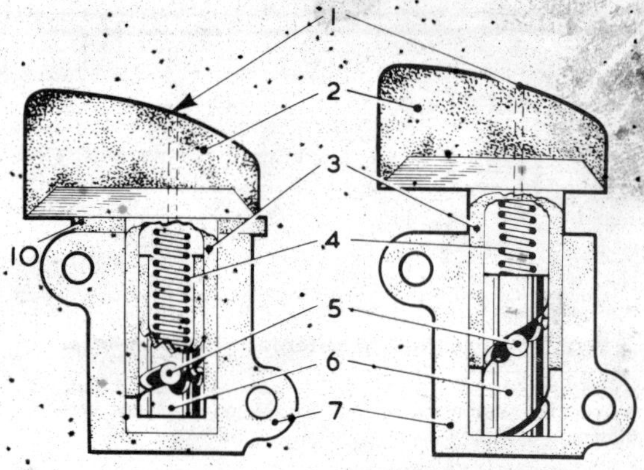

FIG 1:20 Section through adjuster mechanism, contracted and expanded

Key to Fig 1:20 See key to **Fig 1:19**

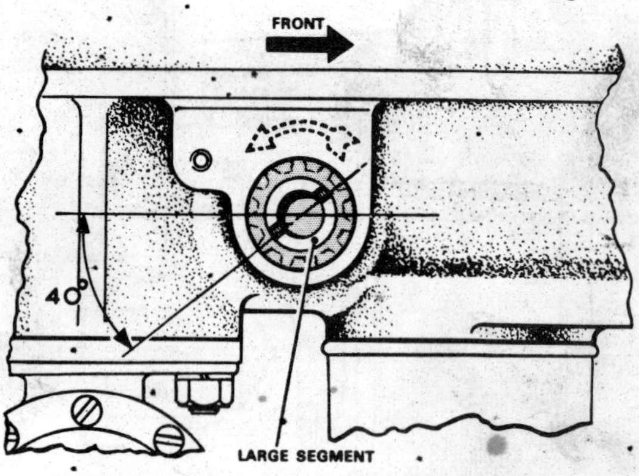

FIG 1:21 Correct position of distributor driving slot after mating the camshaft and distributor shaft

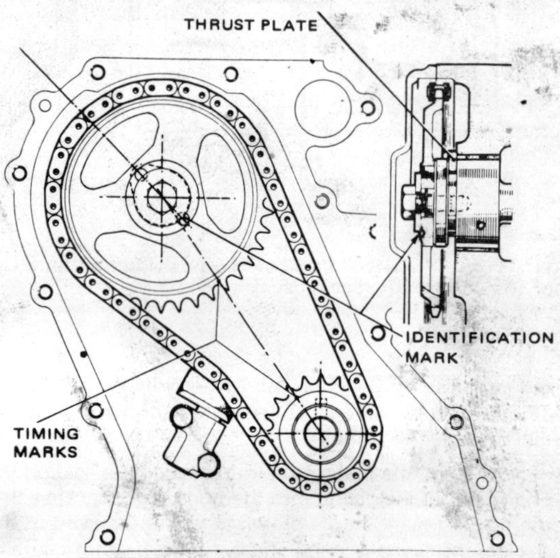

FIG 1:22 Correct location of timing marks on camshaft, (upper) and crankshaft (lower) sprockets

cylinder block. In the event of the cartridge becoming blocked, the relief valve 1, at the top of the cartridge opens permitting unfiltered oil to bypass the cartridge and so maintain the flow through the engine.

Though this is undesirable, it is the better of the two evils, the alternative being starvation of the engine bearing surfaces of lubricant. **The importance of early and regular cartridge renewal cannot, therefore, be over-emphasised.**

When screwed in position, the rubber sealing ring may become attached to the face of the base casting and make the cartridge a little difficult to turn. A 1 inch A/F spanner can be used to grip the outer casing so facilitating turning. This, however, is not likely to occur if the cartridge is first screwed into position until the joint faces meet and then by a further two-thirds of a turn by hand only.

The outlet from the filter goes straight to the transverse oilway, referred to in **Section 1:14,** from which it is distributed to the main and camshaft bearings. The cylinder walls are lubricated by the outflow from the bearings in the connecting rod big-ends. The timing chain is lubricated by an oil duct in the tensioner deriving its supply from a tapping in the forward main-to-camshaft bearing duct.

A vertical oilway from the upper centre camshaft bearing delivers oil to the front rocker support. It then flows along the hollow rocker shaft, over the rockers to drain down the pushrod holes, over the tappets and back into the sump. Drainage from all the other bearings and the timing cover also return direct to the sump. The tappets are provided with drain holes in the sockets below the pushrods to prevent oil accumulating and affecting rocker arm clearances. Oil to the rockers is metered by a special arrangement of drilling in the camshaft at the centre bearing.

1:16 Timing cover oil seal

To renew the oil seal in the timing gear cover, support the outer face of the seal housing and drift out the seal from the inside. Press the new seal into the cover from the outside and support the inner face of the seal housing, use a thick flat steel plate between the press arbor and seal. **FIG 1:18** shows the correct location of the seal, note that the seal contracting spring is to the inside of the timing case.

Apply Shell Retinax A grease to the seal lip before fitting. Do not use oil. If the reason for removal was an oil leak, check the crankshaft pulley diameter that runs inside the cover. It must be free from wear including the smallest scratches and burrs, only a polished unmarked and unworn surface is acceptable, renew if otherwise.

A wider timing cover is employed on the 1500 twin carburetter engine to accommodate the Duplex twin chain, a wider chain tensioner and a rubber damper.

1:17 Timing wheels and chain

Camshaft sprocket wheels used in the 1250 engines are identified by a mark as indicated in **FIG 1:22**, the ones used on the 1500 engines have no mark. The different sprockets are used to obtain different valve timings but allow the same camshaft to be used on the 1250 and 1500SC. The camshaft on the 1500TC is slightly different (see **Section 1:7**), in addition a fixed rubber faced damper is fitted on the driving side of the chain (righthand side).

The chain tensioners:

The components of the chain adjuster are shown in **FIG 1:19** with a sectional view in **FIG 1:20**. The rubber slipper head 2 which is oil and abrasion resistant is bonded to a steel plate mounted on the end of the plunger 3. A light spring 4, assisted by oil pressure, keeps the slipper head against the trailing side of the chain to maintain the tension. Return movement of the plunger is prevented by a limited stop 5 which engages in the nearest toothed gap of the helix in the restraint cylinder 6.

Engine oil enters the tensioner body 7 through the small drilling 9 and is discharged through the hole 1 to lubricate the timing chain.

If the rubber slipper head is worn deeper than .05 inch (1.3 mm) or if there is any signs of the rubber 'picking up' or wearing renew the tensioner complete.

1:18 Reassembly and timing

Reassembly of the engine after inspection, adjustment and renewal of the component parts is a straight reversal of the dismantling sequence but with the additional procedures of timing and adjustment of tappet clearances etc. Briefly summarised, the sequence is as follows.

First, install the crankshaft in the cylinder block tightening the bearing cap screws to 55 lb ft. Insert the pistons in the cylinders, checking that they are the right way round and couple the connecting rod big-ends to the crankshaft, tightening the cap screws to 29 lb ft. Install the camshaft, very carefully until its thrust face is flush with the cylinder block face, fit the thrust plate, a new rear bearing cup and check the camshaft end float with feeler gauges. The end float should be between .004 and .009 inch (.101 and .228 mm) and oversize thrust plates are available to obtain this dimension.

Bolt into position the oil pump and foot strainer. This engages with the skew gear of the camshaft so check that the distributor driving slot is positioned as in **FIG 1:21** with the large segment (the slot is off-centre) below when the timing wheel marking is in the position shown in **FIG 1:22**. If the position is not correct, withdraw the oil pump and readjust the shaft position before re-entering.

Refit the flywheel and clutch.

With pistons 1 and 4 at top dead centre, fit the timing chain and crankshaft sprocket and key so that the timing wheel markings are now as in **FIG 1:22**. Install the chain tensioner.

Fit a new gasket and install the timing gear cover, make sure it is located correctly on the dowels. Refit the water pump and the crankshaft pulley. Fit the oil sump using new gaskets then turn the engine upright and support it on blocks or a frame. Fit the two cylinder head studs.

Fit the dipstick tube and the lefthand engine mounting. Smear the cam bearing faces with graphite grease, oil the sides of the tappers and fit them into their respective bores. Refit the cylinder head with a new gasket, tighten the nuts to the sequence shown in **FIG 1:24** and to a torque of 60 lb ft ($8\frac{1}{4}$ kg m). Assemble the pushrods and rocker gear tightening the nuts to a torque of 17 lb ft (2.35 kg m). Correct location is shown in **FIG 1:23**.

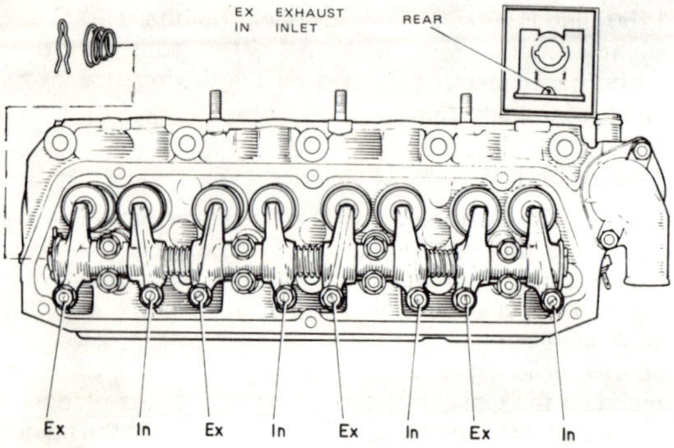

FIG 1:23 Plan view of rocker gear assembly

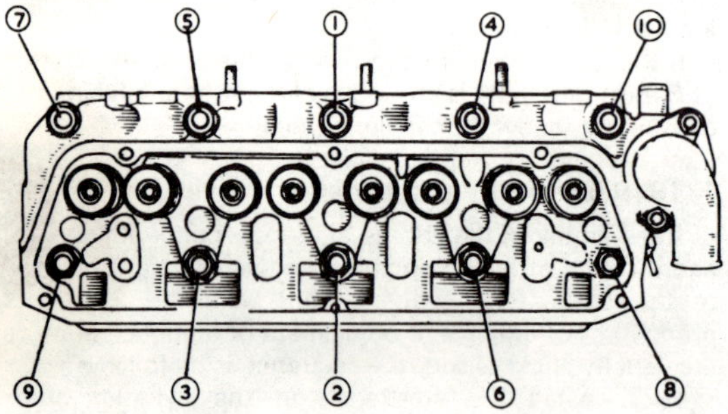

FIG 1:24 Order of tightening cylinder head bolts and nuts

Adjust the rocker gear clearances. Inlet, .008 inch (.20 mm) on the 1250 and the 1500SC and .010 inch (.25 mm) on the 1500TC. Exhaust, .016 inch (.40 mm) for all models. These clearances must be rechecked when the engine is HOT.

Tappet adjustment:

The recommended method of adjusting the tappets on this engine is as follows:

1 Using a $1\frac{5}{16}$ inch A.F. or $\frac{3}{4}$ inch WHIT. ring spanner on the crankshaft pulley retaining bolt, do not turn engine with fan blades, turn the engine until No. 1 cylinder is on TDC compression stroke, the TDC marks on the crankshaft pulley aligned with mark on timing cover and No. 4 cylinder inlet valve just beginning to open. Adjust both valves on No. 1 cylinder.

2 Turn the crankshaft, in the normal direction of rotation, exactly half-a-turn. Adjust both valves on No. 3 cylinder.

3 Turn crankshaft half-a-turn and adjust No. 4 cylinder, both valves.

4 Turn crankshaft a further half-turn and adjust both valves on No. 2 cylinder.

Refit the inlet and exhaust manifolds. Install the distributor and check the timing by referring to **Chapter 3.** Assemble the fuel pump, fan blades and fit the new oil filter cannister.

Assemble the remaining parts and fill the sump with the appropriate oil.

Checking the valve timing:

This method of checking is necessary only when an incorrect replacement of the timing chain is suspected after the timing cover and cylinder heads have been refitted. It suffices as a quick check to confirm or reject ones suspicions.

1 Remove the rocker gear cover and turn the engine to bring the No. 1 piston to TDC at the top of the compression stroke. Adjust the No. 1 exhaust valve rocker clearance to .10 inch (2.54 mm). This is necessary because the timing cannot be checked at normal rocker clearances.

2 Now turn the engine to take the piston through its firing stroke and part of the exhaust stroke and stop turning when the pointer on the crankshaft pulley indicates that the position is about 60 deg. BTDC.

3 Now, very slowly turn the engine and at the same time try to spin the pushrod under the No. 1 exhaust valve rocker. Immediately the pushrod becomes just free to turn, which will indicate the exhaust valve has closed, stop turning the engine and look at the position of the mark on the crankshaft pulley. On 1250 engines the pointer should indicate 25 deg. BTDC. On 1500 engines the pointer should indicate 22 deg. BTDC.

4 If the valve timing is one tooth out, the position on the crankshaft pulley will be 18 deg. or $3\frac{1}{2}$ sections of the spacing marks, before or after the correct position.

5 Readjust the No. 1 exhaust valve to its correct clearance of .016 inch (.40 mm).

1:19 Replacing engine in car

(a) Assuming that the engine has been removed without the gearbox, the latter still being supported in the car on the trolley jack, first make sure the two locating dowels are in position in the engine cylinder block/gearbox face. Engage the first gear on the car.

Raise the engine by crane and manoeuvre over and down into the engine compartment. Then ease it into position, taking care that the gearbox drive shaft splines enter the splined hole of the clutch plate without effort. If necessary, turn the engine or gearshaft to facilitate entry. **Throughout this mating, keep the cylinder block and bellhousing faces parallel.**

Refit the bolts securing the engine block to the bellhousing, and tighten. Lower the engine until the mountings are in position on the front crossbar and secure. The sling may now be removed.

Reinstall the starter and reconnect the heavy duty starter current lead and the solenoid control lead. Connect the battery earth cable to the top fixing bolt of the starter motor.

Reinstall the oil gauge pipe and reconnect the leads to the transducers. Reconnect the fuel feed pipe to the fuel pump, the LT lead to the distributor make-and-break terminal and the HT lead from the distributor to the ignition coil.

Reconnect the radiator and car heating hoses to the engine outlet and cooling pump inlet pipes. Secure with the hose clips. Reconnect the exhaust pipe to the manifold flange, using a new gasket.

Reconnect the leads to the alternator. Reinstall the throttle cable and choke connections. Refit the air filter.

Reinstall the fan on the cooling pump shaft, fit the V-belt coupling fan, alternator and crankcase pulleys and tension by adjusting the alternator mounting. Refill the radiator and the sump and reconnect the battery positive to its cable connector.

The engine is now ready for the trial run.

(b) Should the engine be removed with the gearbox in position, the engine must be made to hang at about 45 deg. from the vertical to enable it to enter the engine compartment. It is then lowered into the engine compartment, slowly turning the engine until it is level with the gearbox, the latter meanwhile being slowly raised on its jack to suit.

Reinstall the bolts securing the front of the engine to the crossmember and those holding the crossmember attached to the gearbox to the body underframe. Reconnect the hydraulic pipe coupling the clutch master cylinder to the slave cylinder and bleed. Reconnect the reverse light switch cable. Replace the screws holding the gearlever in position.

Recouple the propeller shaft and secure. Reconnect the speedometer cable. Subsequent procedure is then as from the paragraph starting 'Reinstall the starter . . .' above.

Finally reinstall the anti-roll bar fixing bolts.

Start the engine. It may take a few turns before firing as it is necessary to prime the carburetters by the fuel pump before an explosive mixture can enter the cylinders. Allow the engine to tick over at about 500 rev/min for a period, then remove the cylinder head cover and check that the oil is flowing freely over the rockers and draining down the pushrod holes. When the engine is hot, check that the valve clearances are as set cold (see **FIG 1:25**). Replace the cover.

After about fifteen minutes, tighten the exhaust nuts and inspect the various oil and water joints for signs of leakage. Tighten where necessary.

FIG 1:25 Setting the rocker to valve clearances with cover removed

The final stage is the tuning of the carburetters for slow-running, the procedure for which is detailed in **Chapter 2**, and the replacement of the engine compartment bonnet.

After the car has taken its first run following an engine overhaul, remember to remove the valve cover and retorque the cylinder head nuts. This will necessitate a recheck of inlet and exhaust valve rocker clearances.

1:20 Exhaust system

The exhaust system comprises a single exhaust manifold coupled to an exhaust pipe through a flange terminating in a silencer with a further expansion box mounted at the rear of the car close to the exhaust pipe exit. The two, silencer and expansion box, are mounted in series and are connected by a slip joint enabling either silencer or expansion box to be replaced individually.

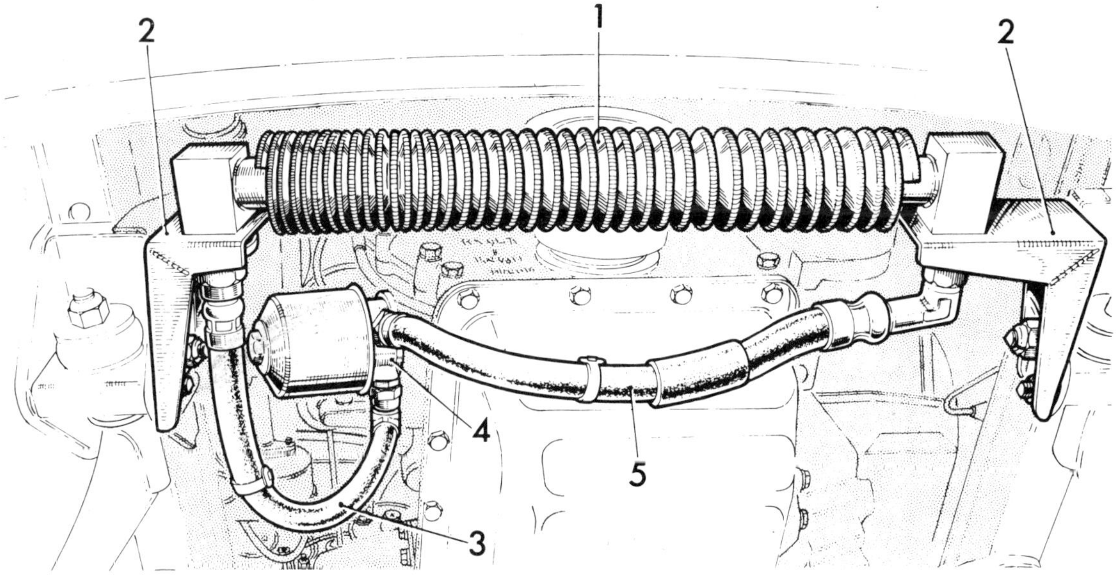

FIG 1:26 Oil cooler details

Key to Fig 1:26 1 Oil cooler 2 Mounting brackets 3 Inlet hose 4 Adaptor block 5 Outlet hose

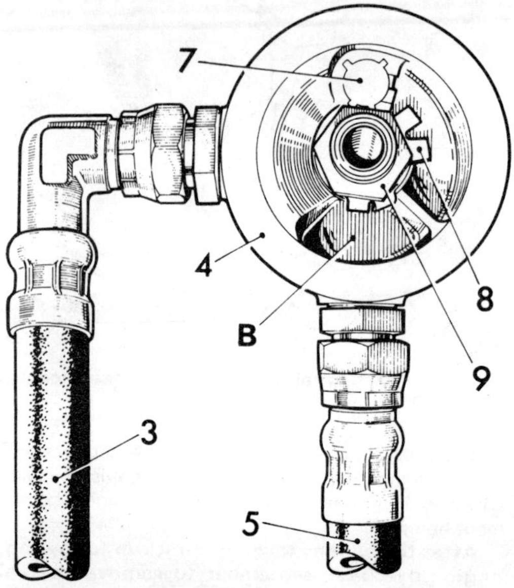

FIG 1 : 27 Filter adaptor

Key to Fig 1 : 27 3 Inlet hose 4 Adaptor block 5 Outlet hose 7 Bypass valve 8 Lockwasher 9 Hexagon union head **B** Leading to filter

When removing a defective silencer or expansion box in which heat and rust have made separation difficult, remember to cut or ease clear the section on the part to be discarded so as to leave the remainder round and undamaged for insertion in the replacement socket.

1 : 21 The oil cooler

The engine oil cooler is fitted to certain models, in front of and below the engine. The installation is shown in **FIG 1 : 26**. Oil from the pump enters the adaptor block 4 directly from the engine and passes through the pipe 3 to the intake end of the cooler 1. After passing through the cooling element the oil then flows through the flexible hose 5 back to the adaptor block where it is directed through the filter, which is screwed onto the block, and back into the engine.

A non-adjustable valve in the adaptor block allows oil to bypass the cooler and flow direct into the filter if any obstruction should develop in the cooler or its connections.

Removal of the oil cooler for cleaning is quite straight forward but a few points on refitting may be of assistance.

Fit the mounting brackets 2 to the side members, noting that the longer bracket is on the lefthand side.

Place the cooler in position through the bracket holes and fit the flat washers, spring washers and nuts.

If the oil filter is to be renewed, remove the filter and unscrew its threaded connector from the cylinder block. Clean all the parts and reassemble as follows:

Check that the rubber sealing ring is in position on the rear face of the adaptor block, then place the locking washer 8 in **FIG 1 : 27** under the hexagon union head 9 before inserting the union through the adaptor block. Partly tighten the union with the adaptor block unions facing downwards.

Fit the two flexible hoses 3 and 5, then tighten the union 9 to a torque of 10 lb ft, taking care to see that the tabs of the lockwasher are kept as far as possible in the anticlockwise direction to prevent any possible slackening.

When fitting the oil filter remember that it should only be tightened by hand.

Run the engine and check for leaks. Check the oil level and top up as necessary.

1 : 22 Fault diagnosis

(a) Engine will not start

1 Flat battery
2 Loose or corroded battery terminals
3 Faulty starter switch
4 Faulty starter motor
5 Faulty ignition coil
6 Disconnected HT lead from distributor to coil
7 Broken HT pencil in distributor cap
8 Broken make-and-break spring
9 Dirty make-and-break contacts
10 Jammed moving contact arm
11 Faulty capacitor
12 Ignition timing slipped
13 Wrongly connected HT leads to plugs
14 Dirty sparking plugs
15 Choked fuel line or carburetter jets
16 Faulty fuel pump
17 Empty fuel tank
18 Air lock in fuel line
19 Jammed starter pinion (Bendix type start)
20 Open circuit in starter solenoid wiring
21 Condensation on plugs, in distributor cap or on HT leads

A little commonsense will tell the probable cause from the many possible ones. If the engine will not turn, suspect the battery, starter switch, and starter in that order. Check also for a jammed pinion. If the engine turns but will not fire, suspect low fuel, damp distributor or plugs, capacitor, carburetter jets, low battery volts, etc.

(b) Engine fires, then stalls

1 Idling jet out of adjustment
2 Choke not out
3 Slow-running adjustment too slow
4 Dirty or over-gapped plugs

(c) Engine runs but without power

1 Ignition timing slipped
2 Automatic advance system not operating
3 Valve springs weak
4 Worn distributor cam
5 Wrong tappet clearances
6 Burnt valves

(d) Engine runs but fades at speed with load

1 Fuel starvation through faulty pump
2 Fuel starvation through wrong needle valve setting
3 Fuel starvation through choked filters
4 Fuel starvation through choked line from tank

(e) Engine fires erratically on idling

1 Wrong idling jet setting
2 Faulty plug
3 Weak valve spring on one cylinder
4 Wrong tappet adjustment on one or more cylinders

(f) Engine 'spits'

1 Water in carburetter
2 Leaking head gasket

(g) Engine 'pinks'

1 Wrong octane fuel
2 Ignition too far advanced

(h) Engine overheats

1 Low water in radiator
2 Slipping fan on pump belt
3 Ignition too far retarded
4 Choked radiator
5 Gasket blown in head

(j) Engine spits back into carburetter

1 Weak inlet valve spring
2 No clearance on inlet valve tappet
3 Sticking inlet valve stem
4 Transposed plug connections

NOTES

CHAPTER 2

CARBURETTERS AND FUEL SYSTEM

2:1 Fuel pump, description

The AC mechanically-operated fuel pump is driven from an eccentric cam on the camshaft midway between the two valve cams for the front cylinder. The pump incorporates its own gauze filter and glass cover bowl which is easily accessible for cleaning at regular intervals.

FIG 2:1 shows a general view of the pump with the filter bowl removed and a section through the pump displaying the working parts.

The cam 7, is held in close contact with the cam lever 6, by the compression spring 4. Both cam lever and link arm 9, are on a common pivot 8, but are loosely connected, raising of the lever depressing the arm to pull the diaphragm 13, down but not necessarily following the lever on its return. The diaphragm 13, is held in an upward direction by the spring 12, and this force, communicated to the link arm by the rod 11, is the one providing the return follow up between the arm and the lever.

In the sealed chamber above the diaphragm, two spring-loaded valves, 1 and 16, control the flow through the pump. When the diaphragm is depressed, valve 16 closes and petrol from the tank is drawn through the inlet union 3, around the inside of the glass bowl and through the filter gauze 17, down into the diaphragm chamber via the valve 1. On the return stroke, the spring 12, pushes the diaphragm upwards, closing the inlet valve 1, and opening the outlet valve 16, forcing the fuel in the chamber 15, through the outlet 14, to the carburetter.

If, however, the float chamber in the carburetter is full and the needle valve closed, the back pressure prevents the valve opening and the diaphragm and rod is restrained from making the full stroke, the loose coupling between the lever and link arm enabling spring 4 to keep the end of the lever in close contact with the cam without attempting to make the diaphragm follow.

In this manner, the amount of fuel delivered in each stroke is regulated by the pump to suit the requirements of the carburetter while quiet operation is ensured by the end of the cam lever always being in close contact with the cam face.

The pump is secured to the engine crankcase by two bolts passing through the flange of the body 10, the diaphragm and pump chamber being secured to the body by six cheese-headed screws. The bowl is retained in place by a wire stirrup and screw, a gasket 2, ensuring a petrol proof seal. The gauze filter is a slip-on fit to the centre column being retained in place by three glass projections within the bowl.

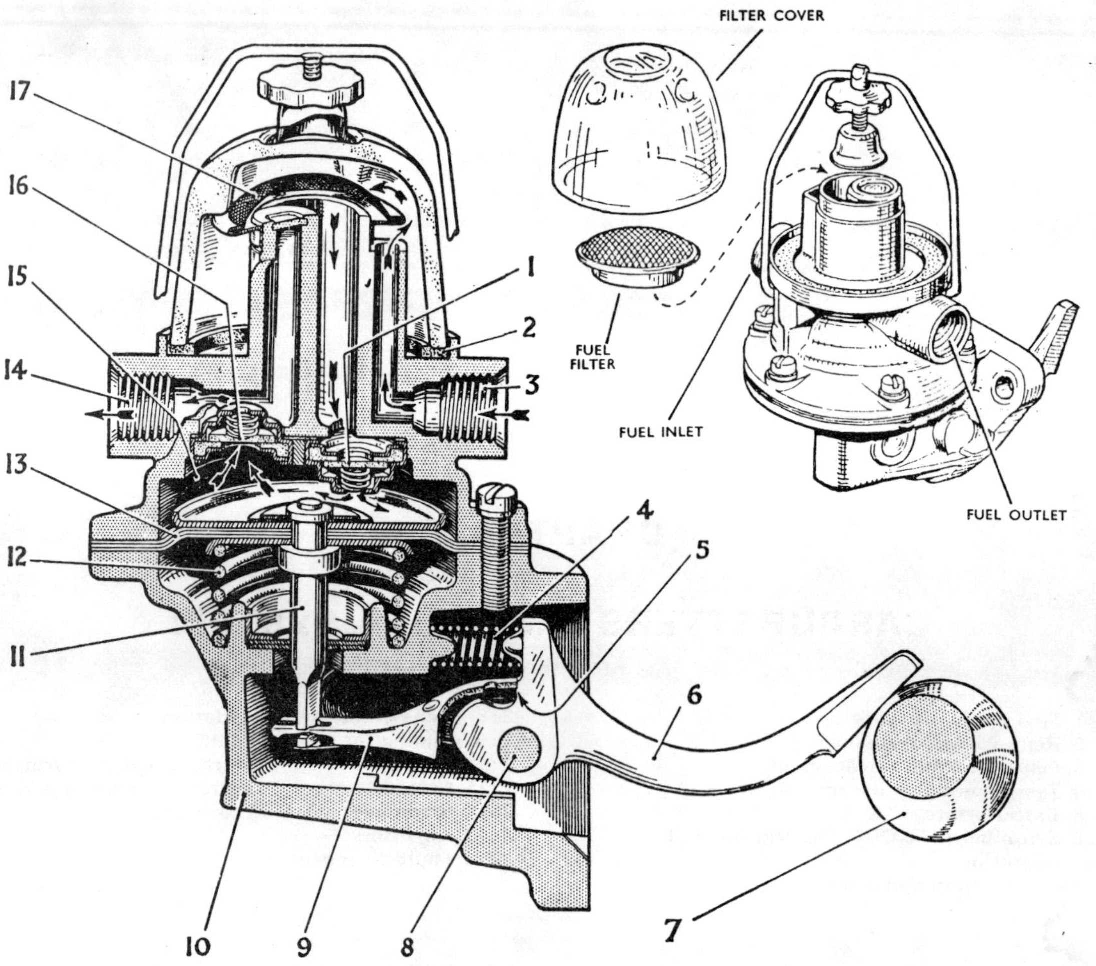

FIG 2:1 General view and section of fuel pump

Key to Fig 2:1 1 Inlet valve 2 Sealing gasket 3 Fuel inlet 4 Cam lever return spring 5 Cam lever to link arm contact area 6 Cam lever 7 Eccentric cam 8 Pivot 9 Link arm 10 Underbody 11 Diaphragm operating rod 12 Spring 13 Diaphragm 14 Fuel outlet 15 Fuel chamber 16 Outlet valve 17 Gauze filter

2:2 Removal and dismantling

To remove the pump from the engine, unscrew the unions to the pipes from the petrol tank, sealing the latter to prevent loss of fuel, and to the carburetter. Loosen and remove the bolts securing the pump body to the crankcase and carefully extract, together with the crankcase sealing gasket. Operate the lever arm a few times to expel the enclosed fuel from the outlet into a convenient receptacle and then transfer to the bench for dismantling.

Prior to dismantling, clean the exterior thoroughly and make a small mark across the flange of the upper and lower halves so that they go together again in the same position on reassembly. Loosen the upper screw and swing the stirrup clear of the bowl. Remove the bowl, sealing ring and filter gauze. Remove the stirrup.

Remove the six screws and separate the two halves of the pump body, the diaphragm still being in the lower half. Turn the diaphragm and pullrod assembly through 90 deg. to free the end of the pullrod from the link arm and remove together with the spring, oil sealing cup and washer. Extract the two cam lever pin retainers and push the pin through to free the cam lever, link arm and associated washers and spring.

The dismantled fuel pump will now appear as in FIG 2:2. **The valves are a press fit into the body and should not be removed unless they have to be replaced. Levering them out of position effectively destroys them.**

2:3 Inspection and replacement

Thoroughly clean all parts in paraffin. Dry off and examine each part for signs of wear. The valve body and valves must be thoroughly clean, the valves seating properly and the valve springs operating effectively. If they are not satisfactory, lever them out of their seatings with a screwdriver and insert new valves, staking them in position with a punch. Always renew the ring gaskets.

The diaphragm and pullrod, a single assembly, must be renewed if there are any signs of wear or cracking. Worn parts must be renewed. Very little wear can be accepted on the rocker arm pin or bearing holes and faces of the cam lever and link arm. Always renew the gaskets at every dismantling. The springs usually are not likely to need replacement unless they are broken or deformed.

Reassembly commences with the installation of the cam lever and link arm on the pin and its assembly into the lower body. Check that the cam lever operates smoothly and that the link arm does not bind. When satisfied, insert the pin retainers, tapping them into place.

Insert the diaphragm spring and place the diaphragm assembly in position over the spring, centring the spring in the cup below the diaphragm. Holding the pump with the cam lever in the 12 o'clock position, rotate the diaphragm until the locating tab on the periphery is at 11 o'clock. In this position, the slot at the base of the rod is parallel with that in the link arm and the diaphragm can be depressed to enable the flattened end to enter the link arm slot.

Holding it in this position, rotate the diaphragm anticlockwise a quarter turn to the 8 o'clock position to engage the link in the fork. The six holes coincide with those in the body flange. Check that the diaphragm now floats up and down on the spring as the cam lever is operated.

To fit the upper half, press the cam lever inwards until the diaphragm rests on the surrounding flange and place the upper half in position, checking that the marks made before dismantling coincide. Insert the six screws and tighten until the heads just engage with the spring washers. Check that the diaphragm flange does not overlap the joint at any point (if it does, the diaphragm is not centred), and then tighten the screws alternately.

Fit the filter gauze, seat the sealing ring, mount the stirrup and screw and position the bowl. Tighten the top screw.

2:4 Testing and installation

It is advisable to give the pump a test before installing in the car. To do this, first make up two unions with metal or rubber pipe extensions, one for the inlet and one for the outlet. Secure the pump upright in a vice the jaws of which grip the underbody lightly and insert the inlet pipe into a container of paraffin a short distance from and slightly below the pump.

Unscrew the stirrup, remove the bowl and filter and pour a little paraffin into the two vertical ducts to wet the valves below. Replace the filter and bowl and secure. With the outlet pipe inserted in a glass measuring jar, start pumping with the cam lever until the glass bowl fills and paraffin starts to flow into the measuring jar. Empty the measuring jar, reinsert the pipe and start to pump the lever about ten times. Measure the amount of paraffin delivered. It should be not less than .5 cc per stroke.

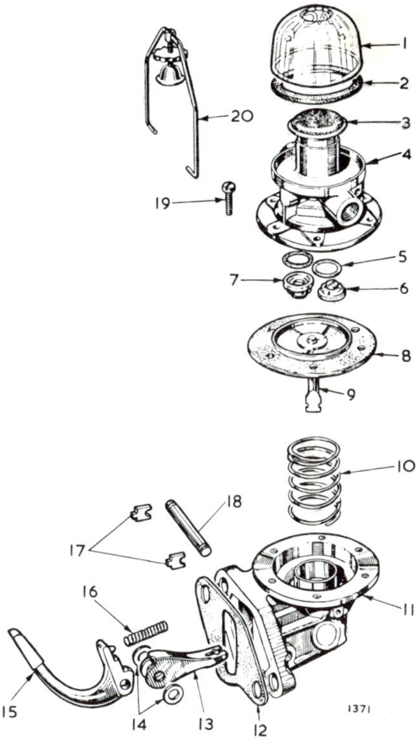

FIG 2:2 Components of petrol pump

Key to Fig 2:2 1 Cover 2 Joint 3 Gauze 4 Body upper 5 Gaskets 6 Valve outlet 7 Valve inlet 8 Diaphragm 9 Rod 10 Spring 11 Body lower 12 Joint 13 Link 14 Washers 15 Rocker arm 16 Spring 17 Retainer 18 Pin 19 Screw 20 Clip

Next, operate the cam lever for a while and check that no air bubbles enter the bowl or emerge from the tube in the measuring jar. Air bubbles here indicate an air leak in the diaphragm chamber.

Finally, remove the inlet pipe connection and cover the inlet with a finger and then operate the lever. One should feel a distinct suction on the finger pad and, on removal, there should be a slight inrush of air.

Providing the pump passes all these tests, it may be reinstalled in the engine. First, mount the pump in position with the gasket properly located over the flange faces, check that the cam lever is resting on the camshaft eccentric and then insert the securing bolts (or, if the pump is attached by studs already inserted in the engine fit the securing nuts and washers) and tighten.

Recouple the pipe from the fuel tank to the inlet side and the pipe to the carburetter to the outlet side, then press the engine starter button from within the engine compartment and check that the bowl fills and fuel reaches the carburetter. Switch on and start the engine.

While the engine is running, check the unions for petrol leaks and the pump mounting flange for oil leaks

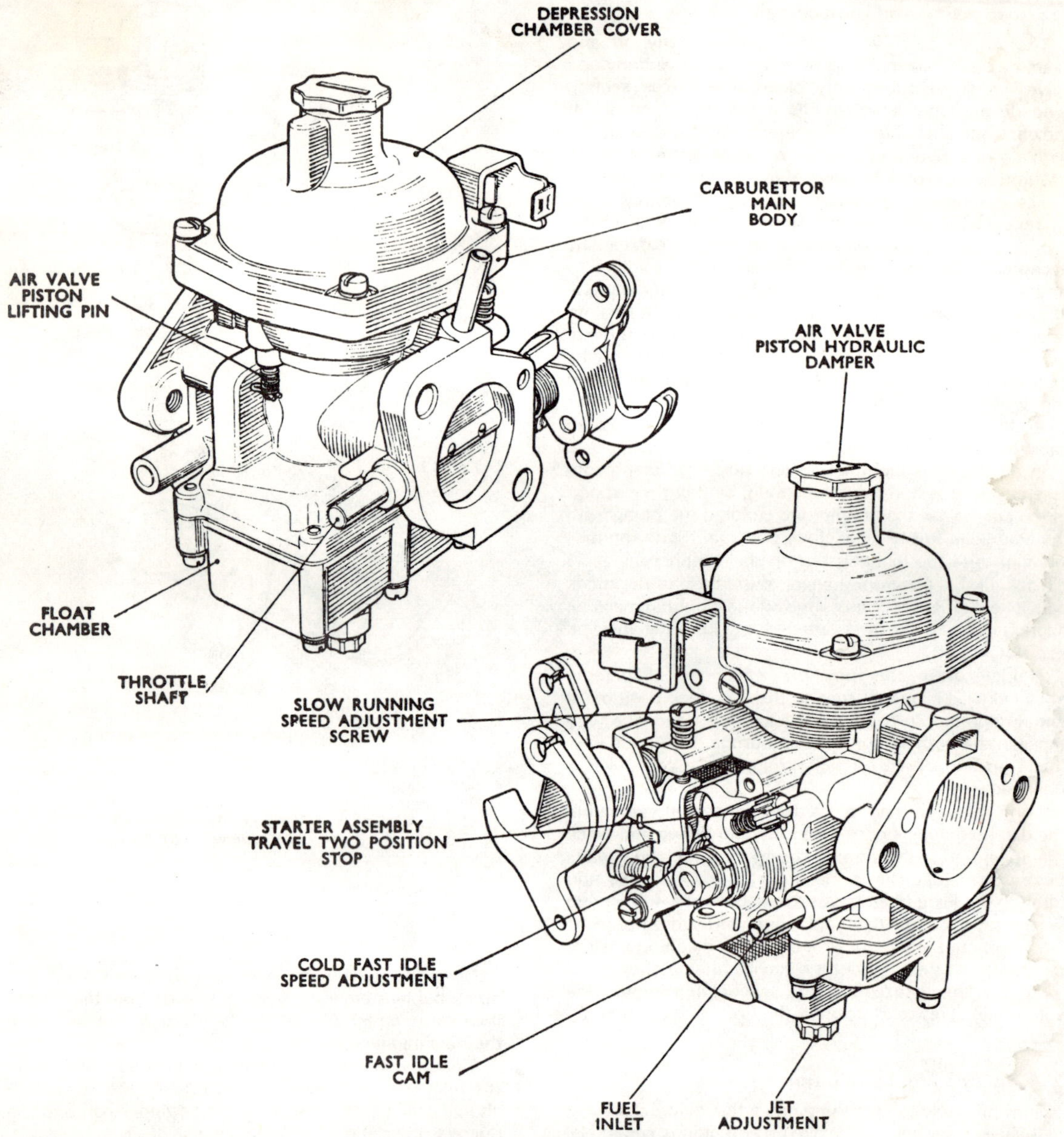

FIG 2:3 Stromberg 150 CDS Carburetter

from the sump. When running and without back pressure from the carburetter float chamber, the pump should be able to deliver one pint of fuel a minute with the engine turning at 1500 to 2000 rev/min. Since the camshaft runs at half engine speed, this corresponds to 750 to 1000 pump strokes per minute.

2:5 Carburetters

The carburetter in general use is the Stromberg 150CDS, made by Zenith. The Plymouth Cricket and models for the USA are fitted with the Stromberg CDSE embodying exhaust and crankcase emission control to meet local requirements and regulations. The GT model has a twin carburetter installations and so has the GLS Saloon which now replaces the GT.

2:6 Stromberg 150.CDS. Description and operation

The Stromberg carburetter is a constant depression pattern with side draught induction and incorporates a separate starter assembly. The general appearance, with the main parts named, is shown in **FIG 2:3**. A part sectional view (see **FIG 2:4**) enables the operational features to be understood from the following description.

When the engine is not running, the air valve piston 9, rests on the carburetter body 5, in the draught tube virtually obstructing it. Fuel in the float chamber 19, is maintained at the proper level by the float 20, the arm of which, pivoting on the spindle 13, in bracket 14, controls the needle valve 12, admitting fuel to the chamber from the inlet 10.

The jet 24, is retained in the centralizing bush 11, and its retaining screw 18, by the opposing forces of the spring 22, and jet adjustment screw 17, fuel being admitted to the jet via side holes in the retaining and jet adjustment screws from the encircling float chamber. A close fitting O-ring 15, seals the float chamber where it encircles the jet retaining screw.

Rise and fall of the air valve piston 9, taking with it the tapered fuel metering needle 21, concentric with the jet, is controlled by the differential pressure between the upper chamber 31, and lower chamber 4, the latter being open to the atmosphere via the hole 6, and the former being connected to the draught tube via holes 25, in the lower end of the piston. The two chambers are separated by the diaphragm 3, which is clamped to the piston by the ring 29.

Normally, the piston is held on the seating by spring 30, which is, however, not strong enough to overcome the full lift of the piston by the differential pressures, the piston rising and falling with charges in the depression within the draught tube, varying the width of the annular orifice, or jet, created by the needle within the hole in the jet body 24.

A dashpot comprising a piston on the spindle 1, attached to a screw in the air chamber cover 32, working in the cylinder 2, of the piston, stabilizes the hunting which might occur from cyclic changes in the differential pressures and also provides a delay feature giving a temporary enrichment of mixture on sudden acceleration.

With the throttle butterfly valve 27, closed on the stop 28, enriched vapour is introduced into the draught tube by the starter assembly (see **FIG 2:5**). This comprises two discs, 37 and 41, on the valve spindle 36, the inner disc being drilled with a number of holes giving access to an annular groove 38, leading to the port 39, in the draught tube. The same disc has, on the opposite side, another annular channel giving access to the annular channel in the second disc which communicates with the perforations or holes. With the starting control in full operation, the discs are turned to permit the flow of fuel, drawn from the float chamber via duct 40, to be routed between the two discs and through the holes into the port 39, the amount of fuel being progressively decreased as the control is pushed in, reducing the number of holes uncovered. At the same time, the cam 34, opens the throttle valve via the arm and adjusting screw 42, so regulating the amount of air and fuel entering the inlet manifold.

Normally, the full use of the starting control is not necessary and a second two-position stop 33, limits the extent of withdrawal for all but the coldest conditions. In winter, this stop can be set for full starting control utilising the full number of metering holes.

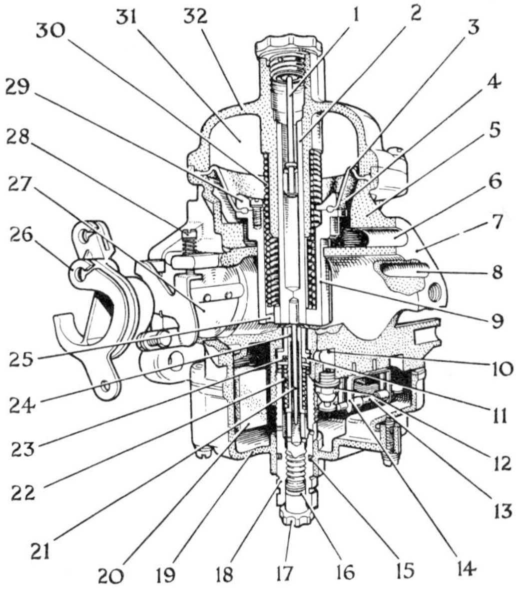

FIG 2:4 Section through Stromberg carburetter

Key to Fig 2:4 1 Dashpot piston 2 Dashpot cylinder 3 Diaphragm 4 Lower chamber 5 Body 6 Air hole to lower chamber 7 Air filter mounting flange 8 Air hole to float chamber 9 Air valve piston 10 Fuel inlet 11 Centralizing bush 12 Needle valve 13 Spindle 14 Bracket 15 O-ring seal 16 O-ring seal 17 Jet adjustment screw 18 Centralizing bush retaining screw 19 Float chamber 20 Float 21 Metering needle 22 Jet spring 23 O-ring seal 24 Jet 25 Depression transfer hole 26 Throttle lever 27 Butterfly valve 28 Slow-running adjustment screw 29 Diaphragm retaining ring 30 Air valve piston return spring 31 Upper chamber 32 Depression chamber cover

Operation of the carburetter can be understood by examining four stages; slow-running, an intermediate stage of throttle opening and the two conditions of full throttle, with low and high engine speeds (see **FIG 2:6**).

At idling speed and the engine ticking over, the throttle valve is opened only a trifle, set by the slow-running adjustment screw 28. The position of the piston is then as in (A), just raised from the stop permitting a small amount of air to pass at high velocity across the jet orifice which is choked back by the almost fully inserted metering needle 21. By suitably designing the taper of the needle the ratio of fuel to air is set to suit the engine at this speed.

As the accelerator is depressed, the throttle butterfly valve opens as in (B), air velocity across the bottom of the piston increases and the pressure above the diaphragm falls as the air is drawn down the hole 25. The piston valve rises, increasing the fuel content, while the velocity falls until a position of equilibrium is reached in which air flow is balanced against fuel content for the setting of the butterfly valve.

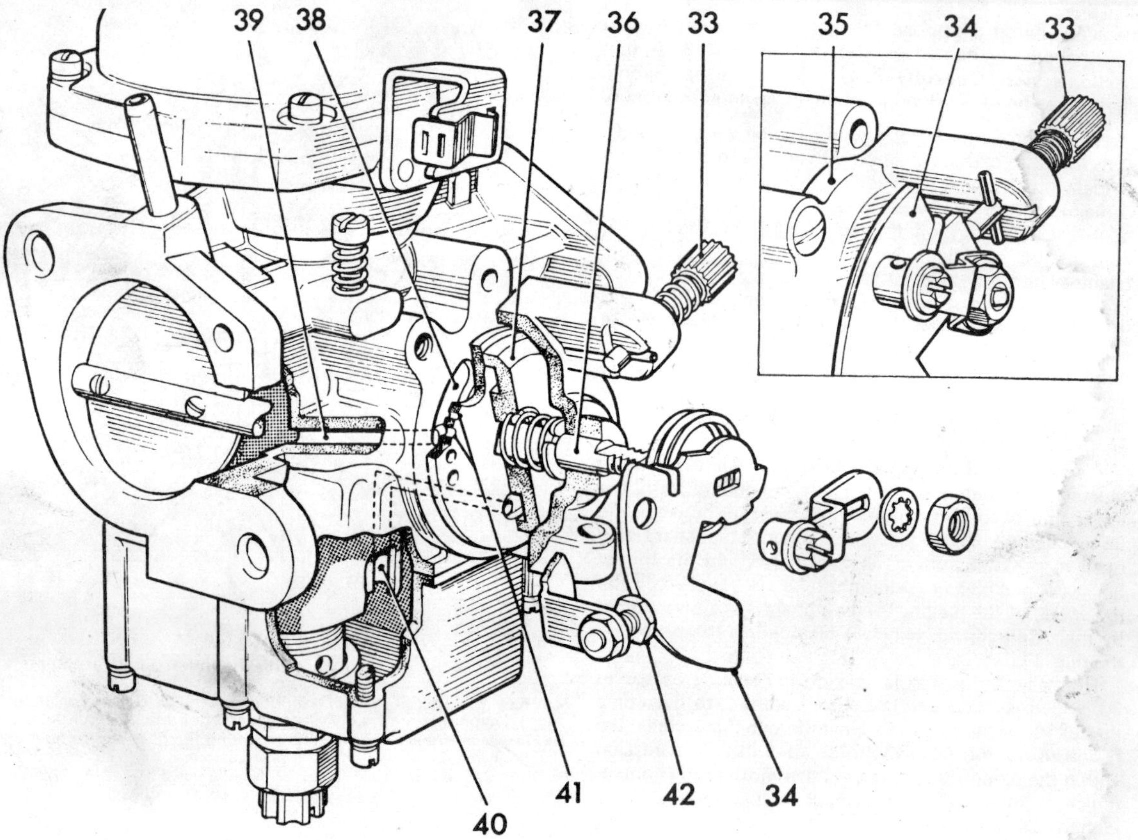

FIG 2:5 **Starter assembly detail on Stromberg 150.CDS Carburetter**

Key to Fig 2:5 33 Two position stop 34 Fast idling cam 35 Outer housing 36 Valve spindle 37 Disc valve 38 Annular channel to port 39 Port to throttle bore 40 Fuel duct 41 Metering holes 42 Adjusting screw

At full throttle, with the engine speed reduced by load, the piston again takes up a position where the air velocity past the bottom of the piston is balanced against fuel content to give the best ratio irrespective of the restriction, within reason, of the butterfly valve (C).

At lesser load, if the throttle is suddenly opened, the increased velocity draws air from the upper chamber raising the piston, which is restricted in its upward movement by the hydraulic damper, causing a richer mixture to be formed for acceleration purposes. During the acceleration phase, the piston rises steadily maintaining a constant depression over the jet and enlarging the jet size, by withdrawing the needle, as the volume of air increases, so maintaining the required fuel/air ratio for the full range of engine requirements of speed and load.

2:7 Dismantling and inspection

Disconnect the fuel pipe from the pump, the throttle and the starting control cables. Remove the air filter. Unbolt and remove the carburetter from the manifold taking care to preserve the gasket. Thoroughly clean the exterior and transfer to the bench.

Remove the screws securing the float chamber and draw it free from the jet bushing retaining screw, slightly twisting meanwhile to ease it from the sealing O-ring 15. Remove the jet adjusting screw, hydraulic damper and depression chamber cover. Lift out the air valve piston, needle and diaphragm assembly. Blow the fuel feed holes in the starter assembly clear by applying compressed air to the hole 40, in the float chamber, moving the starter assembly across its full travel several times with the stop screw (33 in **FIG 2:5**) fully out.

Blow clean all other ports and drillings and wash the extracted components in paraffin or petrol. Examine all components for signs of wear or distortion.

If it is necessary to replace the diaphragm, remove the four screws securing the retaining ring 29, to the piston and replace by a new diaphragm, taking care to see that the tabs are properly located in their annular recesses. **(This change can be carried out without removing the carburetter from the engine, if necessary, access being obtained by simple removal of the depression chamber cover 32).**

Check operation of the valve damper piston. When the cylinder is filled with clean Super Shell oil (not a low viscosity grade), the piston should be able to fall freely but be drawn up slowly with some resistance when lifted by a finger.

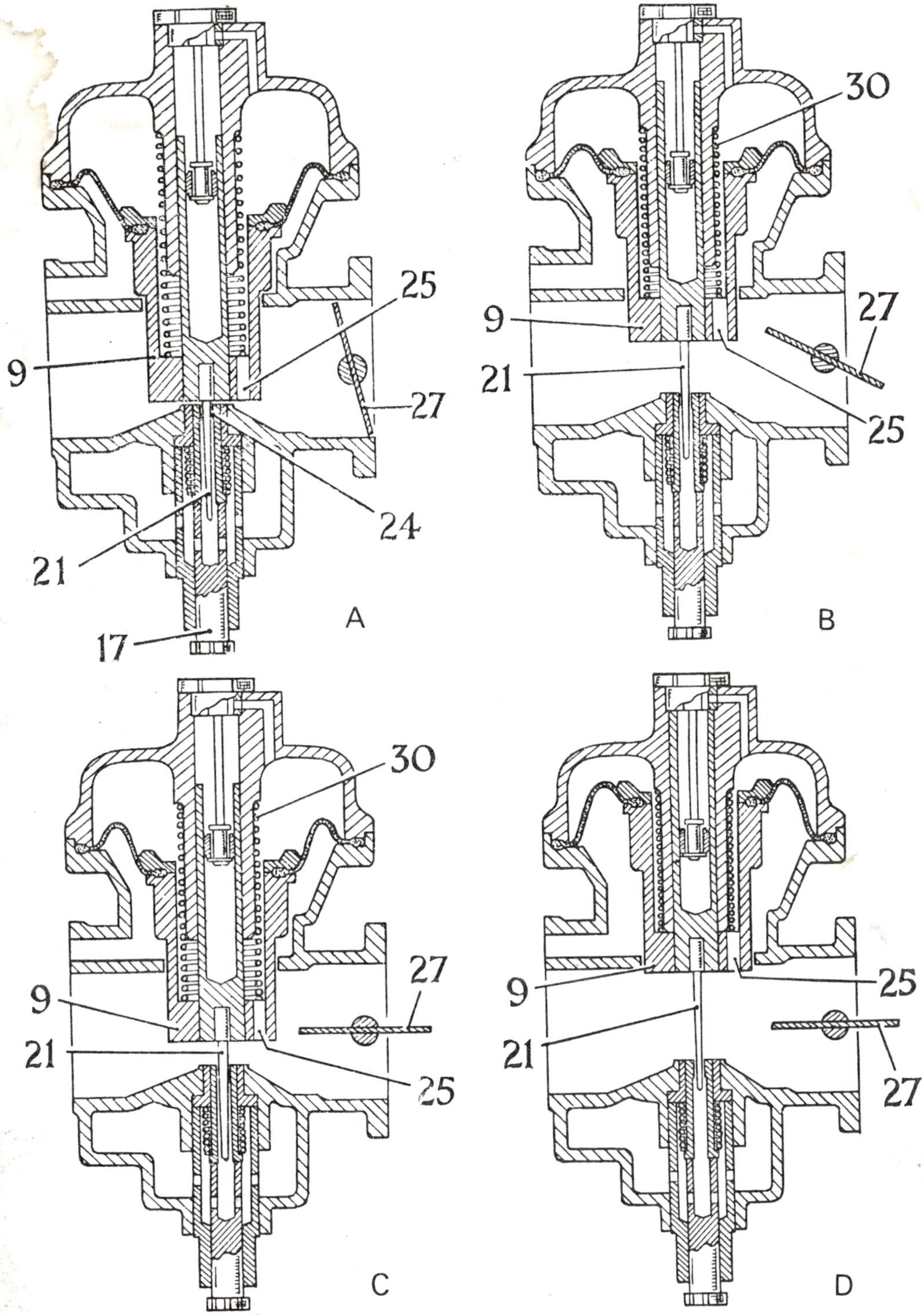

FIG 2:6 Operational phases of Stromberg carburetter. (A) Slow-running. (B) Half throttle. (C) Full throttle, engine under load. (D) Full throttle, full speed. For key (see FIG 2:4)

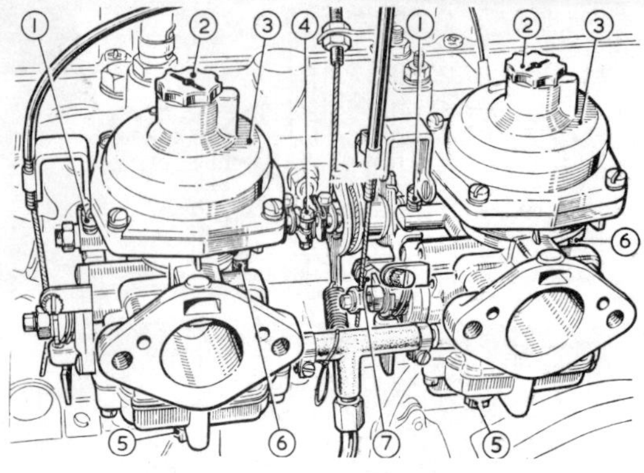

FIG 2:7 Setting twin Stromberg carburetters. Figures refer to text references

There is no need to dismantle the carburetter any further but particular care must be taken not to bend or remove the needle from the end of the piston. This is factory set and centralized in the jet orifice.

Float setting:

This check or adjustment is only necessary when flooding or excessive fuel consumption occurs. With the float chamber removed, invert the carburetter and measure the two highest and the two lowest points of the float from the float chamber mounting flange. The highest points of the float should be .63 inch (16 mm) above the

FIG 2:8 Interconnections on Exhaust Emission Control system

Key to Fig 2:8 1 Carburetter 2 Control valve pipe interconnection 3 Control valve 4 Inlet manifold to control valve connection, large bore 5 Vacuum advance line 6 Vacuum retard line 9 Crankcase emission pipe 10 Flame trap 11 Vacuum advance capsule 12 Distributor 13 Vacuum retard capsule

flange and the lowest points .35 inch (9 mm) above the flange.

To correct, bend the float arm extension in the required direction. The float arm is the one that contacts the float needle but take care to ensure that having bent the arm it is contacting the needle valve centre at 90 deg. Small corrections can be made by placing an extra washer under the float needle valve assembly.

2:8 Reassembly and installation

Reassembly and installation is a simple reversal of the removal and dismantling procedure. After installation, unscrew the top of the chamber cover and withdraw the dashpot piston, top up with the Super Shell oil to within $\frac{1}{4}$ inch of the top of the bore 2, re-insert the piston and screw the top home. If it does not operate smoothly, extract the old oil and replace by fresh, clean oil.

2:9 Tuning for slow-running (FIG 2:4)

Dealing first with a **single carburetter** installation, first remove the dashpot piston damper 1 and insert a metal rod into the cylinder 2, to hold the piston down while the jet adjusting screw 17 is turned to meet it at the jet and piston faces. Check that the piston is free in its bore by lifting it, using the air valve piston lifting pin (see **FIG 2:3**) and allowing it to fall. A sound should be heard as the piston bottoms on the jet face. If the piston does not fall freely, the jet will need centralizing. Loosen the bushing retaining screw a half turn and screw in the jet adjusting screw so that it again contacts the piston and give the retaining screw 18, a sharp tap, on one of its hexagon faces, to reseat the bushing. Unscrew the jet adjusting screw and retighten the bushing retaining screw. Again check for free fall.

Slacken off the jet adjusting screw two turns. Re-insert the dashpot piston, top up with oil, and start the engine, allowing it to reach operating temperature before proceeding farther. Adjust slow-running screw 28, to give a speed of 700 to 750 rev/min, but if automatic transmission is fitted the idling speed should be 600 rev/min. Readjust the jet adjusting screw half a turn either way to find the best position for smooth running. If it alters engine speed, correct by the screw 28.

With the two-position stop as in the insert to **FIG 2:5**, set the cam 34, to its full back position resting on the stop. The cams are stamped with identifying letters, either SA or M. The M cam was introduced to reduce excessive fast speed under choke conditions. The correct clearance for an SA cam is between .040 and .050 inch (1.02 and 1.27 mm). The correct clearance for an M cam is between .030 and .040 inch (.76 and 1.02 mm). The carburetter is now set for both slow idling with the starting control set for normal, and fast idling when it is set for starting conditions.

Adjustment in a **twin carburetter** installation is a trifle more complex. First carry out the adjustments and checks for each carburetter as for a single carburetter installation, but setting back the jet adjustment screws two full turns exactly instead of only half a turn. Now unscrew the fast idling adjustment screw 7 (see **FIG 2:7**) **rear carburetter only** until it is clear of the cam. Loosen the clamping bolt between the two spindles 4.

Now set the slow-running screws 1, both so that a thin piece of paper is lightly gripped between the ends and the throttle levers. Remove the paper and turn the screws clockwise exactly two turns in each case, opening each throttle by the same amount. Re-tighten the clamp 4.

Run the engine until warm and make similar adjustments to both carburetters by turning the jet adjusting screws 5, one way or the other but by not more than half a turn. This is a similar procedure to the single carburetter installation.

Finally, remove the air cleaner and listen carefully to the hissing intake at each inlet and and make slight individual adjustments to one carburetter only by slackening the clamp 4, and advancing or retarding the throttle opening. Retighten the clamp and replace the air cleaner. If necessary readjust the idling speed to between 600 and 650 rev/min.

2:10 Exhaust emission control, single carburetter

The exhaust emission control system, developed to minimize carbon monoxide and unburnt fuel in the exhaust gases, as fitted to single Stromberg carburetter installations comprises a modified CDS carburetter, designated CDSE, a control valve and a distributor with overrun retard control. These are interconnected by small bore tubing as in **FIG 2:8** and a crankcase emission pipe, with flame trap 10, routes oil vapours into the air intake.

The main differences are in the running jet, which is not adjustable from below as in the CDS carburetter, and the incorporation of a throttle bypass valve, a temperature control valve and a slow-running air control screw. These are shown in detail in **FIG 2:9** and **FIG 2:10**.

The carburetter and the differentially controlled distributor vacuum advance device are interconnected as in **FIG 2:11**. The control valve 3, opens under engine overrun conditions when the inlet manifold vacuum falls below 21 inches Hg and, via the interconnecting tubing, applies the same depression to the throttle bypass valve 4, and distributor retard capsule 2.

Under normal conditions, and particularly in heavy traffic necessitating long periods of idling and slow-running, the higher engine temperatures combined with the richer mixtures necessary for good acceleration from a standstill, results in an exhaust content of unburnt fuel and incomplete combustion in a proportion of the remainder which is rich in carbon monoxide. In the Stromberg and similar carburetters, tuning of the main jet for good acceleration tends to favour this condition.

In the CDSE, the main jet is factory fixed, not adjustable, and the metering needle is spring-loaded. This effectively prevents the production of an excessively over-rich mixture at low speeds, still further dilution being provided by extra air admitted through the temperature controlled bypass valve when the engine is over-hot. In this manner, almost perfect combustion is achieved in the majority of engine running conditions at normal and low speeds.

To overcome this, the control valve 3, opens when the depression is excessive (of the order of 21 inches Hg as against a more normal maximum of 11 to 15 inches Hg) and this, in turn, operates the throttle bypass valve 4, enabling more air to be mixed with the fuel and reducing the flow over the jet. At the same time the ignition is

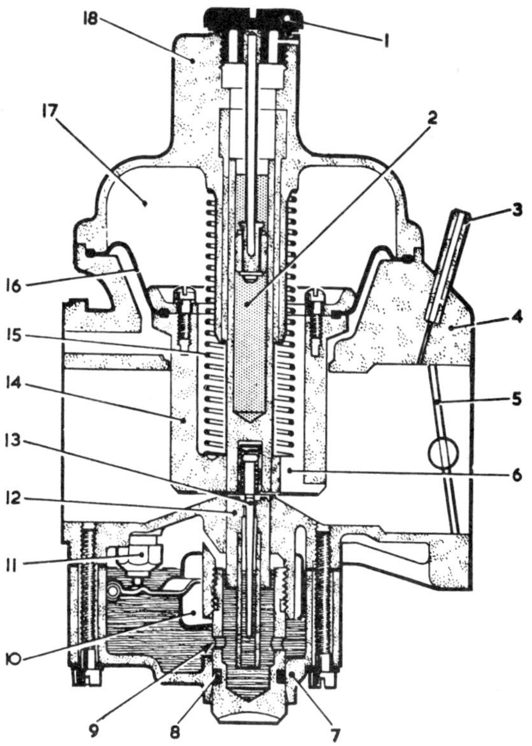

FIG 2:9 Section through CDSE carburetter

Key to Fig 2:9 1 Cap and piston for dashpot 2 Dashpot cylinder with oil 3 Vacuum advance connection 4 Body 5 Butterfly valve 6 Vent to upper chamber 7 Float chamber 8 O-ring seal 9 Fuel feed hole 10 Float 11 Needle valve 12 Main jet 13 Metering needle 14 Piston valve 15 Spring 16 Diaphragm 17 Upper chamber 18 Depression chamber cover

retarded permitting easier burning of the fuel within the cylinders.

On completion of the over-run and with the intake depression returning to normal, valve 3 closes and the controlled bleed 7, permits the depression in the retard capsule and behind the bypass valve to fall, so restoring normal operation.

Servicing of the CDSE carburetter to ensure the correct exhaust conditions necessitates the use of special equipment (vacuum gauges, an electronic diagnostic unit, etc), and should not be undertaken by the owner-mechanic. Otherwise the installation may be no better than a normal one and some risk of offending local regulations, where such are concerned with exhaust gas composition, may result.

2:11 Exhaust emission control, twin carburetter

The twin CDSE installation differs from the single in that there is no vacuum retard feature nor is there a control valve. In addition, the operation of the bypass valve depends on the differential depression across the piston valve, opening to permit additional air to enter the induction system if the differential is excessive.

The general arrangement is shown in **FIG 2:12**.

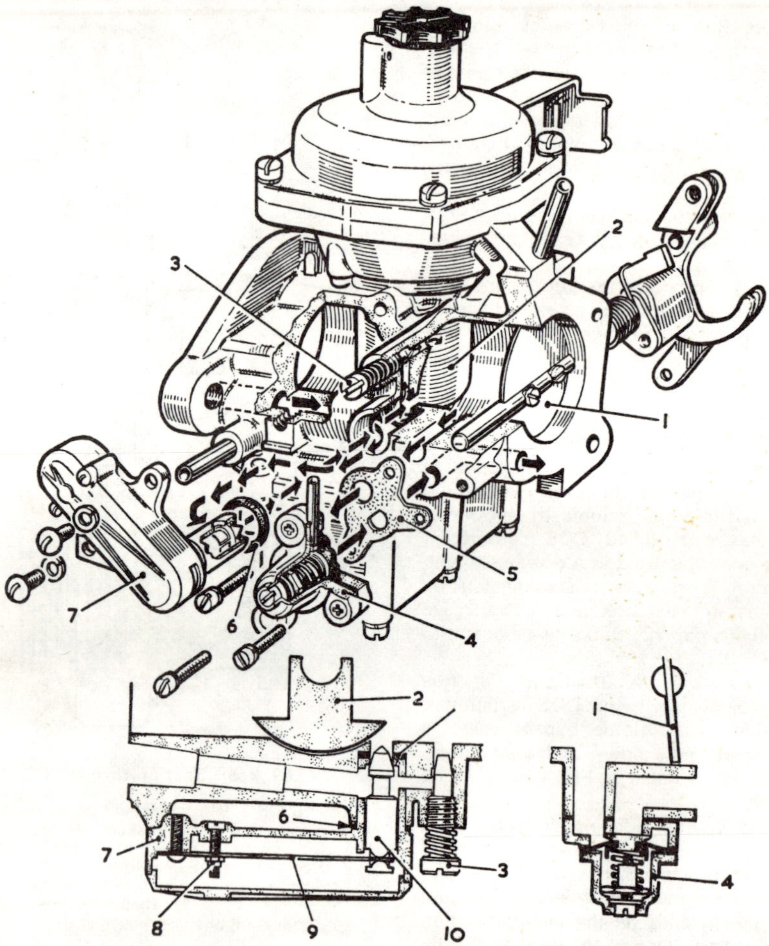

FIG 2:10 CDSE carburetter detail showing detail of bypass valve and temperature control valve

Key to Fig 2:10 1 Butterfly valve 2 Piston valve 3 Slow-running air adjustment 4 Bypass valve 5 Gasket 6 Joint ring 7 Temperature control valve 8 Leaf adjustment 9 Bi-metal leaf 10 Air inlet valve

To synchronize twin CDSE carburetters remove the air cleaner, tying the end of the throttle to the adjacent stop 7 (see **FIG 2:13,** left) and disconnect throttle cable at carburetter. Slacken cam follower screw 1, clear of cam and unscrew adjustment screws 2 and 3, on both carburetters clear of their abutments. Remove screw 4, from differential linkage.

Compress spring peg 5, by pushing screwdriver blade between tag 6, and peg head 5, and retain by piece of wire shaped as in inset 10. Close both throttles and now screw down 2 and 3 until they just rest on the abutments and the throttles are about to open. **Open front throttle by exactly two turns of 2.** Repeat on rear throttle screw 3. Set 4 until it just touches tag 6 and remove wire to release spring peg 5. The carburetters are now synchronized.

With the engine warm, adjust idling speed to 950 rev/min (750 rev/min if the transmission is automatic) by screw 2, screw 3 being set clear of its abutment. Listen to intake hiss and equalize by slight adjustment of 4. Finally, reset 3 to just contact its abutment plate.

Adjust the cam follower gap 1, to .05 inch and tighten the locknut. Reinstall the throttle cable and air cleaner and transfer the throttle spring back to the cleaner bracket.

2:12 Stromberg 150 CD3 carburetter

Some later models may be fitted with the CD3 series carburetter which is similar to the CDSE unit shown in **FIG 2:9** in that there is no jet adjustment. The CD3 carburetter has provision for small mixture adjustments by moving the needle up and down with an adjusting screw which is turned with a special tool. The adjusting screw and tool are shown in **FIG 2:14**. The adjusting screw must not be turned more than one turn in either direction of the datum position. The datum position is when the needle shoulder, or if the 'Delrin' washer is fitted the lower face of the washer, is flush with the bottom of the guide rod. It is essential that the needle is set in this position before adjustment is made.

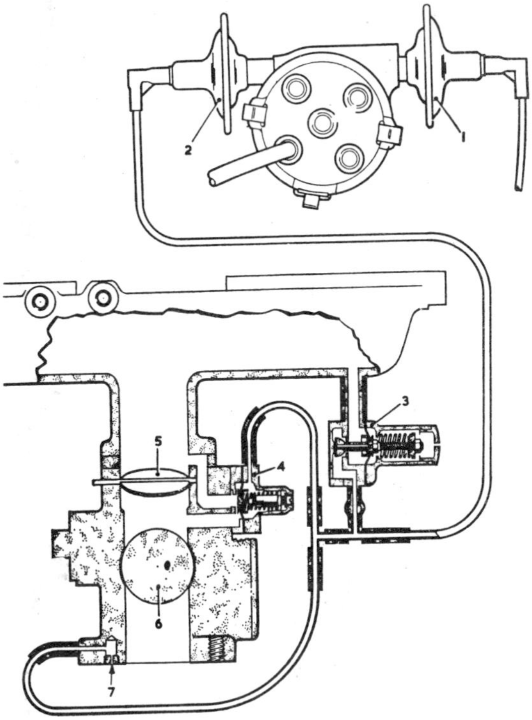

FIG 2:11 Schematic arrangement of Exhaust Emission Control system

Key to Fig 2:11 1 Vacuum advance capsule 2 Vacuum retard capsule 3 Control valve 4 Bypass valve 5 Butterfly throttle valve 6 Piston valve 7 Air bleed nipple

With the engine at normal running temperature the damper is removed and the adjusting tool fitted into the guide rod so that the location on the outer body of the tool locates in the guide rod. The outer body of the adjusting tool must be located and held still during adjustment to avoid damage to the air valve piston diaphragm. The inner 'Allen' key of the tool is then located into the adjusting screw. The mixture can be adjusted by turning the adjustment screw up to one full turn in either direction from the datum position. Raising the needle, by turning the adjusting screw clockwise, richens the mixture whilst lowering the needle, by turning the screw anticlockwise, weakens the mixture.

Whilst making adjustments to the needle adjusting screw the engine may have a tendency to 'stall', allow the engine to recover between each fractional adjustment by holding the engine speed at a fast idle for a few seconds to clear the manifold.

2:13 Air filters

The air filter fitted to the single Stromberg installations is shown, dismantled, in **FIG 2:15**. It comprises a removable cover 1, and main body 4, housing the renewable filter element 3, sealed between the gaskets 2. The assembly is secured to the carburetter intake flange by two studs 7, passing through the cover.

The renewable element is of the dry type and does not need wetting with oil or other fluid. The intake can be

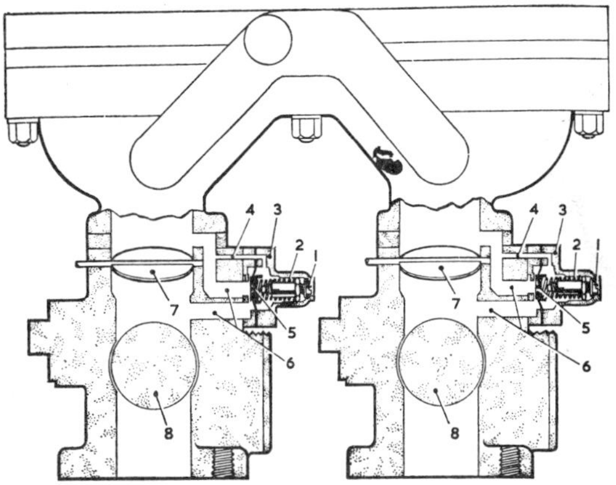

FIG 2:12 Schematic arrangement of twin carburetter Exhaust Emission control system

Key to Fig 2:12 1 Bypass valve 2 Spring 3 Valve body 4 Bypass passage 5 Diaphragm 6 Bypass ports 7 Butterfly valve 8 Piston valve

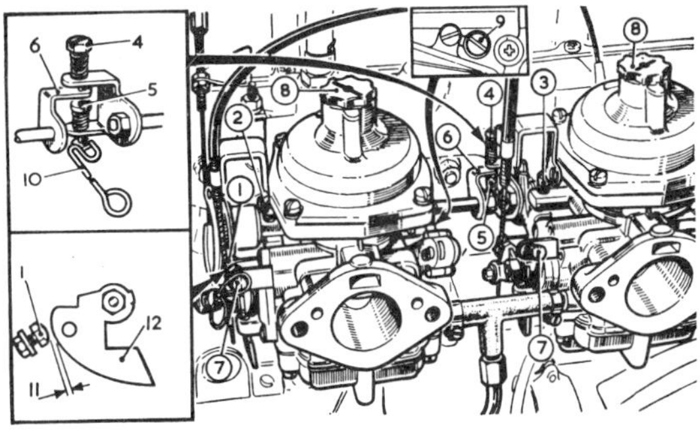

FIG 2:13 Synchronizing twin CDSE carburetters. Figures refer to text references

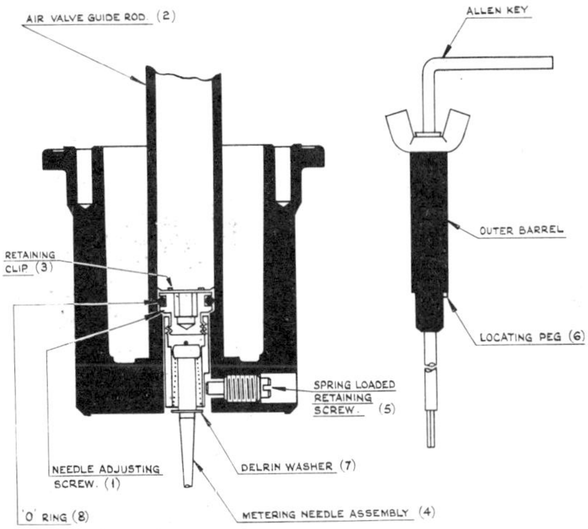

FIG 2:14 Adjusting the air valve needle on Stromberg CD3 carburetter

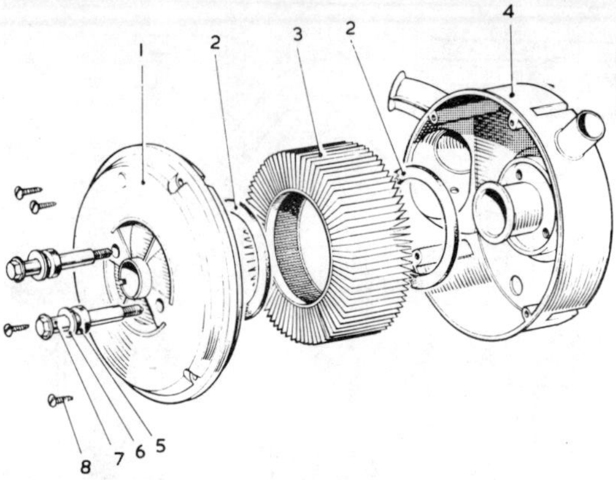

FIG 2:15 Air cleaner for single Stromberg carburetter. Figures refer to text references

turned to alternative positions to draw air from straight-ahead, summer position, of from within the engine compartment close to the exhaust manifold for winter conditions.

Do not attempt to clean an old filter element; always fit a new one and change it at reasonable intervals according to the time of year, and ambient conditions. In dusty or foggy surroundings, the element becomes clogged faster than in clean and fairly dry environments. **Whenever an element is renewed or cleaned, always take the opportunity of cleaning the exterior and interior of the housings, so preventing an early deposit of old dust on the new element.**

A modified form of filter is fitted to twin carburetter installations.

2:14 Fault diagnosis

The fuel system is dependent on the ignition and valve timing and settings and these should first be checked when trouble arises before assuming that it is the carburetter or pump which is at fault.

(a) Engine will not start

1 Low fuel in tank
2 Faulty fuel pump
3 Choked filter gauzes
4 Sticking float or needle valve
5 Air leaks in induction system
6 Over-rich mixture through too much choke

A faulty pump can be checked by disconnecting the fuel pipe at the carburetter and turning the engine over by the starter. If the pump is operating, fuel will flow from the pipe.

A common start trouble can be traced to 6. It may be necessary to remove and dry the sparking plugs. When this has been done, set the throttle to half position, switch on and again try to start.

(b) Engine starts but quickly stalls

1 Too low an idling setting
2 Not enough choke setting

(c) Engine shows poor acceleration

1 Piston valve sticking
2 Wrong jet setting
3 Bent or worn jet needle
4 Lack of or wrong grade of oil in piston damper

(d) Engine loses power at speed

1 Choked air filter
2 Blocked fuel filter
3 Faulty fuel pump

(e) Engine idles unevenly

1 Wrong setting of mixture control screw
2 Piston valve sticking
3 Low oil level in dashpot

An unusual, but not unknown, cause of loss of power on acceleration with the Stromberg carburetter is a leak in the tube between the manifold and vacuum advance unit. Sometimes the tube may have slipped off the connection at either end in which case the ignition fails to advance and the fuel vapour is diluted by the air escaping into the manifold through the open inlet tube.

CHAPTER 3

THE IGNITION SYSTEM

3:1 The ignition system

The ignition system is conventional, comprising an ignition coil, distributor and breaker with both centrifugal and vacuum advance features. The system is negative earthed.

Maximum engine performance under all conditions of load and engine speed is dependent on several features. These include cylinder head temperature, grade and temperature of the fuel vapour, compression ratio of the engine and the intervals before top dead centre at which ignition commences. Some are a function of engine design based on predicted engine and ambient vapour temperatures and the cooling system is devised to achieve these temperatures when running under normal conditions. The variables are engine speed and load and, to deal with these, a variable ignition advance system is incorporated.

Variations of speed are dealt with by a centrifugal advance mechanism which increases the interval between ignition and top dead centre as the speed increases. Variations in load are dealt with by a secondary system, increasing or decreasing the centrifugal advance as the demand on the fuel induction varies.

In the Lucas 25D distributor, as fitted, the contact breaker and capacitor are mounted on a plate, moveable through a small arc by the vacuum advance capsule. The cam and camshaft, passing through the central hole enabling the cam face to bear on the contact breaker lever, are loosely mounted on an action plate secured to, and rotating with, the distributor shaft. The link between the cam and action plate is by springs and the centrifugal weights which, as they move outwards with increase in rotational speed, turn the cam through a small arc in relation to the action plate to advance the instant of contact break.

The vacuum capsule, on the other hand, acting on the breaker mounting plate moved it in the opposite direction to give a further advance when the induction manifold depression is high, corresponding with fast engine speed at a given throttle opening. When load reduces the speed at the same opening, the degree of vacuum controlled advance is reduced proportionately.

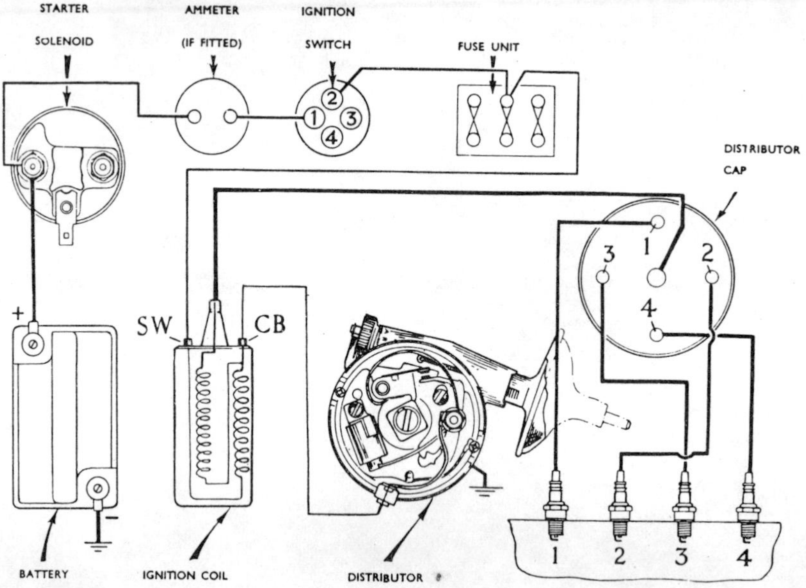

FIG 3:1 Schematic diagram of the ignition system

The ignition system, with the route of wiring from the battery to the ignition coil, is shown in **FIG 3:1.** In some cases, the connection to the ignition coil is taken direct from the ignition switch and not from the fuse-board.

The ignition coil is wound as an auto-transformer. That is to say, the primary and secondary windings are connected in series, the common junction being connected to the contact breaker with the positive feed from the battery going to the opposite terminal of the LT winding via the ignition switch. (In some car systems, the feed is routed to the common point and the breaker contacts are between the free end of the LT winding and earth. Though the connections in the diagram are the preferred alternative, it is immaterial to operation which way round they are connected.)

When the contact breaker points are closed, current flows through the coil primary winding setting up a magnetic field which is intensified by the soft iron core of the coil. Each time the contact breaker points open, the battery current is cut off and the magnetic field collapses, inducing a high voltage in the secondary winding. When the contacts open the current surge to the contacts, which is increased by the influence of the secondary winding charge, is checked by the capacitor, so reducing arcing at the contacts. The charge in the capacitor reverses through the primary winding which causes the magnetic field to collapse faster thereby increasing the induced charge in the secondary winding, this reversal is known as a back EMF or back electromotive force.

3:2 Automatic ignition timing and controls

Ignition timing therefore is adjustable under three headings, static, centrifugal and vacuum. The static timing is set by the meshing of the distributor skew gear with that on the camshaft and this has to be set for the breaker contacts to open at 6 to 10 deg. nominal, before top dead centre assuming a fuel with an octane rating of 96 to 98. The first degree of fine adjustment is by the clamping bolt immediately beneath the distributor body and the second, or vernier, adjustment is by means of the knurled control on the opposite site end to the vacuum assembly on the distributor body.

This timing can be set by means of the 5 deg. timing V-notches on the rim of the crankshaft pulley, the last of these, when the engine crankshaft is rotated clockwise from the front, centring against the pointer on the timing case cover at top dead centre (see **FIG 3:2**).

It is sometimes convenient to mark the pulley adjacent to the timing notches to show the exact position. If this is done and the two coarse controls are set with the contacts opening at this position for No. 1 cylinder, the vernier control being at mid-point, the final adjustment can then be made while fine-tuning by means of the vernier.

The centrifugal control is factory-adjusted by the weights and springs installed and, providing that the weights are not binding either on their pivots or on faces and that the springs are not over-extended, there is no adjustment that can be carried out for centrifugal advance. This is 13 to 15 deg. at 2600 rev/min for the single carburetter or 12 to 14 deg. at 1800 rev/min for the twin carburetter installation.

There is a difference in centrifugal advance according to whether the engine is running up or running down and the setting is based on a running down engine. The setting of centrifugal advance and the curve relating speed to advance can be checked by reference to the Distributor

Service Number stamped on the body immediately below vernier control (see **Technical Data**).

The vacuum advance unit is also factory set and cannot be altered. Refer to **Technical Data** for the identification markings.

3:3 Removing and dismantling the distributor

Release the securing caps and remove the distributor cover, disconnect the HT leads and transfer to a safe place. Remove the rotor arm from the spindle. Disconnect the feed pipe to the vacuum capsule. Disconnect the LT lead. Remove the fixing clamp bolt beneath the distributor body and then extract the distributor, complete with driving dog from the distributor mounting plate on the engine. Transfer to the bench. During the dismantling operation make a careful note of the positions in which the various components are fitted. For example, the tongue of the driving dog is offset, so note the relationship between the dog and the rotor electrode and maintain this position when reassembling; otherwise the timing will be 180 deg. out.

Commence dismantling by removing the vacuum advance capsule. This is done by removing the spring from the pillar on the breaker mounting plate 14 (see **FIG 3 : 3**) and then removing the two screws securing the breaker baseplate 4, to the distributor body. The breaker mounting plate and base plate can then be slipped over the cam, the LT terminal slipping out of its socket in the body.

Remove the circlip and vernier adjusting screw 10, from the micrometer timing screw, easing the latter with capsule from the body, at the same time retrieving the ratchet and spring assembly from the cavity adjacent to the micrometer timing screw rim.

Extract the pin from the dog 8, at the foot of the distributor shaft, together with the thrust washer 9, and extract the shaft from the body, taking care to retrieve the distance collar 11. Dismantle the centrifugal device by, first, removing the two springs from the pillars on the action plate 12, extracting the screw in the centre of the cam 13, and easing the cam and plate away from the action plate. This releases the two weights 5.

To dismantle the breaker mounting plate, remove the nut 22, insulating collar 23, from the pillar 26, together with the insulating washer 25, spring 24 and connections from the screw pillar 26. The contact breaker lever 18 and insulating washer 19, can now be eased from pillar 21. By removing screw 3, the fixed contact and plate 20, can next be extracted. All that is left to remove is the capacitor 16, secured by its own screw to the breaker mounting plate 14.

The distributor is now completely dismantled.

3:4 Inspection and reassembly

Thoroughly clean and examine all parts for signs of wear. In particular, examine the surfaces of the breaker contacts and replace the lever with moving contact and the fixed contact plate if necessary. **Clean the surfaces of new contacts which are protected by a coating of preserving film while in store.**

Check the fit of the shaft in the bearing bush and, if the shaft is not scored but the fit is sloppy, replace the bushing

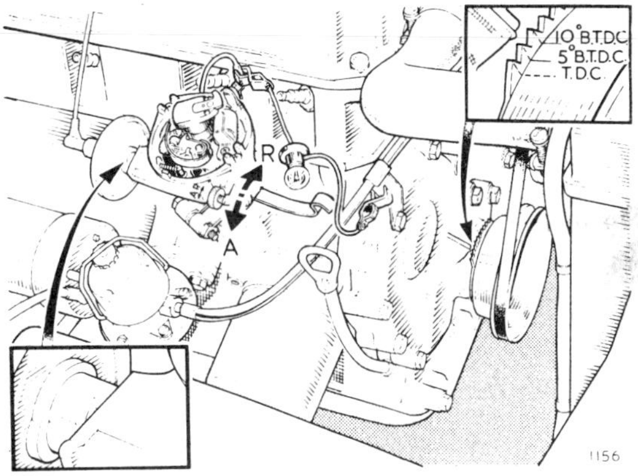

FIG 3:2 Adjustment and timing mark details. Inset shows vernier scale

9. This is a sintered copper/iron bush stepped externally to a larger diameter for $\frac{3}{4}$ inch from the bottom. Prepare a new bush for fitting by immersing it in clean SAE.30 or 40 engine oil for 24 hours and then, using a shouldered mandrel, drive out the old bush from the body end and insert the new one. This will be an easy push fit until the larger diameter commences to enter and the final stage is to press it home in a vice or press by steady pressure. **Do not use a drift and hammer for insertion.** It is fully home when the lower end is flush and the upper end is slightly proud.

Drill the shaft drain hole taking care to remove all swarf. Rinse through with engine oil, lubricate the shaft and insert it in the bushing. It is likely to be a tight fit and may need light tapping at the lower end to remove but, after a few insertions and withdrawals, the fit will ease considerably.

When it can be rotated without undue effort, re-oil and run in by turning the shaft in a lathe or by a drill in a test rig for about 15 minutes. It will then be free enough to extract, wipe clean, re-oil and insert for good.

The bushing, being sintered, must not be reamed to size or drilled as either process will destroy the inner surface and impair its self-lubricating properties. If it is necessary to fit a new bush at short notice, it may be soaked in hot oil (100°C) for 2 hours instead of in cold for 24 and allowed to cool.

Reassembly is straightforward, starting with insertion of the shaft and distance collar, smearing each surface with clean engine oil. Re-install the vacuum capsule and secure by the milled nut with its spring and ratchet assembly and circlip. Replace washer, dog and pin.

Reassemble the centrifugal timing weights, seeing that they are free on the pivots when the cam foot and cam is secured to the shaft by the centre screw, and refit the springs. These, of course, should be replaced if they are at all extended. Lightly oil or grease the surfaces of each part.

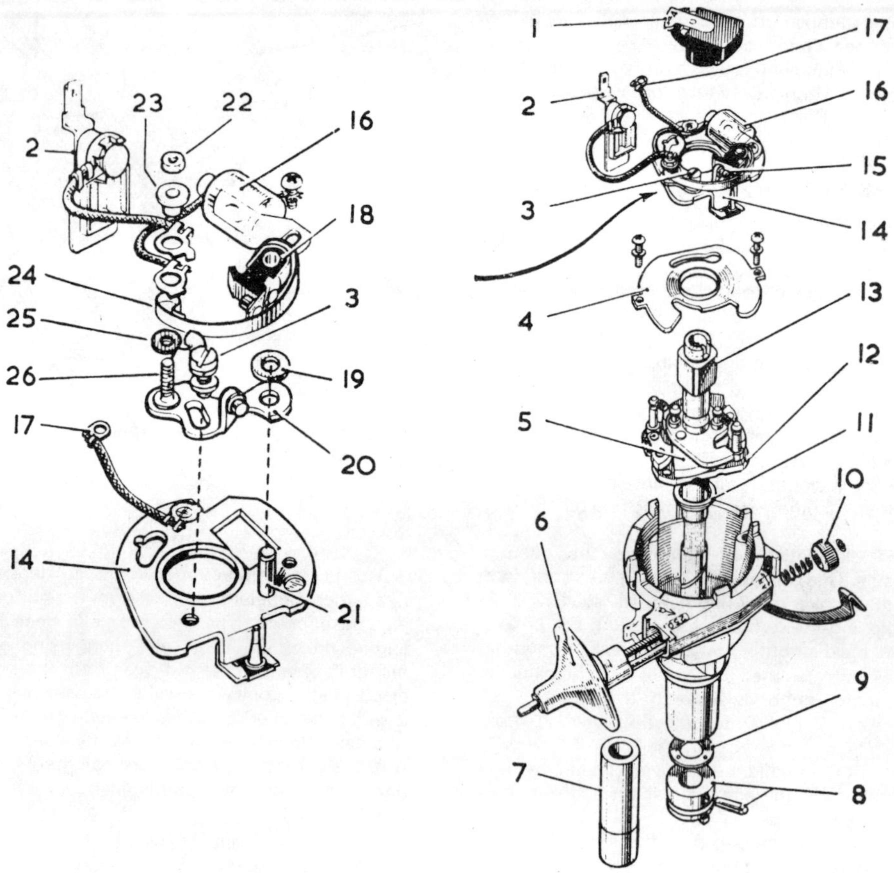

FIG 3:3 Component parts of the ignition distributor

Key to Fig 3:3 1 Rotor 2 Low-tension connection 3 Fixed contact plate retaining screw 4 Breaker base plate 5 Weight 6 Vacuum capsule 7 Bush 8 Dog and pin 9 Thrust washer 10 Vernier adjusting screw, spring and circlip 11 Distance collar 12 Action plate 13 Cam 14 Breaker mounting plate 15 Contacts 16 Capacitor 17 Earth lead and tag 18 Contact breaker lever 19 Insulating washer 20 Fixed contact and plate 21 Pillar 22 Nut 23 Insulating bush 24 Spring 25 Insulating washer 26 Screw pillar

Now reassemble the contact breaker and capacitor on its mounting plate taking care that all connections, insulating collars and washers are in the same places as during dismantling. Mount the assembly on the base plate by inserting the underside rivet head into the keyhole slot and turning, then fit the assembly in the body securing by the two screws, under one of which the earth connection 17, is placed. Reconnect the end of the spring from the vacuum unit to the stepped pillar on the breaker mounting plate. Slide the terminal block 2, into position.

Rotate the cam until the moving contact is separated from the fixed contact by the largest amount—with the contact breaker lever 18, resting on the top of one of the four cam peaks—and adjust the fixed contact to give a gap between the two contact faces of .015 inch. **FIG 3:4** shows how this adjustment is made with a screwdriver blade, the screw 3, being very slightly slackened during the adjustment and retightened after. Finally, fit the rotor arm into position, centre the vernier control adjustment, and replace the distributor cap.

3:5 Installation and timing

Check that No. 1 piston is at top dead centre on the compression stroke. This can be done by removing the cylinder head cover, and turning the crankshaft until the timing mark on the pulley indicates top dead centre with both valves on No. 1 cylinder head closed. The crankshaft can be turned easily by means of the pulley if all sparking plugs are removed from the cylinders. Alternatively, jack up one rear wheel, put the gearlever into top gear and use the wheel to turn the crankshaft. The handbrake, of course, must be off and the other rear wheel chocked fore and aft.

Insert the distributor shaft into the mounting and, with the rotor arm pointing to No. 1 cylinder contact in the cap, push it home until the dog has meshed with the slot in the oil pump shaft driving end. Take up the slack in the clamping screw under the distributor body until the body can just be rotated in the mounting. Turn the crankshaft back until the 8 deg. mark on the pulley is opposite the pointer, rotate the body in the direction of the arrows on the vernier barrel a few deg. until the contacts have open and closed, then reverse the direction to the point at which they just begin to open. Holding the body in this position, secure the clamping screw.

Turn the crankshaft through one complete revolution to 8 deg. before top dead centre on No. 4 cylinder and check that the contacts are again just beginning to open. Check that when fully open, the gap is .015 inch as set. Replace the sparking plugs, distributor cap, LT connection to contact breaker, HT leads to ignition coil and sparking plugs and the vacuum advance pipeline to the capsule.

The distributor is now set for running.

There are a number of ways of setting timing, simple and sophisticated, recommended in various publications including stroboscopic analysis of vacuum and centrifugal advance characteristics. The straightforward procedure outlined is, however, quite effective in bringing timing within the range of fine vernier adjustment and the fine tuning can then be done with the engine running to get the best response. Since neither the vacuum advance nor centrifugal advance features are capable of local adjustment, there is little point in the owner-mechanic going through complex testing procedures. If, after all other checks have failed, engine performance still seems to be below standard and the automatic advance features are being suspected, the obvious step is to replace the distributor with a new one from the agent and return the old one for examination and reconditioning.

For really high performance tuning, allowances have to be made for the grade of fuel used and the local barometric conditions. These are within the setting of the vernier control but, for all normal purposes, once this has been set, no further adjustment should be necessary.

Timing marks:

The timing marks are the thirteen V-notches behind the belt groove of the crankshaft pulley. The notch spacings represent 5 deg. intervals ranging from 60 deg. BTDC to TDC. These marks are used to measure the number of crankshaft degrees BTDC when setting the static ignition timing or checking the amount of centrifugal and vacuum advance with a stroboscopic timing light and a tachometer.

Vernier control:

The vernier control shown in **FIG 3:2** provides a means for finer adjustments to be made when a different type or grade of fuel is used. One complete turn of the knurled nut is equivalent to 3 deg. of crankshaft rotation and a vernier space, shown in the inset, is equivalent to 4 deg. of crankshaft rotation.

The knurled nut should be rotated clockwise to retard the ignition and anticlockwise to advance, indicated by the arrows and the letters A and R.

Timing, static method:

1 Turn the engine to bring No. 1 piston up to TDC on the compression stroke, this can be checked with the plugs removed and placing a thumb or finger over the No. 1 plug orifice. As the piston approaches TDC on the compression stroke, considerable pressure will be felt.

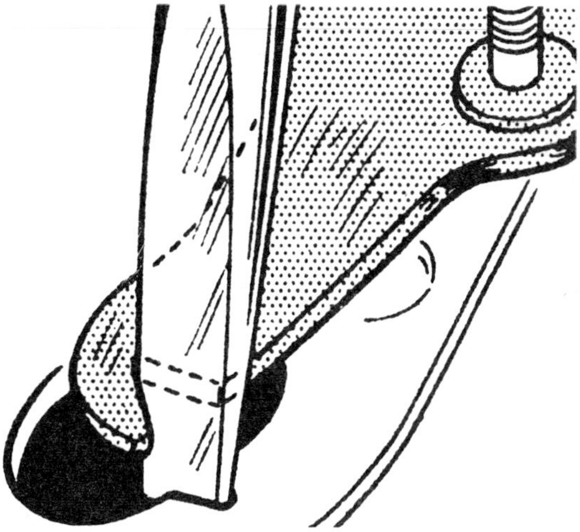

FIG 3:4 Adjusting fixed point

2 Set the engine to the required number of degrees BTDC. This will be 6 to 8 deg. for the 1250 and the 1500SC with HC and LC engines. 7 to 9 deg. for the 1500TC and 7 deg. if the engine is equipped with an exhaust emission control system.
3 Set the vernier adjustment to the midway position.
4 Remove the distributor cap and connect a 12-volt bulb between the LT terminal on the distributor and a good earth as shown in **FIG 3:2**. Switch on the ignition.
5 Slacken the distributor clamp screw and turn the body of the distributor anticlockwise, then clockwise to take up any play. Slowly turn the body clockwise until the bulb just lights, which indicates the points have just opened.
6 Tighten the clamp screw, not too tightly otherwise it will distort the clamp.
7 Check the setting by turning the engine one full revolution until the bulb lights again, then look at the pulley timing marks to ensure that the pointer is against the correct degree marking.
8 Switch off the ignition, remove the test light and refit the cap.
9 Finer adjustments should be made by adjusting the vernier to give the best performance from a particular fuel or to eliminate 'pinking' when excessive carbon deposits have formed in the engine.

Timing, Stroboscopic:

1 Disconnect the vacuum advance pipe from the carburetter. This is to ensure that the vacuum advance unit does not begin to operate when the engine is running and give a false reading.
2 Clean the timing marks on the pulley and using quick drying white paint, a wax crayon or a dye pen mark the correct degree line appropriate to the engine (see Timing, static or **Technical Data**).
3 Connect a reliable tachometer to the engine and connect the stroboscopic light to the manufacturers instructions.
4 Start the engine and adjust the engine speed to obtain 1000 rev/min.

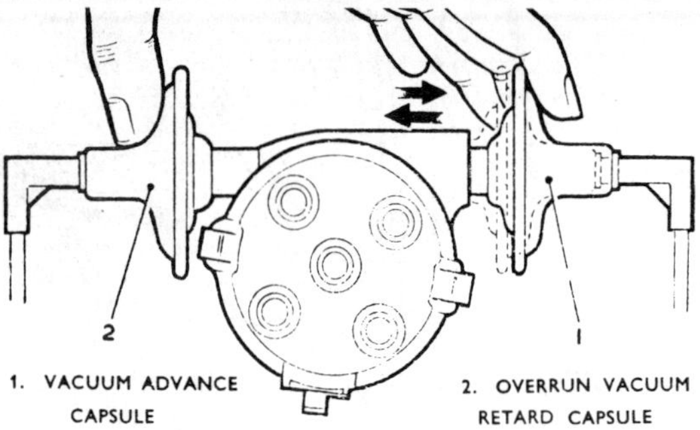

FIG 3:5 Checking freedom of capsule operation on exhaust emission control distributor

5 Project the stroboscopic light beam on to the timing case pointer **but take care not to collide with the revolving fan.** When the ignition timing is correct the painted position on the pulley will appear 'stationary' opposite the timing case pointer. If necessary the distributor body can be rotated, whilst the engine is running, to align the mark.
6 After completion, reconnect the vacuum advance pipe and readjust the idling speed.

Checking the centrifugal advance:

1 Carry out operations 1 to 3 under Timing, stroboscopic.
2 Start the engine and increase the speed to 3000 rev/min.
3 The distance between the painted line and the pointer, should increase and decrease smoothly whilst increasing or decreasing engine speed. Any jerky movement of the mark will indicate a sticking mechanism. Rectify before checking the vacuum advance.

Checking vacuum advance:

4 Reconnect the vacuum pipe and adjust the engine speed to 1500 rev/min. By connecting and disconnecting the tube from the carburetter a definite movement of the mark in relation to the pointer will be noticeable.
5 A blockage in the pipe, sticking of the contact breaker plate, a leaking diaphragm or a defective unit will prevent a correct vacuum advance.

3:6 Exhaust emission control

The distributor on cars fitted with exhaust emission control may incorporate two vacuum capsules, one of which is used to retard ignition during periods of engine overrun (see **Chapter 2, Section 2:13**). The degree of retardation is dependent on the depression in the inlet to the cylinder—that is, the manifold—whereas the degree of advance is dependent on the depression in the area between the throttle valve and piston valve in the carburetter. (This second capsule is not present on twin carburetter exhaust emission control installations.)

The retard capsule acts in an opposite sense to the advance capsule and, if nothing is binding, it should be possible to concertina the two towards each other (see **FIG 3:5**). Otherwise, no adjustment is possible. Moreover, in the single carburetter installation, the vernier control having been disposed with, timing has to be accurately set by rotation of the distributor body in its mounting clamp. The retard capsule is operable over an angle of 12 deg., the vacuum advance angle being the same as for a normal installation, that is 6 to 8 deg.

Servicing is limited to a check on contact breaker gaps, condition of sparking plugs, timing and a visual inspection of the vacuum pipelines and junctions.

3:7 High-tension cables

The HT cables between the distributor and the coil and sparking plugs are high resistance core cables to minimize radio interference both on the internal radio, if fitted, and external radio and television equipment.

Any indication of deterioration of the insulation should be countered by complete renewal of all HT cables. Termination of high resistance cables at the distributor and sparking plug/ignition coil ends is a job calling for care and special terminals since the conductor is nothing more than a coating of graphite on a plastic core. Normal methods of checking continuity are not possible, the only satisfactory test being on a clean plug from the ignition coil direct when operating the contact breaker manually. The plug, of course, is clamped to the cylinder block and not inserted in the cylinder head.

3:8 Sparking plugs

The standard pattern of sparking plug is the Champion N.9.Y with single carburetter, and N.7.Y with twin carburetters, with the gap set at .025 inch. Plugs should be removed for examination and adjustment of gap at regular intervals. The state of the plug can then be used as an indication of engine running conditions.

A wet plug is an indication of faulty ignition combined with over-rich fuel mixture. It is found usually in engines after an extended period of unsuccessful starting with the choke out. Clean or burn off the excess fuel and readjust the gap before reinstallation.

A gummy deposit on the plug is an indication of oil fouling in the cylinder which can be traced to worn pistons or piston rings or a badly worn cylinder. The only way oil can enter the cylinder is via the gap between the piston and cylinder walls. Presence of oil shows that the sealing is not efficient.

A dry, sooty deposit usually indicates an over-rich fuel mixture, incomplete burning through an over-retarded ignition, or is evidence of continual misfiring through a faulty plug or defective contact breaker points or HT cables.

The correct deposit is dry, hard and white but if this is accompanied by badly corroded or burned electrodes, the chances are that the engine is running overheated.

Although sparking plugs can be cleaned and the gaps reset, the cost of a new set is so small and the effect on performance so significant that complete replacement is usually advisable. One word of warning, **when setting the gap always bend the outer electrode, never the inner one or you may crack the central insulator.**

3:9 Modifications

The Lucas 25D.4 distributor and 11C.12 ignition coil are used on all home models but an alternative coil, HA.12 may be found on some overseas models. The distributor itself is standard except for differences in the vacuum advance module and in the weights and springs of the centrifugal device to suit individual engine performances in certain cars. These are indicated by changes in the Despatch or Service number engraved on the distributor body just below the vernier control. The number to be found on the rotor arm indicates the mean degree of advance by the centrifugal assembly. The vacuum advance data can be determined from the capsule marking (see **Section 3:2**).

Service numbers to be found on the home market 1250 single carburetter installations are 41302, with a 16 deg. centrifugal advance and a 5-14-11 capsule on the 1500 single carburetter installation a 41303 with 4-14-8 capsule is installed on low-compression ratio engines or a 41304 with 5-11-7 capsule on the high-compression ratio versions.

3:10 Fault diagnosis

(a) Engine will not fire

1 Low battery volts
2 Dirty contact breaker
3 Faulty capacitor
4 Broken contact breaker spring
5 Broken or disconnected LT lead
6 Broken or disconnected HT lead
7 Faulty ignition coil
8 Faulty ignition switch
9 Condensation on or in distributor cap
10 Broken carbon pencil in distributor cap
11 Wet or faulty plugs
12 Excessive contact breaker gap setting
13 HT leads crossed over

Low battery volts may not show across the battery terminals on open circuit but, if a cell is poor, when the starting current—of the order of 280 to 370 amps—is flowing the voltage across the ignition coil may drop below 9 volts, the minimum for creating a healthy spark. Even with a good battery, on a very cold day the starting current can be high enough to prevent ignition until just after the starter motor has been switched off, an excellent reason for not keeping the starter switch closed for more than a few seconds at a time. A series of short starts is far more likely to get the engine to fire.

(b) Engine misfires

1 Faulty plug or plugs
2 Carbon track on distributor cap
3 Moisture on sparking plugs
4 Faulty HT lead to one plug
5 Plug contacts bridged by carbon
6 Sticking contact breaker

(c) Accelerator poor

1 Ignition too far retarded
2 Centrifugal weights seized
3 Centrifugal springs broken
4 Distributor clamp loose
5 Excessive contact breaker gap
6 Plugs need renewing

(d) Engine 'pinks'

1 Ignition too far advanced
2 Fuel octane value too low
3 Ignition timing slipped
4 Distributor cam worn
5 Vacuum advance not operating

NOTES

CHAPTER 4

COOLING AND AIR CONDITIONING

4:1 The cooling system

Engine cooling is by a conventional system, comprising radiator, fan and circulating pump, which also serves as the heat source for the air heating and ventilation system. The general layout is given in **FIG 4:1**, the coolant being circulated through the system by the impeller pump 1, driven by V-belt from the crankshaft pulley. A fan, bolted to the pump drive pulley, circulates air through the radiator 2. The flow of water through the system is regulated by the thermostat 3, to achieve an early normal engine temperature after starting from cold and thereafter controlling the flow through the cylinder block 9, and head 7 to regulate the temperature regardless of changes in load, speed and ambient conditions.

In order to maintain a fairly high coolant temperature without excessive evaporation, the system is pressurized by a filler cap which incorporates a spring-loaded valve system discharging excess water on expansion to overflow.

Within the cylinder block, the coolant circulates round the cylinder walls to pass to the cylinder head through vertical channels where it is jet-directed on to the valve seat inserts 8 ensuring that these parts are adequately cooled.

With the thermostat closed, water circulates between the cylinder head and engine block via the bypass 4 and through the water valve 3, in the closed position. As engine temperature increases, the thermostat operates to open the second route through the radiator and the circulation is then divided between the radiator and bypass routes in varying proportion dependent on the coolant temperature. Only when the temperature exceeds 95°C is the bypass route closed diverting all coolant through the radiator (see **FIG 4:2**).

The water valve is in the air heating and ventilation system. Opening of this valve diverts coolant in the bypass circuit into the heater 6, through which the ventilating air is routed.

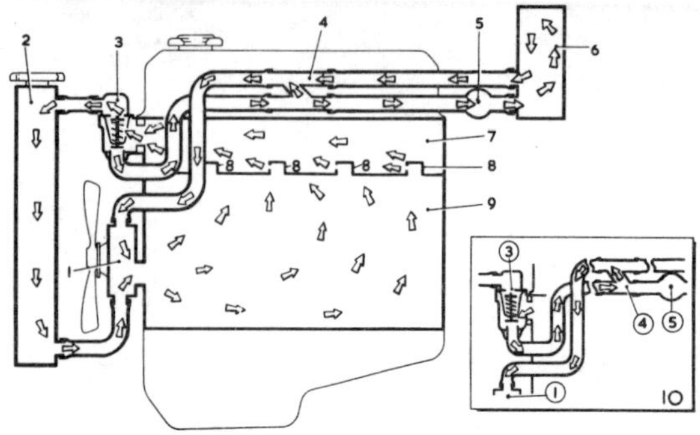

FIG 4:1 Diagrammatic view of cooling system

Key to Fig 4:1 1 Pump 2 Radiator 3 Thermostat 4 Bypass 5 Heater control valve 6 Heater unit 7 Cylinder head 8 Jets in cylinder head 9 Cylinder block Inset shows flow when bypass route is closed

The temperature of the coolant at the thermostat is monitored at all times by a transmitter in the front end of the cylinder head electrically connected to a temperature indicator on the dashboard. The normal operating temperature is between 82°C and 95°C.

It will be appreciated that when the coolant exceeds 95°C, closing the bypass circuit, the air heating system becomes inoperative. The use of a radiator blind during exceptionally cold weather, in order to raise engine coolant temperature, may have the effect of cutting out air warming unless an eye is kept on the temperature gauge and the blind adjusted to keep the coolant temperature below 95°C.

The radiator cap pressurizes the system to 9 lb/sq in above normal atmospheric. The effect of this is to increase the boiling point of the water coolant to around 112°C. **It is therefore dangerous to remove the radiator cap when the engine has been running hot as the water will flash into scalding steam the moment the system pressure is lowered to that of the surrounding atmosphere.**

The system is drained by a cock at the bottom of the radiator and also by a drain cock on the lefthand side of the cylinder block. Water will not flow, however, unless the radiator cap is first removed and the heater will not drain unless the control lever is placed in the 'HOT' position.

For winter conditions, the system must be filled with an antifreeze coolant, a mixture of ethylene glycol and water with a corrosion inhibiting additive. Many proprietary glycol and inhibitor compounds are available all of which are suitable providing that they are mixed with water to the proportions listed on the containers.

Generally speaking, a 20 per cent solution—one part glycol to 4 parts water by volume—gives full protection down to 15°C of frost (17°F) a 30 per cent solution down to 30°C of frost, a 40 per cent solution down to 45°C of frost and a solution comprising equal parts of glycol and water down to 65°C of frost (—33°F). These, however, relate to persistent temperatures over a fairly long period but for night frosts followed by a rise in temperature during the following day, the protection can be extended by at least another 20°C of frost. Much, however, depends on the environment—whether the air is still or a wind is blowing and whether the car is in an exposed position or under shelter. A car completely submerged in a snowdrift is less liable to freeze than one in the open and exposed to a biting wind.

The air conditioning and heating system draws fresh air from the exterior of the car and circulates it throughout the interior with part bypassed through the heater to raise the ambient temperature. It does not recirculate the air already in the car and air extractors at the side rear enable the foul air to escape as the fresh air enters even when all windows are closed.

4:2 Maintenance and servicing

Normal maintenance comprises a check of water level at regular intervals and an examination of the hoses and connections for signs of leaks at the joints or general deterioration of the rubber connections.

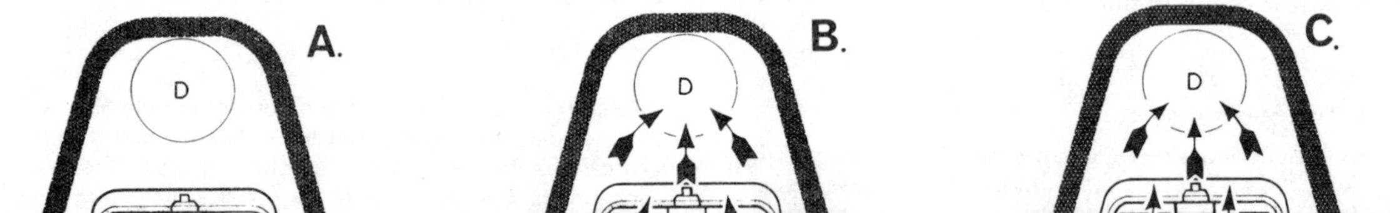

FIG 4:2 Principle of thermostat operation. A shows the flow with thermostat closed; B is the flow when the upper valve is opened and C is the flow with bypass closed

At least twice every year, drain the radiator and heating system and flush out. If the drained coolant is clean and contains the antifreeze, it can be re-used after allowing any sediment to settle out in the container used for storage. If it is rusty, refill with fresh antifreeze solution or water according to the time of the year. Antifreeze solution with present day inhibitors can remain in the system without detriment, providing that it is clean, throughout the year. When topping up, use fresh water unless the loss is through leaks in the hoses. Topping up should then be with antifreeze solution to avoid too much dilution.

When filling with antifreeze solution, make sure that the cylinder head nuts are tight as any leakage into the cylinders or oil passages by the ethylene glycol can cause serious damage.

Check the exterior of the radiator grilles for accumulations off dirt and dead insects and brush clean. Check the fan belt for tightness and adjust as necessary.

Always use fresh tap-water for filling the radiator. It is not generally realised that rain-water, though pure in regard to mineral content, contains a fairly high porportion of dissolved carbon dioxide and this carbonic acid attacks the metal of the radiator tubes fairly rapidly. If rain-water is the only coolant available, boil first to expel the carbon dioxide.

Should the tap-water be hard and, as the result of frequent topping up, lime accumulations occur in the system, these must be removed before they clog up the

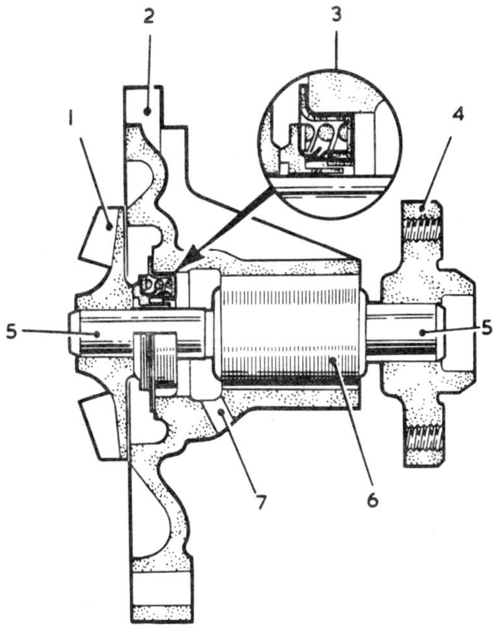

FIG 4:3 Diagrammatic view through the pump

Key to Fig 4:3 1 Impeller 2 Body 3 Seal, pressure type 4 Hub 5/6 Spindle and bearing 7 Drain hole

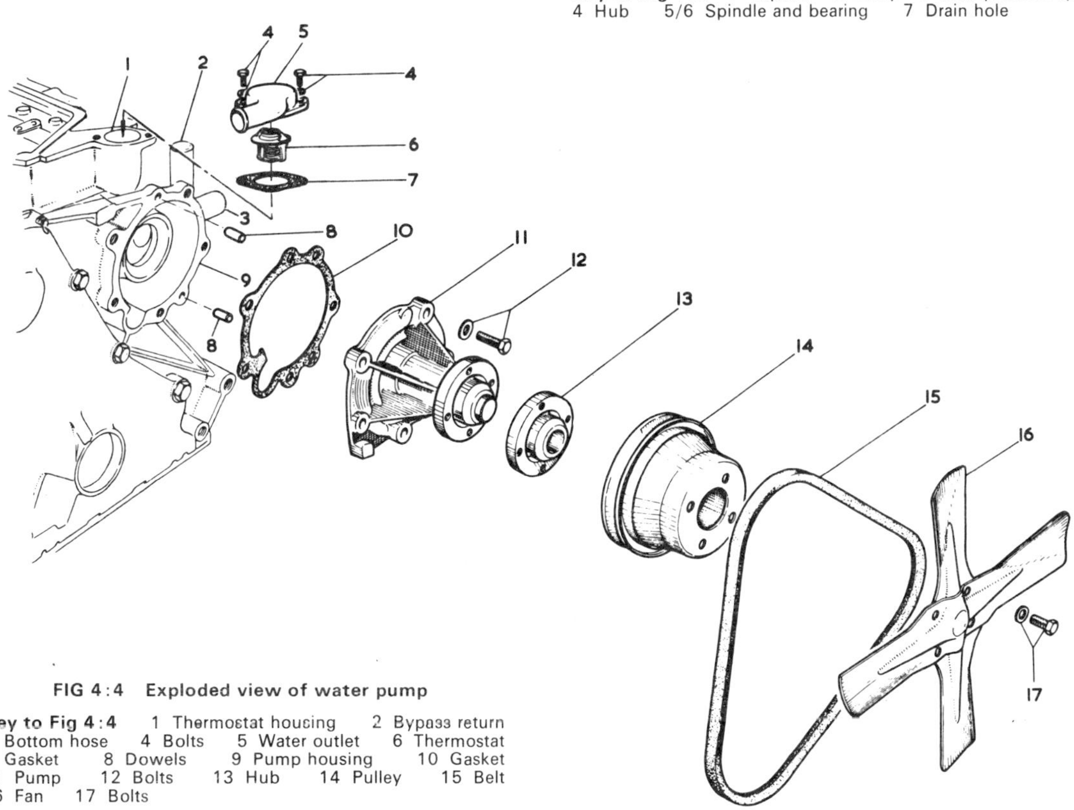

FIG 4:4 Exploded view of water pump

Key to Fig 4:4 1 Thermostat housing 2 Bypass return 3 Bottom hose 4 Bolts 5 Water outlet 6 Thermostat 7 Gasket 8 Dowels 9 Pump housing 10 Gasket 11 Pump 12 Bolts 13 Hub 14 Pulley 15 Belt 16 Fan 17 Bolts

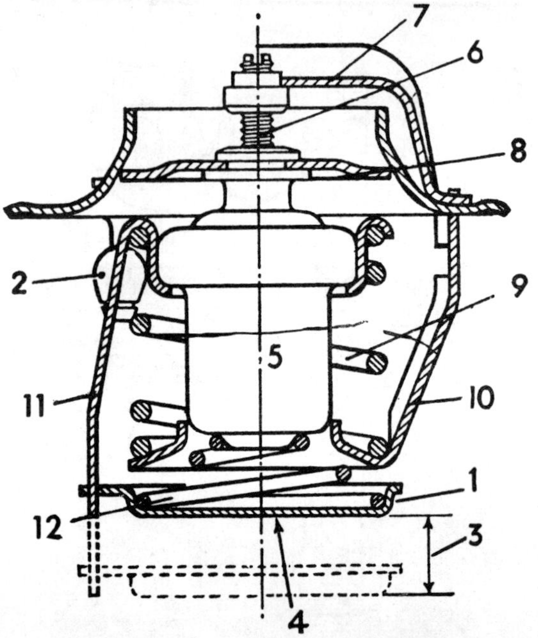

FIG 4:5 Section through thermostat

Key to Fig 4:5 1 Bypass valve, open 2 Jiggle pin 3 Bypass valve travel 4 Bypass valve 5 Expansion element 6 Central rod 7 Upper fixed member 8 Main radiator valve 9 Spring 10 Lower fixed member 11 Lower moving member 12 Bypass valve seating spring

small bore radiator passages. Generally speaking, in a pressurized system, topping up should be rare and the liming troubles experienced in non-pressurized systems are unlikely.

Draining of the heater in the air conditioning system is through the radiator drain cock. When the latter is open and the heater control is set to 'Hot', open the water valve. Similarly, draining will be accelerated if the engine is first run up to normal temperature enabling the thermostat to open and air to enter the bypass channel and cylinder head. Alternatively, disconnect and remove the temperature transmitter from the thermostat housing.

After refilling the system, open the heater control valve and run the engine for a while to charge the heater circuit. Afterwards, top up the radiator.

At each service inspection, examine the seal and seating of the radiator filler cap and replace if these are not in perfect condition.

4:3 Water pump, removal

The following instructions are given for the 1250 and 1500SC. On the 1500TC the fan cannot be removed without first removing the radiator. The fan blades and hub are a plastic moulding and the fan should not be used as a means of turning the engine.

To remove the water pump, first drain the system and then disconnect the radiator bottom hose and heater hose to the pump. Slacken the belt adjustment and remove the fan belt.

Remove the screws and washers securing the fan blade to the pump pulley and remove the fan and pulley. Disconnect the belt tightening strap from the pump. Remove the five bolts securing the pump to the timing case, ease the pump clear and transfer to the bench for dismantling.

To dismantle, first examine the section diagram **FIG 4:3** and the exploded view **FIG 4:4.** Note that the fan pulley centre 4, is a press fit on one end of the pump spindle 5, and the impeller 1 is a press fit on the other end beyond the water thrower and sealing unit 3. The bearing and pump spindle 6 is a sealed and prelubricated unit and cannot be dismantled. **Do not wash the pump or this component in paraffin or petrol as it will dissolve the lubricant and no provision for repacking has been made.**

4:4 Water pump, inspection

Clean and inspect all parts and examine for signs of wear or mechanical failure. Rotate the shaft in the bearing and feel for any roughness or excessive play. Examine pump body and impeller housing for signs of binding on the faces through end play and, in particular, to the mating surfaces where they contact the gasket.

Note that the water seal has a carbon face mounted in a rubber housing, the face being spring-loaded to bear on the front face of the impeller. If the face is scored or worn or the spring is weakened, replace the pump to ensure that the seal will be watertight when reassembled.

The correct location of the bearing in the pump depends on the press fit in the body and any attempt to dismantle is likely to result in a deterioration of the fit with consequent loss of efficiency. **Do not, therefore, attempt to dismantle the pump but, should it show signs of deterioration, return it to the Chrysler agent in exchange for a new one.**

4:5 Water pump installation

Remove any traces of old gasket on the mating surfaces of block and pump and clean up. Lightly smear the surfaces with clean grease and fit a new gasket. Insert the bolts and tighten evenly and firmly to achieve a watertight joint.

Re-install the alternator/generator adjusting strap and re-secure the fan blade on to the pulley centre. Refit the V-belt and adjust tension to give about $\frac{5}{8}$ inch total play on the centre of the longest run. Re-install the hoses, fitting new hoses and/or clips as may be necessary.

4:6 Thermostat operation and renewal

The thermostat is housed in the front cylinder head water connection which also serves as the union to the radiator and bypass hoses. This unit is shown dismantled in **FIG 4:4.** It comprises two castings 1 and 5, bolted together with an intervening gasket to form a cavity in which the thermostat 6 is contained, the lower half 3, being an integral part of the cylinder head. The upper half 1, is the connection for the hose to the cylinder head.

A section through the thermostat is shown in **FIG 4:5.** The thermostat comprises a wax filled expansion element 5, sliding on a central rod 6, secured to the upper fixed member 7, and carrying the main radiator valve 8. The rod is threaded at the upper end as a means of setting the operational range.

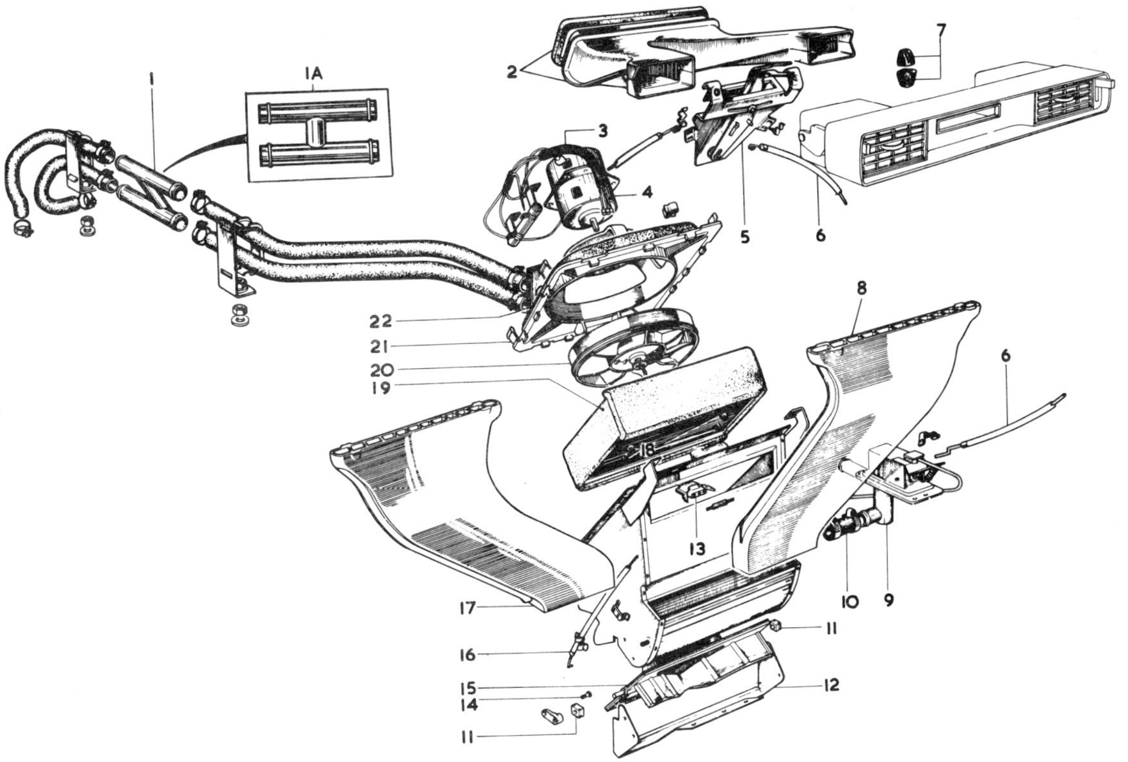

FIG 4:6 Exploded view of fan heater unit

Key to Fig 4:6 1 Bypass with alternative type at 1A 2 Face vent 3 Fan harness 4 Fan motor 5 Control assembly 6 Valve control cable 7 Control lever knob 8, 17 Demister ducts 9 Water valve and capillary 10 Hose and clips 11 Flap valve bearings 12 Deflector plate 13 Socket 14 Trunnion 15 Flap valve 16 Flap valve cable 18 Capillary clips 19 Heater unit 20 Fan 21 Top cover 22 Bulkhead seal

Normally, the valve 8, is kept closed by the spring 9, interposed between the lower fixed member 10, and the collar of the lower moving member 11, around the element flange. At the same time, the bypass valve 4, supported on the moving member 11, is kept open.

The coolant, circulating around the element body, causes the wax to expand with rising temperature. The body of the element, together with the upper and lower valves, moves downwards on the rod to open the main valve 8, and partially close the valve 4, on to its seating in the lower housing. When the temperature reaches 95°C, the bypass valve is firmly seated closing the bypass circuit. The coil spring 12, interposed between the base of the expansion element and the valve, then takes up any further expansion.

Failure of the thermostat can be due to a number of causes but, without exception, these can be remedied only by replacement with a new thermostat. To remove the thermostat, first drain the radiator system to below thermostat level and then disconnect the upper hose from the housing. Remove the two nuts securing the two halves of the housing and take off the upper half. The thermostat can then be extracted, the interior cleaned and seatings examined, and a new thermostat inserted.

Clean the joint faces, renew the gasket and smear both faces with a thin film of grease. Refit the upper half of the housing, tighten down the nuts and remake the hose joint. **When reassembling the thermostat in the housing, check that the jiggle pin 2, is uppermost. The purpose of this is to ensure that no air is trapped in the lower half of the assembly, preventing the element from being fully immersed in the coolant.**

During the operation, it may be convenient to disconnect the cable to the water temperature transmitter in the lower part of the housing. **Take particular care not to earth the lead as, should the ignition switch be turned on, it may damage the indicator on the instrument panel.**

The water temperature transmitter comprises a temperature-sensitive element coupled to the temperature indicator on the instrument panel. The circuit is voltage-dependent and is, therefore, connected to the battery through a voltage stabilizer.

To replace the transmitter, drain the system to below thermostat housing level, unscrew the faulty unit and replace by a new one. The transmitter cannot be repaired.

4:7 Air conditioning, operation

The air conditioning unit is mounted centrally behind the dashboard and comprises heater unit, fan and air

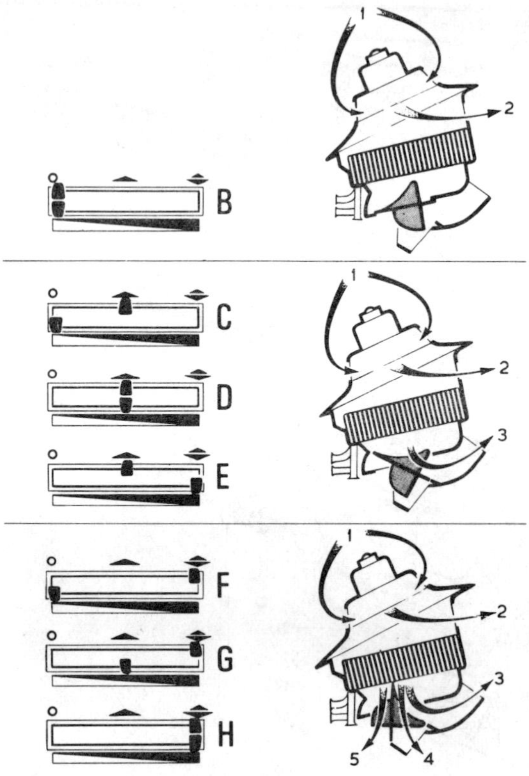

FIG 4:7 Positions of controls with resultant air flows

Key to Fig 4:7 1 Ram air inlet 2 Fresh air to face vents 3 Air to windscreen 4 Air to rear of car 5 Air to front of car

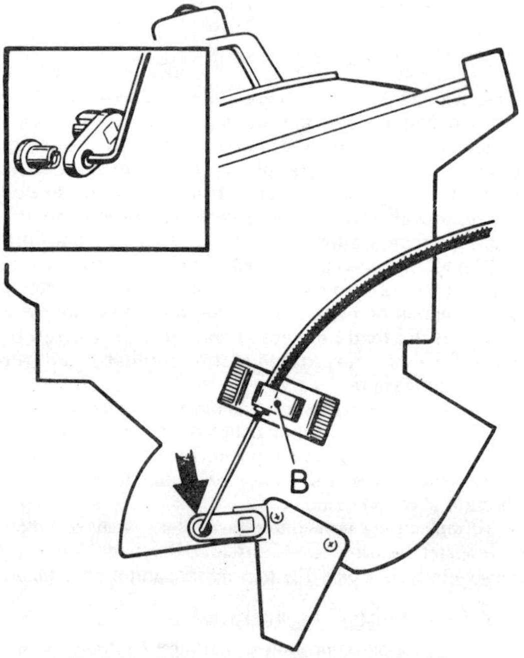

FIG 4:8 Adjustment to flap control cable

mixing valves with two control levers, one of which regulates the temperature of the air and the other its distribution between the car interior and the windscreen. The fresh air is drawn in through a horizontal grille below the windscreen at the front of the car and is channelled to outlets in the car and on the facia shelf. Separate ducts to face vents at each end of the facia panel provide a flow of cold air, regardless of the setting of the heater controls, at face level. The outlets to these are controlled at the vents.

Normally, the air flow is by ram air as the car is travelling but this can be accelerated, or induced when the car is at rest, by a twospeed fan within the unit. The flow of hot water through the heater is controlled by the water valve, cable operated from the dashboard. The general arrangement is shown in **FIG 4:6**.

The air temperature control operates a flap valve in the unit body and a piston-type water valve through a torsion spring link. The distribution control operates a flap valve diverting the air stream between the demister ducts and the car interior. In the 'Off' position, no air enters the car other than that through the two face level vents.

Control settings and the effect on the flaps and heater valve for the six main positions are given in **FIG 4:7.** With both controls at 'Off', no air passes through the heater or into the car other than via the face vents. This can be ram air or accelerated by switching on the fan.

With the upper control to 'Screen' cold air passes over the lower flap and is diverted upwards to the demister ducts. With the same control at 'Screen' the flap is lowered still farther to admit air to both car and screen.

With the lower control at centre, the heater flap is moved to mid-position and the water valve opened. The resultant mixture of hot and cold air is then diverted to windscreen or screen and car interior according to the position of the upper control. With the lower control at 'Hot', the flap moves over to divert all air through the heater, other than that to the face vents, and this again is distributed to windscreen or screen and car interior as set by the upper control.

Strictly speaking, the upper control should be used as a three-position one but intermediate positions on the lower control can be selected to regulate the temperature of the air conditioning stream. **As already mentioned, the air heating is inoperative when the radiator coolant temperature exceeds 95°C.**

The flaps are operated by Bowden type cables from the levers in the control assembly. The adjustment is made by a pinch nut on the lever arm at the flap end. The distribution control is on the lefthand side and the heater control on the righthand side of the unit.

To adjust the distribution control, push the upper control lever fully to the left (Off) and loosen the pinch nut **B** (see **FIG 4:8**). Move the lever as far as it will go in the direction of the arrow and retighten the pinch nut.

To adjust the heater control, push the lower control lever to the left (Cold) and loosen the pinch nut **A** (see **FIG 4:9**). Hold the flap lever over to the left as far as it will go and tighten pinch nut **A.** Always check that the cable sheath is fully gripped at each end by the clamps before making the adjustments.

4:8 Air conditioning, maintenance

Generally speaking, the air conditioning unit is not likely to need maintenance during the life of the vehicle.

The only possible faults that are likely to arise is a fan motor failure or a leak in the heater radiator. It is then necessary to remove the unit from the car to effect the necessary repair or replacement. Procedure is as follows:

First disconnect the battery, drain the cooling system and disconnect the two hoses to the water valve where they pass through the bulkhead. If a radio is fitted, this must next be removed and then the underscuttle apron. Uncouple and release the face vent hoses at each side of the unit. The position of these can be seen in the exploded view of the heating and ventilating unit (see **FIG 4:6**).

Remove the two screws securing the heater assembly at the upper mounting points. Ease away, complete with controls, to the left until the heater pipes are clear of the bulkhead aperture with the front flange clear of the supporting ledge. Draw into the passenger side. The unit can then be removed from the car.

To replace the heater, release the socket 13 (see **FIG 4:6**) and the plastic clips securing the top cover assembly and lift off, complete with fan unit. Underneath, remove the seven self-tapping screws holding the deflector plate in position, then remove the deflector plate 12. **Note the position of the bearings 11, one having a wider slot than the other,** then set the valve 15 in mid-position and prise out the bearings. Remove the flap valve from the housing.

Carefully release the capillary tube from the clips 18, release the water valve clip 10, bulkhead seal 22, and then unscrew the water valve 9, withdrawing it as far as possible. Turn the heater casing over and withdraw, first, the heater unit and then the valve and capillary assembly (see **FIG 4:10**).

The water valve and capillary tube are supplied as a single assembly. Should it be necessary to replace the unit, the capillary tube must first be shaped to the form of the one it supersedes using, if possible, a simple template (see **FIG 4:10,** right).

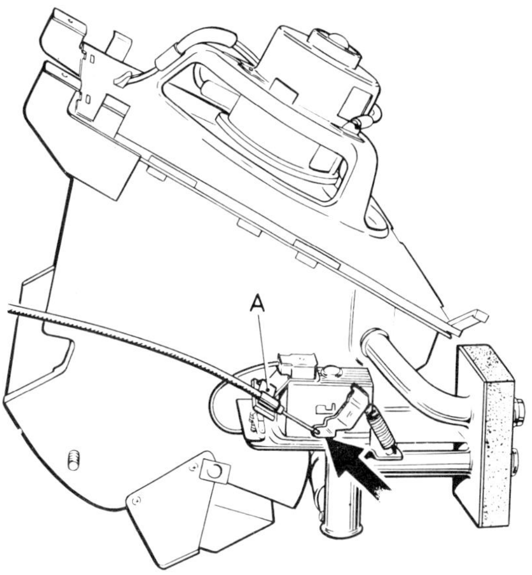

FIG 4:9 Adjustment to water valve control cable

To replace the fan unit, remove the heater from the car and release the top assembly as already described, then prise off the fan securing clip on the motor shaft and pull off the fan 20. Disconnect the motor cables, noting the position of each, and release the motor unit by pulling off the three clips.

Reinstallation is a simple reversal of the above dismantling sequences.

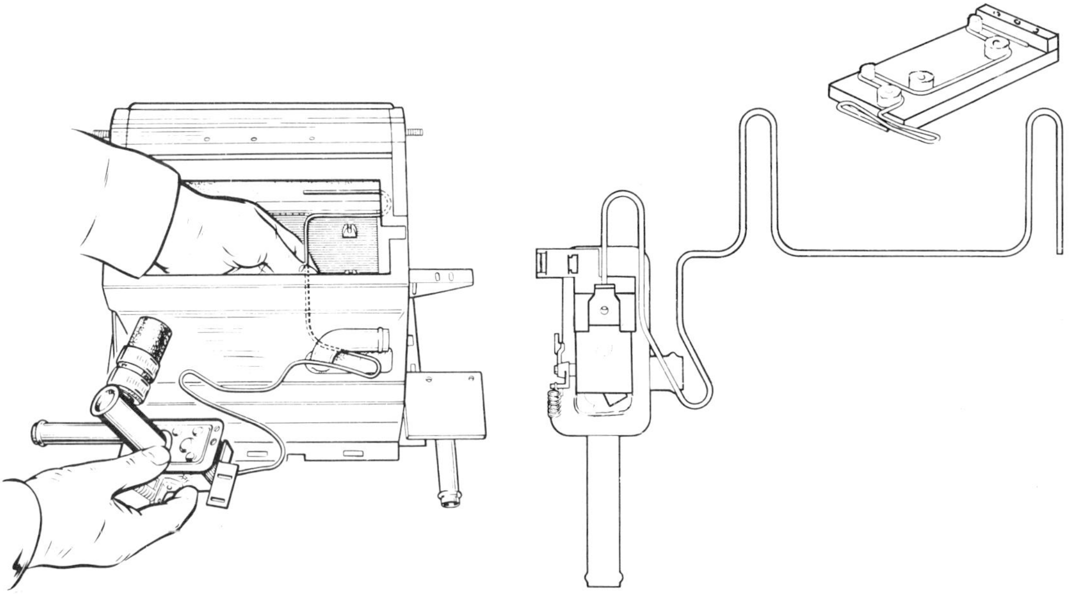

4:10 Removing water valve and capillary with, right, capillary shaping before installation

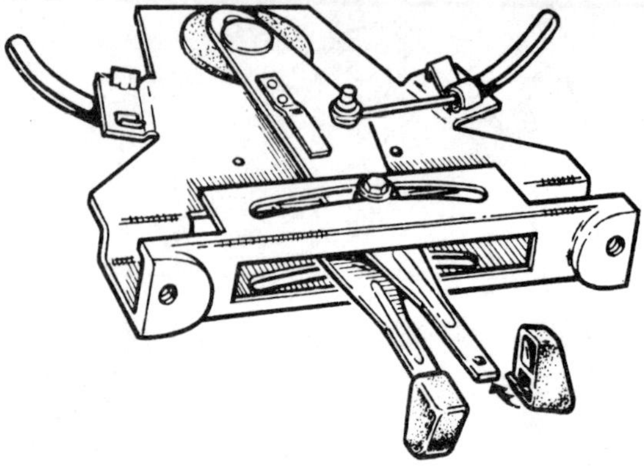

FIG 4:11 View of control assembly removed from panel

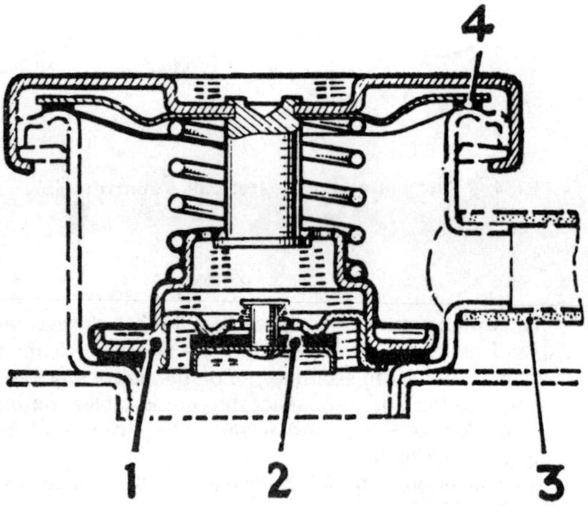

4:12 Section through radiator filler cap

Key to Fig 4:12 1 Expansion valve 2 Vacuum valve 3 Overflow pipe 4 Seal

4:9 Radiator and filler cap

To remove the radiator, first drain the cooling system, disconnect and remove the top and bottom hose connections.

Unscrew and remove the four fixing bolts and carefully lift from the seating taking care not to damage the radiator fins meanwhile. Small leaks in the radiator can be repaired by soldering but, as one leak is usually the sign of a general deterioration, it is far better to replace the radiator as a whole.

If the radiator drain cock is stiff, remove the complete cock by unscrewing it from the lower compartment and dismantle on the bench. Apply a thin film of grease to the cock before reassembling and ensure that the cock is watertight but can be turned with ease. **Never strain the cock while in position or either the cock may be broken or the radiator shell may be ruptured.**

The radiator filler cap (see **FIG 4:12**) incorporates two spring-loaded valves. The larger one of these opens upwards to relieve pressure in the radiator and to vent the coolant via the side duct 3, to the overflow. The smaller one 2, opens downwards when the contents of the system contract to admit air, the system being sealed by the filler neck seal 4.

At frequent intervals, examine these seals and replace by a new filler cap if they are faulty.

4:10 Fault diagnosis

(a) Frequent topping up of radiator

1 Leaks in hose connections or from joints
2 Faulty filler cap
3 Leak in heater system
4 Leaking drain cock or valves
5 Leaking cylinder head gasket

The last is a serious condition occurring after an engine overhaul through failure to check cylinder head nut tightness after a few hours running. It is usually accompanied by loss of power and occasionally by excessive condensation from the exhaust. **Immediate strip down and a new gasket is imperative if further damage is to be avoided.**

(b) Temperature gauge indicates excessive temperature

1 Broken or loose fan belt
2 Low water level in radiator
3 Obstructions in radiator passages
4 Fault on temperature gauge
5 Faulty thermostat

With this form of thermostat, a capsule failure prevents circulation through the radiator. If a replacement thermostat is not immediately available **leave the faulty thermostat out of the housing and remake the housing joint.**

CHAPTER 5

CLUTCH AND PROPELLER SHAFT

5:1 Clutch description

The clutch is of the dry, single plate type with a diaphragm pressure spring and with a spring cushioned hub as part of the driven plate. The hub and hub plate are coupled, through helical springs, to the cushion disc which is integral with the driven plate, faced on both sides with bonded asbestos brake material (Ferodo). This ensures smooth engagement between the engine and gearbox drive shaft by damping out cyclic accelerations and retardations. The special diaphragm pressure spring maintains a constant load on the pressure plate irrespective of the degree of clutch withdrawal or wear on the friction facings.

The drive from the engine is communicated to the gearbox drive shaft by clamping the facing ring of the driven plate between the pressure plate, part of the clutch withdrawal mechanism, and a machined facing on the engine flywheel. This pressure is applied by the diaphragm, secured at nine points to the clutch cover, against rings which act as a fulcrum around which the diaphragm bells when the centre section, divided into a group of eighteen radial segments, is deflected by the central release plate. The torque between the pressure plate and clutch cover is taken by three tangential straps and contact between the periphery of the diaphragm and the pressure plate is maintained by clips at the diaphragm end of the straps, so preventing noise arising from any loose association between the two members.

The belling of the diaphragm has the effect of releasing the circumferential pressure on the driven plate the clips slightly withdrawing the pressure plate. The clutch housing can then rotate with the engine crankshaft without transmitting the torque to the gearbox drive shaft.

A section through the clutch, as withdrawn from the bellhousing, is shown in **FIG 5:1** with the main components illustrated in the exploded view in **FIG 5:2**. In both of these the facing ring is omitted as part of the flywheel assembly but this does not affect the general description of operation.

The diaphragm 5, pivoted about the spring rings 3, and secured to the clutch coverplate 6, by the studs 4, in the rest state applies a pressure to the plate 2, to clamp the

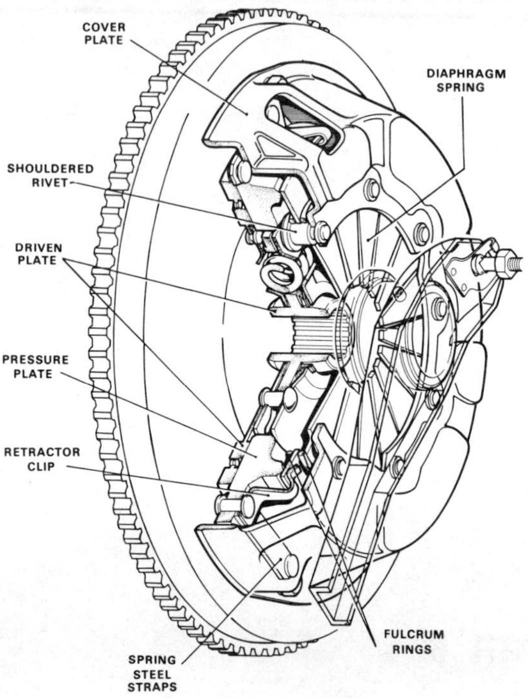

FIG 5:1 Diagrammatic part section through Avenger clutch assembly showing the component parts. The thrust pad and withdrawal lever are ghosted to show the position in relation to the diaphragm spring fingers

friction surfaces of the driven plate 1, to the machined facing on the flywheel. The engine torque is, therefore, transmitted from the flywheel to the clutch cover, to which it is attached by nine bolts, via the drive straps to the pressure plate and via the clamped friction pads to the driven plate mounted on the splined shaft of the gearbox drive shaft.

Movement of the clutch withdrawal lever, transmitted to the thrust pad assembly, applies pressure to the release plate in the centre of the diaphragm 5, causing this to move to the left. The segments, each acting as a separate lever around the fulcrum 3, force the outer periphery of the diaphragm to the right, taking with it the pressure plate 2 and releasing the clamp on the driven plate.

Movement of the clutch withdrawal lever (see **FIG 5:3**) is by a cable link coupled to the clutch pedal.

5:2 Removal and dismantling

To remove the clutch, raise the car on stands and remove the gearbox as described in **Section 6:3**. If, of course, clutch overhaul is being part of a general engine overhaul, the engine and gearbox will have been extracted and the separation then takes place on the bench.

The clutch cover is secured to the flywheel by six bolts and three dowels. Slacken the bolts evenly all round, half a turn per bolt before proceeding to the next, so as to avoid any chance of distorting the assembly. Remove the bolts and separate the clutch cover from the flywheel taking care not to allow the driven plate, which now will be free, from dropping to the garage floor.

The clutch removal lever and thrust pad will, of course, be retained in the bellhousing on the gearbox and, should it be necessary to dismantle this, release the end of the withdrawal cable and return spring from the end of the lever—this will have been done usually as part of the gearbox dismantling—and slide the lever in the direction of the arrow (see **FIG 5:3**) to release the end from the fulcrum post. The lever may then be withdrawn from the gearbox drive shaft and separation of the thrust pad from the lever effected as a second operation.

5:3 Inspection and reassembly

Examine the driven plate for wear of the friction surfaces. If these are worn or badly ridged renew the driven plate.

Examine the hub splines for signs of excessive wear and check for backlash on the gearbox drive shaft.

Examine the facing ring on the flywheel. If this is ridged, the flywheel will have to be removed and refaced.

Examine the clutch assembly. If the pressure plate is ridged or there is any other fault, the clutch plate assembly must be renewed as a whole. **It is not possible to dismantle or repair a clutch assembly.**

Check the condition of the thrust pad assembly and renew if necessary.

To reassemble:

First, replace the thrust pad assembly and withdrawal lever if the latter has been dismantled. Check that the securing clips are in place.

To refit the clutch assembly and driven plate to the flywheel, first place the driven plate in position, with the face marked 'this side to flywheel' the right way round, and locate with a spare primary shaft or special tool RG.541. **This is important. Unless this is done, it will not be possible to insert the gearbox drive shaft into the driven plate hub.**

Locate the clutch assembly on the flywheel by means of the dowels, insert the securing screws and tighten evenly, half a turn at a time until all are tight to a torque of 16 lb ft. Remove the locating shaft or tool.

Refit the gearbox, taking care when meshing the hub and drive shaft, and couple up the control cable.

5:4 The clutch control

An exploded view of the clutch cable control is shown in **FIG 5:4**. The action is simple. The clutch pedal 11, pulling on the clevis attached to the cable of the Bowden type control 8, withdraws the end of the lever 2, pivoted at fulcrum point 3, against the tension of the return spring 4. The tension of the latter is sufficient not only for holding off the lever and thrust pad from the clutch diaphragm, but also to overcome the friction of the cable in the sleeve and the weight of the clutch pedal on its

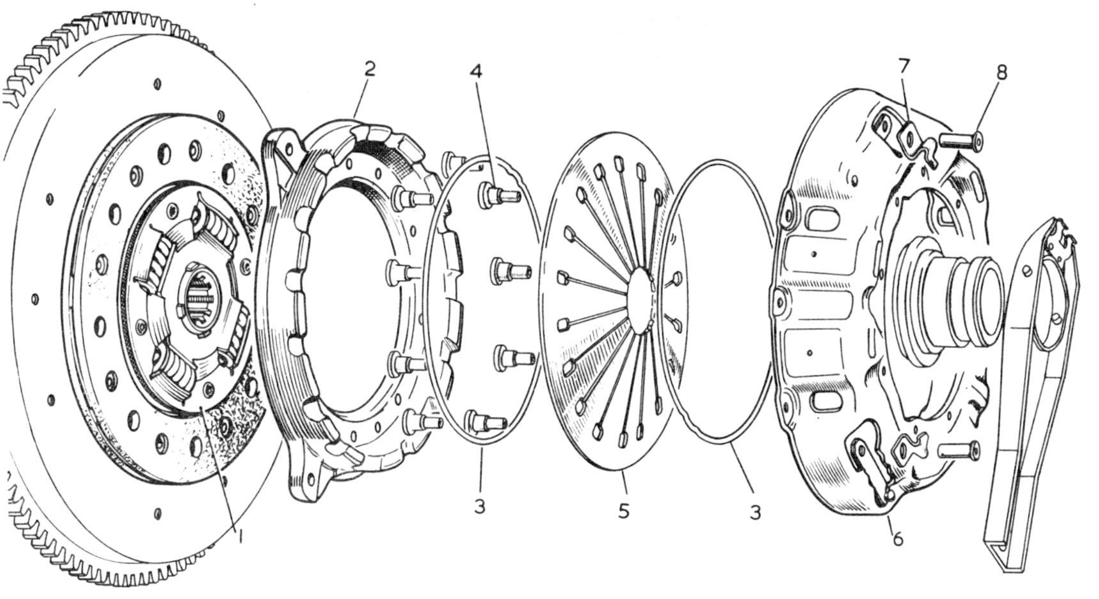

FIG 5:2 Exploded view of the clutch assembly

Key to Fig 5:2 1 Cushioned driven plate 2 Pressure plate 3 Fulcrum rings 4 Rivets 5 Diaphragm 6 Coverplate 7 Clip 8 Clip and strap rivet

shaft 10. Weakening of the pull-off spring, or excessive dryness of the cable in the sleeve and/or the pedal on the shaft can result in a slipping clutch. These points must, therefore, be given attention and lubricated as necessary.

To dismantle for a replacement of the cable assembly, release the pull-off spring and unscrew the adjuster and locknut 5 and 6. At the pedal end, extract the clevis pin at the upper end of the pedal and separate the cable from the pedal arm. The rubber boot 9 can then be pushed through the bulkead into the engine compartment by first withdrawing the tapered end of the sleeve from the abutment barrel where it has been acting as a key holding the boot in place. The cable can then be released from the supporting clips in the engine compartment 12 and a new one installed in its place.

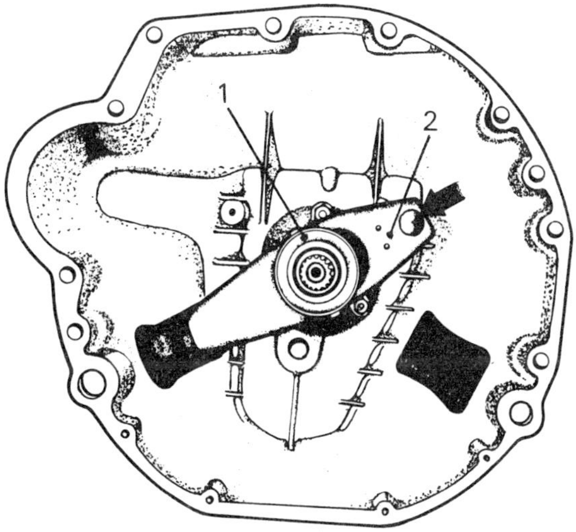

FIG 5:3 Interior view of bellhousing showing the position of the thrust pad and bearing 1, and withdrawal lever 2, with the fulcrum pivot point arrowed

5:5 Installation

Installation of the clutch control cable is a simple reversal of the dismantling procedure with only one minor change in sequence. The clevis and cable end at the engine bulkhead is first passed through the hole and the boot 9, which is divided to permit passage of the cable into the boot behind the clevis, is fitted to the cable and then inserted from the pedal side into the bulkhead aperture. When it is fully home, the metal surround of the bulkhead fitting into the slot behind the flat part, the barrel is parted sufficiently to enable the tapered end of the nylon abutment to enter and the abutment and sleeve pushed home to lock the boot into place.

After assembly, set the adjuster nut on the control cable so that there is $\frac{3}{16}$ inch free play at the withdrawal lever end before the thrust pad bears on the diaphragm within (see **FIG 5:5**). Lock with the locknut.

Replacement of a broken cable within a sleeve is not to be recommended. In the event of trouble with the cable assembly, renew the complete unit.

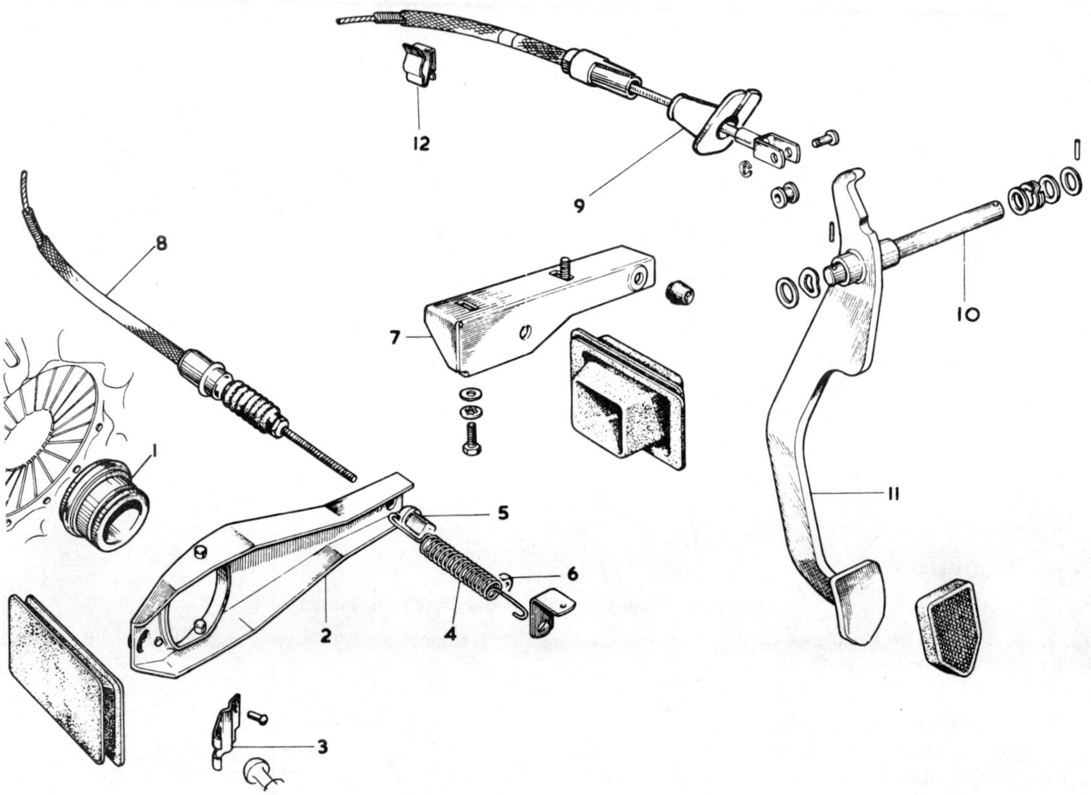

FIG 5:4 Exploded view of clutch control on the Avenger

Key to Fig 5:4 1 Thrust pad and bearing 2 Withdrawal lever 3 Fulcrum pivot and clip 4 Return spring 5/6 Adjuster and locknut 7 Pedal stop plate 8 Clutch cable assembly 9 Bulkhead boot 10 Pedal shaft 11 Pedal 12 Cable clip

5:6 Maintenance and servicing

The clutch control system, being extremely simple, needs no special maintenance other than a regular check of free play in the withdrawal lever.

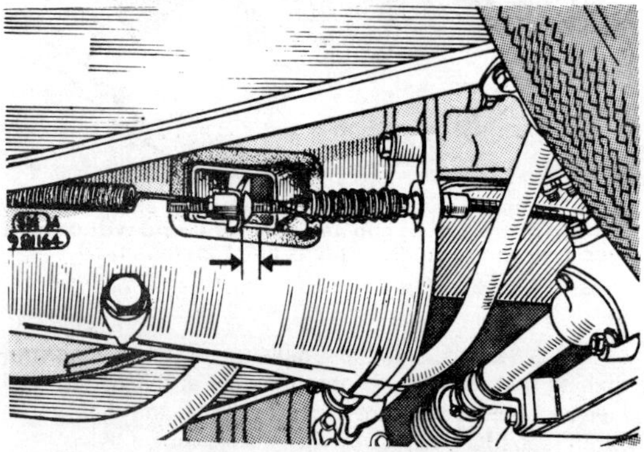

FIG 5:5 Adjustment point for clutch withdrawal free movement. The distance between the arrows from full withdrawal to contact between thrust pad and diaphragm fingers should be set to $\frac{3}{16}$ inch

5:7 Propeller shaft and bearing

The tubular propeller shaft terminates at both the gearbox and differential in universal joints with sealed needle bearings. These are lubricated for life and do not require periodical lubrication. The sliding spline drive end is enclosed within the gearbox and is lubricated by the gearbox oil. The rear, driven, end is flange-coupled to the drive shaft of the differential.

In certain models, a bonded rubber damper has been incorporated in the propeller shaft at the rear end; in others the shaft is plain.

Should it become necessary to remove the propeller shaft, remove the nuts from the rear axle coupling, place a drip tray under the gearbox to catch any oil, pull the shaft forward to clear the coupling, lower and then withdraw the shaft rearwards. Reinstallation is a reversal of this procedure.

The universal joints can be dismantled by first removing the circlips 2 (see **FIG 5:6**) then tapping gently on one radius of an ear of the yoke. The needle bearings will emerge and can be extracted. Check that all are present

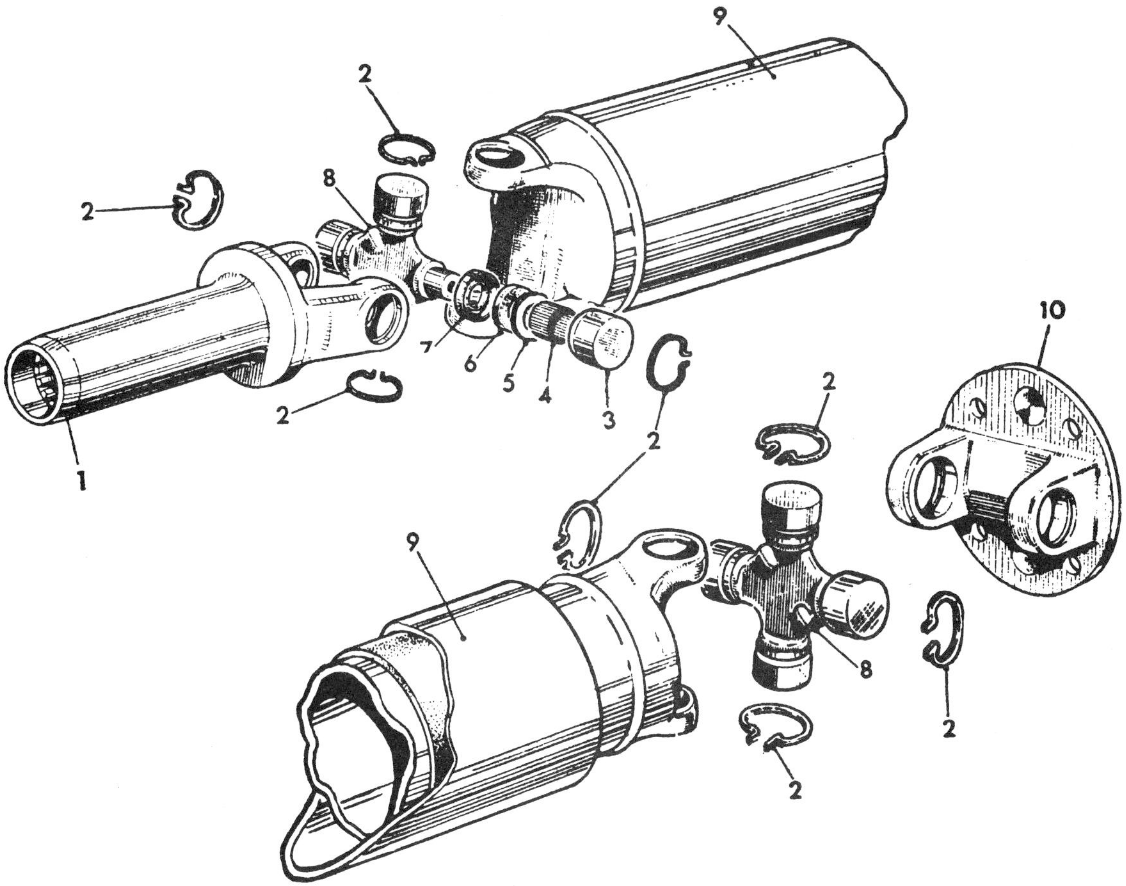

FIG 5:6 Exploded view of universal joints at gearbox end (above) and differential end (below)

Key to Fig 5:6 1 Gearbox drive shaft 2 Circlip 3/4/5 Needle bearing 6 Gasket 7 Gasket retainer 8 Spider journal 9 Tubular propeller shaft 10 Flange connector-to-differential coupling

and record the number for reassembly. Repeat for the opposite bearing. Turn the joint through 90 deg. and repeat for the other two sides. Extract the journals and spider. Wash all parts in paraffin or petrol and examine for wear. Replace parts worn or marked with corrosion.

Reassemble, packing the bearings with Retinax 'A' filling the race about one-third full with the roller in position. Install new gaskets and seals. **In the case of the inner yokes, these can be replaced only as a complete shaft since the yokes are welded to and balanced with the shaft.**

Insert the journal in the flange yoke holes, gently tap the bearing assembly into position and, when all are positioned, fit new snap rings. Tap lightly all round to relieve pressure, if any, in the assemblies.

5:8 Fault diagnosis

(a) Clutch will not disengage

1 Broken clutch cable
2 Wrong cable adjustment

(b) Clutch will not engage

1 Worn driven plate facings
2 Grease on facings
3 Wrong cable adjustment
4 Broken return spring

(c) Clutch judders

1 Worn driven plate
2 Grease on facings

NOTES

CHAPTER 6

MANUAL GEARBOX

6:1 Operation of gearbox

The gearbox is of conventional type with four forward and a reverse gears. The forward gears are all synchromesh, the gear teeth being of helical pattern, permanently meshed, to give quiet operation. The reverse gear is obtained by an intermediate gear sliding between spur gears on the layshaft and drive shaft.

The gearbox is in two parts, a forward bellhousing integral with the gearcase, within which is the clutch withdrawal mechanism, and a rear cover supporting the drive shaft extension, speedometer drive and gear selector mechanism. The two sections are bolted together. The gearcase has a pressed steel top cover giving access to the gears within (see **FIG 6:1**).

The main gear components comprise a first-motion shaft, transmitting the torque from the engine through the clutch to the gearbox, a layshaft and a third-motion shaft, transmitting the torque from the gearbox to the rear transmission via the propeller shaft, each with its cluster of gears, together with the gear selector rods and forks. The third motion shaft is supported at the forward end in needle bearings within the first motion shaft and in a ballbearing in the rear wall of the gearcase.

The drive from the first motion shaft (A in **FIG 6:2**) is transmitted to the layshaft **C**, via the first pair of helical cut gears, 3a, 3b at the forward end of the gearbox. Adjacent to the drive gear and integral with the first motion shaft is a tooth wheel 4, which is engaged with the inner teeth of the sliding sleeve 5, to provide top, or direct, drive.

In all other gears, the drive is via the layshaft and through one of the three pairs of helical cut gears 6, 7 or 8, the driven gear of each being a sliding fit on the third motion shaft with each having a tooth wheel, on the side adjacent to the sleeve, as an integral part.

Gear selection is by movement of one of the two sliding sleeves 5 or 9, which are splined to a central hub keyed to the third motion shaft. The internal splines of each sleeve, when moved left or right by the selector fork and rod, mesh simultaneously with the tooth wheel of the adjacent driven gear and those of the hub to provide a positive drive to the third motion shaft while leaving the remaining pairs of helical gears free to rotate without taking load.

The synchronizing feature is provided by a tooth wheel interposed on the shaft between the sleeve hub and a driven gear. The tooth wheel is friction driven on one side by the driven gear and locked by dogs on the other

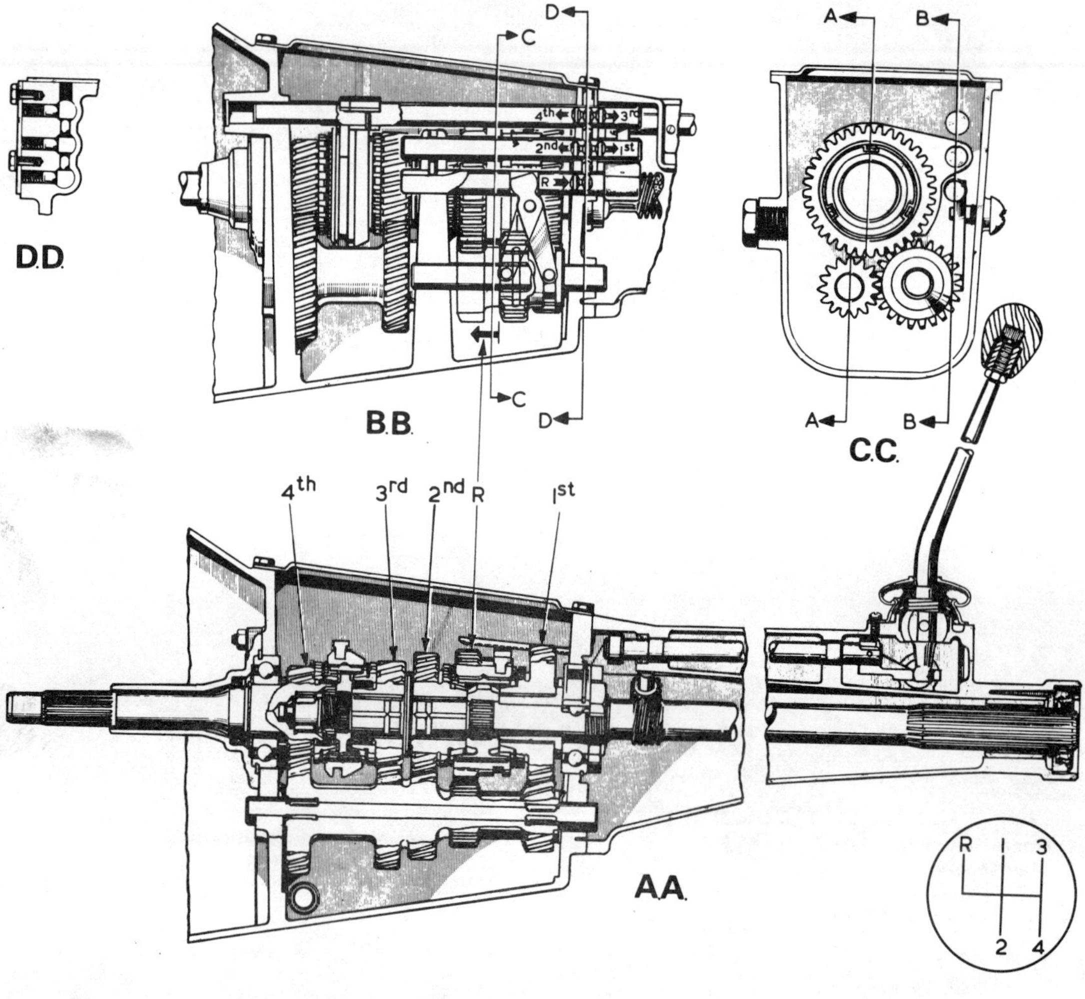

FIG 6:1 Sectional view through the Avenger fourspeed gearbox

immediately prior to engagement with the tooth wheel by the sleeve to ensure that both sleeve and driven gear are at the same speed of rotation before positive meshing.

The sleeves are moved by forked arms 10, 11, embracing the circumferential groove of the sleeves, the arms being mounted on rods passing through the end wall and a short projecting inner side wall of the gearcase, as shifted by the gear selector lever. Engagement of the lever with the centre rod and fork 11, enables the first or second gear to be selected by movement of the sleeve 9 in either direction. Engagement of the lever with the upper rod and fork 10 enables the third gear or direct drive to be selected by movement of sleeve 5 in either direction while movement of the lower rod and lever serves to slide the intermediate gear 14 into mesh between the spur gears 17 and 18 on the layshaft and third motion shaft respectively. This provides a direct drive but with reversed motion.

Positive movement of the forks and rods is ensured by spring-loaded detent pins in the rear side wall of the gearcase entering one of three grooved recesses in the rods. The first gear provides a ratio of 3.317:1, the second a ratio of 2.029:1, the third a ratio of 1.366:1 and top gear is direct. The reverse gear provides a ratio of 3.450:1. These gear ratios are, of course, further modified by that of the crownwheel and pinion in the differential to give the true crankshaft to rear axle ratio.

6:2 Maintenance

Maintenance of the gearbox is confined to periodical checking on the oil level and topping up with Shell Super Motor or equivalent grade oil. Filling is done through a hole on the righthand side of the gearbox which is closed by a screw plug. The oil must reach the bottom level of the hole. The content of the gearbox, when full, is 3 pints

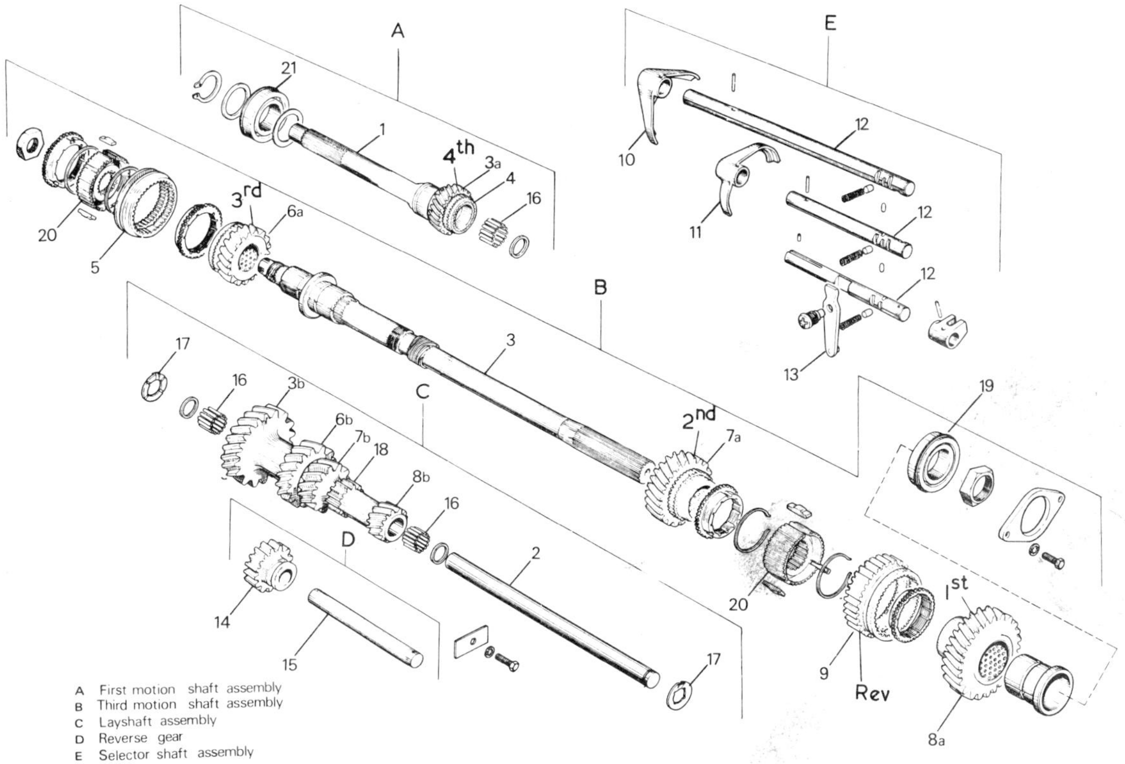

FIG 6:2 Exploded view of the gear trains and shafts

Key to Fig 6:2 1 First motion shaft 2 Layshaft 3 Third motion shaft 4 Tooth wheel 5, 9 Sliding sleeves 6a/6b Third speed gears 7a/7b Second speed gears 8a/8b First speed gears 10/11 Selector forks 12 Selector rods 13 Fulcrum lever 14 Intermediate spur gear 15 Intermediate gearshaft 16 Needle rollers 17 Thrust washers 18 Reverse spur gear on laygear 19 Third motion shaft bearing 20 Synchronizing hub assemblies 21 First motion shaft bearing

but there is no necessity for draining and refilling during the life of the car unless there has been some mechanical failure within the gearbox. Similarly, after a complete overhaul, the original oil can be re-used if it is not obviously contaminated.

The gearchange lever and shaft also receive their lubrication from the gearbox by splash and need no adjustment or servicing.

It always pays to keep a good ear to gearbox noise as this can disclose incipient troubles before they reach a dangerous stage. A finger lightly applied to the end of the gearchange lever will sense any damaged or chipped gears while the car is running. While no sound should come from the gearbox in any of the forward gears, there will always be a small degree of whine with the reverse gears since they are not helical-cut and even the best of spur gears are not dead silent in operation.

6:3 Gearbox removal

1 Drive the car onto ramps or over a pit and drain the oil from the gearbox. Disconnect the battery earth lead.

2 Disconnect the throttle control rod from the carburetter by removing the retaining clip from the rod and then the rod from the coupling.

3 To remove the starter motor, take out the nuts and bolts retaining the battery earth lead, starter shield and the motor.

4 If a centre console is fitted, to remove it, first release the gearlever gaiter by pushing inside the console. Take out the rear compartment ashtray to expose two screws at the rear of the console. Now remove all the securing screws, slide the console forward and upwards to clear the handbrake and gearlever.

5 Take off the gearshift lever and covers.

6 Remove the propeller shaft as described in **Chapter 5, Section 5:7**.

7 Disconnect the speedometer drive cable and the clutch withdrawal cable, move the clutch cable forward away from the withdrawal lever.

8 Remove the inspection cover from the forward lower section of the bellhousing.

9 Uncouple the exhaust pipe from the manifold.

10 Disconnect the reverse switch cables (if fitted).

11 Support the weight of the engine with a jack and place a block of wood between the jack pad and the engine to distribute the weight and protect the engine.

12 Remove the rear support mounting from the body and lower the gearbox just enough to gain access to the bellhousing upper securing bolts and nuts. Remove

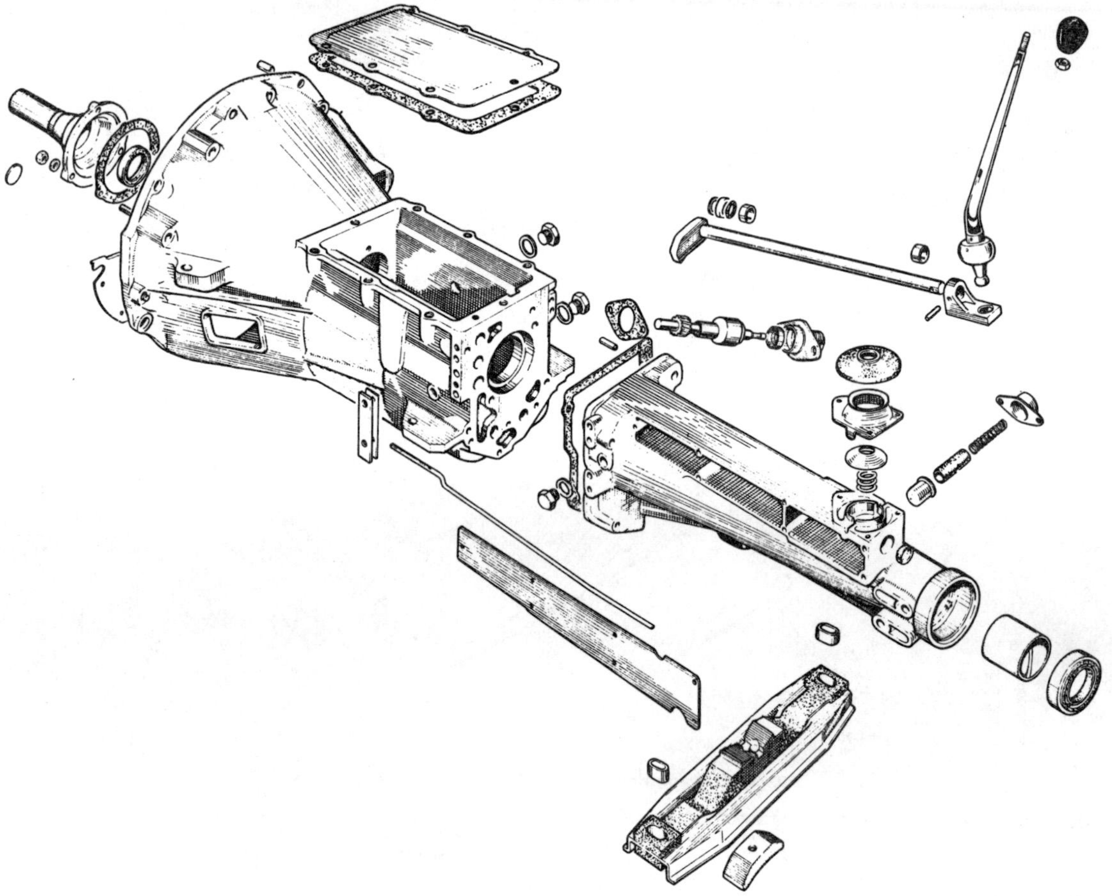

FIG 6:3 Exploded view of gearcase, end cover and gearbox support member

them and the lower ones and withdraw the gearbox from underneath the car.

13 During the final stages of removal do not allow the weight of the gearbox to be supported on the first motion shaft otherwise the clutch driven plate will be distorted.

6:4 Dismantling and inspection

Wash out the interior of the gearbox with paraffin, draining the liquid through the lower drain plug. Clean the exterior with a proprietary detergent liquid and dry.

Remove the two bolts securing the speedometer gear housing to the rear section and remove. Check the condition of the rear oil seal and if it is worn to the point of replacement, extract it before removing the rear cover. This is secured in position by five bolts and, as some are longer than the others, note the position of the longer bolts for replacement.

Twist the gearlever shaft counterclockwise in its seating to disengage it from the selector rods and then pull the rear cover back to separate it from the gearbox. **If the oil seal is satisfactory, this operation must be carried out carefully so that it is not damaged on the drive shaft.** Extract the oil feed pipe, a push fit in the rear cover and gearcase.

Unbolt and remove the gearcase cover and gasket, unbolt and remove the detent spring coverplate at the rear lefthand top corner and extract the springs and pins. With a $\frac{1}{8}$ inch pin punch, drive out the roll pins in the gear selector forks and remove both forks and rods. Extract the interlock plungers in the vertical bore between the selector rods. These may be seen in the detail **DD** in **FIG 6:1. The reverse selector shaft is left in position for the time being.**

Engage two gears simultaneously by moving the sleeves on the hubs by hand to lock the shafts, remove the rear bearing clamp plate and then unscrew the $1\frac{5}{8}$ inch self-locking nut on the third motion shaft. Return the sleeves to the neutral position. At the rear remove the small locking plate securing the ends of the layshaft and reverse gear spindles.

Obtain a length of shaft the same diameter as that of the layshaft but only as long as the laygear cluster—a special set of dummy layshafts are available from the Chrysler agent under part No. RG.543—and insert it from the front end into the layshaft bearing, driving it home until the true layshaft has been ejected at the opposite end. Centre the dummy layshaft so that the laygear cluster is free to drop into the bottom of the gearcase.

Remove the clutch withdrawal lever and bearing pad from the first motion shaft within the bellhousing end, extract the nuts and withdraw the front bearing cover (see **FIG 6:4**). Using a drift from within the gearbox, drive the bearing forward until there is a $\frac{1}{8}$ inch gap between the gearcase face and bearing retainer ring. **Be careful not to damage the oil thrower** (see **FIG 6:5**). Using a pair of angled levers, extract the bearing from the gearcase (see **FIG 6:6**). The first motion shaft will come out at the same time together with the needle rollers and abutment washer in the counterbored end where it supports the third motion shaft. **There should be 23 rollers present. Check the number and, if any are absent, locate them from within the gearcase before proceeding further.**

Remove the third motion shaft from the gearcase bearing by tapping the splined end with a hide mallet supporting the gear assembly in the gearcase meanwhile. When it is free of the bearing, extract the bearing from the gearcase (see **FIG 6:7**) and this will enable the shaft, complete with gears and hubs, to be eased out of the enclosure (see **FIG 6:8**). To prevent the 1st/2nd gear clusters from being displaced during removal, a tubular spacer 1 inch long by $1\frac{1}{4}$ inch ID can be fitted over the end of the shaft and retained in position by the rear nut screwed on finger tight as shown in **FIG 6:8**.

Extract the layshaft from the bottom of the gearcase together with the two thrust washers. The reverse selector pivot bolt can now be removed, the fulcrum lever extracted and the selector rod withdrawn. Take care to retrieve the detent pin and spring, if these have not already been removed, and the selector shaft guide peg.

The next stage is to remove the intermediate shaft and gear. The shaft is a drive fit in the inner wall and must be extracted through the outer wall, that is, drifted to the rear. If drifted in the opposite direction, the forward wall of the gearcase will be damaged.

The end of the shaft in the cavity below the coverplate is grooved to take a special adaptor which can be attached to a slide hammer for extraction. The adaptor is tool No. RG.3072-3 for use with slide hammer RG.3072. Alternatively, the shaft can be tapped out from within the gearcase by careful application of light ball-end hammer. **It is not advisable to use the outer wall of the gearcase as a backing for a screw type ejection tool as it may distort or crack.**

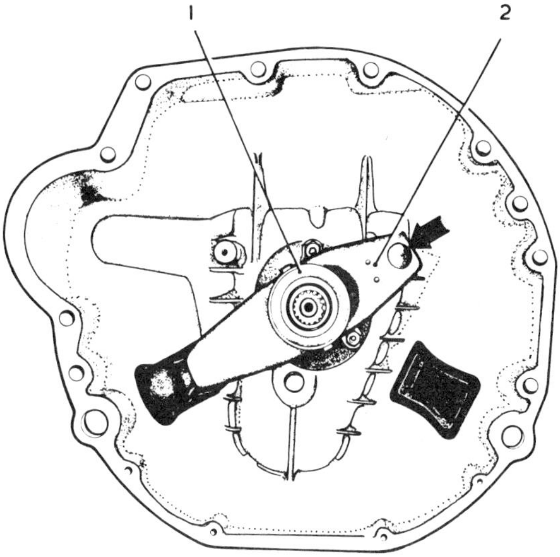

FIG 6:4 View inside bellhousing showing clutch withdrawal lever. To remove, detach from fulcrum pillar by pushing in the direction of the arrow

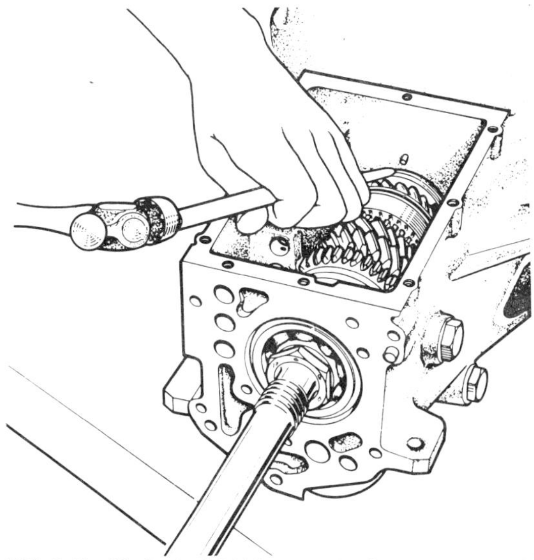

FIG 6:5 Method of drifting out the first motion shaft bearing

Inspect the first motion shaft for signs of wear, particularly in the splined end which should be checked in the clutch driven plate for backlash, examine the needle rollers for wear or pitting, renewing the whole set if one or more have this indication, and reassemble in the opposite order to dismantling.

Wash out the bearing and check for smooth running by spinning the outer race. If satisfactory, re-oil the race immediately after inspection to prevent the ingress of moisture. If not satisfactory, extract the bearing in a press and fit a new one. The bearing incorporates a predetermined amount of end float and has a 'spot' classification denoted by faint rings on the outer edge of the track. When replacing the bearing, fit one with identical spot markings to the one removed.

If, for any reason, the bearing has to be removed from the first motion shaft, always fit a new one and a fresh circlip. When reinstalling the needle bearings, use a small quantity of grease to hold them in place until reinstalled in the gearbox.

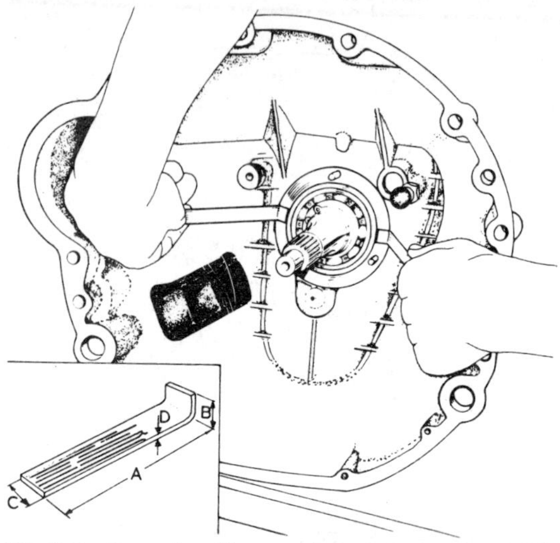

FIG 6:6 Removing first motion shaft bearing with cranked levers. Inset shows the shape and dimensions of the levers

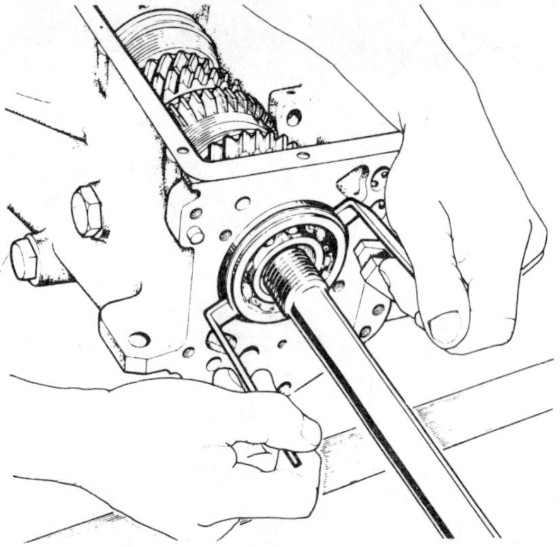

FIG 6:7 Removing the third motion shaft bearing with cranked levers

Inspect the layshaft and laygear assembly for wear or corrosion and remove the needle rollers and abutment washers for cleaning and examination. There should be 26 needle rollers at each end. After inspection, reassemble on the dummy shaft with the needle rollers held in position by a small quantity of grease. Should it be necessary to replace the laygear, the end float of the assembly in the gearcase must be checked and, if necessary, the front thrust washer changed to keep it within the prescribed limits of .006 and .010 inch. Three front washers are available but the rear washer is always of the one thickness, .070 to .072 inch.

Turning to the third motion shaft, examine the condition of the gears and synchronizing hubs, if satisfactory, wash clean in petrol or white spirit, dry and oil ready for installation. Should it be necessary to dismantle the assembly for the replacement of any component, first study the exploded view in **FIG 6:2,** then remove the dummy spacer and nut from the rear end and slide the first and second gear assembly, with synchronizing hub and cones, clear of the shaft. Lay out in order on a clean sheet of paper ready for reinstallation in the correct sequence.

Next, remove the front self-locking nut with a suitable ring spanner, securing the shaft against rotation by some suitable means other than gripping the shaft in a vice. If no other means is available, insert the propeller shaft coupling in a vice between protected jaws and use the spline socket to hold the splined ends of the shaft against rotation (see **FIG 6:9**). **Discard the nut. A new self-locking nut must be fitted on reassembly.**

Slide off the third and top gear assembly and synchronizing hubs and lay out in order on the sheet of paper. Each component can now be examined individually and replaced as necessary.

When inspection is completed and any necessary replacements obtained, reassemble in the reverse order, lightly oiling the components before fitting. Tighten the front nut, plain side towards the hub, to a torque of 70 lb ft. Replace the rear nut and spacer finger tight until after assembly in the gearcase. Inspect the intermediate gear and shaft, layshaft and other components, replacing as necessary.

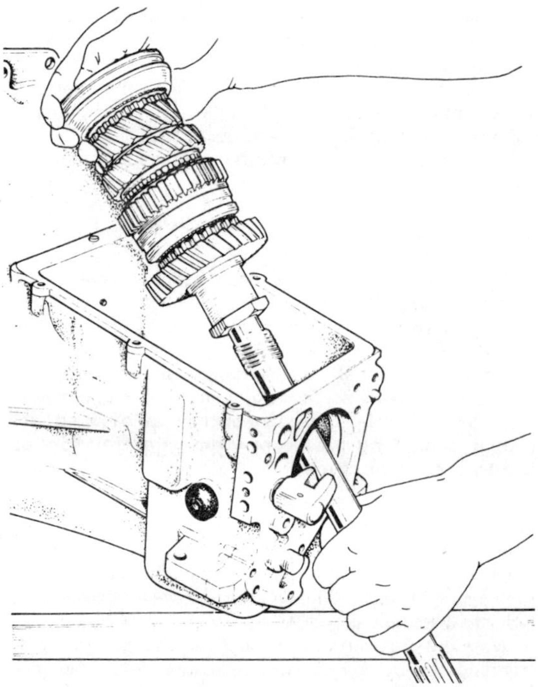

FIG 6:8 Extracting the third motion shaft from the gearcase

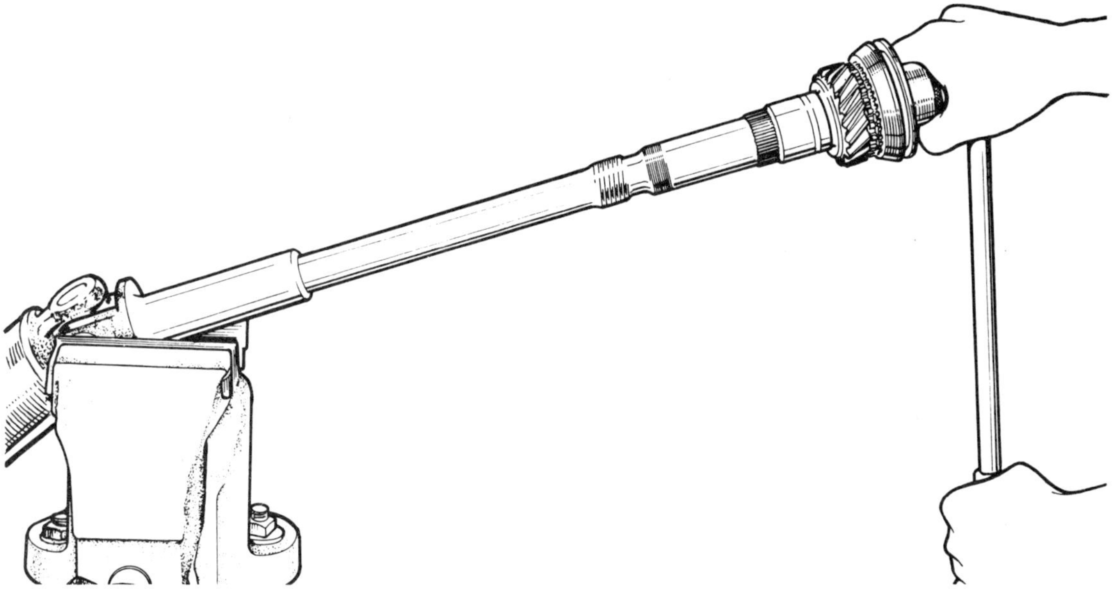

FIG 6:9 Method of securing third motion shaft against turning while removing the end nut by using the universal joint socket in a vice as the locking element

6:5 Reassembly and installation

Reassembly commences with the installation of the intermediate spur gear and spindle, securing the latter in place by means of the lock plate. Lubricate each part generously with SAE.90 oil before installation. Next, install the dummy shaft and laygear assembly in the bottom of the gearcase, fit the thrust washers into position, tags seated in the slots in the gearcase and the thinner washer at the front end, holding them in place with grease while the laygear is lifted into position and the layshaft driven home, displacing the dummy layshaft. Check the end float which should be between .006 and .01 inch as already stated.

Insert cords under the layshaft, replace the layshaft by the dummy and once again lower the laygear to the bottom of the gearcase with the cords hanging over the sides. This is done to prevent damaging the laygear teeth during installation of the third motion shaft and bearing. Reinsert the third motion shaft by a reverse of the procedure outlined in **FIG 6:8**, remove the rear nut and dummy spacer and **discard the nut**. Fit the rear bearing over the shaft with the retainer ring at the rear and tap into position until retainer ring is in contact with the casing.

Set up in a press with the inner ring of the bearing supported on blocks and press the bearing home (see **FIG 6:10**) taking care to see that the dogs, slots and plates of the synchronizing hubs are properly located, remove the assembly from the press and install the first motion shaft, drifting the bearing outer ring home evenly until fully seated, checking that both third motion shaft and first motion shaft turn smoothly, without excessive end play, and independently. Reinstall the laygear and shaft, using the cords to lift into position, and remove the cords. Fit the sealing ring and front cover tightening the nuts to a torque of 6 lb ft.

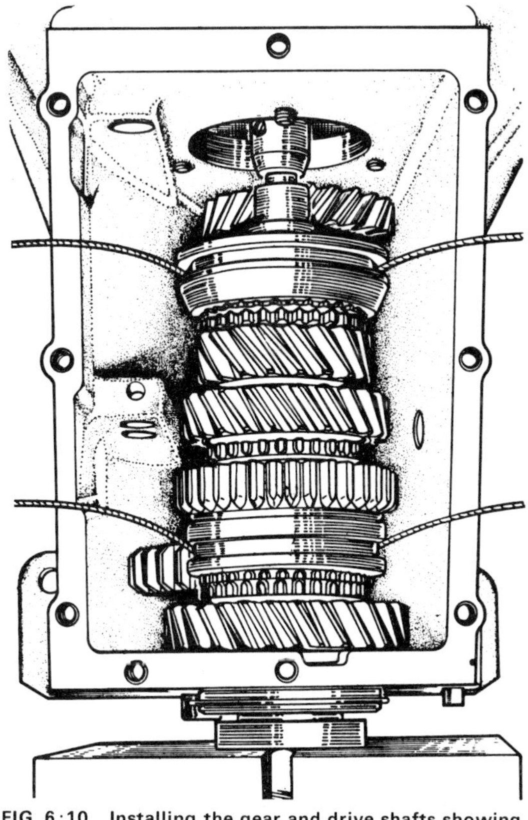

FIG 6:10 Installing the gear and drive shafts showing the cords ready to mesh the layshaft and laygear when in position

Reinstall the reverse selector shaft and guide peg, fit the pivot bolt and fulcrum lever into place and then the two selector forks and rods with the interlock plungers in position.

Remove the rear bearing clamp plate, slide both reverse and fourth gears into mesh to lock the third motion shaft and then fit a new rear nut tightening it to a torque of 70 lb ft. Insert detent plungers and springs and refit the coverplate and disengage the reverse gear and fourth gear to bring the gearbox to the neutral position. Check that the gears will now engage properly by movement of the selector rods and that it is not possible to engage two gears at once.

Reinstall the oil pipe in the rear cover, smear the rear oil seal with grease and bolt the rear cover into position with the gearshift lever properly engaged with the selector rods and forks. Reinstall the speedometer gear and bearing, joint and cover and, finally refit the top cover and gasket.

All that remains before installation in the car is to replace the clutch withdrawal lever and bearing pad.

Reinstallation is a simple reversal of the removal procedure taking care to ensure, before inserting the first motion shaft end into the clutch driven plate, that it has been properly centred as set out in **Chapter 5**. After installation, refill the gearbox with three pints of Shell Super motor oil.

6:6 Gearshift adjustment

The gearshift lever needs no special adjustment. The simple and robust linkage between the lower end of the gearlever and the selector rods is not likely to wear in the normal life of the car. The only parts which are likely to deteriorate are the rubber cover to the ball cavity and, possibly, the springs to the ball seating and reverse gear pad. These are easily replaced and reference to the exploded view in **FIG 6:3** will make the operation simple.

6:7 Fault diagnosis

(a) Forward gears will not mesh silently

1 Clutch not releasing (on all gears)
2 Synchromesh not operating (1st, 2nd, 3rd or top gears)

(b) Noisy forward gears

1 Worn or damaged helical gears

(c) Noisy reverse gear

1 Worn reverse or intermediate gear
2 Intermediate gear improperly meshed

(d) Gears slip out while travelling

1 Worn spring or detent of selector mechanisms
2 Damaged or worn selector forks

CHAPTER 7

AUTOMATIC TRANSMISSION

7:1 Description of automatic gearbox

The Borg Warner Model 35 automatic transmission comprises two main components, a torque converter and a hydraulically operated gearbox embodying a set of epicyclic gears with controls providing three forward speeds and a reverse.

Both the torque converter, and the gearchange mechanism share a common oil supply and pump. The gearchanges are effected by the application of internal clutches and external brake bands to elements of the planetary gears in ordered sequence. This is set by the selection of gear from a lever by the driver, engine speed as regulated by the throttle control and torque as determined by a governor.

The torque converter comprises an impeller, bolted to the engine crankshaft through a special adaptor plate, the outer blades of which circulate the fluid through the peripheral vanes of a turbine rotor coupled to the gearshaft. The fluid returns through inner vanes of the rotor and a stationary set of vanes back to the impeller (see **FIG 7:1**).

The shape of the vanes is such that, when the impeller is turning at a rate faster than that of the turbine rotor, the drive is combined with a degree of torque multiplication. This ranges from 2.3:1 at full throttle with the car stationary in gear, decreasing to 1:1 when impeller is running at about ten per cent above rotor speed. From this point the device acts as a simple fluid coupling, without torque multiplication.

The transmission can be considered as two distinct mechanisms, a mechanical group, comprising planetary gears, clutches and band brakes, and an engine-driven hydraulic pump, valves, regulators and a governor.

The physical arrangement can be seen from the sectional view in **FIG 7:2**. The torque converter is on the left, the gear trains on the right and the hydraulic channels and valves in the section beneath. The hydraulic governor is in the extension housing with the speedometer drive beyond.

A schematic view of the transmission is given in **FIG 7:3**, with a more detailed cutaway view of the clutch and gear trains in **FIG 7:4**. The front clutch 6, links the

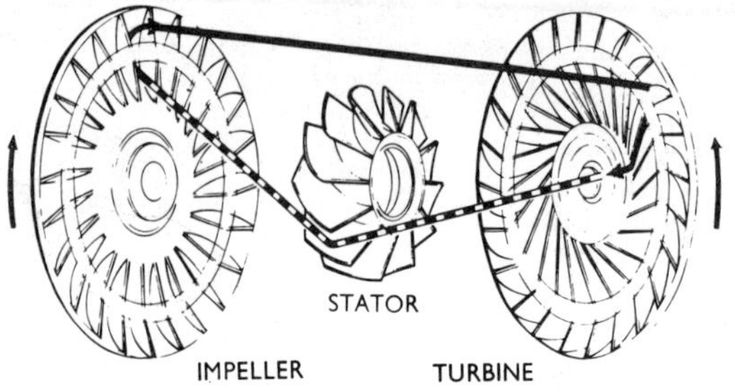

FIG 7:1 Diagrammatic impression of torque converter operation

input shaft 5, with the forward sun gears 13. The rear clutch links the input shaft 5, with the reverse sun gear 17, the latter being locked by the external brake band 8, in certain gear configurations. A unidirectional clutch 9, prevents the pinion carrier 11, from rotating in a direction opposite to that of the engine and permits the gearbox to freewheel in 1st gear. The rear brake band 10, when applied, locks the pinion carrier against rotation in either direction. The annulus 12, transmits the drive from the planetary pinions 15 and 16.

The planetary gear set comprises two sun gears, two sets of pinions, a pinion carrier and a ring gear or annulus. The teeth are helical involute throughout for quietness and efficient torque transmission. In all forward gears, the drive is through the forward sun gear 13 (see **FIG 7:4**), leaving by the ring gear 12. In reverse, the drive is through the reverse sun gear. Six pinions in all are mounted on the planet carrier. Three are long pinions meshing between the reverse sun gear and the internal teeth of the annulus at one end and between the forward sun gear, via the second set of three pinions and the annulus teeth at the other.

Selection of gear is, primarily, by the gear selection lever. This provides six positions, 1, 2, Drive, Neutral, Reverse and Park, indicated by the initial letters on a scale adjacent to the lever.

In the drive position D, bottom gear is mechanically obtained on selection. Changing up is then automatic according to throttle setting and torque. This is done by the hydraulic control mechanism. In P, the car is braked positively by a pawl mechanism providing a third brake apart from the hand- and footbrake. **It must never be engaged while the car is in motion or serious damage to the transmission will result.**

The hydraulic control derives its supply of oil from a single pump, driven from the input shaft, to give pressures ranging from 57 lb/sq in to 160 lb/sq in according to speed. Part of the output is routed to the hydraulic converter and part is converted to lower pressures in regulator valves for other purposes within the transmission.

Apart from non-return valves, there are eight valves—two regulator, two shift, one manual, one throttle, one servo orifice and one modulator—a governor, two brake servos and two clutch servos interconnected by a complex network of channels. The manual valve is operated mechanically by the gear selector lever and the throttle valve by a cam linked with the throttle by a cable. All others are hydraulically operated and provide the automatic feature of the transmission.

The function of the manual valve, mechanically linked to the gear selector lever, is to direct the hydraulic fluid to, or exhaust it from, the clutch and servo pistons. In this manner the initial stages of power flow from the engine, through the gears, to the drive shaft is set up.

The throttle valve is set by a cam, cable-linked to the throttle control. Depression of the accelerator pedal, therefore, acts on both the carburetter butterfly valve and the throttle valve in a proportion set by the shape or contour of the cam. Actually, this is two valves in a common body each having a separate function and interlinked by a spring. The first is the downshift valve the function of which, at full accelerator depression, is to delay upshifts or effect downshifts at maximum engine speeds. This is the 'kick-down' feature which enables the driver to achieve the effect of a changedown with a manual gearbox to get increased acceleration if needed.

The second is the throttle valve proper which floats between the downshift valve spring and its own return spring, the return force being amplified by governor controlled throttle pressure. It transmits hydraulic pressure, via the primary regulator valve, to control the clutch and servo units operating on the brake bands of the sun wheel and annulus. This regulates the clutch and brake band capacities to suit current operating conditions.

The governor valve is centrifugally operated and regulates the pressure to the modulator, shift and servo orifice valves according to output shaft speed. The regulator valves are, in effect, pressure reducing valves modifying the pump pressure to suit the requirements of the torque converter, overall lubrication and the exhaust to the pump inlets. The modulator valve acts as a hydraulic relay applying the differing pressures required by the throttle valve according to the condition of the governor.

Though the underlying principles of the transmission are relatively simple, their translation into an effective and smooth running, reliable mechanism is the result of much development and experiment with valve dimensions, spring pressures and channel proportions all of which are permanently set in the dimensions of the component parts. The only adjustments are the purely mechanical ones of taking up wear in the planetary brake bands, the linkage between the carburetter and the downshift cam and the link between the gear selector lever and the manual valve. The sole faults that are likely to occur in the valve and hydraulic system are those due either to the use of wrong hydraulic fluid, allowing the fluid level to fall too low or the admission of dirt or grit into the hydraulic system.

The adjustments to the linkages are made while the transmission is in the car. Adjustments to the planetary brake bands necessitate removal of the unit to a bench.

7:2 Gear selection

Manual gear selection is by a short gearlever mounted centrally between the driver and passenger seats. This may be either of two types, T-head with rod linkage (see **FIG 7:6**) or club-head with cable linkage (see **FIG 7:7**). Once the gearlever has been moved to the

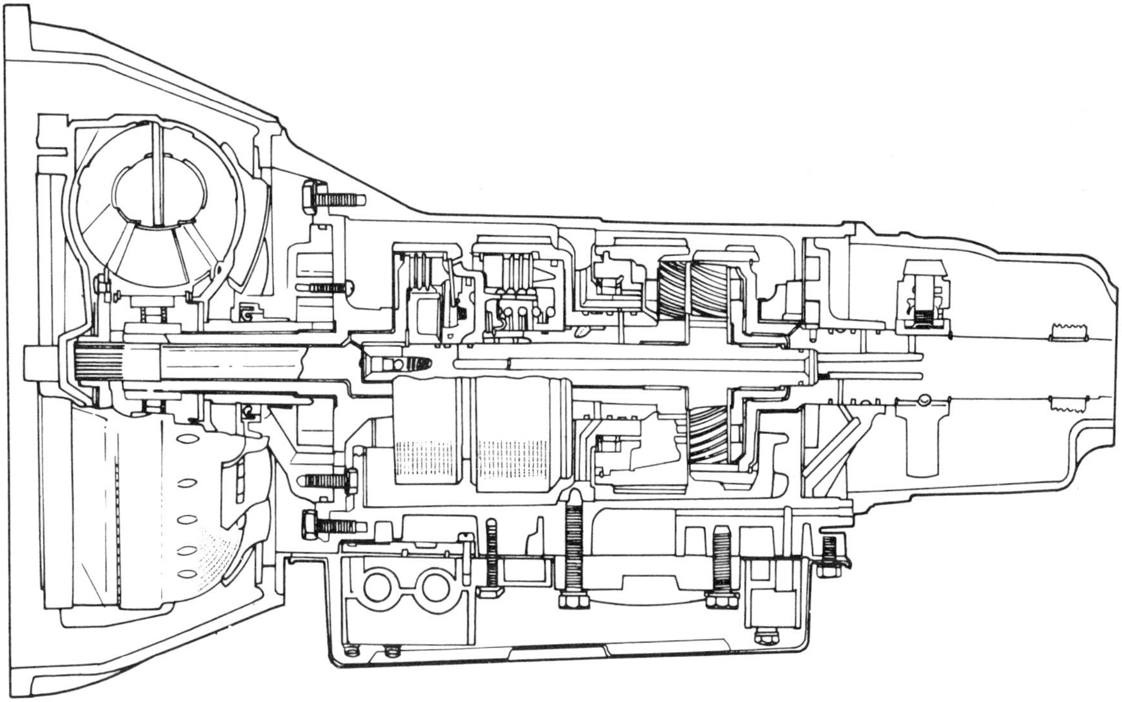

FIG 7 : 2 Section through complete gearbox and converter

D or 2 position, subsequent gear selection is automatic as already described. In D the change is automatic through the three forward gears but when 2 is selected changes occur, up and down, between the 1st and 2nd gear only. Only in the the 1 position is automatic shift to other gears inhibited.

In each type of lever, the movement is controlled by a gate, shown inset, which provides movement between Drive and Neutral without depression of the button in the lever head. To engage any of the other positions, the button must first be depressed but, with the exception of the parking position, return to D or N is effected without further depression of the button. With the lever moved to P, however, it is then permanently locked and cannot accidentally be dislodged. Depression of the button is necessary to release the lever before engagement of any of the Drive or the Neutral positions.

Indication of the selected gear position is given by pointers against an engraved plate which, in the T-head assembly, is rear illuminated when the ignition switch is turned on. The plate is not illuminated with the club-head assembly. The exploded views of the two arrangements in **FIGS 7 : 6** and **7 : 7** enable dismantling and reassembly to be effected without more than a cursory explanation. With the T-head arrangement, bulb renewal is by first removing the console and carpet around the indicator unit, extracting the four screws holding the unit to the floor tunnel, prising the forked end of the plastic coupling rod 5 clear of the selector lever—this must be done carefully as as not to damage the rod fork—and lifting the upper half of the assembly with the engraved plate and bulb holder out of the housing. The bulb 6 can then be replaced.

With the club-head lever, the gearlever 21 passes through a slot in the indicator body 10, and through a hole in the flexible indicator strip 11. This is sandwiched between the upper indicator cover 13, and the body, the angled contour of which provides the friction control. The engraved plate is housed within a slot in the cover, being prevented from end-to-end movement by the slot, the two pointers on the indicator strip embracing the stepped edges of the plate to give the required indication while the upward pressure of the strip holds the plate in position.

A switch mounted on the gearbox (see **FIG 7 : 10**) inhibits operation of the starter motor when the engine is in any of the Drive positions. The switch is in the solenoid circuit of the starter and, should the engine stall while the car is in motion, the gearlever must be returned to N before the starter button can be operated. **Unlike installations with two hydraulic pumps in the gearbox, with the engine stalled no pressure is exerted on the servos and reverse drive from the transmission is not effective in restarting the engine. The lever must be moved to N and the starter button depressed while the car is still in motion to restart the engine after which the lever can be returned to D or other selected drive position. For the same reason, tow-starting is not possible should the battery be discharged to a point at which the starter cannot be operated.**

No provision is made for a starting handle but there is a manual button on the starter solenoid which can be

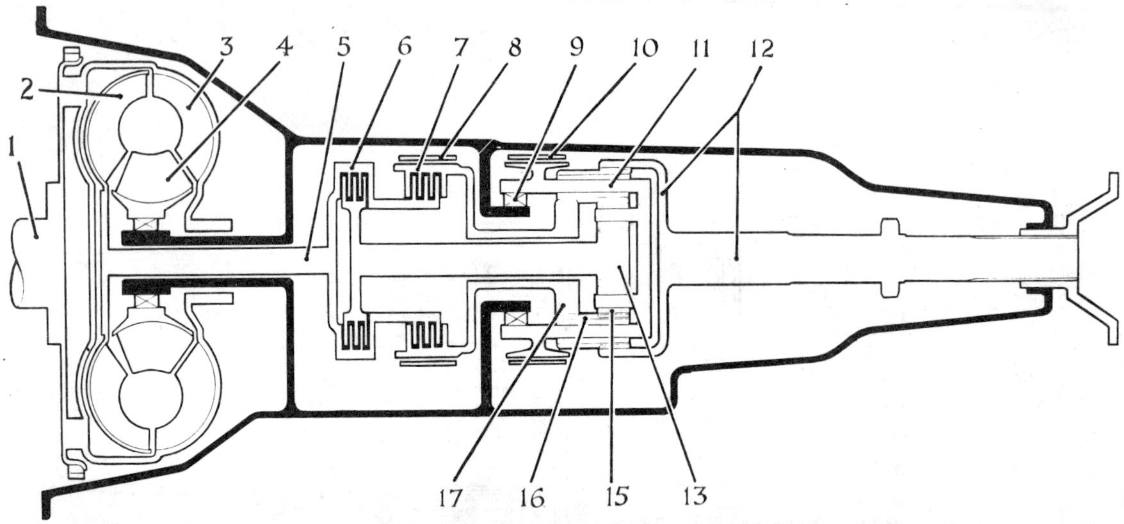

FIG 7:3 Schematic view of transmission unit

Key to Fig 7:3 1 Engine crankshaft 2 Turbine blading 3 Impeller blading 4 Stator blading 5 Gearshaft 6 Front clutch 7 Rear clutch 8 Front brake band 9 Uni-directional clutch 10 Rear brake band 11 Pinion carrier 12 Annulus and drive shaft 13 Forward sun gear 14 Parking pawl teeth 15 Short planetary pinion 16 Long planetary pinion 17 Reverse sun gear

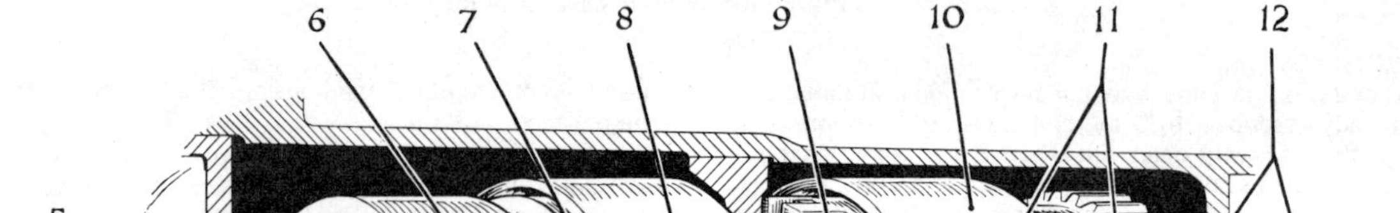

FIG 7:4 Cutaway section through clutches and planetary gears

Key to Fig 7:4 1 to 17 See Fig 7:3 18 Rear clutch piston 19 Rear clutch return spring 20 Rear clutch plates 21 Front clutch piston 22 Front clutch diaphragm spring 23 Front clutch plates operated from the engine compartment. **As this over-rides the safety switch on the gearbox, it must not be operated unless the gear selector lever is in the P position. In some cases, cars fitted with the automatic gearbox have the manual button on the starter solenoid covered by a metal cap to prevent operation.**

A second pair of contacts on the switch operates the reversing light when the selector lever is moved to R.

To adjust the linkage, first set the selector lever to D. On the T-head installation, loosen the nut 1 (see **FIG 7:6**) and move the lever 3 by operation of the rod 2, to bring it as far back as possible. This is the P position. Move it forward three 'clicks' to the D position and tighten the nut 1.

On the club-head installation, remove the clevis pin 2 (see **FIG 7:7**) and slacken the clamp fixing bolts 3. At the gearbox end, move the lever 1, as far forward as possible, to the P position and then back three 'clicks'. Re-insert the clevis pin and secure. Finally, pull the outer cable cover back as far as possible to take up any slack and to position the cable clamp correctly in the elongated holes of the bracket 4, and tighten the bolts 3.

With either installation, check operation by moving the selector lever through all positions noting the positive feel of the lever as each position is engaged or by listening for the slight clicks as they do.

Manual selection of the 1 or 2 positions with the car in motion must not be carried out at speeds above 30 mile/hr or 50 mile/hr respectively to avoid overspeeding of the engine or overstressing of the rear transmission. If towing to a garage is necessary, this can be done for short distances with the gear in neutral so long as the towing speed does not exceed 30 mile/hr. For longer distances, up to about 25 miles, the fluid in the transmission must be increased by about 4 pints to ensure lubrication of the gears by splash in place of the normal hydraulic flow provided by the engine driven pump. The extra fluid must, of course be drained off before returning the car to normal use. For towing over distances above 25 miles, support the rear of the car with the wheels off the road from the towing vehicle.

The parking position P, is particularly useful for holding the car on steep gradients but it should always be applied in addition to, and not as a substitute for, the handbrake. If it is released without the hand- or footbrake being applied, the car will immediately commence to roll and attempts to re-engage it can only result in damage.

When stopping on slight upward gradients, if the engine tick-over has been properly set, the car will remain stationary in Drive and not roll back. If the gradient is a little steeper, roll-back can be stopped by a light application of the accelerator ready for a quick move off. On level ground, the engine should be set to give a very slow crawl forward. The footbrake should always be applied before selecting gear and the foot transferred to the accelerator after the gear has been engaged. A very slight kick can be felt as the servo clutches operate. If the kick is heavy, the engine idling speed is too high.

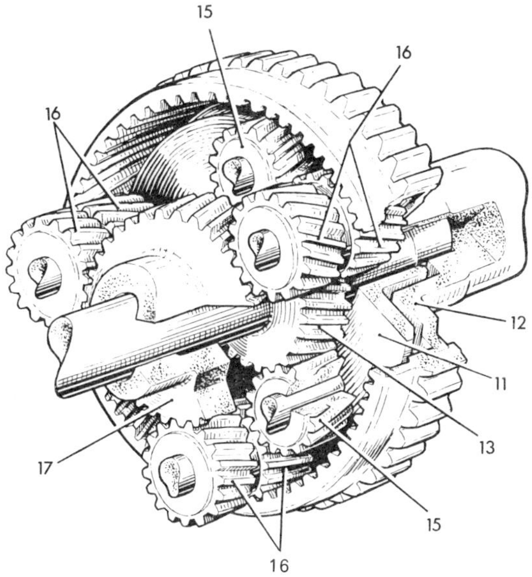

FIG 7:5 **Cutaway section of planetary set**. For key to numbers, see **Figs 7:3** and **7:4**

7:3 The torque converter

The torque converter is a sealed unit with the impeller as an integral part of the housing, a stator mounted on a unidirectional clutch supported on the tube projecting from the gearbox and the turbine rotor splined to the gearshaft housed within the tube. Cooling blades and a drive ring are welded to the outer casing of the converter and the general view when extracted from the gearbox is shown in **FIG 7:8.** The sleeve seen projecting from the converter provides the drive to the front pump rotor, the projections fitting into the slots visible in **FIG 7:9.** Within this sleeve is the converter support tube, the splined end carrying the unidirectional clutch and stator. The gear-shaft passes through the support tube to enter the splined boss of the turbine rotor.

The three units, impeller, stator and rotor, are self-supporting within the converter and the withdrawal of support tube or shaft does not affect their mechanical relationship. The hydraulic fluid from the pump enters the converter via an annular clearance between the sleeve and support tube, returning via a similar clearance between support tube and gearshaft.

The starter ring gear is shrunk on to the drive ring and the whole is mounted on an adaptor plate secured to the flywheel flange on the engine crankshaft by six bolts with hardened steel washers, four similar bolts and washers being used to secure the drive ring to the adaptor plate (see **FIG 7:10**).

7:4 Power flow in gears

Torque transmission, or power flow, in the various gears is shown diagrammatically in **FIG 7:11.**

In the first of these, the gear selector is set in either N or P. The front and rear clutches are released and the rotor shaft turns without transmitting torque to either of the sun

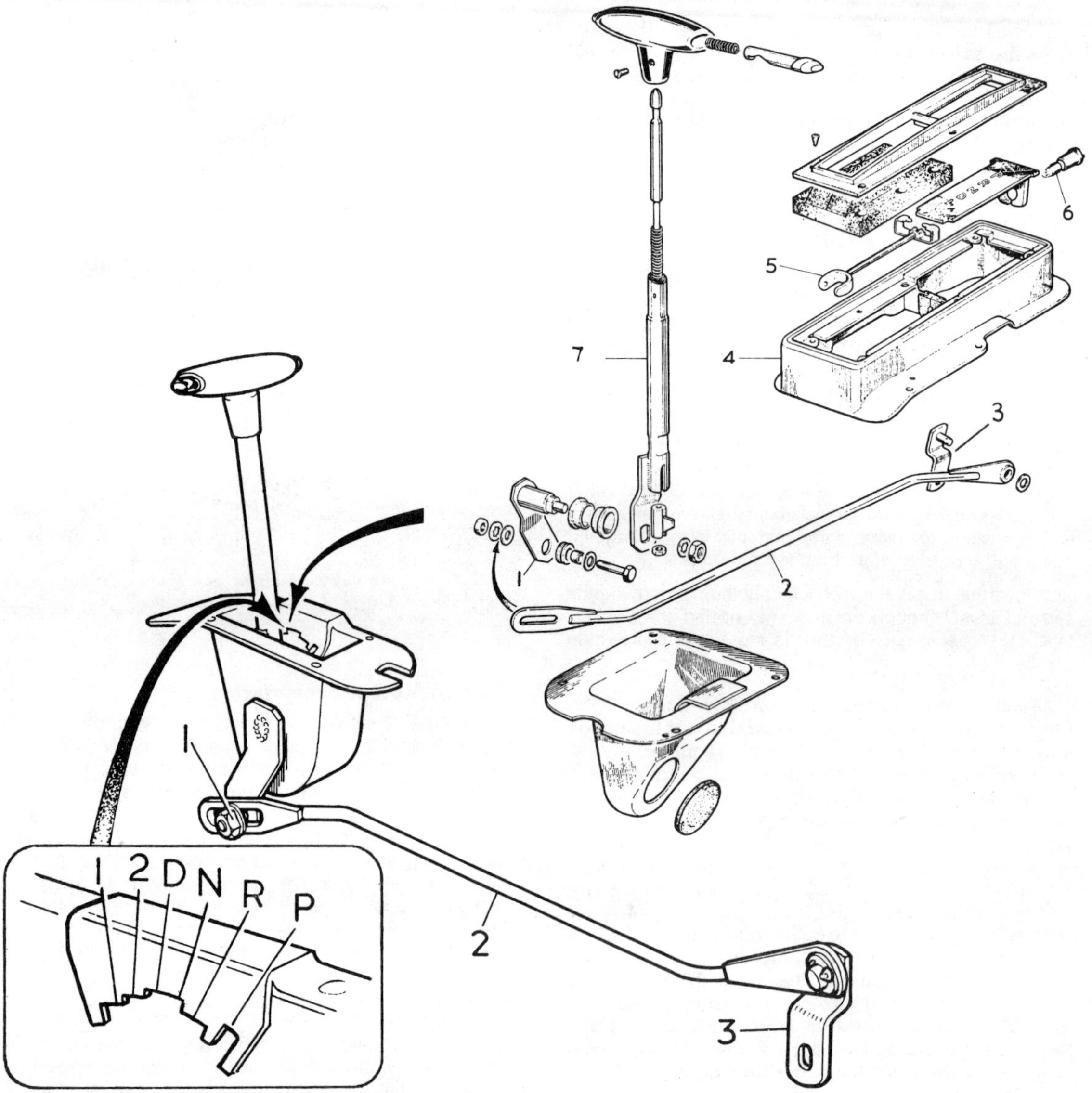

FIG 7 : 6 T-head pattern gear selector lever showing, above, an exploded view and, below, the setting adjustment point

Key to Fig 7 : 6 1 Adjusting nut 2 Control rod 3 Lever arm 4 Housing 5 Forked coupling rod 6 Indicator lamp bulb 7 Gear selector lever

wheels. The only difference between the two positions is that, in P, the pawl brake is applied mechanically through linkage with the selector shaft and, purely for constructional reasons, the rear brake band is applied if the engine is running.

When the Drive position is selected, the front clutch is applied connecting the converter to the forward sun gear. The unidirectional clutch prevents the pinion carrier from turning and the torque is transmitted through the pinions to the annulus providing a gear reduction of 2.393:1. On the overrun, the unidirectional clutch releases the forward drive and the car freewheels.

At a suitable point, set by the combination of governor pressure and throttle setting, the front brake band is applied holding the reverse sun gear, which has been freewheeling, stationary. This has the effect of reducing the gear ratio to 1.45:1.

With a further increase in engine speed for a given throttle setting, the front clutch is applied, connecting the converter to the forward sun gear. At the same time, the

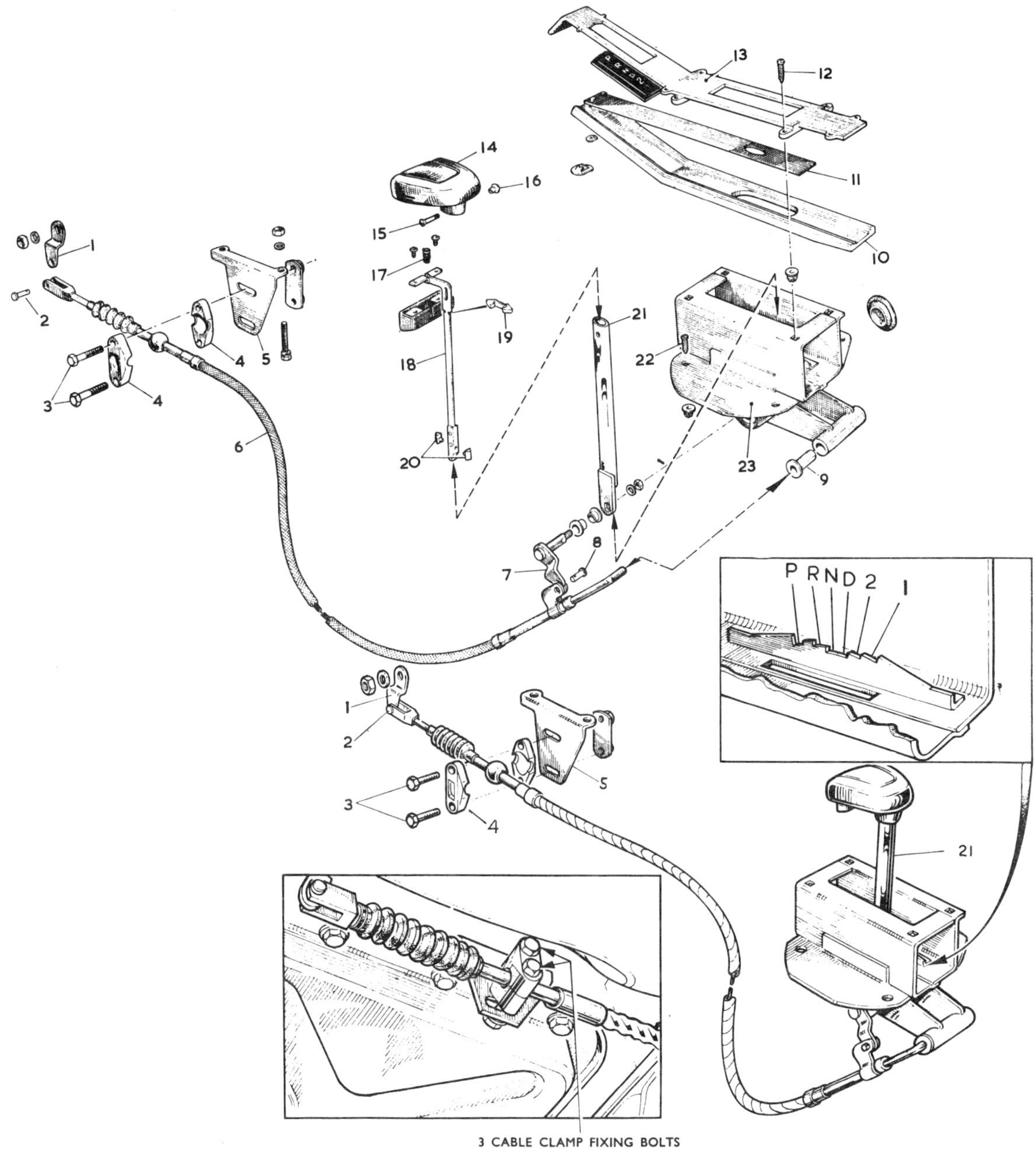

FIG 7:7 Club head pattern gear selector lever showing, above, an exploded view and, below, the cable adjustment point

Key to Fig 7:7 1 Lever arm 2 Clevis pin 3 Clamp bolts 4 Cable sleeve clamp 5 Clamp bracket 6 Control cable 7 Lever 8 Clevis pin 9 Bush 10 Lower indicator body 11 Indicator strip 12 Bolt 13 Upper indicator body 14 Club head 15/16 Screw and nut 17 Spring 18 Release rod 19/20 Plastic guide and guide blocks 21 Gear selector lever 22 Screw 23 Fulcrum assembly

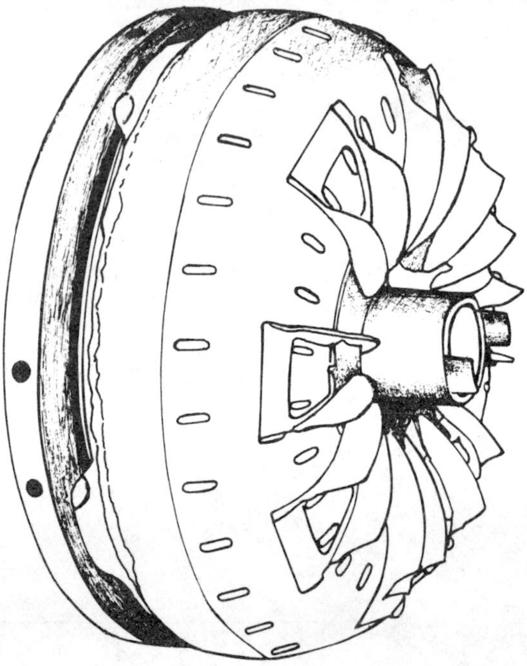

FIG 7:8 View of torque converter removed from the engine and housing. The starter gear ring is not fitted in the picture

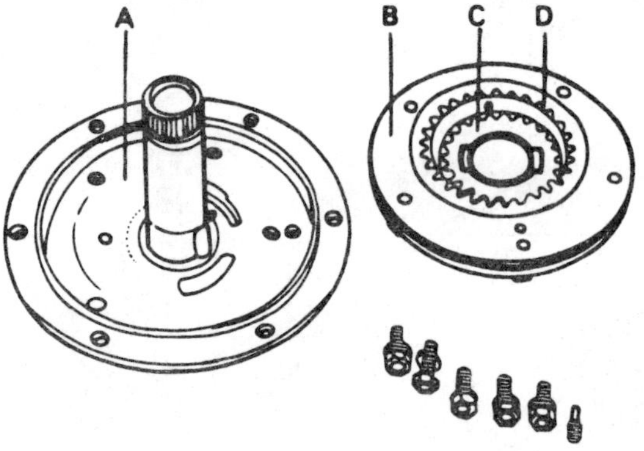

FIG 7:9 Front pump dismantled to show, **A** the converter support assembly, **B** the pump body, **C** the pump driven gear with drive sockets and **D** the pump driven gear

front brake band is released. With both sun gears now locked together, the gearing rotates as a whole to give a direct drive from converter to drive shaft.

Changing up and down from second to top gear is, therefore, effected by switching the locking between front band and rear clutch, while changes between bottom and second are effected by applying or releasing the front brake band.

When Reverse is selected, the front clutch is released and both the rear clutch and rear brake band are applied. The latter holds the pinion carrier stationary and the drive is now through the rear sun wheel, via the gears on the carrier to the annulus and drive shaft, the intermediate gear in the pinion carrier reversing the direction of rotation of the annulus to that of the converter. The reduction ratio is now 2.094:1.

If 1 is selected instead of D, the rear brake band is applied instead of using the unidirectional feature of the built-in clutch. The gear ratio is the same as for Drive, namely 2.393:1, but the car can no longer freewheel and the engine can therefore be used for braking when descending hills. The other features of the 1 drive are inherent in the hydraulic system, but, in effect, the application of 1 when the car is stationary inhibits a change-up into second gear while a shift from Drive to 1 in second or top gear produces an immediate change-down into the gear below. In a change from D (top gear), a further change to low takes place when the speed of the car is reduced by braking to below 5 mile/hr. The same effect can be achieved between 5 and 20 mile/hr by use of the accelerator kick-down with the selector lever at 1.

With 2 selected, automatic changes between 1 and 2 are obtainable, the freewheel facility in 1 being restored but a change to D is inhibited. This is particularly useful on ice covered roads. The incorporation of the two drive positions with the normal D, or top, gear enables full manual gearchanges to be effected, if desired, with an automatic gearbox.

7:5 The hydraulic system

The hydraulic system is complex and not easy to understand or dismantle. Even garage mechanics of long experience and skill have to undergo a course at the makers before they are able to dismantle, repair and re-adjust the hydraulics satisfactorily, so it is not advisable for the owner/mechanic to attempt to dismantle the assembly even under the most favourable home garage conditions. Fortunately, the makers supply a valve and body assembly as a complete unit and, should trouble be traced to this area of the transmission, replacement of the unit is the recommended remedy. The procedure is dealt with in **Section 7:6.**

Operation of the system in the various settings of selector lever and throttle are outlined below with schematic diagrams to enable the owner/mechanic to appreciate something of what is going on during a journey.

Lever in Neutral (N) (see FIG 7:12):

With the engine running, the pump circulates the fluid to the primary regulator valve, manual valve and throttle valve, the former adjusting pressure to the torque converter and, via the secondary regulator valve, lubrication for the front gear trains. The latter serves as a pressure relief valve, exhausting to the pump inlet via 24, while ensuring that lubrication to the rear end of the gear train, via 23, is not maintained at the expense of that to the converter and front gear trains via 21. Both of the clutches are free and neither of the servo brake bands are applied. Fluid returned to the pump via 24 passes either to the sump or to the pump inlet.

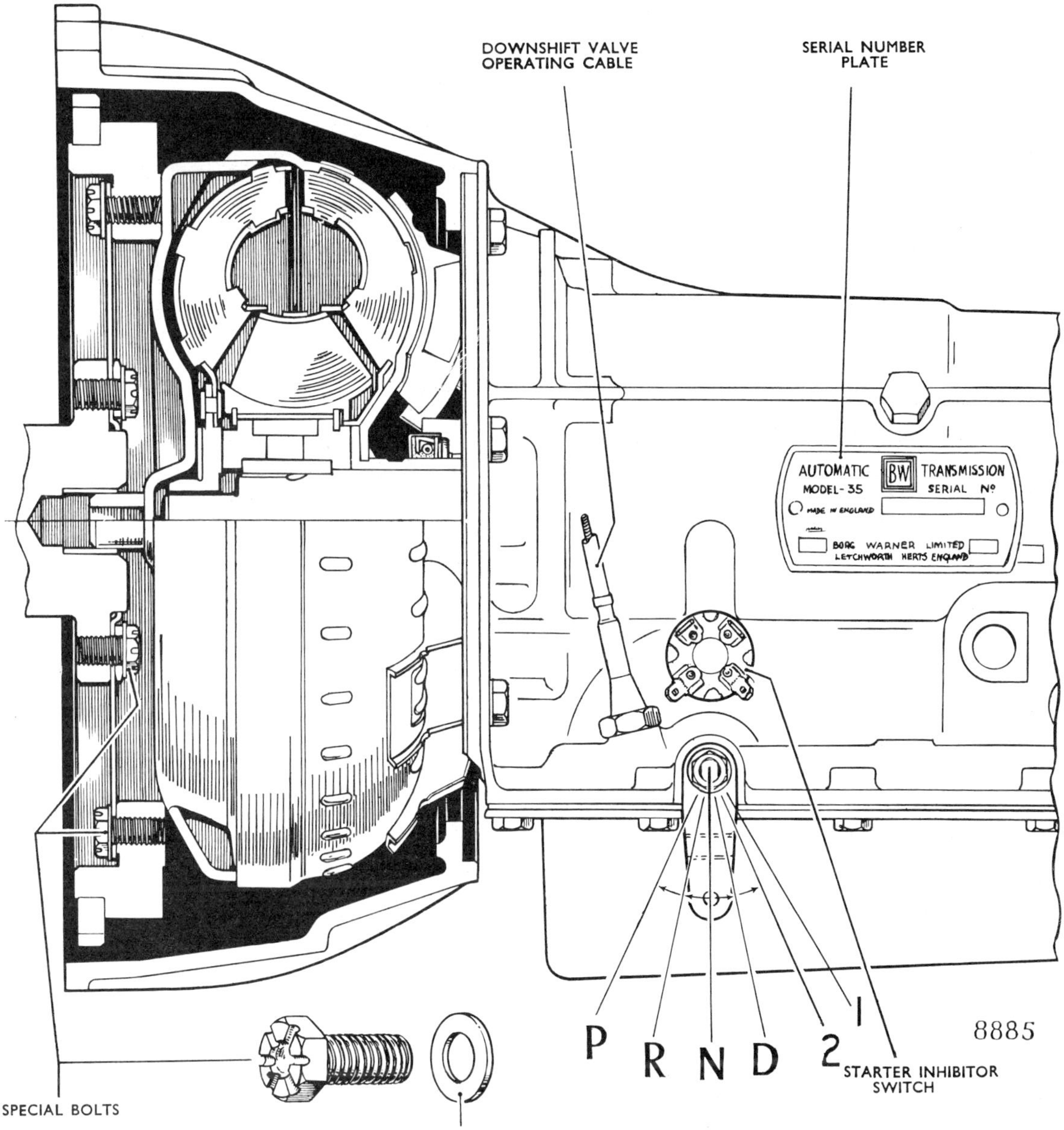

FIG 7:10 Part section through converter and housing showing the bolts securing the adaptor plate to crankshaft flange and converter and the positions of the operating cable connector, starter inhibition switch, gear selector lever and serial number plate

Lever in Park (P) (see FIG 7:13):

With the engine running, the hydraulic system is the same as for Neutral with the addition of a feed to the rear servo brake band. An extension to the selector rod lever setting the manual valve operates a toggle mechanism inserting a robust pawl into dog-teeth integral with the driven shaft annulus or ring gear.

Strictly speaking, the application of the rear servo brake band has no useful purpose but the arrangement is the result of an extremely simple design of manual control valve.

Lever in Reverse (R) (see FIG 7:14):

With the engine running and the pump circulating the hydraulic fluid, the manual valve opens the line to shift valves 1/2 and 2/3. The former redirects the pressure to apply the rear servo while the latter applies the rear clutch and, via the servo-orifice valve (which serves no purpose at this stage) the front servo. The function of the throttle pressure line is to regulate the degree of pressure applied to the clutches and servos to suit the torques as a function of engine speed and throttle setting.

The application of the clutches and brakes is then as described in **Section 7:4** for Reverse.

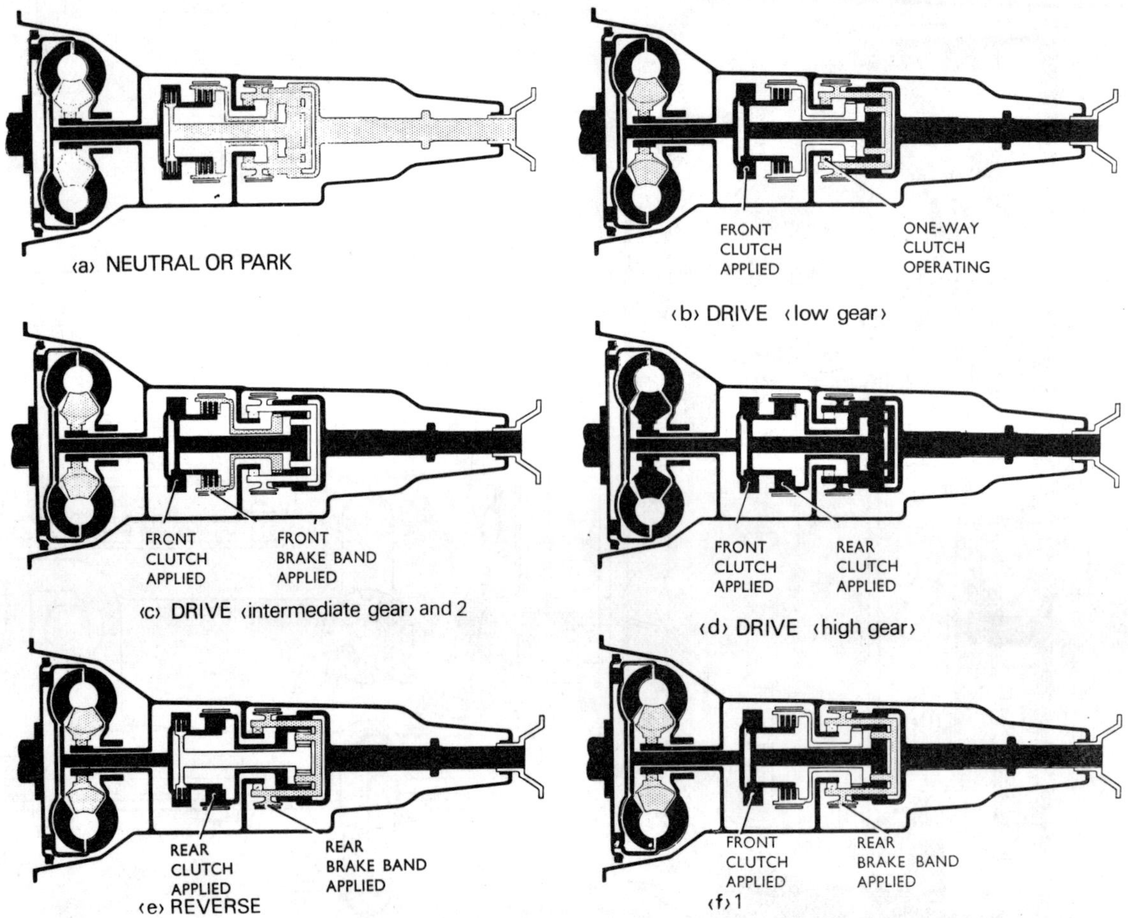

FIG 7:11 Power flow diagram for the main selector positions and hydraulically selected secondary positions

Lever in Drive (D) (see FIGS 7:15, 7:16 and 7:17):

The manual valve applies pressure to the front clutch at the same time opening the hydraulic lines to the shift valve 2/3, 1/2 and to the governor valve.

With the throttle in full open position as illustrated, the pressure 9, regulated by the modulator valve balancing governor pressure against feedback throttle pressure, opposes the throttle pressure in the primary regulator valve to adjust line pressure in the interests of smooth gear-shifts. As the engine speed increases with fall-off in torque for a given throttle setting, the governor commences to regulate the flow and pressure of fluid to the shift valves, servo orifice and modulator valve 2, balancing the throttle pressure 9, so adjusting the degree of application of the front clutch.

From this point onwards, the control of fluid flow through the primary regulator valve, supplying the converter and lubrication, is set by the opposing forced and modulated throttle pressures 9 and 8. The former is controlled by the setting of the throttle valve and the latter by the modulator valve which, in turn, is regulated by governor pressure 2 (see **FIG 7:16**).

The shift takes place when the governor pressure 2 at one side of the 1/2 shift valve opposes the integral spring pressure and shift valve plunger pressure 10, to a point at which line pressure 5 is admitted to the front servo line 19, applying the front brake band. In the kick-down position as shown, the downshift cam has operated the throttle pressure line 9, to the modulated throttle pressure line 11, opposing the governor pressure in the two shift valves. The action of these is then inhibited and the changedown takes place or change-up is prevented, at least until the kick-down has been stopped or excessively high engine speed has caused the governor to resume control.

As the engine speed increases with reduced torque in intermediate gear, the governor pressure 2 also increases until a point is reached at which shift valve 2/3 also moves up to open the line 15, to both the rear clutch, applying it, and to the servo orifice control valve which is regulated by governor pressure 2. When this is sufficient to move the piston, fluid is admitted to the opposite side of the front servo and the brake band is released. With the two clutches engaged, the through drive is effected (see **FIG 7:17**).

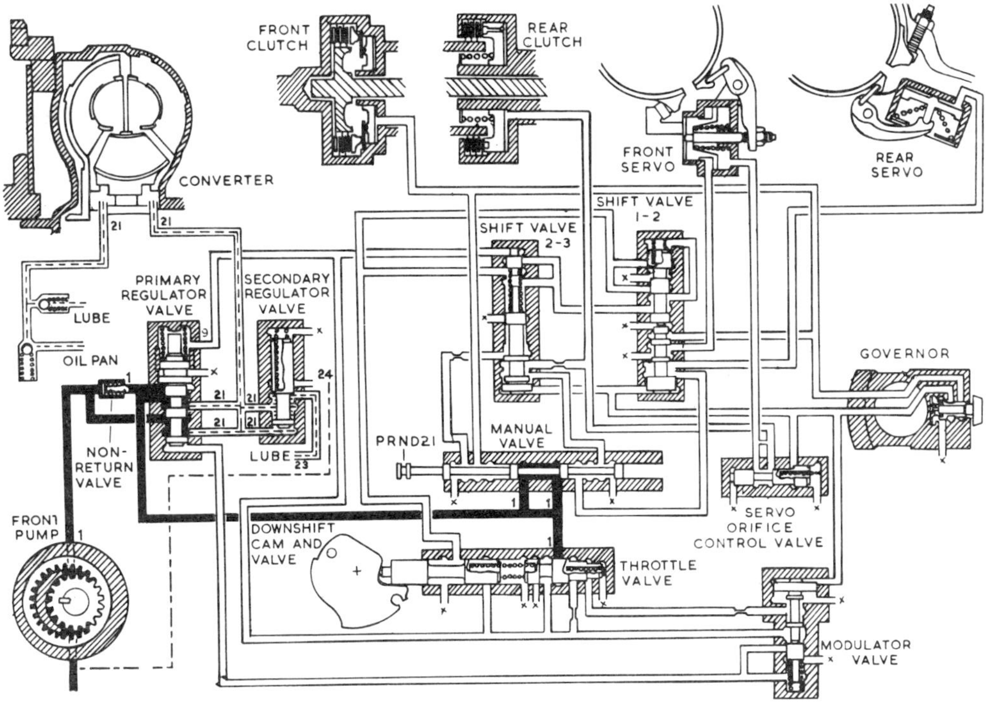

FIG 7:12 Operation of hydraulic circuit in N

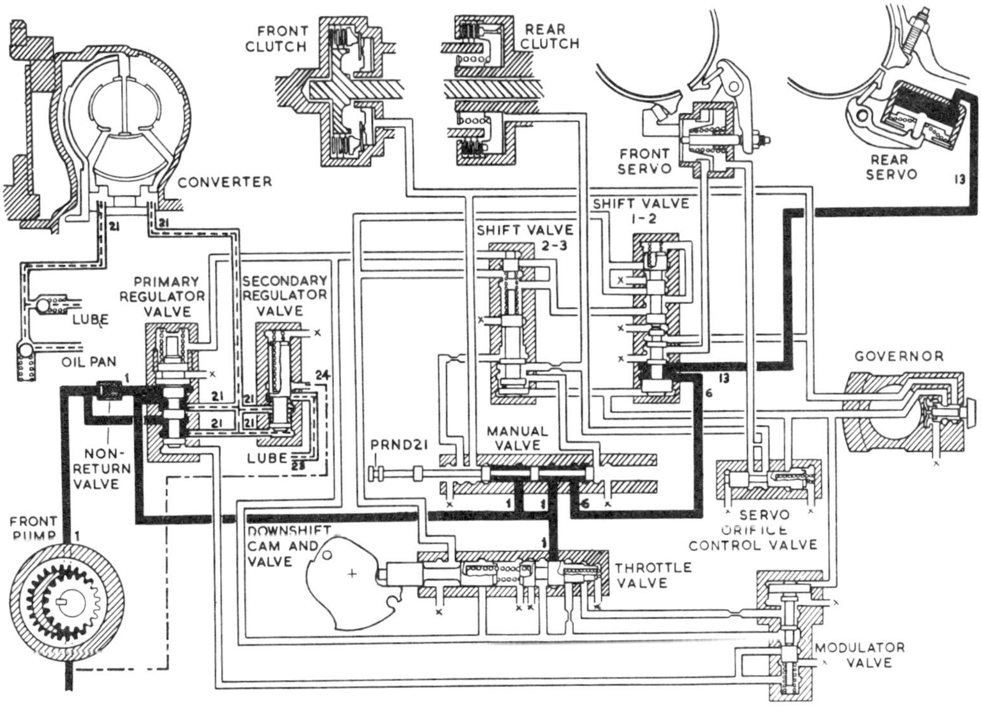

FIG 7:13 Operation of hydraulic circuit in P

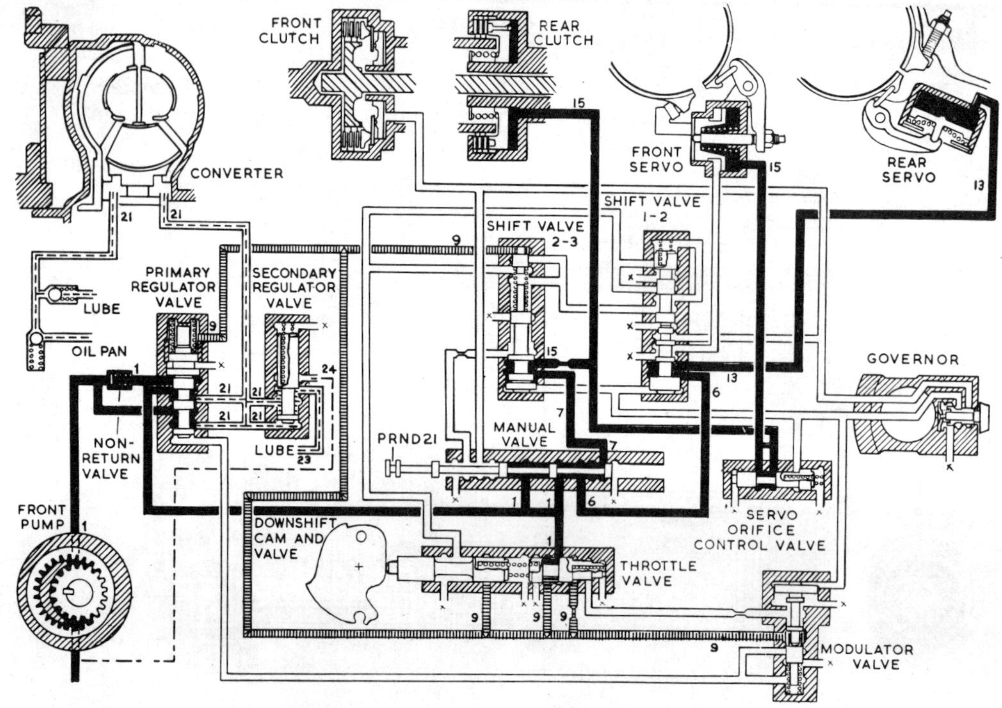

FIG 7:14 Operation of hydraulic circuit in R

Any further retardation merely serves to reduce the throttle pressure and the transmission remains in top. Even when the car is coasting with the throttle closed, as in **FIG 7:17**, the existence of governor pressure is sufficient to prevent changedown. The only conditions which will induce a changedown is a serious fall in speed with load, resulting in a fall in governor pressure, or a sudden rise in throttle pressure as would result from a heavy depression of the accelerator either of which, or a combination of both, will result in shift valve 2/3 closing to release the rear clutch and permit the 1/2 valve side of the front servo to overcome the rapidly falling counter pressure from the servo orifice control valve.

It must be appreciated that the operation of the valves and hydraulic pressures is not a step-by-step process but a constantly varying and inter-related condition which is functioning entirely in accordance with road and engine speed conditions, related to throttle opening, on a pre-arranged performance graph. The examples shown are merely typical conditions existing at selected points on this performance graph. Even the applications of the clutches and servos is a graduated process giving smooth transitions from gear-to-gear, not just an on-off step. The exception to this is the front clutch which is directly applied by selection of any of the forward gears, the feed coming from the manual valve alone. The other three controls are dependent upon the position of the shift valves.

Lever in 1 (see FIG 7:18)

The manual valve has sealed off the pressure to the shift valve 2/3 and provided a direct feed via 6 and 13 to the rear servo. Governor pressure acting on the two shift valves is unable to effect any changes and the bottom gear remains selected from a standing start.

If the transmission is already in D and running in top gear (see **FIG 7:17**), the effect of moving the manual valve to 1 is to open the line 3, from shift valve 2/3 to exhaust and the line 15 pressure drops releasing the rear clutch. A downshift to second gear results, governor pressure moving shift valve 1/2 up to seal off 6 and couple 13 to exhaust while opening 5 to 19, the front servo release. This is then the condition in **FIG 7:16.**

When engine speed has decreased further through braking, the governor pressure drops and shift valve 1/2 moves down to open the line from the manual valve, via 6 and 13, to apply the rear servo. This is then the condition in **FIG 7:18.** It will be noticed that, though the power flow in D (low) and 1 are identical (see **FIG 7:11**), in the former the pinion carrier is held stationary in one direction only by the freewheel whereas in the latter it is held stationary to movement in either direction by the rear servo and brake band.

Lever in 2 (see FIG 7:19)

With the lever in 2, the transmission acts as a two-speed unit.

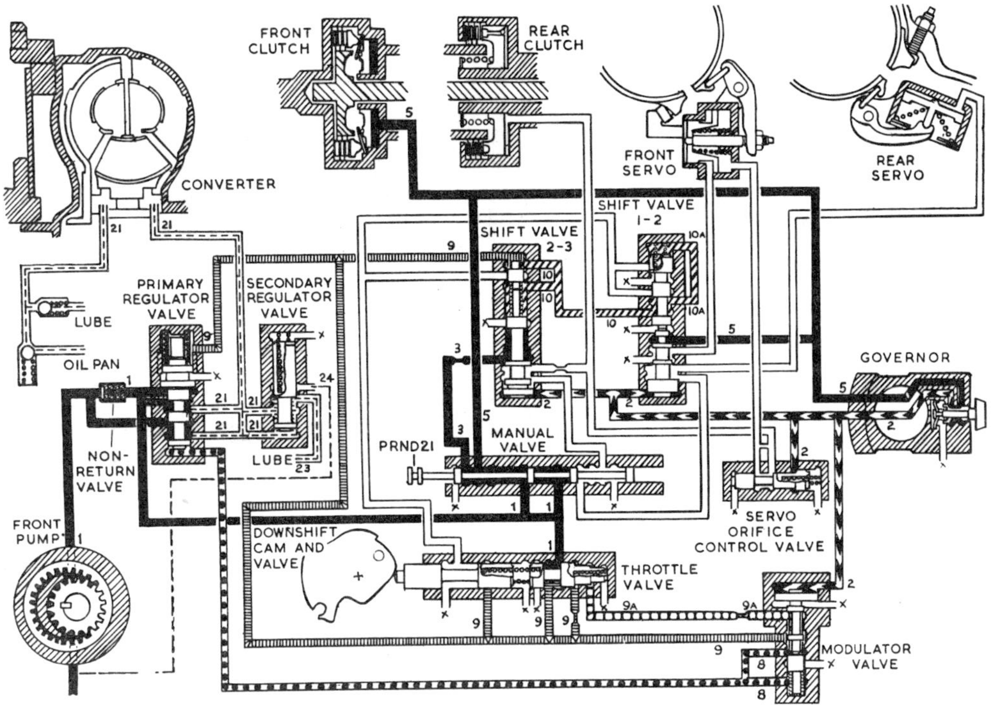

FIG 7:15 Operation of hydraulic circuit in D (low)

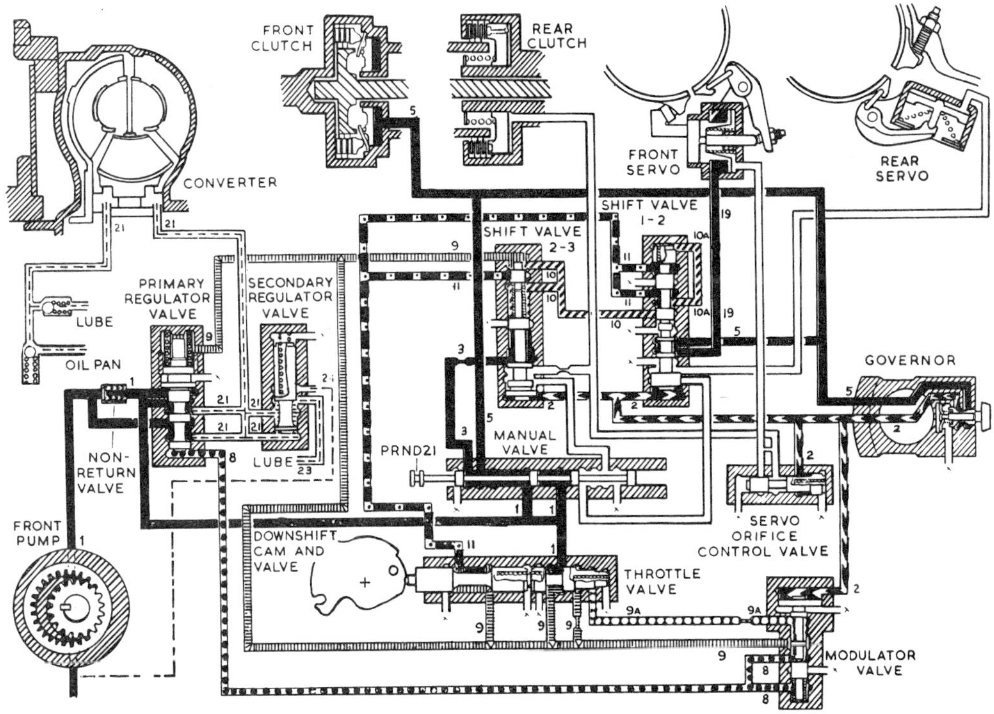

FIG 7:16 Operation of hydraulic circuit in D (intermediate)

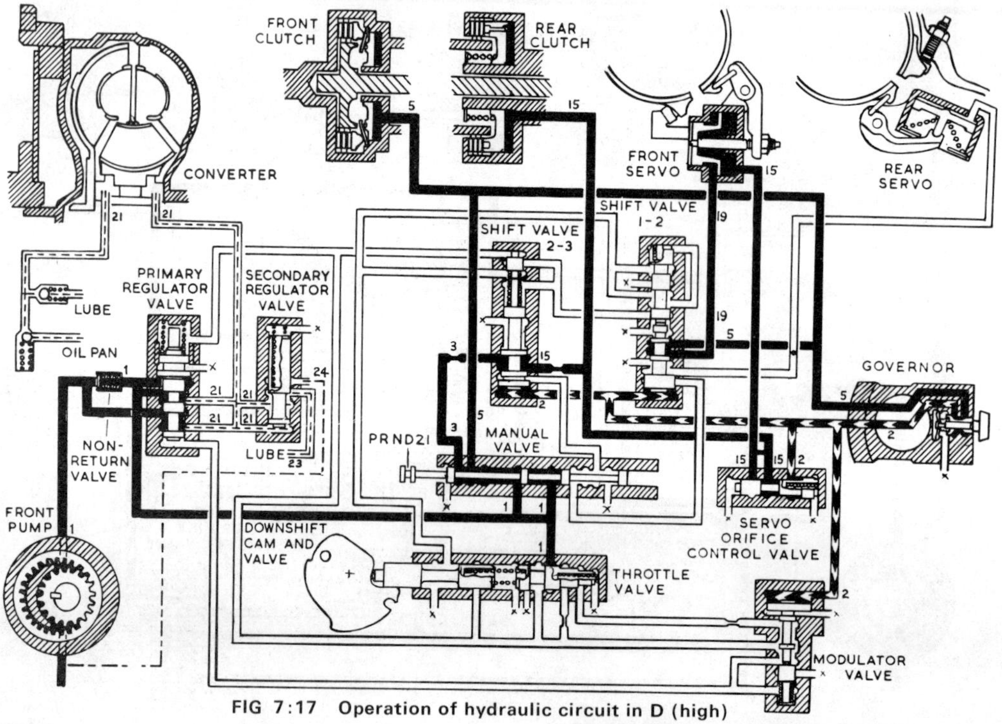

FIG 7:17 Operation of hydraulic circuit in D (high)

LINE OR DIRECTED LINE PRESSURE
CONVERTER PRESSURE
GOVERNOR PRESSURE
THROTTLE PRESSURE
FORCED THROTTLE PRESSURE
MODULATED THROTTLE PRESSURE
THROTTLE PRESSURE CONTROLLED BY MODULATOR VALVE
SHIFT VALVE PLUNGER PRESSURE
EXHAUST

In this position, the manual valve seals off line 3 to the shift valve 2/3 which then operates only under the opposing forces of the valve spring and governor pressure. Line pressure to the rear clutch servo is, therefore, inhibited and no change to top gear can take place. Governor controlled changes between 1st and 2nd (intermediate and low) are still operative with engine braking only in the intermediate gear. In 2, the car will freewheel down a gradient in 1st applying engine braking when the combination of throttle setting and governor speed effects a change to 2nd. Releasing the throttle and braking will restore the 1st position and the freewheel. **This is particularly valuable when driving on icy roads where the removal of the foot from the accelerator pedal but without applying the brakes restores the freewheel immediately the engine speed falls to idling. With the lever in 1, no free-wheeling is available and skid correction is not then automatic.**

The general rule, therefore, is to use position 1 for engine braking on steep gradients but position 2 for icy road conditions.

7:6 Dismantling and inspection

Raise the front of the car and mount on stands. Remove the drain plug and drain the fluid from the gearbox. **If the engine has been running recently before dismantling has been commenced, take care in draining as the temperature of the fluid can be above scalding point.** The drain plug has a hollow hexagon head and requires an Allen key $\frac{1}{4}$ inch A/F to remove it. Draining the main gearcase will not allow the fluid to drain from the converter, so it is advisable to refit the plug before removing the converter/gearbox unit from the engine.

Disconnect the starter motor lead and remove the dip-stick tube securing bolt. Loosen and remove the bell-housing bolts noting that one also secures the battery earth lead. Remove the upper mounting bolt and that securing the transmission filler tube to the support bracket. Disconnect the exhaust pipe from the manifold. Disconnect the downshift cable at the clevis pin and remove the connection to the inhibitor switch.

Mark the propeller shaft coupling flange for subsequent remarrying, loosen and remove the coupling bolts and lower the shaft at the rear to enable it to be withdrawn from the gearbox coupling splines. Free the handbrake cables from their supports under the car. Unbolt and remove the starter motor.

Through the starter motor hole, loosen and remove the converter-to-adaptor securing bolts (see **FIG 7:20**) rotating the crankshaft to bring each bolt opposite the hole. Loosen and remove the four bolts securing the engine rear plate to the converter and engine support bracket. Loosen and remove the speedometer cable and driven gear.

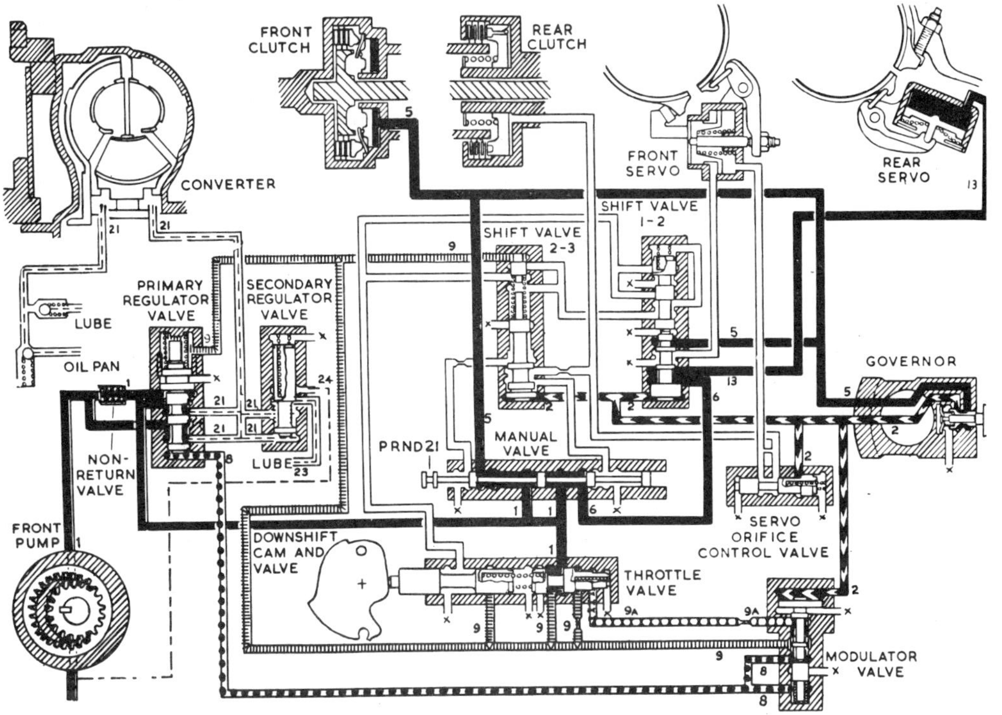

FIG 7:18 Operation of hydraulic circuit in 1

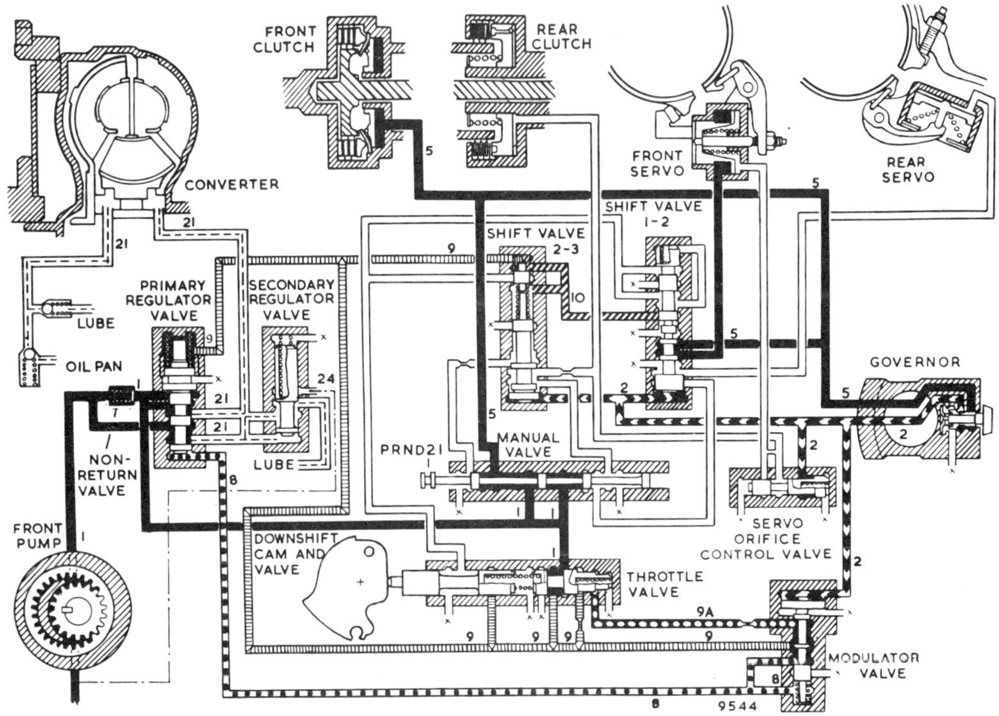

FIG 7:19 Operation of hydraulic circuit in 2

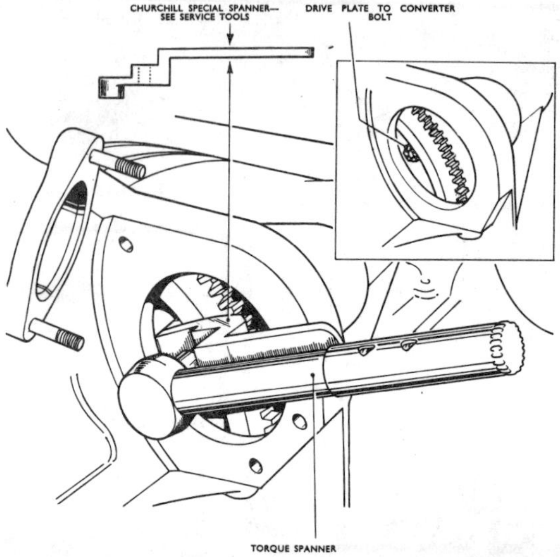

FIG 7:20 Diagram showing access to bolts securing the converter to the adaptor plate through the starter aperture using the Churchill cranked spanner with torque spanner attached for tightening to a 28 lb ft setting

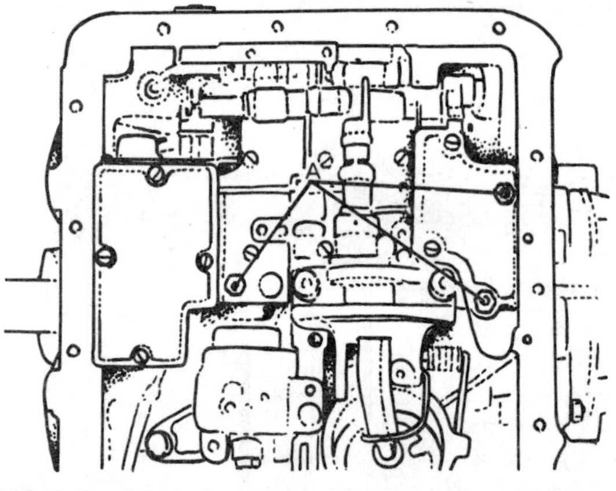

FIG 7:21 View of underside of transmission unit with oil pan removed showing, at A, the valve assembly securing bolts

Place jacks under both the engine and gearbox and take their weight. Unbolt and remove the engine rear support from both engine and underframe, ease the gearbox rearwards to free it from the engine—**the engine rear plate will be released by this and may fall away from the locating dowels**—lower it on the jack and transfer to the bench or stand.

Place a tray under the joint between the converter housing and gearbox, remove the six bolts and spring washers securing the housing and carefully break the joint to enable the fluid within to drain away. Remove the housing.

The oil pan is of relatively light construction and, if the assembly is allowed to bear on it, some distortion will occur affecting the position of the oil tubes above. The weight must always be taken on the main casing and a special bench cradle, T62P.7035.BW is available for this purpose.

There may be some slight differences in the above procedure resulting from production changes in layout from time to time. However, these should become evident as the work proceeds and if a note is taken at the time, the reassembly will present no untoward difficulty.

Clean the exterior of the transmission and converter housings and drain the remnants of the hydraulic fluid from the transmission through the drain hole in the pan if this has not already been done.

Examine the converter body for signs of damage and check that the sleeve with the turbine rotor within rotates in the bearing without roughness or excessive friction. If any trouble has been experienced or there is any suspicion as to its efficient operation, fit a new converter returning the other to the makers for reconstruction. **The units being welded together, are not suitable for local repair.**

Turn the transmission over and mount on a suitable cradle with the hydraulics section uppermost. Unbolt and remove the oil pan. The pan supports four oil tubes each of which is a push fit into its socket. These can easily be damaged if the gearbox is allowed to rest its weight on the oil pan, so be careful. With the pan removed, carefully lever out the tubes, noting their positions for reinstatement. Unscrew the four studs securing the filter in place, clean the filter in petrol or carbon tetrachloride and allow to dry. **Do not use any fluffy material to wash or wipe down.**

Now remove the valve body assembly by extracting the three $\frac{7}{16}$ inch bolts indicated in **FIG 7:21**. (Two of these may have already been extracted when removing the filter). Detach the cable from the downshift cam and carefully lift clear of the four oil tubes in the front of the gearbox. The two larger diameter tubes are the front pump inlet and outlet and the smaller are the feed and return for fluid to the converter. **Do not attempt to dismantle the valve body assembly.** The front pump is next to be removed giving access to the gear train from the front clutch end.

The two clutch assemblies may now be extracted, the front clutch by just pulling clear and the rear assembly, complete with forward sun gear, by easing through the open front clutch band. Separation is second procedure. The clutch band can then be squeezed together to free it from the servo and withdrawn through the front opening. The servo unit is secured by two $\frac{5}{16}$ inch bolts.

To remove the planet gears, the centre support must first be extracted. This is secured by two centre screws and the forward screw of the pair retaining the rear servo unit. Separation of the support and gears assembly is external to the casing after extraction. The rear brake band can be extracted through the front end, tilting it slightly on withdrawal.

The governor can be serviced on the drive shaft. To remove the rear cover, unscrew the five bolts and spring washers and withdraw.

Examine all bushes, thrust washers, friction surfaces of clutch plates and drums for signs of scoring and the brake bands for signs of burning. Replace all oil seals and any parts obviously damaged or worn.

The foregoing brief summary of dismantling assumes that minimum work is needed and, in the majority of cases, it is only to service one part which is suspect. For a fuller instruction, secure from the Chrysler agent the Borg Warner workshop manual WSM.139.

7:7 Reassembly and installation

Reassembly is a straightforward reverse process to dismantling, bearing in mind the following points. First, absolute cleanliness must be observed at all stages and the use of rags should be dispensed with or, at the minimum, only lint-free materials. Freshly washed nylon rag is quite suitable.

Always renew all gaskets and oil seals. Immediately before reassembly, all parts must have been cleaned in petrol or carbon tetrachloride and dipped in clean transmission fluid to facilitate installation.

All nuts and screws must be tightened to the appropriate torque as detailed in the Appendix as many of the threads are of light alloy and overtightening may damage them and render the fixing insecure. Be particularly careful not to cross threads when inserting. If possible, start the thread with the fingers and take up slack with a tubular socket spanner without the use of a tommy bar or other lever device, using the torque wrench as the final stage.

From full dismantling, the assembly sequence is:

(a) insert shift rod, lever and parking pawls
(b) insert drive (output) shaft and annulus
(c) install rear coverplate
(d) fit governor and speedometer drive pinion
(e) install rear band and servo
(f) insert centre support and planet gear group
(g) install front servo and band
(n) install rear clutch
(i) install front clutch
(j) install front pump
(k) fit extension housing
(l) fit pump and converter oil tubes and install valve assembly
(m) fit four supply tubes and install oil pan
(n) install converter and housing in car
(o) reinstall transmission on housing in car
(p) reconnect propeller shaft and resupport gearbox on mounting
(q) remake all connections, electrical and mechanical, dissembled during the preparatory phase of dismantling.

Adjustments:

During the reassembly, certain adjustments have to be made. The first of these is for the front brake band (see **FIG 7:22a**) and procedure is as follows. Slacken the adjustment locknut. With a torque screwdriver tighten the adjusting screw to a torque of 10 lb in, then slacken off exactly four turns and secure with the locknut. **This is done with the oil pan removed.**

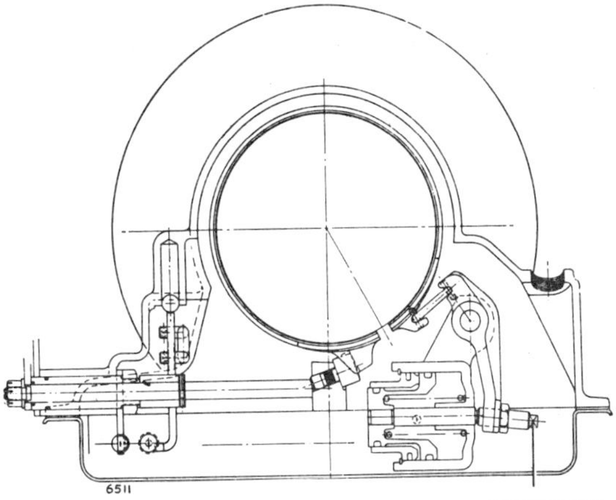

FIG 7:22a Adjustment of front brake band

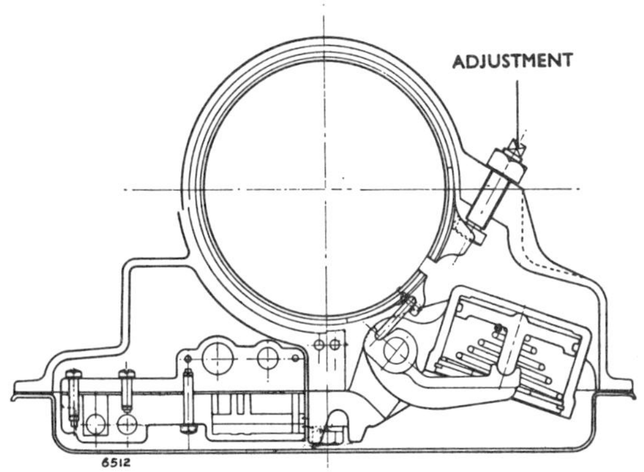

FIG 7:22b Adjustment of rear brake band

The rear brake band adjustment is external on the right-hand wall of the case (see **FIG 7:22b**). Again, slacken the locknut, tighten the adjusting screw to a torque of 10 lb ft and slacken off one complete turn. Tighten the locknut.

To adjust the starter inhibitor switch, mounted above the gearshift lever on the transmission, place the selector lever in the D or L position. Couple the reverse connections (these tabs are set over at 45 deg.) to a battery and lamp and screw in the switch body to the unit until the lamp is extinguished. Make a mark on the body against a mark on the transmission casing and transfer the connections to the other two tags. Screw in further, counting the number of turns and parts of a turn, until the lamp is again illuminated. Turn back half this number to achieve a mid-point setting and secure with the locknut. Remake the proper connections.

To set the downshift valve cable, run the engine until warm and set the idling speed at 500 rev/min against a reliable tachometer, with the selector lever in N. Apply the handbrake and chock the wheels. Stop the engine.

Check that the downshift cable and sleeve are secure at the transmission end, then adjust the nut at the throttle lever end (see **FIG 7:23**) until the end of the sleeve just

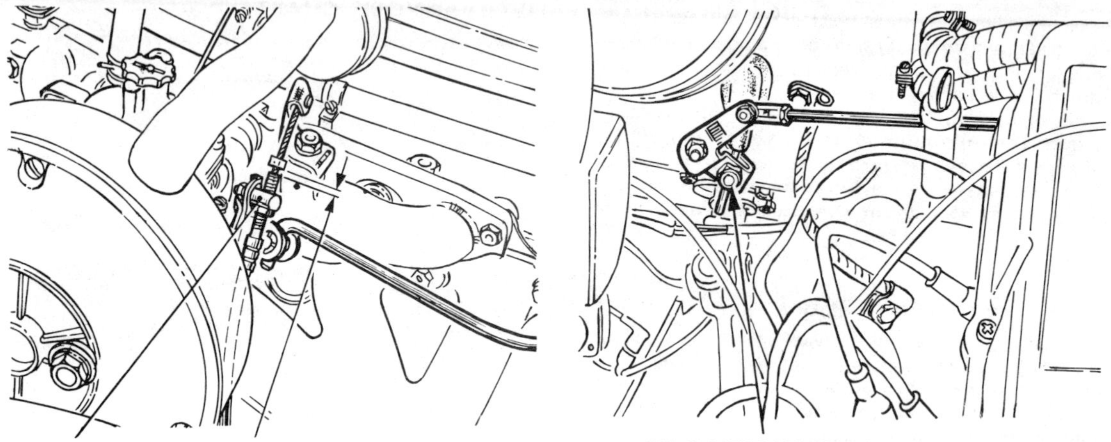

FIG 7:23 Adjustment of downshift cable, left, and throttle linkage, right, with Stromberg CDS carburetter

abuts the adjustment stop crimped to the cable; that is, so that there is no free play in the sleeve. Set back until the gap shown is .03 to .06 inch. Secure by the locknut. Select D and note the fall in engine speed. This should be about 100 to 200 rev/min. Full throttle adjustment should be set to give 1 inch clearance below the accelerator pedal when fully depressed to the wide open throttle position.

The only other adjustment is that for the selector lever which has already been detailed.

7:8 Maintenance

Maintenance is restricted to periodic checks of the hydraulic fluid using the dipstick in the breather tube to the rear of the engine. This should be done every 3000 miles and the check must be carried out on a level surface after the fluid has attained normal running temperature and while the engine is running. Bring the level up to the 'High' mark **but do not overfill.**

Routine fluid changes are unnecessary. At each service period, check the condition of the oil pan underside and the ventilating grilles beneath the converter housing. Clear away any caked road dirt or mud as the surfaces play an important part in cooling.

7:9 Modification

Certain modifications have taken place since the Model 35 transmission was introduced. Generally speaking, these are only of significance when re-ordering new parts for replacement of their own counterparts. Providing that the unit serial number, from the plate just above and to the right of the selector lever, is quoted, the correct part will be sent automatically.

In all, two major changes in design of the transmission have taken place giving three versions of the Model 35 which are different in certain essentials. The original offered five drive selector positions, **Park, Reverse, Drive, Lock-up** and **Neutral,** and embodied two pumps, one driven from the converter input shaft and the second from the output shaft. The latter enabled a push start to be effected since hydraulic pressure, essential to the operation of the clutch and brake servos, was available from the rear pump when the motor was stationary or had stalled.

The first change was the incorporation of an additional low gear position between L and D, which was nominated D2, the D position becoming D1. The change in the hydraulic assembly necessitated the introduction of an extra valve, the D1/D2 control valve, and this arrangement was available with or without the second pump. The second change is to the form described above and fitted to the Avenger and allied models in which only the front pump is incorporated.

7:10 Fault diagnosis

Most faults in the transmission system can be located by a sequential process since an observed irregularity can be traced to more than one cause. The adjoining table shows how the most common symptoms can be checked to identify the cause in the quickest possible time. Clearly, those causes which do not need unit removal must be checked before the longer process is embarked upon. Intelligent use of the chart avoids this. Operations G to L do not need unit removal from the car but do need draining of the hydraulic fluid and lowering of the oil pan.

QUICK REFERENCE FAULT DIAGNOSIS CHART

NUMBERS INDICATE THE RECOMMENDED SEQUENCE OF FAULT INVESTIGATION

Fault	Operations that do not require unit removal															Operations requiring unit removal									
	A	B	C	D	E	F	G	H	J	K(1)	K(2)	L	M	N	O	*	p	q	r(1)	r(2)	s	t	u	v	w
No automatic upshifts																									
No 1-2 shift	.	1	.	.	.	.	.	3	4	.	5	2	.	.	.	6	.	7	.	.	.	.	.	.	.
No 2-3 shift	.	1	.	.	.	.	.	.	4	.	5	2	.	.	3	6	.	.	.	.	7	.	.	.	.
Incorrect shift speeds—quality of shift affected																									
Incorrect shift speeds	.	.	1	.	2	.	.	.	5	.	3	4	.	.	6	.	.	.	.	.	.	.	.	.	.
Loss of kickdown	.	.	1	.	2	.	.	.	.	.	3	.	.	.	.	.	.	.	.	.	.	.	.	.	.
Slip on 1-2 shift	1	3	.	.	2	.	.	4	5	.	6	.	.	.	.	7	.	8	9	.	.	.	.	.	.
Slip on 2-3 shift	1	2	.	.	3	.	.	.	5	.	6	.	.	.	4	7	.	8	.	.	9	.	.	.	.
Harsh 1-2 shift	.	.	.	.	1	.	.	2	.	.	3	4	.	.	.	5	.	.	7	.	.	6	.	.	.
Harsh 2-3 shift	.	.	.	.	1	.	.	2	.	.	3	.	.	.	.	4	.	.	.	.	5	.	.	.	.
Harsh 3-2 shift	.	.	.	.	.	.	.	1	3	.	2	.	.	.	.	4	.	5	.	.	6	.	.	.	.
Harsh 2-1 shift	.	.	.	1	2	.	.	.	.	.	.	.	.	.	.	3	.	.	4	.	.	5	.	.	.
Seizure 1-2	.	.	.	.	.	1	.	.	.	2	.	.	.	.	.	3	.	.	.	.	4	5	.	.	.
Seizure 2-3	.	.	.	.	.	.	.	1	2	3	.	.	.	.	.	.	.	.	.	.	.	.	.	.	.
Loss of drive—slip on take off																									
No forward drive	1	2	.	.	3	.	.	.	.	.	4	5	.	.	.	6	.	.	7	8	.	9	.	10a	10b
No drive in reverse	1	2	.	.	.	3	6	.	.	.	5	.	.	.	4	7	.	.	.	.	8	.	9	.	.
Slip or squawk in L	1	2	.	.	3	.	.	.	.	.	4	.	.	.	.	5	8	.	6	7	.	.	.	.	.
Slip or squawk in R	1	2	.	.	3	4	5	.	.	.	6	.	.	.	.	7	10	.	.	.	8	.	9	.	.
Incorrect operation in L																									
Upshifts occur with L selected	.	1	.	.	.	.	.	.	.	3	.	2	.	.	.	.	.	.	.	.	.	.	.	.	.
Excessive downshift delay—no engine braking. L selected from 30 m.p.h.	.	1	.	.	.	.	.	2	3	.	4	.	.	.	.	.	.	.	.	.	.	.	.	.	.
Miscellaneous																									
Incorrect starter or reverse lamp operation	.	1	.	.	.	.	.	.	.	.	.	.	2	.	.	.	.	.	.	.	.	.	.	.	.
P position not holding vehicle	.	1	.	.	.	.	.	.	.	.	.	.	.	2	.	.	.	.	.	.	.	.	.	.	.
Bumpy D, L, or R engagement	.	.	.	1	2	.	.	.	.	.	3	.	.	.	.	4	.	.	5	.	6	.	.	.	.
Delayed D, L, or R engagement	1	2	.	.	.	.	5	.	.	.	4	.	.	.	3	6	10	.	7	8	9	.	.	.	.
No neutral drive in neutral	.	1	.	.	.	.	.	.	.	2	.	.	.	.	.	3	.	.	4	.	.	.	.	.	.
Drag in R	.	.	.	.	.	.	.	1	.	.	.	.	.	.	.	2	.	.	3	.	.	.	.	.	.
Overheating	1	.	.	.	.	3	.	2	.	.	.	.	.	.	.	4	.	.	.	.	.	.	.	.	5

Key to Table

- **A** Check fluid level
- **B** Adjust manual linkage
- **C** Check carburetter full throttle
- **D** Adjust engine idling speed
- **E** Adjust downshift cable
- **F** Adjust rear brake band
- **G** Examine rear servo
- **H** Adjust front brake band
- **J** Examine front servo
- **K1** Check valve block screws for tightness
- **K2** Remove and clean valve block
- **L** Remove and clear governor
- **M** Readjust starter inhibitor switch
- **N** Check pawl mechanism
- **O** Check fit of rear clutch supply tube
- ***** Remove transmission unit
- **p** Examine front pump and drive
- **q** Check front friction band
- **r1** Examine front clutch assembly and forward sun wheel seals
- **r2** Examine plug in forward end of drive shaft
- **s** Examine rear clutch assembly and seals
- **t** Check uni-directional clutch
- **u** Check rear friction band
- **v** Examine planetary gear set
- **w** Replace hydrokinetic converter

NOTES

CHAPTER 8

REAR AXLE AND SUSPENSION

8:1 Rear axle, description

The rear axle is of the semi-floating pattern with a hypoid gear final drive. The casing is of unit construction incorporating the differential carrier and coverplate and the axle tubes are welded into the sides of the carrier. The differential drive pinion, supported on taper roller bearings is preloaded and adjusted by a collapsible spacer, the differential assembly being supported, on its bearings, in the casing by caps and bolts.

The crownwheel is bolted to the differential cage which supports, in usual manner, the free and side bevels on taper roller bearings preloaded by shims and adjuster nuts with a locking plate. A filler plug for lubricant is provided in the differential casing cover at the rear but there is no drain plug. Draining, when necessary, is by removal of the coverplate. A plastic breather is provided at the top side of one of the two axle casings.

The halfshafts are splined to mesh with the internal splines of the side bevels in the differential and are supported within the casing at the outer ends in ball-bearings held in position against lateral movement by a seating on the inner lip of the bearing housing and externally by shims and a locking plate. The bearings are designed to take side thrust, in addition to vertical loads, in either direction substantially greater than that to be expected under the most adverse cornering conditions in normal service.

The brake backplate is clamped between a backing plate and gasket and the endplates of the axle casing, secured by four bolts, the backplate supporting the brake cylinders of the rear hydraulic drum brakes and the mechanical linkage of the handbrake. Acceleration and braking torque reactions on the axle casing are taken by two outer swinging arms and two inner reaction links between brackets welded to the axle casing and brackets welded to the sidemembers of the chassis. The coupling is through resilient bushings in each case. The outer axle brackets also provide the bushed lower mount for the dampers, also of the direct acting telescopic pattern, the dampers being inclined to both the axle and body underframe.

An exploded view of the rear axle is shown in **FIG 8:1** with a sectional view through the assembly in **FIG 8:3**. The component parts of the differential assembly is shown in **FIG 8:2**.

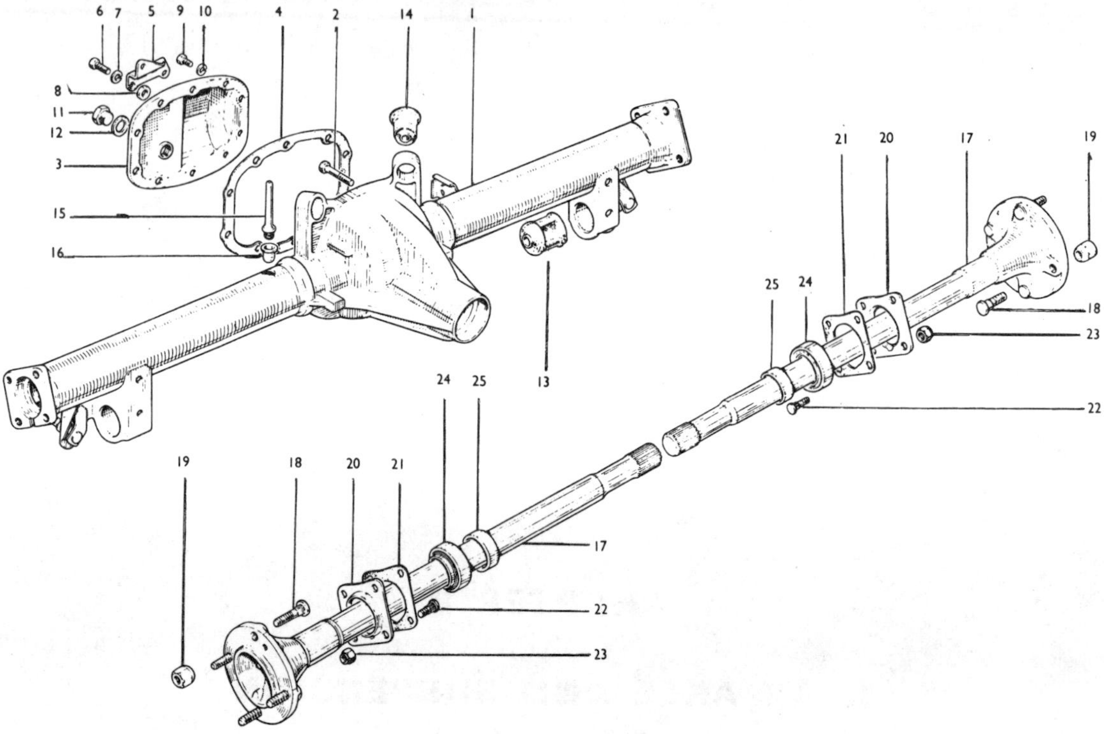

FIG 8:1 Exploded view of rear axle and axle casing

Key to Fig 8:1 1 Axle casing 2 Bearing cap bolt 3 Coverplate 4 Coverplate gasket 5 Brake pipe bracket 6 Coverplate bolts 7 Spring washer 8 Distance piece 9 Coverplate bolts, short 11 Oil filler plug 12 Washer 13/14 Mounting bushes 15/16 Breather and seating 17 Halfshaft 18/19 Wheel nut and stud 20 Retaining plate 21 Gasket 22/23 Nut and bolt 24 Axleshaft bearing 25 Bearing retainer collar

8:2 Dismantling and servicing

Raise the car on stands, remove the road wheels and clean all dirt and grease from the drums and backing plates. Note any indications of oil or grease leakage from the hydraulic brake connections, cylinders, bearings etc., and record for remedial action during the servicing.

Release the handbrake, extract the countersunk screws retaining the brake drum on the hub plate and pull the brake drums clear. Remove the four self-locking nuts securing the axle shaft backing plate to the casing end plates—these also secure the brake drum backing plate—and bolt to the hub plate by means of the wheel nuts, the base of a sliding hammer, such as special RG.188/1 adapter fitted to an RG.16A tool, and draw the axle with bearing out of the casing (see **FIG 8:4**). Repeat with the second halfshaft.

Mark the propeller shaft and bevel shaft coupling flanges to ensure identical mating on reassembly, remove the coupling bolts and lower the propeller shaft to the ground. Place a drip tray beneath the differential casing and slacken the cover bolts, easing the cover clear of the casing to allow the oil from within to drain away. Unbolt and remove the cover.

Remove the nuts securing the bearing caps of the differential housing, mark the caps so that they, too, can be returned to their original positions, remove the adjusting nut locking plates and withdraw the differential assembly complete with bearings, shims and adjusting nuts. **Be particularly careful to note the position of each shim and washer as these determine the adjustment between crownwheel and bevel. If it is not necessary to replace any part, reassembly will be facilitated and expedited by returning each shim and washer to its original position, otherwise a protracted setting operation will be necessary.**

Secure the coupling flange against turning, slacken and remove the self-locking nut to release the coupling from the shaft. This may require a puller. Extract the dust cover 20 and oil seal 19 (see **FIG 8:2**) and carefully tap out the bevel pinion rearwards from the axle casing. The shim 15, rear taper bearing 16, and collapsible spacer 17, will come away with the bevel and shaft and the forward taper bearing 18, can be extracted separately. **Discard the collapsible spacer 17, and self-locking nut 22, as these must be renewed at each servicing.**

This completes the dismantling of the rear axle into its major components. Further dismantling of the differential is described in **Section 8:4**.

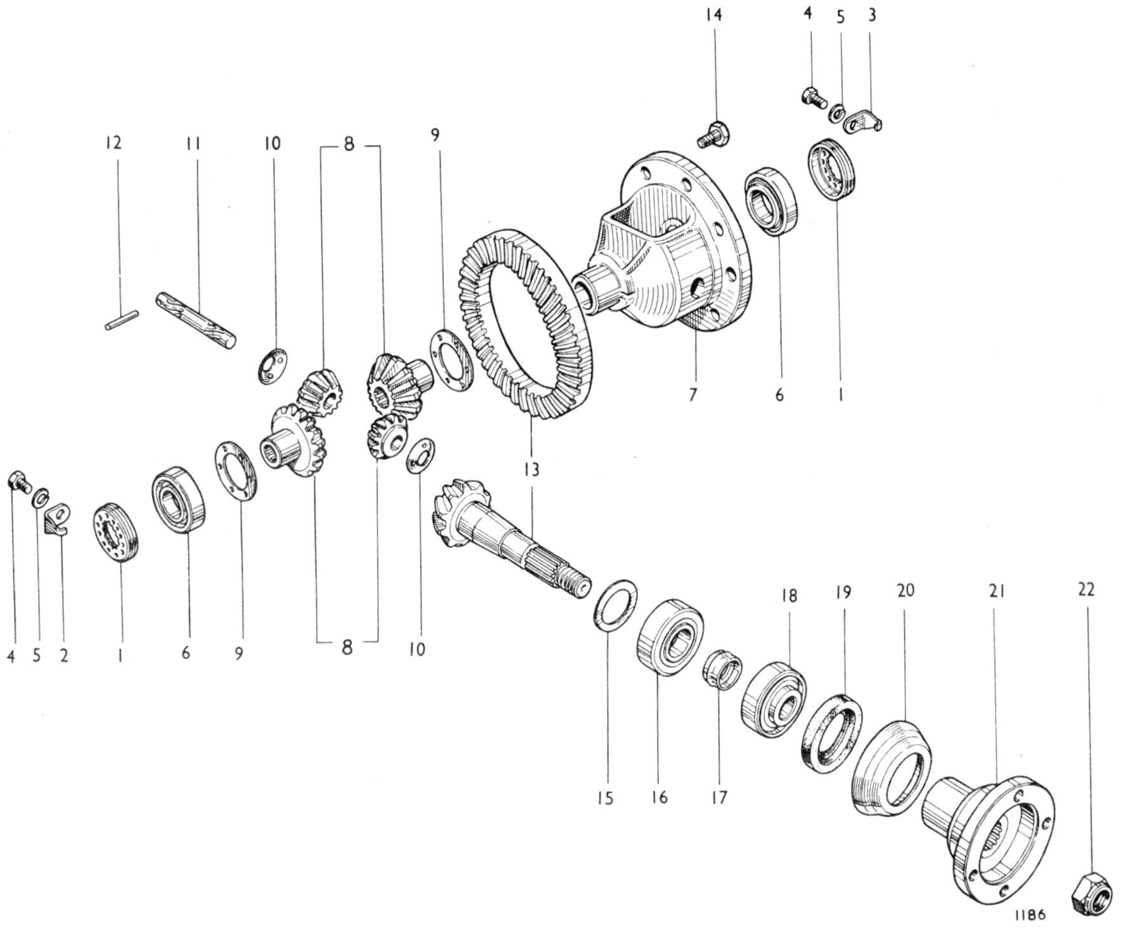

FIG 8:2 Exploded view of differential

Key to Fig 8:2 1 Adjuster 2/3 Locking plates 4 Bolt 5 Washer 6 Differential cage bearing 7 Differential cage 8 Side and free bevels 9 Thrust washers 10 Free bevel thrust washers 11 Free bevel shaft 12 Locking pin 13 Crownwheel and bevel shaft 14 Crownwheel bolts 15 Shim 16 Rear bevel pinion bearing 17 Collapsible spacer 18 Front bevel pinion bearing 19 Oil seal 20 Dust cover 21 Flange coupling 22 Self-locking nut

8:3 Inspection and reassembly, rear axle

Transfer all parts to the bench and thoroughly clean and degrease. Examine the halfshafts for signs of rubbing and, in particular, the splined ends for wear or distortion. Check the splined ends for free but close engagement with the mating female splines of the differential side bevels. There must be no rotational play in either direction or spline wear will develop rapidly.

If the splines are worn, remember to check the inner splines of the side bevels for wear at the same time. Though most halfshafts shear at the ends of the splines, this is often a shock failure occasioned by play in the splines themselves. It is then useless to replace the halfshafts if the wear in the side bevels has not been rectified. **On the Avenger, the halfshaft is integral with the hub plate and the two cannot be separated.**

The halfshaft bearing is a sealed bearing and should therefore not be washed in solvents such as petrol, etc. If the bearing is serviceable it must not be removed from halfshaft as this renders the bearing unfit for further service.

The bearing is a press fit on the halfshaft and will require a minimum ram force of 1 ton (1016 kg) to fully seat it against the abutment face of the axle shaft. The retaining collar is also a press fit and will require a minimum force of 1120 lb (508 kg) to fit it in position. If these minimum forces are not met the fitting will not be acceptable and it will be necessary to renew either the bearing, retainer or axle shaft. Obviously, a 10T or 20T press will be necessary, equipped with a load gauge and the necessary special tools to remove and refit the bearing and retainer. These special tools are numbered P4090.6 (bearing remover), 4090.2A and 2d (replacers) with a taper base 370.

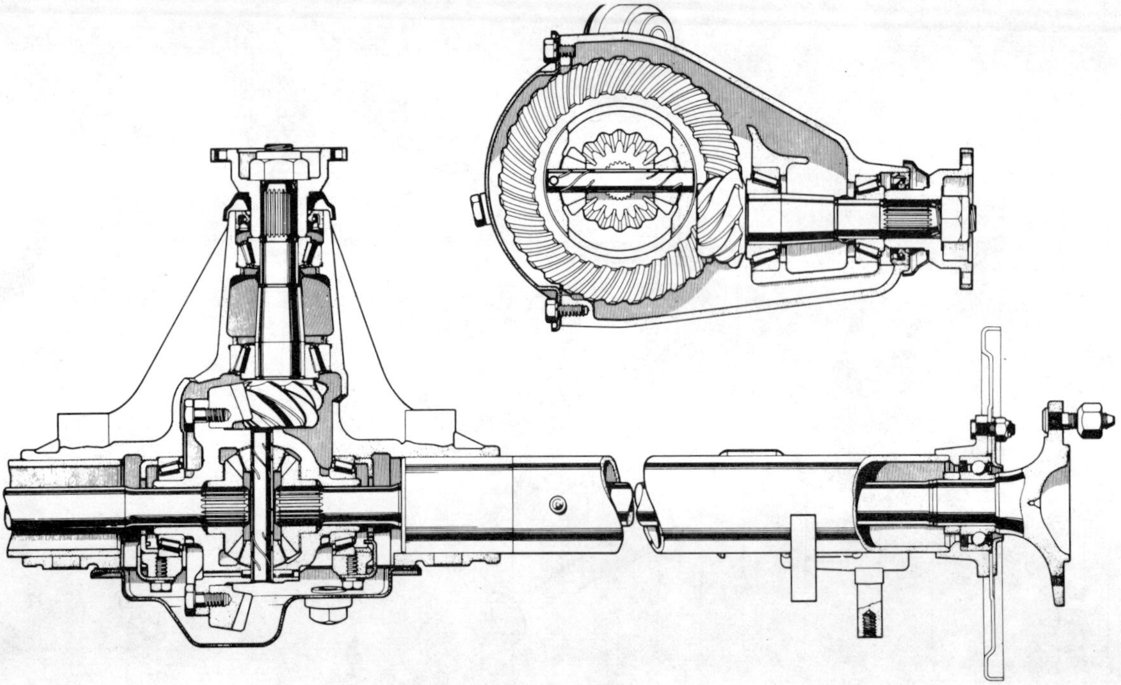

FIG 8:3 Section through rear axle and differential assembly

This equipment will not be easily borrowed and in many instances it will be unobtainable, it is therefore advisable to have this work done by a Chrysler service garage. For those fortunate enough to be able to obtain and use the equipment the removal and reinstallation is shown in **FIG 8:5**. The bearing and the retainer must be scrapped after the removal and new parts obtained. The bearing is located with its extended boss towards the hub flange and the retainer plate with its swaged centre also towards the hub flange.

The halfshaft is now ready for reinstallation. Lightly oil the splines and check that the shaft is clean, and insert it carefully into the axle casing, easing the splines into position in the differential side bevels without force. Push home until the bearing outer ring is entering the housing and the retaining plate is correctly positioned over the four studs. The latter are a drive fit into the axle casing end flange.

With a hide mallet applied to the hub plate and using light blows, drive the halfshaft and bearing home until the bearing outer ring is fully seated. **To do this, the force driving the outer bearing ring into position has to be transmitted through the ballrace and excessive hammering loads could damage the ball or bearing ring surfaces. Discretion must, therefore, be exercised. The alternative of pulling the bearing into position by means of the retaining plate is not feasible as the plate may be distorted with resultant excessive axle shaft end play.**

Finally, install the four self-locking nuts to the retaining plate bolts, tightening each one to a torque of 14 lb ft. The remainder of the installation sequence is a simple reversal of the dismantling operation.

8:4 Dismantling the differential

Dealing, first with the differential cage assembly, after cleaning at the bench, unbolt and remove the crownwheel. Before actually separating the crownwheel from the cage, make identification marks so that it can be returned to the same position after servicing. The bolts, eight in all, are of special design which do not need any locking device. Should they be damaged or lost during the operation, use only the correct bolts secured from the Chrysler agent.

Knock out the locking pin 12 (see **FIG 8:2**) to release the free bevels shaft 11, push out the shaft and rotate the free bevels by turning one side bevel with the other held stationary until the free bevels 8, are opposite to the openings in the differential cage 7. Remove the free bevels, together with the thrust washers 10.

The side bevels and thrust washers 9, can now be removed. **Again, note the position of the side bevel and related washer to the side of the differential cage so that they can be returned to their original position. The washers have been selected to eliminate play in the differential pinion train. Unless it is necessary to change a bevel—in which case it is advisable to install a complete new set—the original washers can be used.**

The bearings and bearing caps need not be dismantled unless the bearings are so badly affected as to need replacement. A special press is required to extract the bearing from the cage. The inner ring/race assembly is separate from the outer ring but, when replacement is necessary, the complete assembly must be changed.

After inspection and replacement of all damaged or worn components, reassembly of the differential can be commenced. Thoroughly clean out the interior of the axle casing and the differential housing. Commence by re-installing the bevel shaft and pinion in reverse order to dismantling. Fit a new collapsible spacer 17, and re-assemble in the reverse order to dismantling.

If it is found that the original shimming was not satisfactory, fresh shims will have to be selected and installed. The function of the shims is to ensure a correct relative position between the axis of the crownwheel and to apply a degree of preloading on the bearings so that there shall be no longitudinal play.

A range of four thicknesses of shim is available, .003, .005, .010 and .020 inch, for insertion between the bevel pinion and inner taper bearing (see **FIG 8:6**). To select the right shim thickness, a special gauge comprising a dummy pinion and mandrel, Tool No. RG.545, is required. This is inserted in place of the true bevel pinion on the two taper roller bearings without shims and is bolted in position. The mandrel is clamped between the two differential cage bearing seats by the bearing caps (see **FIG 8:7**). The dummy bevel nut is then tightened until the shaft just begins to bind when turned by hand. In this state, the distance between the table and the underside of the mandrel is determined by feeler gauge. The thickness of the gap, so determined, is the required shim thickness to be fitted. The shims are installed in position **A** (see **FIG 8:6**) with the bearing pressed on to the shaft above them.

To preload the bevel pinion, after assembly with a new collapsible spacer in position but with the coupling flange nut only finger tight, first tighten the nut until the end float disappears and then rotate the shaft several times in each direction to settle the bearings. Wind a cord around the flange and attach to a 20 lb spring balance (see **FIG 8:8**). Tighten the nut slowly and progressively until the resistance to turning is between 6 and 11 lb for original bearings or between 8 and 15 lb for new bearings. **It is important that, once set, the nut shall not be backed off. If overtightened, the assembly must be taken down and a new collapsible spacer inserted.**

Now reassemble the differential cage and crownwheel, tightening the crownwheel nuts to a torque of 47 lb ft, lightly oiling the shafts and gears as assembly proceeds. Insert into the axle casing with the crownwheel meshing with the bevel pinion and the outer bearing tracks on the bearings and backed by the adjuster nuts, secure by the bearing caps and screw down the bolts finger tight. Rotate the adjuster nuts back and forward to ensure that they are correctly located in the threads of the cap. Tighten the bolts to 20 lb ft.

Screw in both adjuster nuts until backlash between the crownwheel and bevel is a minimum and there is no end play in the cage mount. The assembly is now ready for preloading.

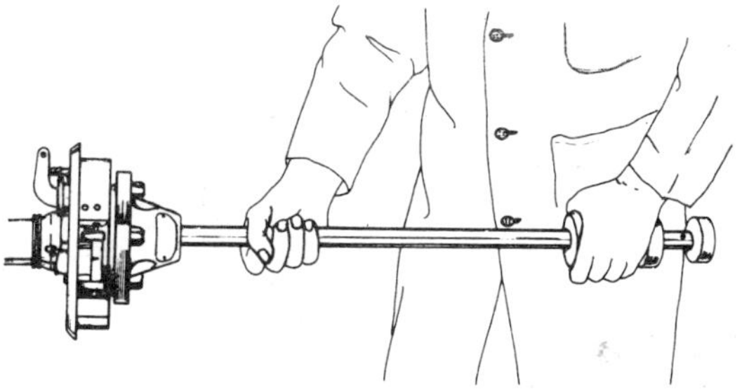

FIG 8:4 Extracting halfshaft with slide hammer and adapter

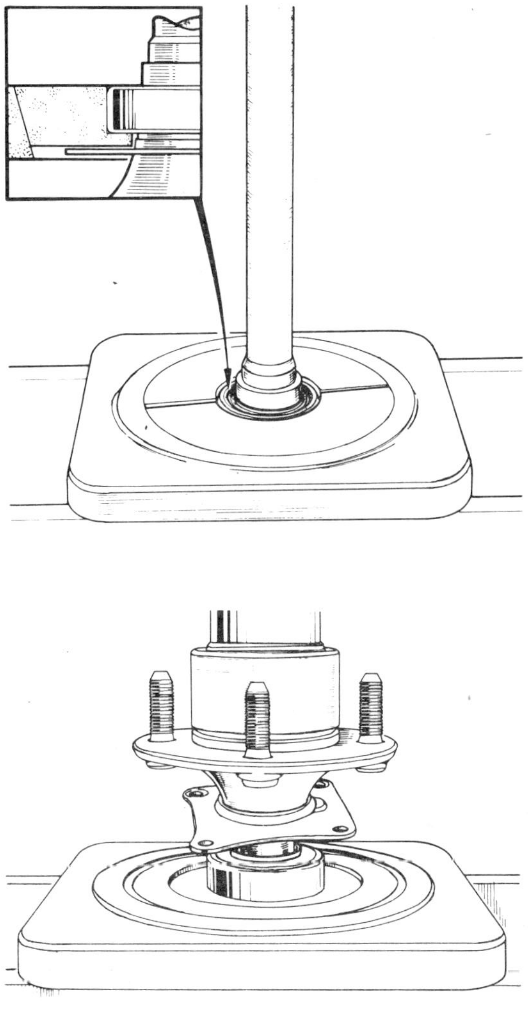

FIG 8:5 Removal (above) and reinstallation (below) of halfshaft bearing in press

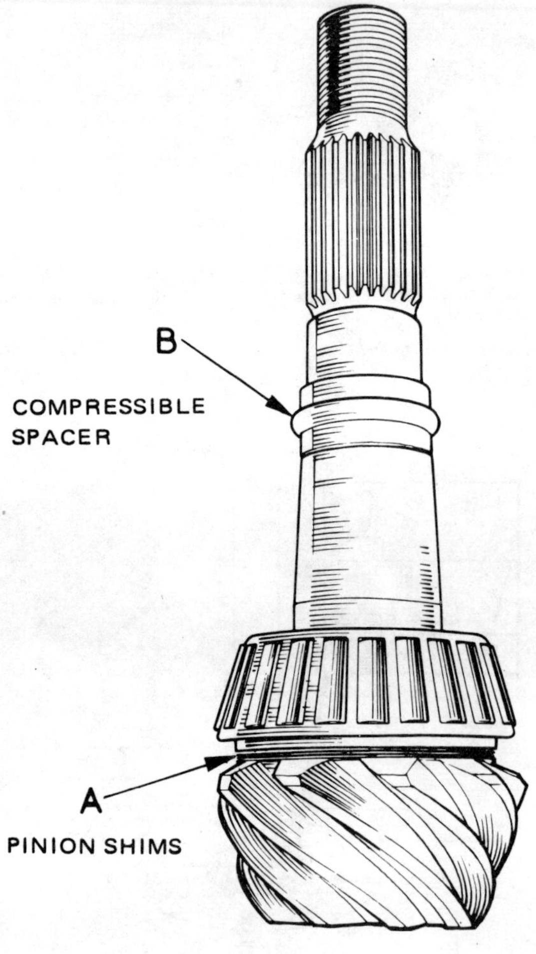

FIG 8:6 Bevel shaft and pinion showing position of shims, A, and collapsible spacer, B

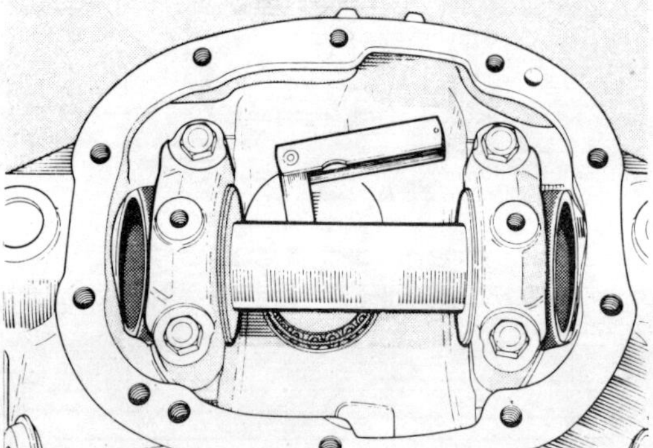

FIG 8:7 Method of checking shim thickness for bevel shaft

8:5 Preloading the differential

Set up a clock gauge on the casing as in **FIG 8:9** to determine backlash on the crownwheel teeth, then turn the two adjuster nuts equally, by means of the special pin wrenches, in the same direction until a backlash movement of .004 inch is indicated. That is to say, the cage as a whole is moved across the housing without affecting end play to bring the crownwheel and bevel pinions into the correct meshing.

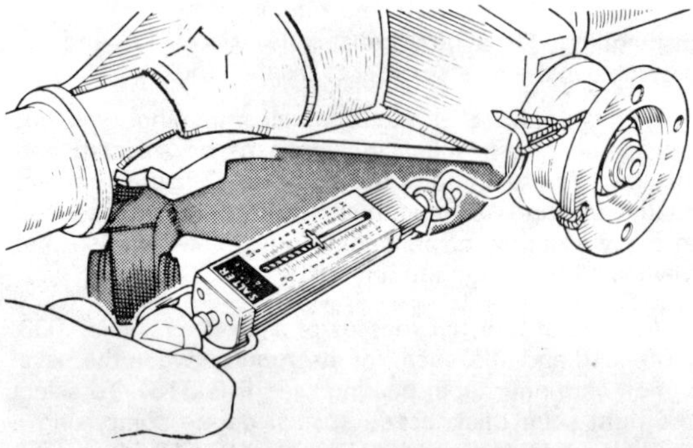

FIG 8:8 Torque check on bevel shaft after assembly and adjustment of self-locking nut

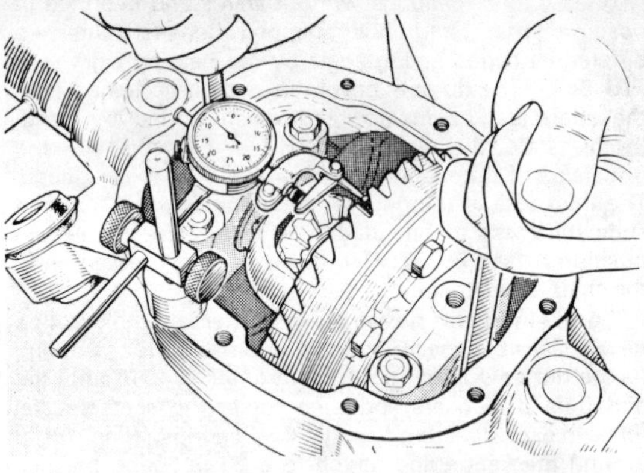

FIG 8:9 Determination of crownwheel backlash with dial gauge

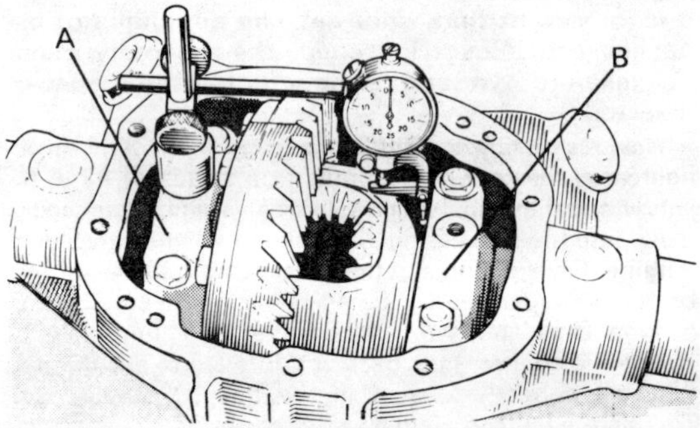

FIG 8:10 Method of determining preload on differential cage bearings

Key to Fig 8:10 **A** Crownwheel side bearing cap **B** Cage side bearing cap

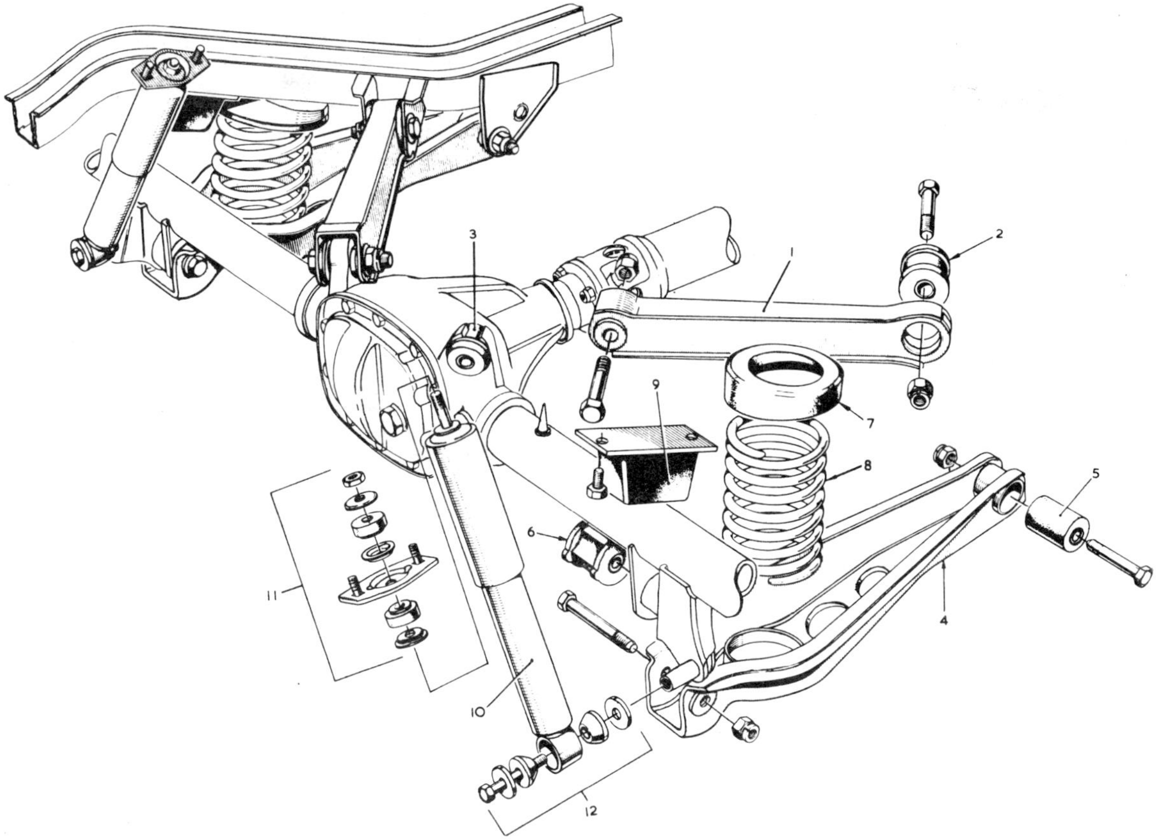

FIG 8:11 Schematic view of rear suspension

Key to Fig 8:11 1 Torque reaction link 2/3 Rubber bushes 4 Swinging arm 5 Pivot bush 6 Swinging arm to axle bush 7 Coil spring bearing cap 8 Coil spring 9 Rubber bump stop 10 Damper 11 Damper upper mount assembly 12 Damper lower mount assembly

Re-position the gauge as in **FIG 8:10** with the tip of the indicator in contact with the inner face of the cage side bearing cap B in **FIG 8:10**. Slacken off the cage side bearing adjuster to release any preload, do not alter crownwheel side bearing adjuster during this operation. Set gauge to zero and tighten cage side bearing adjuster until gauge reads .0015 inch (.038 mm). This adjustment sets the carrier bearing preload and crownwheel to pinion backlash. Check backlash is between .005 to .009 inch (.13 to .23 mm). Check pinion preload, with cord and spring balance as in **FIG 8:8**, which should have increased by 4 to 5 lb (1.8 to 2.3 kg) over pinion only figure. Finally tighten bearing caps to 36 lb/ft (5 kg/m).

8:6 Installation of the differential

With the differential correctly assembled in the axle case housing, reinstall the two half shafts as already described and re-couple the propeller shaft to the bevel pinion coupling flange. Check that the two halves of the coupling are accurately mated as before dismantling and then tighten the coupling bolts to a torque of 17 lb ft.

Fit a new cover gasket in position and replace the rear housing cover tightening the bolts to a torque of 14 lb ft. Fill the casing up to the level of the filler plug with Shell Spirax 90.EP oil or equivalent and insert and tighten the filler plug. Check for oil leaks and see that the plastic breather tube is not blocked.

8:7 Rear suspension

The rear suspension comprises a pair of substantial swinging arms, hinged at the forward end to brackets welded to the chassis sidemembers, supporting the rear axle and two coil springs in compression between the free ends of the swinging arms and the underside members of the chassis. The swinging arm bearings are live-rubber bushed at each end. The damper is coupled between a bushed mount on the axle casing outboard of the swinging arm and the underframe and lies at an angle to the vertical. Torque reactions on the axle casing are taken by substantial hinged links, also live rubber bushed, between the chassis and brackets either side of the differential housing on the axle casing. A general view of the suspension is shown in **FIG 8:11**.

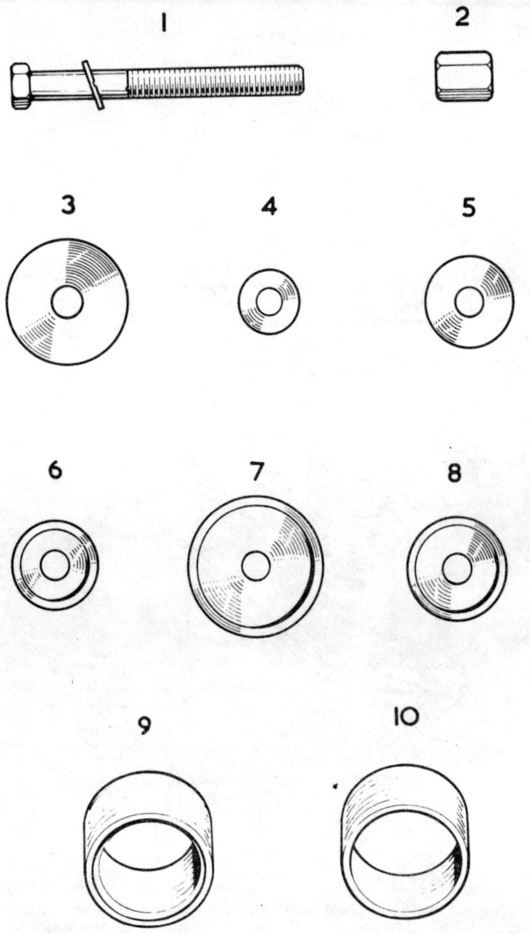

FIG 8:12 Tool set for rubber bush replacement Part No. RG.551

8:8 Dismantling and inspection

Jack-up the car and make safe on stands, remove the rear wheels. When using the jack, take care not to foul the cover to the differential casing or a serious oil leak may develop. Locate the stands under the body sidemembers in front of and close to the lower link front bracket.

Take the weight of the axle close to one end and support it while the damper bolt is withdrawn and the lower half of the unit pulled clear of the mount on the axle bracket. Unless it is desired to replace the damper, this may now be collapsed to its shortest length and left in situ while the rest of the suspension is dismantled.

Lower the swinging arm on the jack sufficiently to enable the coil spring to be withdrawn. Repeat on the other side. Examine the springs and check for free length, 11.72 inches for standard springs, 11.51 inches for heavy duty. Replace as necessary. Heavy duty springs are identified by a single stripe of orange paint across the spring, these springs are normally fitted to cars which are exported to countries with a preponderance of unmetalled roads, or to the Estate versions.

Clean the swinging arms and examine for signs of damage or distortion. Withdraw the rear bolts and allow the swinging arm to pivot downwards on the rear bolt and bush. Examine the condition of the bushes and, if perished or swollen, withdraw the rear bolt and extract the swinging arm to undertake bush renewal. Repeat with the upper swinging arms.

8:9 Overhaul and reinstallation

The only major item of overhaul is the replacement of the live rubber bushes in the pivot ends of the four arms, two swinging arms and two upper torque reaction arms. A special tool is required for this operation. It comprises a bolt and nut, six washers and two collars (see **FIG 8:12**). The use of the tool for removing and reinstalling bushes and the appropriate components from the set are shown in **FIG 8:13.** The only point to note is the direction of removal and insertion for the upper link front bush. If either is attempted in the reverse direction, damage to the housing and bush may result.

The remainder of the suspension reinstallation is a simple reversal of the dismantling sequence.

8:10 Dampers

The hydraulic double-acting dampers are of the sealed pattern and cannot be dismantled. In the event of a failure, replacement is the only remedy.

A word of warning. Do not attempt to disconnect a damper with the wheels off the ground and unsupported. The weight of the car must be on the wheels or the axle casing must be supported on stands before removal is attempted.

When ordering a replacement damper, check the number of the one removed with that on the replacement.

8:11 Coil springs

The standard and heavy duty coil springs are both wound on an inside diameter of 3.517 inches, the heavy duty unit, identified by the single orange stripe, being slightly shorter—11.51 inches free length as against 11.72 inches—but with a marginally increased number of turns 8.49 as against 8.09.

It is, of course, important that both rear coil springs should be of the same type.

8:12 Fault diagnosis

(a) Rear of car out of level

1 Uneven tyre pressures
2 Weak or broken spring
3 Faulty damper
4 Unbalanced loading

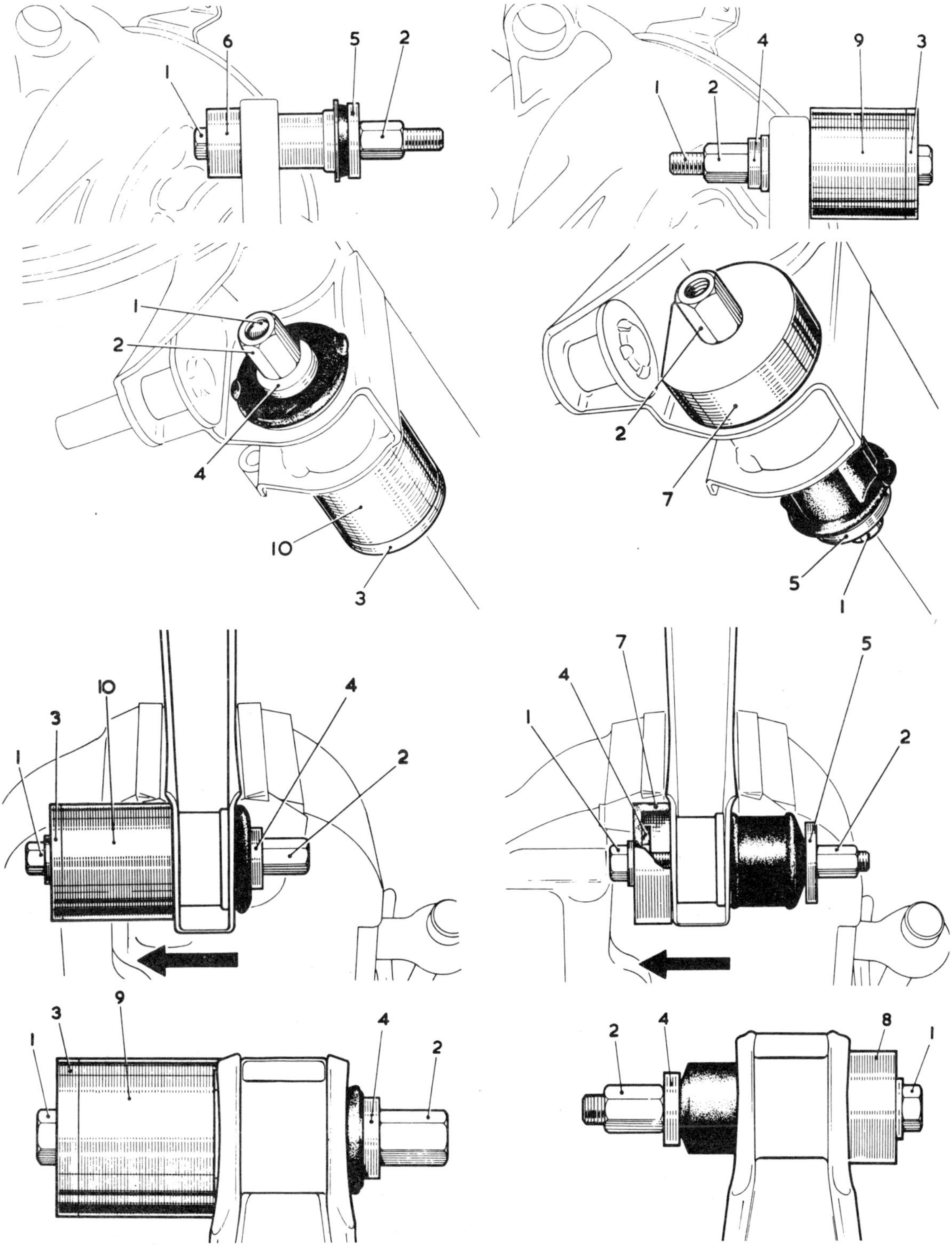

FIG 8:13 Use of tool set components in removing (left) and reinstalling (right) rubber bushes to rear suspension. Reading from top to bottom, upper link rear bush, lower link rear bush, upper link front bush and lower link front bush. The numbers refer to the accessories from the set in Fig 8:12

(b) Uneven rear tyre wear

1 Uneven tyre pressures
2 Weak or broken spring on one side
3 Handbrake out of adjustment

(c) Excessive road vibration

1 Faulty damper
2 Rear wheels out of balance
3 Propeller shaft out of balance
4 Loose coupling nuts

(d) Noisy differential

1 Worn bearings
2 Wear on crown or bevel wheels
3 Wrong shimming
4 Lack of oil in differential

(e) Car tends to pull to one side

1 Flat tyre
2 Brake shoe binding
3 Rear axle out of alignment

CHAPTER 9

FRONT SUSPENSION, HUBS AND WHEELS

9:1 Description of suspension

The front suspension comprises a pair of vertically mounted independent Macpherson pattern strut assemblies and a centre crossmember with swinging control arms. The strut assemblies are secured at their upper end to the front wing valances and at the lower end to swinging control arms pivoted on the crossmember. These two mounting points determine castor, camber and steering axis which are non-adjustable.

The tubular struts each contain the direct acting hydraulic damper, the outer tube acting as both a reservoir for the fluid and the turning member of the stub axle and steering arm which, with the stub axle casting, are solidly connected. A section through the strut assembly and attachment to the swinging arm is shown in **FIG 9:1**. Because of the different brake caliper mountings, the two assemblies are a mirror pair and are not interchangeable.

The riding forces of the car are taken by a rubber mounted thrust bearing at the upper end of each assembly while road shocks are absorbed by the dampers, in conjunction with the coil springs. Rolling tendencies when cornering are controlled by the forward stabilizer bar, secured to the front members by rubber mounted brackets, and connected at both ends to the swing control arms by the vertical link pins shown in **FIG 9:1**. Braking reactions are controlled by the two struts terminating in resilient rubber mountings on the front sidemembers and at the rear in bolts passing through the swinging arm between the stabilizer link pin and hub ball joint.

9:2 Routine maintenance

Routine maintenance is minimal being confined to a check of wear in the swivel bearing at the end of the swinging arms and a check in the play of the hub bearings. Both bearings are grease packed for long life, the swivel bearing not being provided with a grease insertion nipple. The hub bearings have to be dismantled for re-packing with grease.

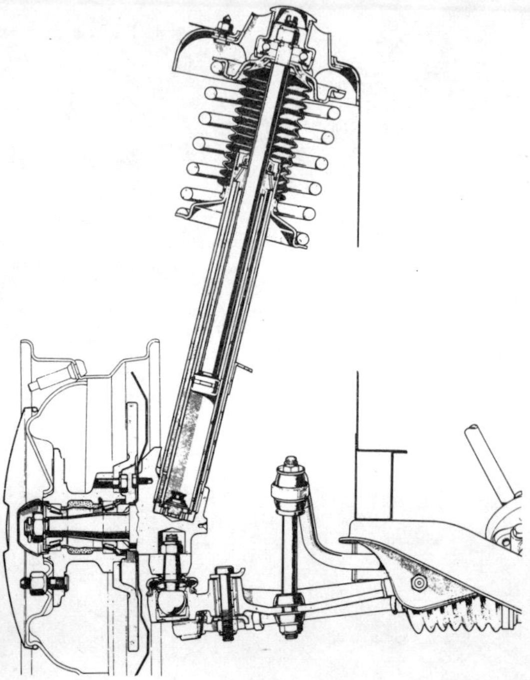

FIG 9:1 Diagrammatic section through strut, damper and hub

9:3 Dismantling and inspection

Should it be necessary to dismantle the suspension for replacement of damaged or worn components, proceed as follows. Apply the handbrake, chock the rear wheel and raise the front of the car on a jack. Be careful not to position the jack so that it fouls the sump. The weight must be taken on the front crossmember. Remove the road wheel on the side to be dismantled. Unbolt and remove the brake caliper with pads and support so that the hydraulic hose is not strained. It is not necessary to disconnect the hydraulic line. Draw off the hub dust cap 29 (see **FIG 9:2**), extract the splitpin 28, and remove the lock cap 27, nut 7, and washer 26. The hub can then be withdrawn by hand as an assembly of hub 19, outer bearing 25, brake disc 9, inner bearing 22, distance piece 23, and grease seal 24.

Clean all parts thoroughly and examine them for signs of wear or deterioration. Renew all oil seals and, where necessary, bearings and wheel studs.

To remove the stabilizer bar 30, remove the nuts and washers 34 to 37, from each end where the bar is secured to the linkpin 33—this can best be done initially when the weight of the car is on the wheels—and unbolt the locating bracket 31. The bar will then come away with the bushes 32, in position. Check the bar for any twisting and the bushes for deterioration. Straighten or replace the bar and replace the bushes as necessary.

To remove the brake reaction struts 38, unbolt the front end from the bracket bush 40, and remove the bolt 45 at the swinging arm end. Withdraw the strut and then dismantle the assembly of washers 41 and rubbers 39. Renew the rubbers if hardened or softened by oil.

To remove the suspension strut assembly, disconnect the steering arm 18, from the foot of the strut by removing the two bolts. The arm will remain part of the steering outer link rod. Unbolt and remove the linkpin 33, from the swinging arm 16, to enable it to be hinged downwards. This frees the strut at the lower end. Suspension strut removal will be facilitated, if before raising the car on the jack, the dust cover 12, is removed and the nut 11, slackened back one turn.

Support the strut assembly and, from above the valance, remove the three nuts securing the bearing housing 8, to the valance. **Do not remove the nut 11, securing the bearing to the strut through the hole in the valance.** Lower the complete assembly from the valance.

Removal of the swinging arm 16, is only necessary if it has been damaged or the bushes 17, have deteriorated.

Removal of the thrust bearing must not be attempted until the coil spring 2, has been clamped in a compressed condition. A convenient way of supporting the assembly—the strut tube 4, obviously must not be gripped in a vice—is to reassemble the front hub and mount on a road wheel. This can then be placed on a bench and the strut steadied by inserting a wedge between the strut and tyre wall. The strut is then moved to a convenient angle for working.

The first step is to compress the spring. A special tool P.5405 is available for this purpose but any method of securely clamping the spring between the mounting plate 3, and a lower coil will do. Compress only sufficient to remove the tension from the bearing unit.

Next, remove the securing nut 11. The special wrench, RG.549 must be used as this has a central screwdriver to fit in the slot at the head of strut to prevent the strut turning when the nut is being loosened (see **FIG 9:3**).

First, remove the dust cap 12, then the nut and washer leaving the strut free for extraction from the bearing and housing 8. Progressively loosen the clamps until the spring is fully extended, remove the clamp and take spring and mounting plate away from the strut.

Should it be necessary to dismantle the in-built damper, push the strut damper rod into the tube and remove the gaiter 5, and retaining plate 6. Unlock and remove the gland sealing nut using gland wrench P.5044, extract the O-ring and gently pull the damper rod to dislodge the guide bush and seal from the strut (see **FIG 9:4**). The piston assembly can now be withdrawn and the oil, which is of no further use, disposed of.

Clean and dry the interior of the cylinder, with petrol, and insert the piston and damper rod back into the stop tube and the assembly into the strut tube. Insert 280 cc of clean fresh oil—Armstrong Fluid 788 or Shell Super motor oil—dividing it equally between the interiors of the stop tube and strut tube. Refit the guide bush, spring washer, cup washer and seal and prime the damper by moving the rod in and out slowly, with long strokes, until an even resistance is felt. Insert a new O-ring and fit a new gland nut, tightening it to a torque of 48 lb ft. Secure by staking with a blunt chisel.

As a general rule damper servicing is restricted to export models only. Home models are dealt with by replacement unless circumstances are exceptional .

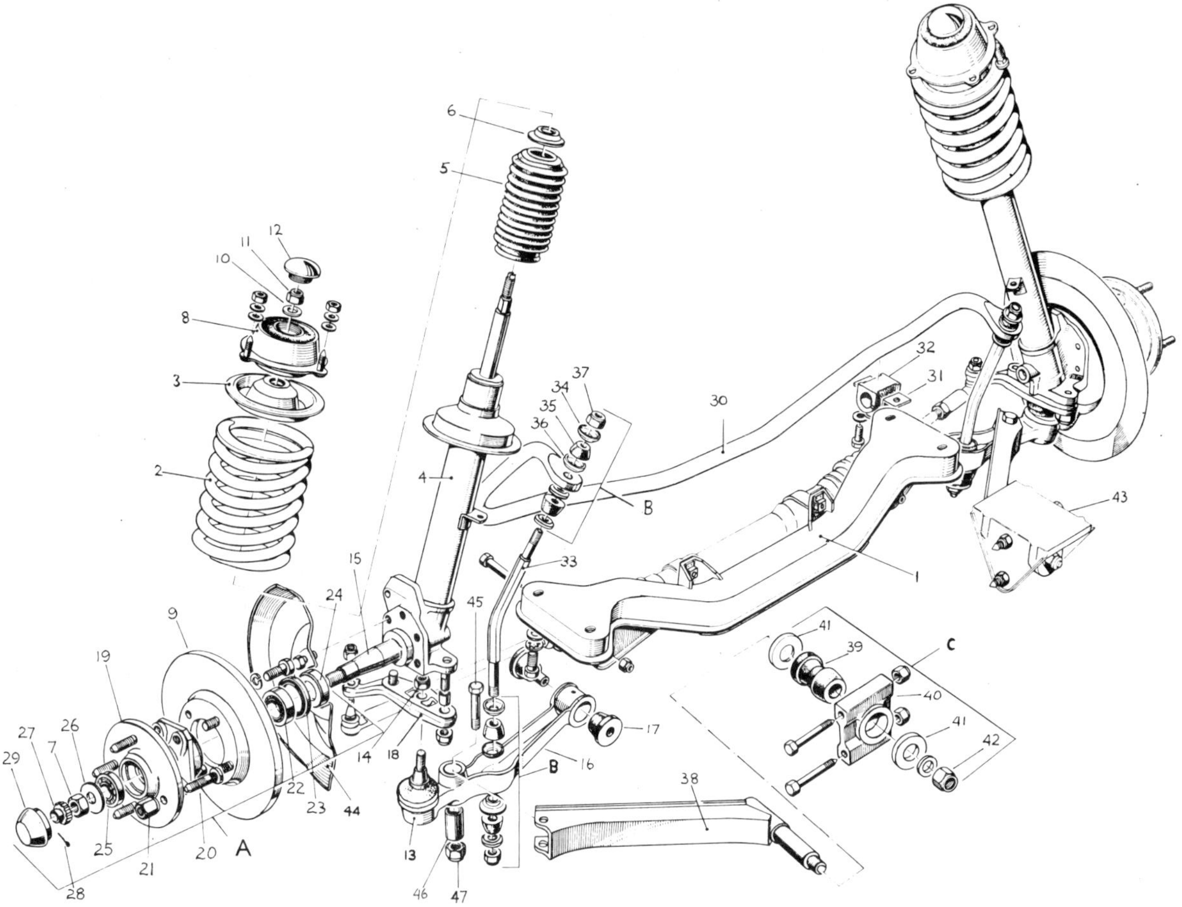

FIG 9:2 Exploded view of suspension

Key to Fig 9:2 1 Crossmember 2 Coil spring 3 Mounting plate 4 Strut, suspension 5 Gaiter 6 Retaining plate 7 Plain nut 8 Bearing housing and bearing 9 Brake disc 10/11 Washer and nut 12 Dust cap 13 Swivel bearing 14 Bearing nut 15 Stub axle 16 Swinging arm 17 Rubber bushes 18 Steering arm 19 Hub plate 20/21 Wheel nut and stud 22 Inner bearing 23 Grease seal 24 Distance piece 25 Outer bearing 26 Washer 27 Lock cap 28 Cotter pin 29 Dust cap 30 Stabilizer bar 31 Bracket 32 Rubber bush 33 Stabilizer linkpin 34 Dished washer 35 Rubber bush 36 Dished washer 37 Nyloc nut 38 Brake reaction strut 39 Rubber damper 40 Reaction rod support bracket 41 Washer 42 Nyloc nut 43 Underframe bracket 44 Brake backplate 45 Bolt, swinging arm to reaction strut 46 Rubber bush 47 Nyloc nut

Fit a new gaiter, fully extend the damper rod, fit the spring and mounting plate in position and compress until the thrust bearing locating rim on the rod projects through the mounting plate. Install the bearing and housing and fit a new nylock nut, tightening to a torque of 30 lb ft. Refit the dust cap.

The remainder of the reassembly is a reversal of the dismantling procedure.

9:4 Reassembly and installation

Reassembly of the complete front suspension is a reversal of the dismantling procedure in regard to the component assemblies with the following points being given careful attention.

All self-locking nuts must be renewed and the old ones discarded. The recommended torque values must be adhered to particularly the 30 lb ft torque figure for the nylock nut at the top of the strut. This should be rechecked when the installation has been completed, the wrench then being inserted through the hole over the nut in the valance. If it is too tight, steering will appear stiff. Conversely, if steering is stiff after reinstallation, the torque on the nut should be rechecked, loosening the nut half a turn and retorqueing.

Renew all rubber mountings, regardless of their condition, if the vehicle has been in service for more than two years. Do not over-tighten them. Check that all bushings, washers and nuts are applied in the proper order, checking against **FIG 9:2** if in doubt.

Before finally mounting the hubs, pack the hub and roller assemblies with Shell Retinax A or equivalent grease. The amount to insert is one and a half capfuls evenly distributed between the outer races in the hub. There must be no grease in the hub cap when fitted (see **FIG 9:5**).

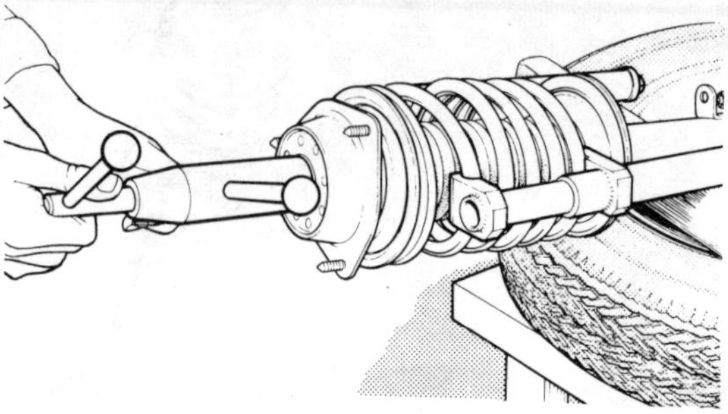

FIG 9:3 Use of gland wrench, RG.549, to loosen strut securing nut

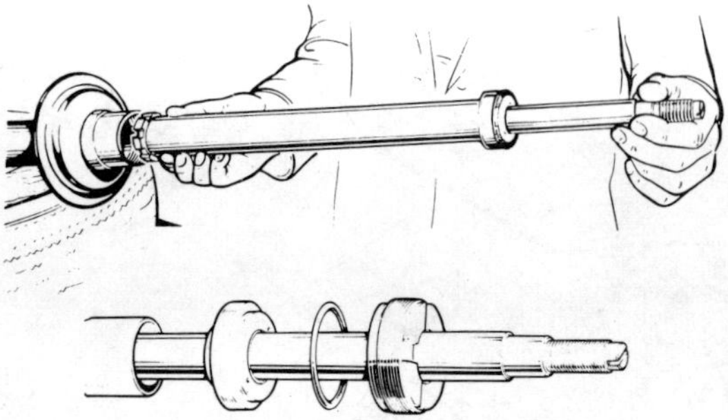

FIG 9:4 Removing damper unit from strut with, below, detail or damper rod sealing arrangements

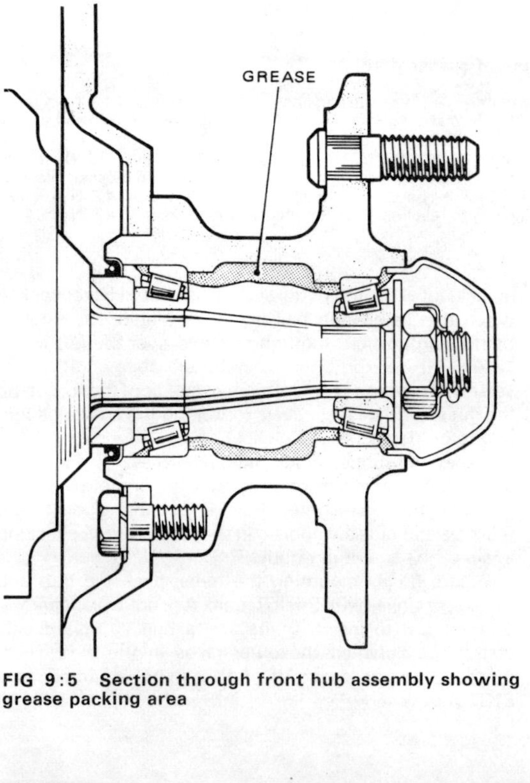

FIG 9:5 Section through front hub assembly showing grease packing area

Adjustment of end float is by the nut on the stub axle. After tightening to a torque setting of 15 lb ft, spinning the hub meanwhile, unscrew the nut by one to one and a half flats. Then check the end play with a dial gauge applied to the hub rim adjacent to the nut. The float must be between .002 and .004 inch. When adjusted, secured by the lock cap and pin.

9:5 Steering geometry

Camber and castor are set and are not adjustable. If these are upset in an accident, they will need to be rectified but this is a matter for the service garage who will have the necessary body jigs.

Toe-in is set by the link arms at the extremities of the track rod. The procedure for checking and setting is explained in **Chapter 10, Section 10:6.**

9:6 Wheels and tyres

The pressed steel wheels are of the safety ledge pattern, the wide bead seat on the outer ledge preventing loss of the tyre at speed should it deflate. The rim size is 4½J x 13 and nuts should be tightened to a torque of 55 lb ft.

Tyre sizes fitted are 5.60 x 13 tubeless crossply or 155 x 13 radial tubeless. Tyre pressures are 22 lb/sq in front and 24 lb/sq in rear. Front radials may be increased by 2 lb/sq in and, with a full passenger load on long journeys, rear pressures may be increased by 4 to 6 lb/sq in.

Either radial or crossply tyres may be fitted providing only that the safety regulations concerning their use are maintained. Briefly, crossply or radial tyres may be fitted all round though radial-ply may affect ground clearance and speedometer accuracy lightly. **The same type of tyre must always be used on nearside and offside, front or rear, and crossply on the front may be fitted with radial-ply on the rear but NEVER radial-ply on the front and crossply on the rear.** Because, however, of the complications arising with a spare tyre, it is safer to fit the same all round and to adhere to the recommended types.

9:7 Modifications

No modifications have been necessary to the original design and the only differences that are likely to be found are the use of alternative types of suspension spring. Both are of the same internal diameter but of different length on nearside and offside wheels. The standard pattern has a free length of 14.4 inches, offside (two white stripes), and 13.3 inches, nearside (two blue stripes). The heavy duty pattern has a free length of 13.29 inches (two green stripes) and 12.32 inches (two brown stripes). These are normally fitted to export models shipped to countries that have unmetalled roads or rough unmade roads. **The same pattern must, of course, be installed on both wheels.**

9:8 Fault diagnosis

(a) Wheels bounce

1 Faulty or worn tyres
2 Tyre pressures too high
3 Weak coil spring
4 Damper not working
5 Wheel or tyre out of alignment

(b) Excessive tyre wear

1 Tyre pressures too low
2 Excessive acceleration or braking
3 Cornering too sharp or fast
4 Excessive hub end float

(c) Car pulls to one side when running

1 Tyres unevenly inflated
2 Tyres unevenly worn
3 Flat tyre

(d) Car pulls to one side when braking

1 Brakes out of adjustment
2 Tyres unevenly worn or inflated

NOTES

CHAPTER 10

THE STEERING SYSTEM

10:1 Description

The steering gear is of the rack and pinion pattern with the ends of the rack rod directly coupled to the steering knuckles and arms through short adjustable links and ball joints. Two types of rack and pinion assembly are installed, according to availability at the time of pro-production, the Burman and the Cam Gears.

The pinion is turned by the articulated steering shaft the upper end of which supports the steering wheel by a conventional taper, spline and nut connection. The upper section of the shaft is supported in the hollow steering column which is secured to the engine bulkhead at the lower end by a through-plate and at the underside of the dashboard by a welded bracket. A two-piece moulded housing around the upper end of the column, shaped to encircle the lower boss of the steering wheel, encloses the column lock control switch and combination ignition switch and shaft lock. A general view of the arrangement is shown in **FIG 10:1** with details of the two patterns of rack and pinion mechanism in **FIGS 10:2** and **10:3**.

10:2 Maintenance

Both rack and pinion assembly and the steering column, with ball pin joints, are lubricated for life and no particular maintenance is needed. Periodical inspection of the joints and rubber shrouds should take place at the 6000 mile interval services and renewed as necessary. Otherwise there should be no reason for interfering with the steering gear unless steering irregularities and excessive play at the wheel give rise to a suspicion that wear has taken place or that the link arms have gone out of adjustment.

10:3 Rack and pinion steering

Reference to the two patterns of rack and pinion mechanism in **FIGS 10:2** and **10:3** will show that the differences are in only minor points of design. In each case, the rack is cut at an angle on the rack rod which is supported in the hollow housing secured across the chassis to the rear of the front suspension. The short

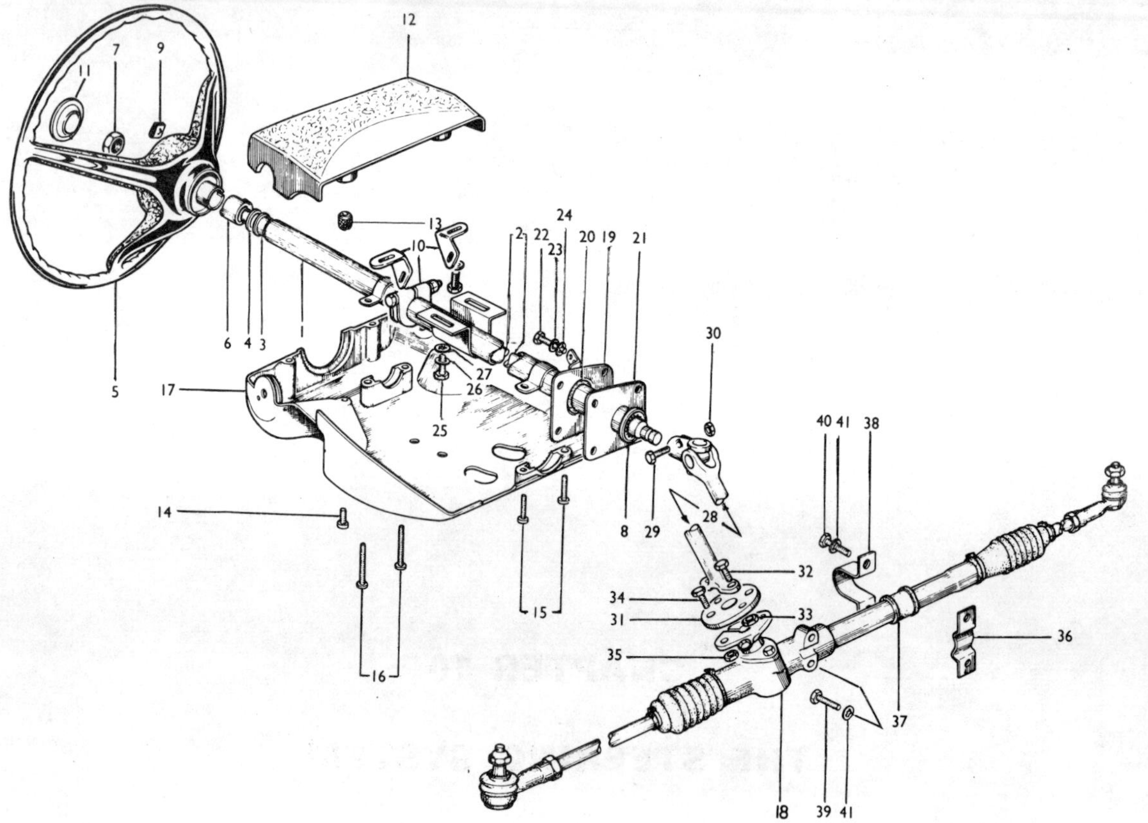

FIG 10:1 Exploded view of steering gear as fitted to the Avenger series of cars

Key to Fig 10:1 1 Steering column 2 Steering shaft 3 Bearing 4 Shims 5 Steering wheel 6 Striker 7/30/33/35 Nuts 8 Sprag washer 9 Clip 10 Clamp assembly 11 Motif 12 Upper cowl 13 Insert 14/15/16 Screws 17 Lower cowl 18 Rack 19 Plate inner 20 Seal 21 Plate, outer 22/29/32/34 Bolts 23/24/26/27/41 Washers 25/39/40 Setscrews 28 Intermediate shaft 31 Coupling 36/38 Brackets 37 Insulator

pinion shaft is mounted at a slight angle to the rack rod in the housing and is kept in mesh by its bearings and a spring-loaded slipper yoke to minimize play in the steering generally.

The ends of the rack rod terminate in ball sockets, lubricated for life and spring-loaded, to accommodate the ball ends of the two adjustable track rods. The latter terminate in the ball pin joints securing them to the front wheel steering arms. The ball joints are hermetically sealed against the ingress of dirt and moisture by substantial rubber bellows and for this reason, **excessive movement from lock to lock with the road wheels jacked off the ground must be avoided as the bellows act as compressors and the build up of pressure within could rupture the bellows or break the joint seals.** This is, of course, not possible at the relatively slower movements possible with the wheels in contact with the road surface.

10:4 Removing steering shaft and column

First disconnect the battery negative terminal to isolate the electrical circuits in the column switch and check that the steering lock is free. Separate the two halves of the moulded housing by extracting the screws and detach it from the column.

Extract the centre motif from the steering wheel. In some cases this is a spring clip attachment removal being by simply prising the motif out with a shaft instrument; in others it is a pad secured in position by lips and is freed by rotating the pad through a few degrees in a counterclockwise direction.

Slacken the nut beneath the motif with a 1 inch AF spanner and pull the wheel upwards to free it from the taper and splines. Before fully releasing it, mark both wheel boss and shaft so that it can be replaced in the same position on reassembly. Extract the nut and take off the steering wheel.

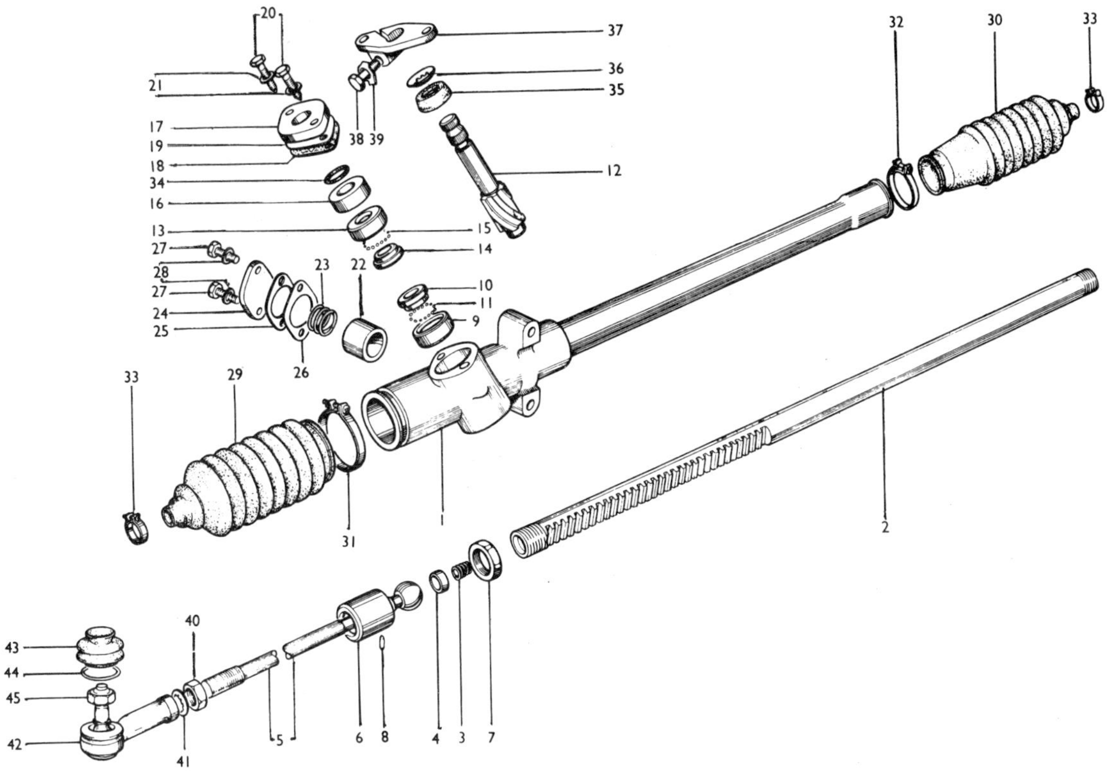

FIG 10:2 Exploded view of Burman type rack and pinion gear

Key to Fig 10:2 1 Rack housing 2 Rack rod 3 Spring 4 Ball seat 5 Link rod 6 Balljoint housing 7 Balljoint locknut 8 Pin 9/10/11 Lower bearing assembly 12 Pinion and shaft 13/14/15 Upper bearing assembly 16 Spacer 17/18/19 Pinion cover, shim and gasket 20/21 Bolts and washers 22 Slipper yoke or pad 23 Spring 24/25/26 Pad cover shim and gasket 27/28 Bolts and washers 29/30 Bellows 31/32 Inner bellows clips 33 Outer bellows clips 34 O-ring 35 Pinion shaft seal 36 Clip 37 Coupling flange 38/39 Setscrew and lockwasher 40/41 Link adjuster locknut and washer 42/45 Ballpin joint 43/44 Boot and clip

At the far side of the bulkhead, slacken and remove the pin 29 (see **FIG 10:1**) to free the lower end of the steering shaft from the universal joint coupling it to the intermediate shaft 28. Remove the four bolts from the floor aperture plate assembly 19 and 21, and unscrew the two bolts and remove with spacers from the column support bracket. Remove the indicator switch from the column after disconnecting the electrical circuits to it and the ignition key and lock.

Slacken the large through bolt on the upper clamp 10, and withdraw the complete column and shaft assembly from within the car.

The steering shaft is secured within the steering column by a circular sprag washer at the foot (see **FIG 10:4**) and the steering wheel at the upper end. With the wheel removed, the shaft can be extracted from the lower end using the steering lock boss as a sliding hammer to push out the lower bush.

Thoroughly clean all parts and examine for signs of damage or corrosion. Reassembly is in the reverse order, lubricating the column splines with Shell Rhodina No. 2 oil and the top bearing with Retinax A grease.

When assembled, due regard having been made to the marks scribed during dismantling to ensure identical positioning of the parts, the end play of the shaft within the column must be checked and, if necessary, adjusted. This is done by means of the sprag washer at the foot of the column which is tapped upwards along the shaft until the end play is reduced to between .008 and .010 inch. A simple method of making this adjustment is to make a shim plate from .010 inch thick material in the form shown in **FIG 10:4** and to insert it between the sprag washer and foot of the steering column before tapping the washer into place. When it is tight against the shim, the latter is removed to give the necessary clearance.

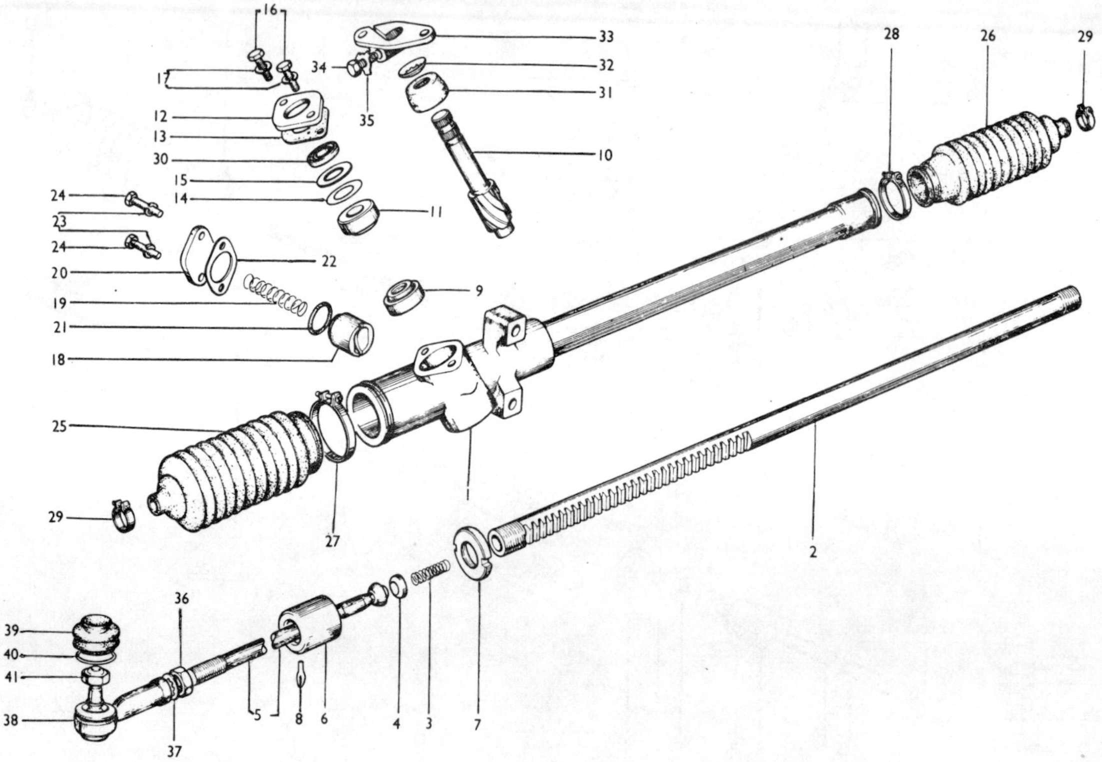

FIG 10:3 Exploded view of Cam Gears type rack and pinion gear

Key to Fig 10:3 1 Rack housing 2 Rack rod 3 Spring 4 Ball seat 5 Link rod 6 Balljoint housing 7 Balljoint locknut 8 Pin 9 Lower bearing 10 Pinion and shaft 11 Upper bearing 12/13 Pinion cover and gasket 14/15 Thrust washer and shim 16/17 Bolts and washers 18 Slipper yoke or pad 19 Spring 20/22 Pad cover and gasket 23/24 Bolt and washer 25/26 Bellows 27/28 Inner bellows blips 29 Outer bellows clips 30 Oil seal 31/32 Boot and clip 33 Coupling flange 34/35 Setscrew and lockwasher 36/37 Link adjuster locknut and washer 38/41 Ballpin joint 39/40 Boot and clip

10:5 Servicing the rack and pinion assembly

To remove the rack and pinion assembly, first support the front of the car on stands after securely chocking the rear wheels. Check operation of the rack and pinion from lock to lock, noting any play and whether the play present is about the same at all points on the traverse from one extreme to the other.

Generally speaking, the steering mechanism is not likely to give trouble until it is so worn out as to need replacement. A new assembly can be obtained from the Chrysler agent and replaced at far less cost in time and trouble than in attempting to repair the old one. Spare parts, like the rack and pinion are not usually available and the steering, being vital to the safety of the car and its occupants, must not be allowed to fall below the minimum standards of wear and adjustment.

If a car has been in service for several years without excessive mileage having been covered, it may be advisable to dismantle, clean and repack with grease. In these circumstances, proceed as follows.

Clean the exterior of the steering box and then remove the clips securing the bellows in place. Unscrew the locknuts at each end of the rack rod to separate the links from the rod and extract the ball pin joints at the far end of the links from the steering arms of the wheel knuckles, using a proper extractor. **Do not use a hammer on any part of the steering.** Take care not to lose the ball spring and seat which will be released from the ball joint with the extraction of the locknut.

Slacken the universal joint bolt and remove it to detach the steering mechanism from the steering shaft, remove the bolts from the housing boss and the securing bracket which together support the assembly on the car underframe. Lower the rack and pinion assembly from the car and transfer to a bench. Thoroughly clean the exterior before proceeding with any further dismantling. Obtain new bellows and clips.

Disconnect the intermediate shaft from the rack and pinion by removing the bolts 34 (see **FIG 10:1**) from the flexible coupling and then slacken the pinch bolt on the coupling flange securing it to the pinion shaft. **Mark the position before detaching the flange from the shaft (see FIG 10:5).**

Extract the two bolts securing the cover to the yoke, or slipper, housing, remove the cover and extract the gasket, shim spring and slipper pad, noting the number and thickness of the shim(s) for replacement. Remove the dust seal and clip from the pinion shaft, extract the two bolts securing the cover, joint and shims in place and extract all three. With a slightly circular motion, withdraw the pinion and shaft together with the upper bearing, spacer and seal assembly. From below, extract the lower bearing assembly. Withdraw the rack and shaft from the housing.

Thoroughly clean and degrease all parts and inspect for wear or damage. Obtain replacements for seals and bellows but if any other parts need replacement, exchange for a complete assembly from the Chrysler agent.

Reassemble in reverse order lubricating each part with Shell Spirax 90.EP oil before assembling. If the same shims are inserted in the position from which they were removed, there should be no need for further adjustment. Should, however, the shims be misplaced, assemble the slipper to the rear of the rack without shims or gaskets, fit the coverplate and push fully home. Holding it in this position, measure the gap between the cover and body flange with feeler gauges and then make up a pack of gaskets with shims between to a total thickness .004 inch more than the measurement taken to give this amount of working clearance between rack and pinion, so preventing undue stiffness without excessive play.

Similarly, adjust the shim thickness of the pinion shaft assembly but, in this case, the thickness of the shim/gasket pack must be .002 inch **less** than that of the measurement to give a degree of preload on the bearings.

After fitting the end bellows fill each with Spirax oil, using a fine nozzle oil can to introduce it, and secure the clips. Reinstall in position on the car, tightening each bolt to the torques set down in the Appendix.

10:6 Steering links

The two track rods are adjustable by screwing the inner shafts in or out of the threaded socket end carrying the ball pin steering arms joints. A locknut on the shaft secures the adjustment, the shaft rotating in the ball joint of the rack rod end.

When reassembling after servicing, adjust both links to the same length before installation and then adjust each equally to correct the front wheel alignment to preserve equal lock to lock movement.

10:7 Front wheel alignment

The only adjustment that can be made on the steering or front wheel alignment without specialized equipment is the toe-in. Camber or castor adjustments, necessitating the changing of shims behind the suspension mounting brackets, are best entrusted to a garage with the necessary equipment and experience. Castor angle—the rearward tilt of the steering axis in relation to the vertical, should be between 1 deg. and 1 deg. 30 mins. The camber angle—that made between the centreline of the tyres viewed from the front and true vertical—should be 1 deg. 45 mins.

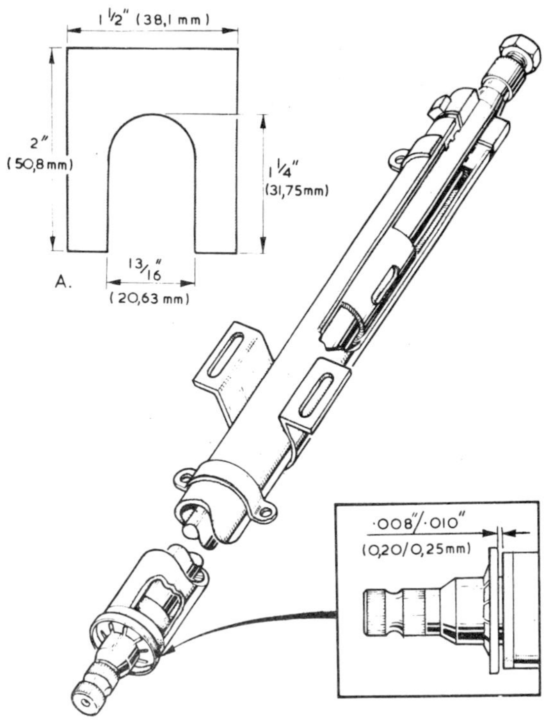

FIG 10:4 Detail of steering column and shaft assembly showing shim and sprag washer for adjusting end float of shaft in column

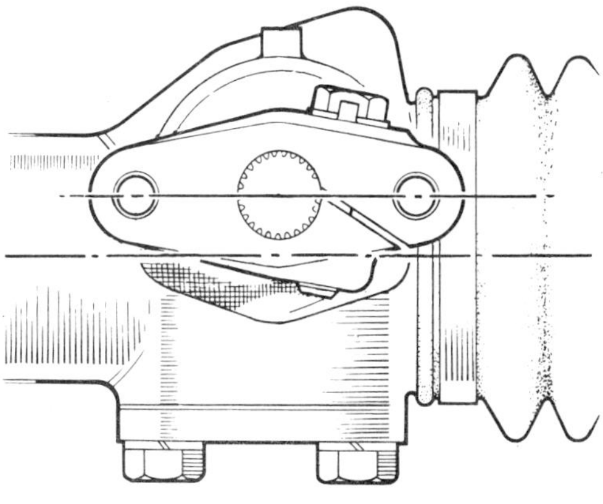

FIG 10:5 Position of pinion shaft coupling flange with the rack centralized in the housing

Toe-in, the difference between the track length at the front and at the rear of the front wheel tyres, should be $\frac{1}{32}$ to $\frac{1}{8}$ inch; that is to say, the measurement between two points on the tyres on a horizontal axis at the front with a track gauge should be this amount **less** than between the same two points when the wheels have rotated 180 deg. and are facing rear.

10:8 Fault diagnosis

(a) Loose steering

1 Slack front wheel bearings
2 Worn ball pin joints to steering arms
3 Loose steering rack mounting
4 Play on ball ends of steering links
5 Worn universal coupling
6 Slack pad adjustment
7 Play in pinion shaft (insufficient preload)

(b) Heavy steering

1 Under-inflated tyres
2 Excessive pressure on steering rack pad
3 Excessive shimming in pinion shaft bearing (excessive preload)

(c) Play in steering

1 Worn rack or pinion
2 Loose or worn link ball joints
3 Worn universal joint
4 Excessive end play on steering shaft in column

(d) Steering wander

1 Play in steering—see (c)
2 Loose wheel nuts
3 Slack rack housing mounts

CHAPTER 11

THE BRAKING SYSTEM

11:1 Description

The braking system is Girling hydraulic operating on disc brakes at the front and drum brakes at the rear with a Girling Type 28 vacuum servo unit interposed between the master and brake cylinders on some models. The cable operated handbrake applies the rear brake shoes only. Brake mechanisms, both disc and drum, are self-adjusting for wear.

Servicing is confined to regular checks of brake fluid level in the reservoirs topping up with Girling amber brake fluid (Specification J.1703) as necessary. Routine maintenance covers, in addition, the checking of brake pads and shoes for wear, checking discs and drums for grooving or scoring, inspecting hydraulic lines and hoses, master and brake cylinder connections, servo air cleaner and vacuum lines and oil seals at the periods set down in the Owner's Service Handbook and renewing as necessary.

11:2 Disc brakes

An exploded view of the front disc brakes is shown in **FIG 11:1.** To dismantle, raise the car on stands or on a garage jack with the rear wheels securely chocked fore and aft and remove the wheels. Withdraw the two pads 16, after extracting the retaining pins 12, and clips 13, together with any anti-squeak shims, not shown, if present.

The brake calipers are secured to the stub axle backing plate by two bolts, not shown, passing through the mounting flange of the calipers. The calipers are located in the cutaway portion of the guard plate 4, which is secured to the backing plate by three bolts and lock-washers 5 and 6, while the brake disc 1 is attached to the hub plate by the three bolts and lockwashers 2 and 3. **The bolts and star washers 17 and 18 hold the two halves of the caliper assembly together and are jig**

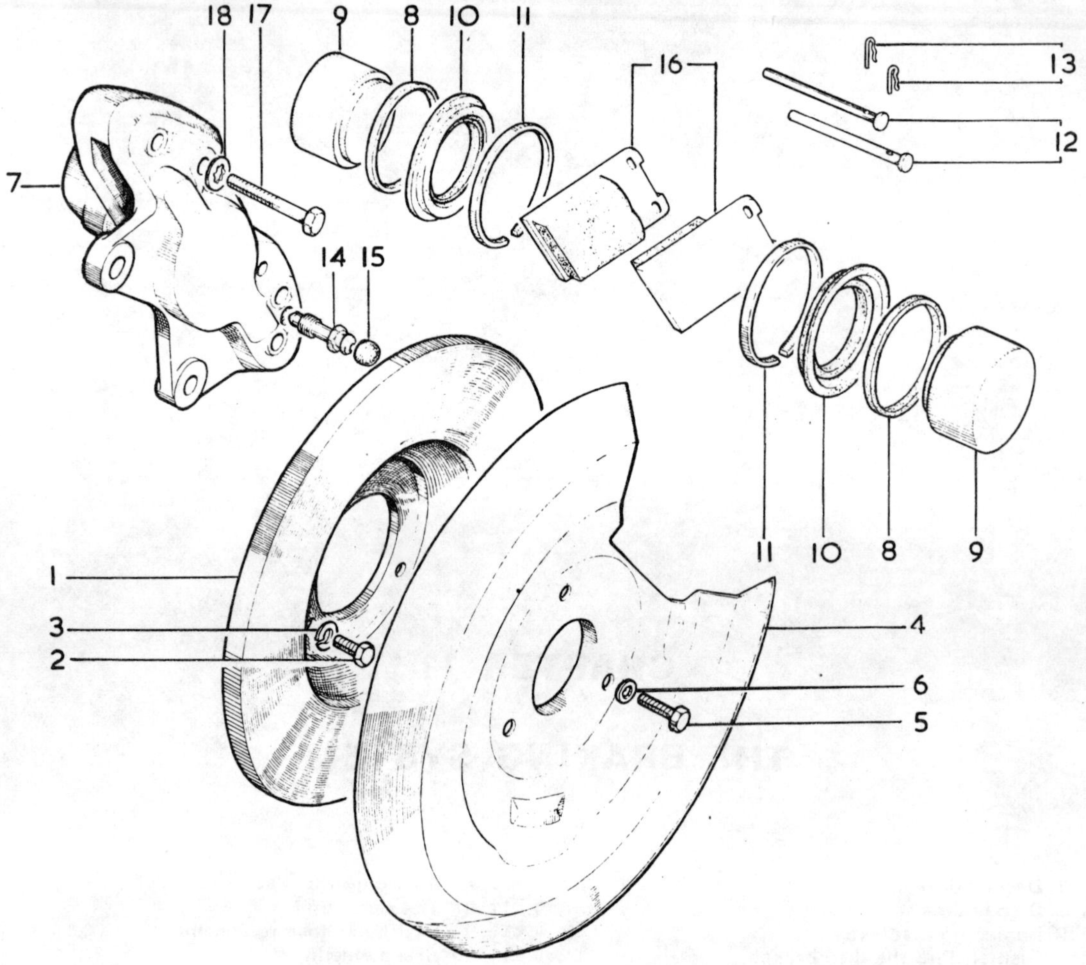

FIG 11:1 Exploded view of disc brake assembly

Key to Fig 11:1 1 Brake disc 2/3/5/6 Bolts and washers 4 Guard plate 7 Caliper body 8 Sealing ring 9 Piston 10 Rubber boot 11 Split ring 12 Pad retaining pins 13 Spring clips 14/15 Bleed screw and dust cover 16 Pads 17/18 Caliper body bolt and washer

fitted at the factory. Do not loosen or remove the bolts in any circumstances or the setting will be upset and only reassembly in the factory jig will restore the calipers to efficient operation.

Hydraulic pressure is applied to the rear of the two brake pads by the pistons 9, sliding in the opposing cylinders of the caliper assemblies being rendered fluid-tight by sealing rings 8, held within grooves in the cylinder walls, and dust-tight by the rubber boot 10 and split ring 11. The sealing ring serves as an adjuster being deformed on the braking stroke to a point at which the piston will slip within the ring. On the return stroke, the only recovery movement of the piston is that caused by the sealing ring returning to its original shape and this is sufficient to withdraw the pads clear of the brake discs. In this manner, the gradual wear of the brake pads is automatically taken up by the corresponding slip of the piston through the sealing ring at the end of each stroke making the brake self-adjusting (see **FIG 11:2**).

11:3 Replacing disc pads

Normally, the braking system will operate efficiently over many years of life with no more attention than the replacement of the disc pads when they have worn to a pad thickness, excluding the backing plate, of below $\frac{1}{8}$ inch. Renewal is quite simple comprising the raising of the car on stands and the extraction of the pads, after removal of the pins and clips, with a pair of thin-nosed pliers. Before inserting the replacements, which of course must be of the same pattern as those extracted, slacken the bleed screw and carefully push the pistons back into the cylinders to re-set them within the sealing ring. A small amount of fluid will escape and, when the pistons are fully back, tighten the bleed screws again.

The pistons should be pushed back with a thin strip of wood covered with a cloth to avoid scoring the surface in contact with the pad and, before inserting the new pads, the faces must be cleaned free from any dirt by rubbing across them with the cloth on the strip moistened with a little petrol.

After reinserting the new pads and replacing the pins and clips, pump the brake pedal a few times to reset the pistons in the seals and check for clearance between pads and disc by rotating the wheel with the brakes off. There should be no rubbing sound at any point. With the brakes partially applied by an assistant, check for the rubbing sound when the pads first contact the disc. An intermittent sound is an indication of disc wear causing runout and if this is excessive to the point at which, with a little more brake pressure, the pads hold at some points while being free at others, the disc will have to be removed and trued-up or replaced.

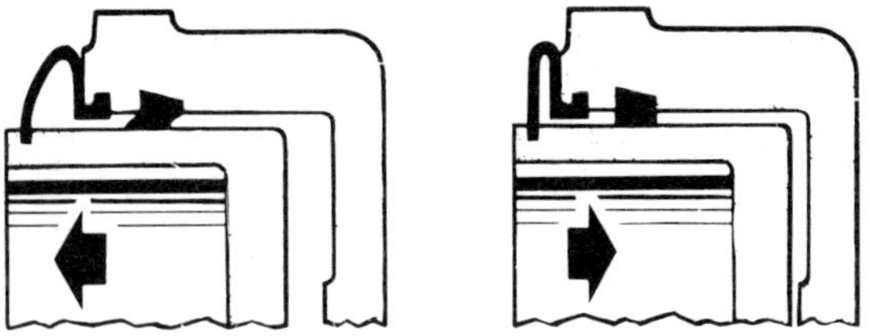

FIG 11 : 2 Diagram showing operation of sealing ring in adjusting for pad wear

After fitting new pads, take the car out and road test at the earliest possible moment, running it slowly for a short distance with the brakes partially applied to bed the pad surfaces in.

The correct replacement pads are faced with Mintex M108GH friction material and are obtainable from the Chrysler service station.

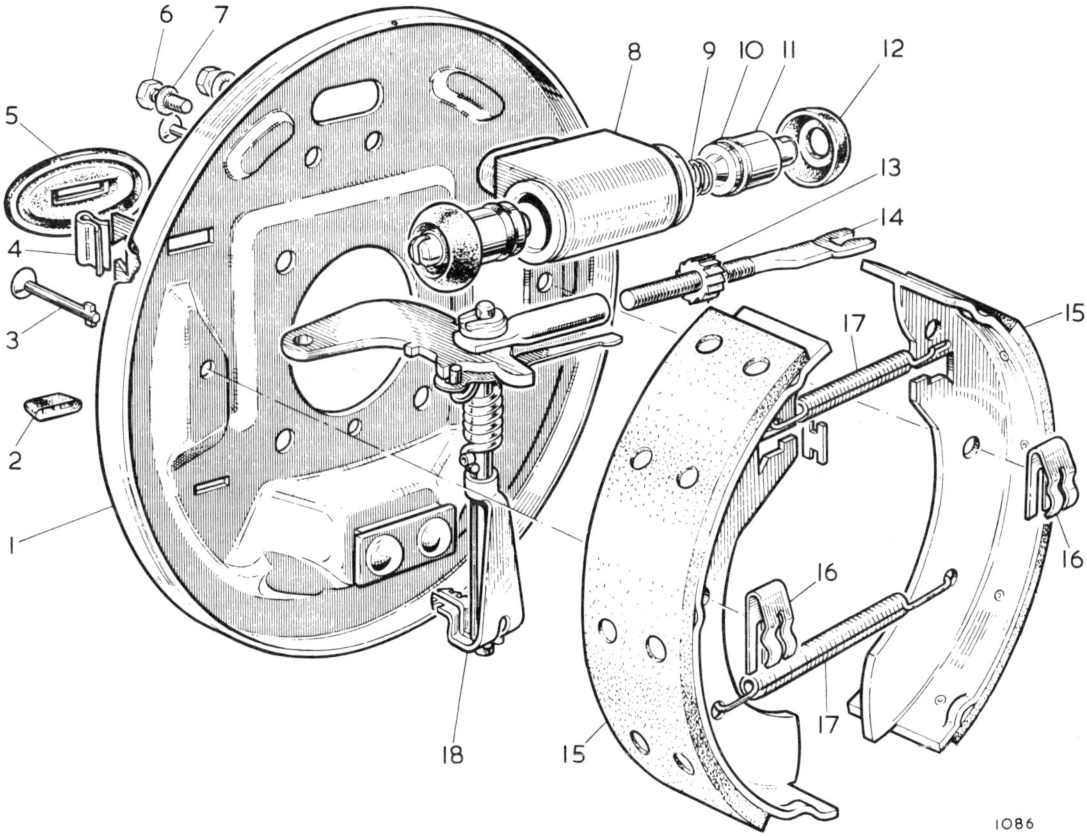

FIG 11 : 3 Exploded view of drum brake assembly

Key to Fig 11 : 3 1 Brake backplate 2 Dirt excluder 3 Hold down pin 4 Clip 5 Dust cover 6/7 Bolt and washer 8 Brake cylinder body 9 Piston return spring 10 Oil seal 11 Piston 12 Rubber boot 13 Ratchet nut 14 Threaded pushrod 15 Brake shoes 16 Hold down clip 17 Brake shoe return springs 18 Handbrake lever assembly

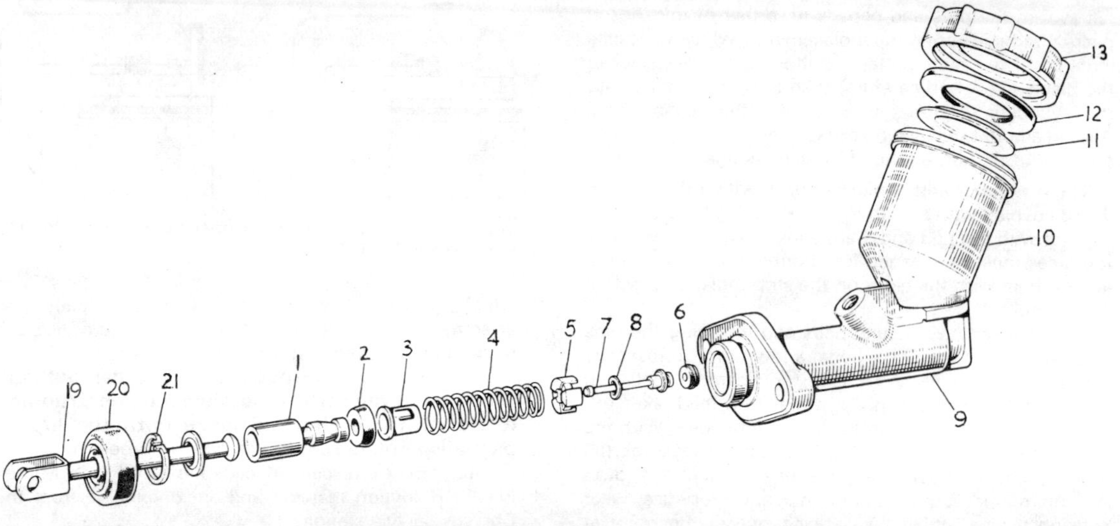

FIG 11:4 Exploded view of manual system master cylinder. For key to numbers, see Fig 11:5

11:4 Dismantling the disc brakes

With the car raised on stands and the brake pads removed, disconnect the hydraulic hoses from the rear of the brake calipers and cap to prevent loss of fluid from the lines. Unbolt the calipers from the backplate and transfer them to the bench for preliminary cleaning and dismantling. Check the condition of the brake discs, cleaning the surrounds, and examine for runout or grooving. Check, also, the state of the hydraulic hoses.

At the bench, after cleaning the caliper assembly externally, remove the bleed screw and drain any fluid from the cylinders. This may be accelerated by pushing the pistons back into the cylinders. Holding one piston back with a cloth pad, eject the second by applying an air line to the bleed screw orifice closing the inlet with a finger. Eject sufficiently to remove the dust cover, extract the cloth pad and hold the piston against re-entry while the second piston is ejected in the same way and the dust cover removed.

Carefully extract each piston, noting which cylinder it comes from so that it can be replaced in the same on on reassembly. From within the cylinders, carefully extract the sealing rings and discard. **Always renew the sealing rings at each major servicing.**

Wash all parts in fresh brake fluid, dry off and examine the bearing surfaces on piston, cylinder and piston faces for scoring or corrosion. If any are present, replace the complete caliper assembly. It is not advisable to refit a new piston into an existing caliper cylinder. **Do not use petrol or other hydrocarbon base fluid to clean the boot or seals as the material is badly affected by such fluids. Use only the approved Girling amber fluid.**

When all parts have passed inspection and new seals obtained, lightly smear the inner surfaces of the cylinders with brake fluid and carefully insert the new sealing rings in the grooves. Lubricate the pistons with fluid and carefully insert them in the cylinders and push back as far as possible. Replace the boots and clips and reinsert the bleed screw. Reinstall in position on the backplate, tightening the securing bolts to a torque of 60 lb ft, and reinsert the brake pads.

Recharge the calipers with brake fluid by pumping the brake pedal with the bleed screw slackened until fluid emerges and then tightening the bleed screw. Check the reservoir level on the master cylinder meanwhile and top-up as necessary.

After both front wheels have been serviced, carry out the bleeding operation as described in **Section 11:10** and road test.

11:5 Dismantling the drum brakes

An exploded view of the rear drum brakes is shown in **FIG 11:3.** Each brake incorporates a leading and trailing shoe both of which are applied by a single double acting cylinder. The lever-operated compensated handbrake linkage incorporates an adjusting device which maintains the brake shoes in correct adjustment in regard to the brake drum regardless of lining wear and this adjustment applies to both footbrake and handbrake application.

The brake shoe linings are secured to the shoes by rivets and, if these are allowed to become proud by wear of the lining material, Don 202GG, scoring of the internal drum surfaces will result.

Maintenance normally comprises the removal of the wheel and brake drum, the blowing out of any dust within the drum and on the shoes and backplate and examination for signs of oil, grease or fluid in the brake assembly. The dust is largely a powder resulting from the wear of the friction material and its presence in any quantity between the shoes surface and drum seriously affects brake performance, particularly when wet. Regular attention to this is, therefore, an important adjunct to safety on the road.

At the same time, an inspection of the condition of the brake cylinder boots, friction lining wear and the general condition of brake return springs, hydraulic hoses etc., can be carried out.

Remove the clips 16, and extract the hold-down pins 3, and lever the bottom web of the leading shoe away from and clear of the fixed abutment on the brake back plate against the pull of the lower return spring 17. Separate the trailing shoe from the handbrake lever mechanism and ease both shoes clear of the brake back plate. The nut and pushrod assembly 13 and 14, will be released at the same time. **Note carefully which is the leading and which is the trailing shoe and, if both brake drums are being serviced simultaneously, which shoes belong to which wheel.** Only if new shoes are being fitted is the precaution unnecessary, though leading and trailing shoes must still not be reversed, and it is always advisable to renew both sets of brake shoes at the same time. Though it is possible to reline old shoes, since factory lined shoes are always available from the stockists, it is not economic to attempt to reline shoes yourself.

Reassembly of the drum brakes is a simple reversal of the dismantling process and should present no difficulties.

11:6 Overhauling the brake cylinders

The brake cylinders are secured to the backplate by two bolts and lockwashers 6 and 7. To dismantle the brake cylinders, first, disconnect the hydraulic hose at the rear and cap to prevent loss of fluid. Remove the two bolts and transfer the cylinder assembly to the bench for servicing. Clean the exterior. **As with all hydraulic cylinder servicing, the surface of the bench should be scrupulously clean and covered, preferably, with a sheet of paper. In many cases, brake troubles have been traced to the presence of tiny particles which have been introduced during servicing under normal workshop conditions which are rarely clean enough for this operation.**

Remove the rubber boots 12, together with the pistons 11 and seals 10. From within the cylinder, extract the return spring 9. Wash all parts in clean brake fluid and examine for wear or scoring. If any is present on the pistons or cylinder, replace the complete assembly. Renew the oil seal and rubber boot at each servicing.

After cleaning and drying, using lint-free cloths for wiping, reassemble in the reverse order, lubricating the

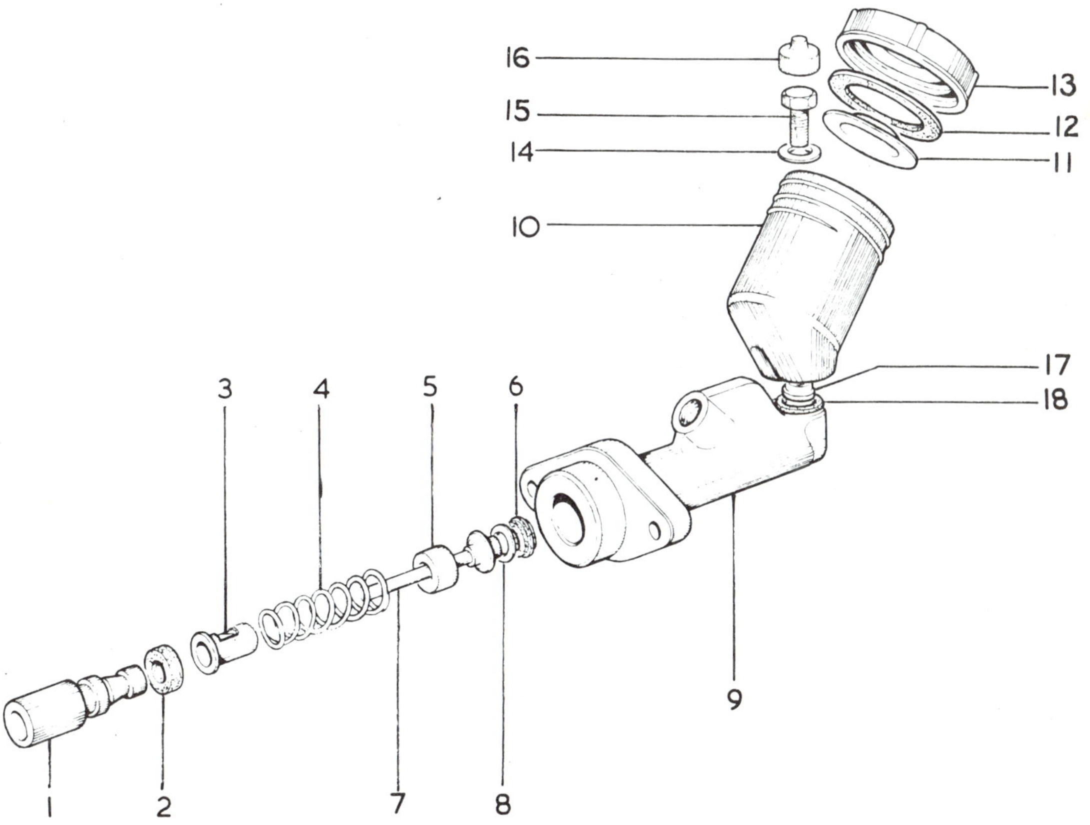

FIG 11:5 Exploded view of servo system master cylinder

Key to Figs 11:4 and 11:5 1 Piston 2 Piston seal 3 Retainer spring thimble 4 Return spring 5 Spacer 6 Seal 7 Valve stem 8 Circlip 9 Cylinder body 10 Fluid reservoir 11/12/13 Baffle, seal and cap 14/15/16 Bolt washer and baffle plate 17/18 Adapter and seal 19 Pushrod 20 Rubber boot 21 Circlip

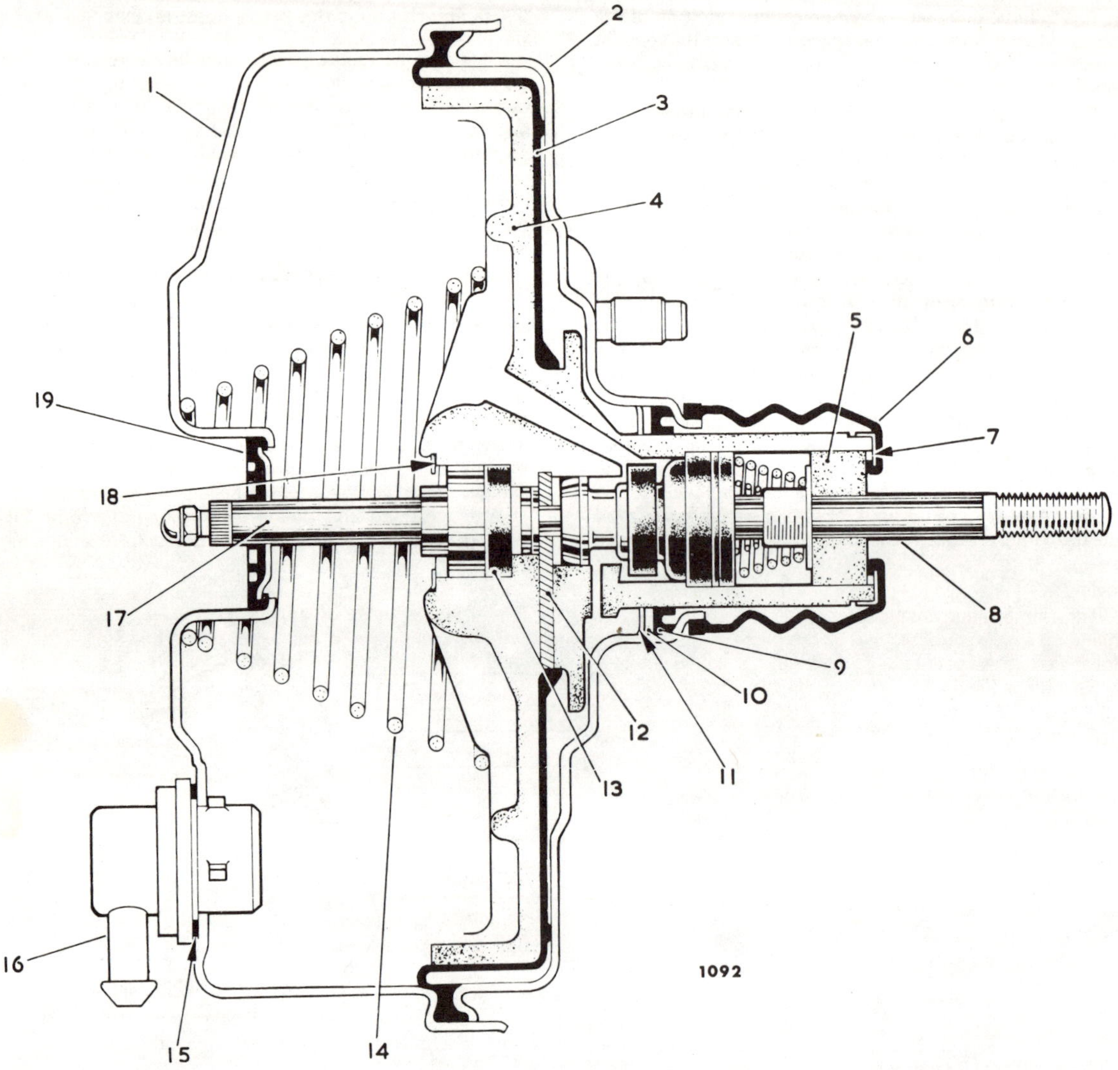

FIG 11:6 Diagrammatic section through vacuum servo unit to show principle of operation

Key to Fig 11:6 1 Front shell 2 Rear shell 3 Diaphragm 4 Diaphragm plate 5 Air filter 6 Dust cover 7 End cap 8 Operating rod assembly 9 Seal 10 Bearing 11 Retainer 12 Stop key 13 Reaction disc 14 Diaphragm return spring 15 O-ring 16 Non-return valve 17 Pushrod 18 Sprag washer 19 Seal and plate assembly

parts with brake fluid before assembly. Reinstall in the backplate securing the fixing bolts to a torque of 18 lb ft. Reconnect the hydraulic line and reinstall the brake shoes. The remainder of the operation is then as for shoe renewal already described, but bleed the brakes after completing.

11:7 Servicing the master cylinder

An exploded view of the master cylinder is shown in **FIG 11:4**. This is the normal pattern as fitted to manual braking installations but where servo braking is incorporated, a slightly modified pattern is used (see **FIG 11:5**). In each case the reservoir is part of the cylinder body assembly to which it is secured by a bolt 14, washer 15 and baffle plate 16.

The piston assembly in each case is similar being held together by a retainer spring thimble the tongue of which is lifted to enable it to be released from the piston 1 and seal 2. The outlet to the hydraulic lines and brake cylinders is via the screw socket on the body immediately to the rear of the reservoir the flange of the body being bolted to the bulkhead on the manual installation or to the servo unit on the servo installation. In the latter, the piston 1 butts directly on to the operating rod of the servo unit; in the former it is abutting the pushrod with clevis end for attachment to the pedal within the protective boot 20, on the end of the cylinder body secured by the washer and circlip 21, within the end of the cylinder.

To service the master cylinder, disconnect the hydraulic line from the outlet and drain the reservoir into a convenient receptacle. On the manual unit, remove the clevis pin securing the operating rod to the brake pedal and unbolt the master cylinder from the bulkhead. On the servo installation, unbolt the master cylinder from the servo unit and transfer to the bench.

At the bench, observing the usual precautions for cleanliness, withdraw the circlip on the manual unit and extract the operating rod and boot. From this point, servicing is identical for manual and servo unit cylinders. Ease the piston assembly out of the cylinder, separate the assembly by lifting the spring tongue on the retainer spring thimble and wash all parts in clean brake fluid. Examine for wear or damage and replace as necessary. Renew all seals and boots. Servicing kits for either type of master cylinder with all parts suitable for replacement are available from the Chrysler stockist. If other parts are damaged or unserviceable, replace the complete master cylinder.

Reassembly and installation is a reversal of the dismantling sequence observing all the precautions outlined for the brake cylinder servicing.

Bleed the brakes as described in **Section 11 : 10**.

11 : 8 The servo unit

The servo unit, where fitted, is the Girling Supervac operated by the depression in the engine induction manifold. It is shown in diagrammatic section in **FIG 11 : 6**. The unit comprises a large diameter piston in the form of a flexible diaphragm supported on a floating circular disc, the diaphragm being sealed at the outer edges between two hermetically sealed chambers. The foremost of these chambers is connected, via a pipe and non-return valve to the engine inlet manifold and is, therefore, always at a pressure lower than atmospheric, depending on the engine running conditions and the effect on inlet depression.

The rear half is open to atmosphere through a piston valve on the central operating rod which passes through the centre of the diaphragm where it is part of a transfer port-communicating between the two chambers. Movement of the rod in a forward direction closes the transfer port and in a rearwards direction closes the atmospheric port. An extension of the rod bears on the master cylinder piston as already described.

Movement of the operating rod is limited within the area of the diaphragm by a stop key which serves to transmit movement of the diaphragm piston outside these limits direct to the rod and, through it, to the piston of the master cylinder.

With the engine running, the differential pressure exerted by the two chambers on the piston is countered to some extent by the substantial diaphragm return spring. Providing that the operating rod is stationary, should the differential pressure overcome the force of the spring, the piston will move forward but, before it reaches the limits set by the stop key, the transfer port is opened and air passes into the forward chamber. This stabilizes the movement and no displacement of the master cylinder piston assembly results.

Forward movement of the control rod on applying the brakes, holds the transfer port closed and the atmospheric port open. The piston then moves forward, to the new position set by the brake pedal so amplifying the manually applied braking force to the extent of the differential pressure times the area of the piston. This is many times that of the normal manual braking effort which is relatively light for substantial braking effect.

On releasing the brake pedal, the operating rod moves to the rear, opening the transfer port and closing the atmospheric port. Pressure being equalized between the two chambers, the diaphragm return spring operates to make the diaphragm follow the control rod to a new position where the transfer port is once again closed. That is to say, in whichever direction the control rod moves under pedal pressure, the diaphragm follows faithfully, adding its effort to that of the piston on the forward stroke only. The whole of this effort is transmitted, via the control rod, to the piston of the master cylinder and, via the hydraulic lines, to the brake cylinders.

The servo unit rarely develops internal faults and needs little maintenance or servicing. Every 30,000 miles (48,000 km) or 30 months whichever is the sooner it will be necessary to renew the filter 5. Service kits are available comprising a dust cover 6, end cap 7, filter 5, a non-return valve 16 and O-ring 15, and a seal and plate assembly 19.

Renewing filter:

1 Uncouple the operating rod from the brake pedal by extracting the splitpin and clevis pin.

2 Unscrew the four securing nuts and washers from the mounting studs, disconnect the hydraulic pipe connections from the master cylinder and the vacuum pipe from the servo unit.

3 Withdraw the servo unit from the bulkhead complete with master cylinder. Note the position of the four tubular spacers behind the unit.

4 Pull back the dust cover 6, extract the end cap 7 and circlip, take out the filter.

5 Cut the new filter diagonally from the outer edge to the centre hole and press it into the neck of the diaphragm plate.

6 If necessary, renew the end cap and dust cover, refit the servo in the reverse order of removal.

7 Bleed the brakes as described in **Section 11 : 10**.

Renewing non-return valve:

1 Disconnect the vacuum pipe from the valve and note the position of the valve in the body so that the new one can be fitted in the same position.

2 Press down on the valve and with a spanner turn the valve anticlockwise about one third of a turn to release the retaining lugs.

3 Fit the new one with a new O-ring in the reverse order. Do not lubricate the seal.

4 A modified valve with a straight nozzle is incorporated on the later models which is not interchangeable. To remove the new type with the hose connected, exert a side load and pull the valve from the body. Lubricate the new grommet with M34 grease before pushing in the new valve.

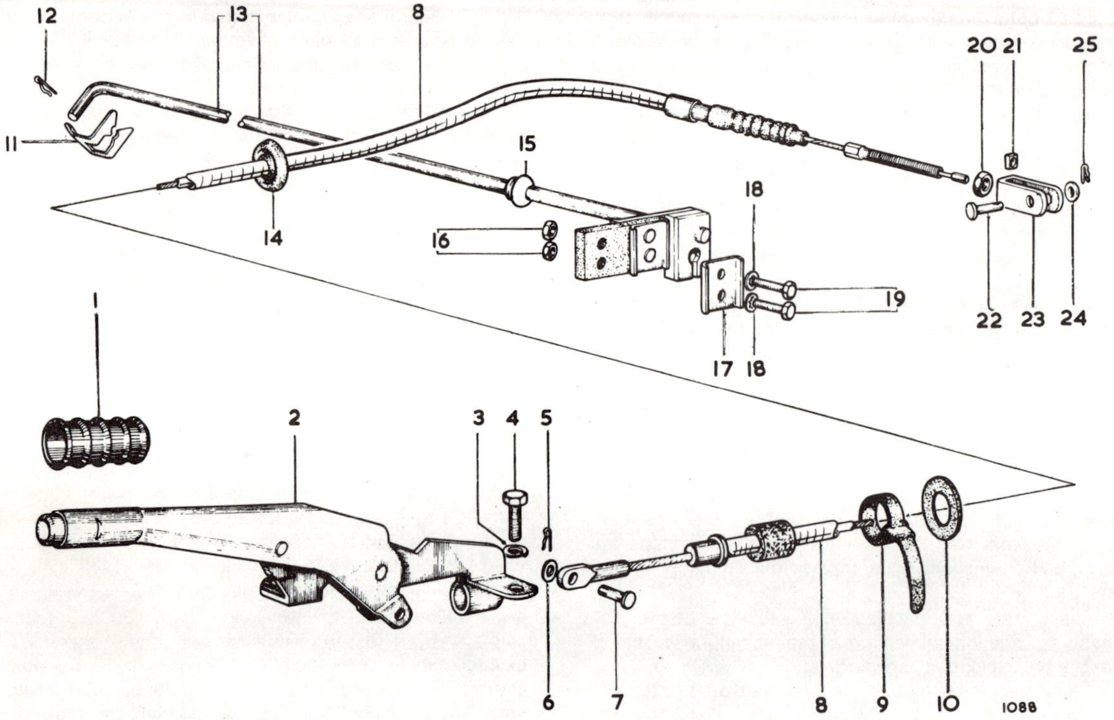

FIG 11 :7 Details of the handbrake cable and lever assembly

Key to Fig 11 :7 1 Grip 2 Lever 3 Washer 4 Setscrew 5 Splitpin 6 Washer 7 Pin 8 Cable 9 Strap 10 Washer 11 Clip 12 Splitpin 13 Rod 14 Grommet 15 Bearing 16 Nut 17 Stiffener 18 Washer 19 Setscrew 20 Locknut 21 Nut 22 Pin 23 Jaw 24 Washer 25 Splitpin

Renewing seal and plate assembly:

1 Complete operations 1 to 3 for renewing filter.
2 Remove the master cylinder.
3 Extract the seal and plate assembly 19 by gripping the centre rib with a pair of pointed nosed pliers.
4 Using the grease supplied in the kit, lubricate the new seal and press the assembly into the servo body.
5 Refit the master cylinder and replace the unit.
6 Bleed the brakes as described in **Section 11 :10**.

11 :9 Hydraulic hose replacement

While little deterioration in the hydraulic lines should be experienced over many years of service, the hose connections between the brake cylinders and the pipe terminations are subject to deterioration by the mud, dirt and oxidation effects of the car exhaust-contaminated atmosphere. It is, therefore, advisable to check these from time to time and replace wherever necessary. The procedure is straightforward and replacement connections are available, ready for installation, from most agents on demand.

When installing new hoses, always hold the end of the hose connector in a grip or spanner while tightening the union nut with another. A twisted hose wears rapidly and, if it does not hang naturally between the pipe and brake cylinder union, slacken the joint and readjust until it does.

11 :10 Brake bleeding

After any adjustment in the hydraulic system, if the fluid level in the reservoir has been allowed to fall to a low level or the braking feel becomes spongy, bleed the brake system to get rid of the air trapped in the hydraulic lines.

To bleed, remove the dust cap from one front brake and fit a short length of plastic tube to the nipple allowing the other end to rest below the surface of a quantity of brake fluid in a glass container. Slacken the bleed valve one turn and, with long steady strokes, operate the brake pedal until the fluid emerging into the container is free from bubbles. With the pedal held right down, tighten the bleed screw and repeat on the other front wheel. Carry out the same operation on the rear wheels. **As the operation is extracting fluid from the system, keep a sharp eye on the level of fluid in the reservoir and top up from time to time. If the level is allowed to fall below the outlet from the reservoir, air will again enter the system and the operation will have to be repeated.**

Fluid in the container may be returned to the storage can for further use but only after allowing it to stand until the entrapped air has been allowed to escape.

11:11 Handbrake adjustment

The handbrake operates on the rear wheels only, serving a dual purpose, primarily as a means of holding the car stationary and secondly as a brake adjuster for the hydraulically operated footbrake.

The application is carried out by the use of Bowden type cables and rod linkage, the inner and outer cables both having a function to perform. Referring to **FIG 11:7** the rear end of the inner cable is connected to an adjustable fork end but the outer casing terminutes at a flexibly mounted bracket on the rear axle casing. The handbrake lever is connected to the inner cable and the outer cable is held by a trunnion bush in the mounting bracket. When the handbrake is applied the lever attached to the inner cable fork end moves to operate the brake and the opposing tension on the outer cable operates the rod through the flexibly mounted bracket.

When adjusting the handbrake, check first that the operating levers are free and that the hydraulic pistons are not binding with the fork and clevis pin removed, apply the handbrake one tooth of the ratchet and adjust the lengths of the cable or rod connection so that the clevis pin can be inserted through the fork and lever without effort or pull on the lever.

11:12 Fault diagnosis

(a) Brakes 'grab'

1 Pads or linings of wrong grade
2 Pads or linings contaminated with lubricants
3 Brake drums worn
4 Servo unit not functioning properly

(b) Brakes holding on

1 Handbrake out of adjustment
2 Brake cylinders seized
3 Master cylinder bypass port blocked
4 Brake pedal return spring broken
5 Shoe return springs weak or broken
6 Obstructed hydraulic line

(c) Brake action spongy

1 Low fluid in reservoir
2 Air in hydraulic lines
The cure for sponginess is, of course, bleeding

(d) Footbrakes fail

1 Low fluid in reservoir
2 Broken hydraulic line
3 Faulty master cylinder seals

(e) Unbalanced braking

1 Unevenly worn tyres
2 Unbalanced tyre pressures
3 Obstructed hydraulic line

NOTES

CHAPTER 12

THE ELECTRICAL SYSTEM

12:1 Description

The electrical system is 12-volt with negative earth return. On some cars for the home market it is derived from a two-brush generator with voltage and current regulator and cut-out and a lead/acid battery. The nominal voltage is 12 but, with the engine running and the battery being charged from the generator, the voltage developed across the system is between 14.4 and 15.6. The maximum charging rate of the generator is 22 amps.

On cars for certain overseas markets, and highly tuned versions on the home market the supply is derived from a belt driven alternator with integral rectifiers and a regulator. That is to say, the alternator is, in reality, a DC generator in which the conventional practice of a rotating field with a stationary armature, or stator, common to AC generators has been adopted with silicon rectifiers taking the place of the commutator and brush rectification in the conventional DC generator. This type of generator is self-regulating over a range of 0 to 34 amps while the rectifiers, being uni-directional to current, also serve as the cut-out when the generator is not running. Voltage regulation is by a built in regulator incorporating transistors.

The micro-circuit regulator makes it of the greatest importance not to reverse polarity at any point on the system or the transistors will be destroyed. Always disconnect the battery negative connections before attempting any change of alternator connection and scrupulously observe the precautions in heavy print at the end of Section 12:3.

12:2 The battery

The battery is a six-cell lead/acid type with a capacity of 33 or 40 amp/hr at the 20 hour discharge rate. The battery normally fitted is the Lucas D7, capacity 33 amp/hr. On cars with automatic transmission a larger battery,

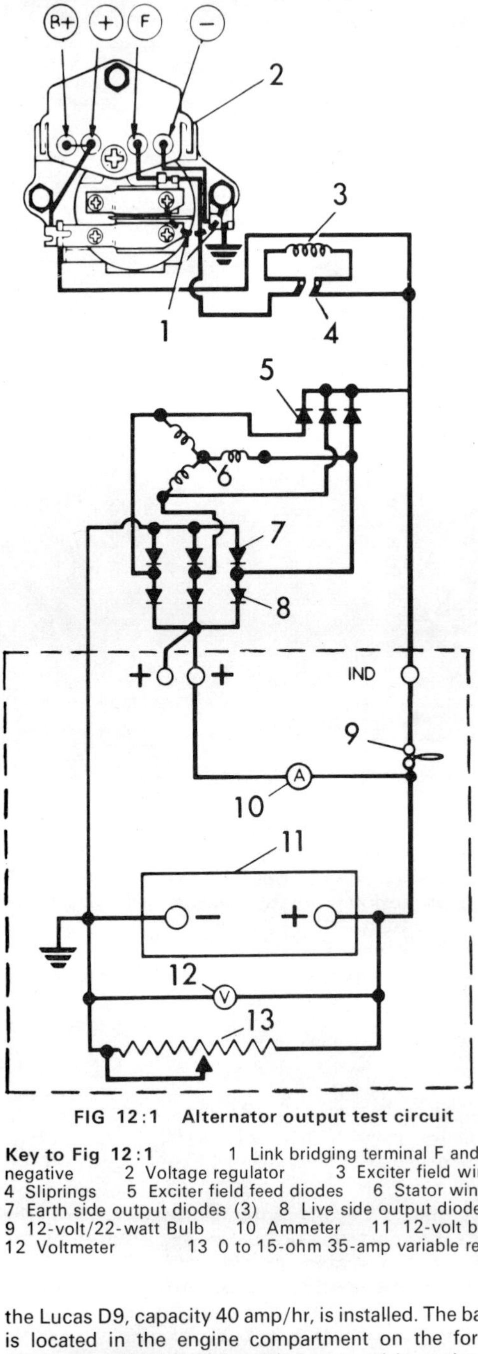

FIG 12:1 Alternator output test circuit

Key to Fig 12:1 1 Link bridging terminal F and (—) negative 2 Voltage regulator 3 Exciter field winding 4 Sliprings 5 Exciter field feed diodes 6 Stator windings 7 Earth side output diodes (3) 8 Live side output diodes (3) 9 12-volt/22-watt Bulb 10 Ammeter 11 12-volt battery 12 Voltmeter 13 0 to 15-ohm 35-amp variable resistor

the Lucas D9, capacity 40 amp/hr, is installed. The battery is located in the engine compartment on the forward righthand side viewed from the rear and is retained on the steel platform by stay bolts and a metal strap.

Maintenance is confined to a periodical check of electrolyte level and topping up with distilled water as necessary. A battery in good condition should have all the cells with the same specific gravity, ranging from 1.27 to 1.29 at full charge falling to 1.11 to 1.13 when discharged. Inability of the battery to deliver heavy starting currents though giving sufficient for other purposes may be due to one faulty cell. The usual method of checking this is by measuring the volts across each cell with a heavy discharge device. **This practice is unsuitable for the Lucas D-type batteries and the only way to check without harming the battery is to test the specific gravity of each cell with a hydrometer, a faulty one being indicated by a lower than average specific gravity.**

12:3 The alternator and regulator

The alternator fitted is the Lucas 16ACR with a built-in voltage regulator. This is a lightweight machine designed for negative earth electrical systems, and comprises a 3-phase star connected stator with a wound rotating field, excitation of the field being from the rectified output of the stator when running and from the battery at starting. Field rectification is half wave, provided from three diodes, and the main current output is rectified by a group of six silicon diodes arranged to give full wave rectification.

The alternator is belt driven from the crankshaft pulley and belt tension must be checked periodically to ensure that the full output is available.

The voltage regulator is of micro-circuit construction specifically designed for operation with the 16ACR alternator and it is set to maintain voltage regulation between 14.1 and 14.5 volts by the makers. The reverse characteristics of the diodes in the alternator make a separate cut-out unnecessary.

An exploded view of the alternator is shown in **FIG FIG 12:2** and the external connections in **FIG 12:1**. Disconnection and dismantling is easy, but unless a full knowledge of the charging circuit and the limitations of diodes and transistors is appreciated—that is, the owner-driver has some knowledge of electronics and electronic equipment—no attempt at servicing should be made. The following precautions must always be observed:

1 **Connections must be made right the first time. Trial and error methods will result in disaster.**
2 **Battery and circuit cables must not be connected or disconnected while the alternator is running.**
3 **The battery earth cable must be disconnected before attempting to remove or install the alternator.**
4 **The alternator must not be run without a load across the output if the field is energized.**
5 **The engine and alternator must never be started with a battery charger or booster still connected.**
6 **Only a moments connection with reverse polarity is sufficient to destroy the diodes. Check carefully that the cables are the right way round before coupling up the battery or starting up the engine.**
7 **If a booster battery is connected in to assist in turning the starter it must be connected in parallel: positive to positive and negative to negative using correct heavy duty cables.**
8 **If arc welding equipment is used on the vehicle the connector must be removed from the alternator and the +ve terminal of the battery disconnected.**

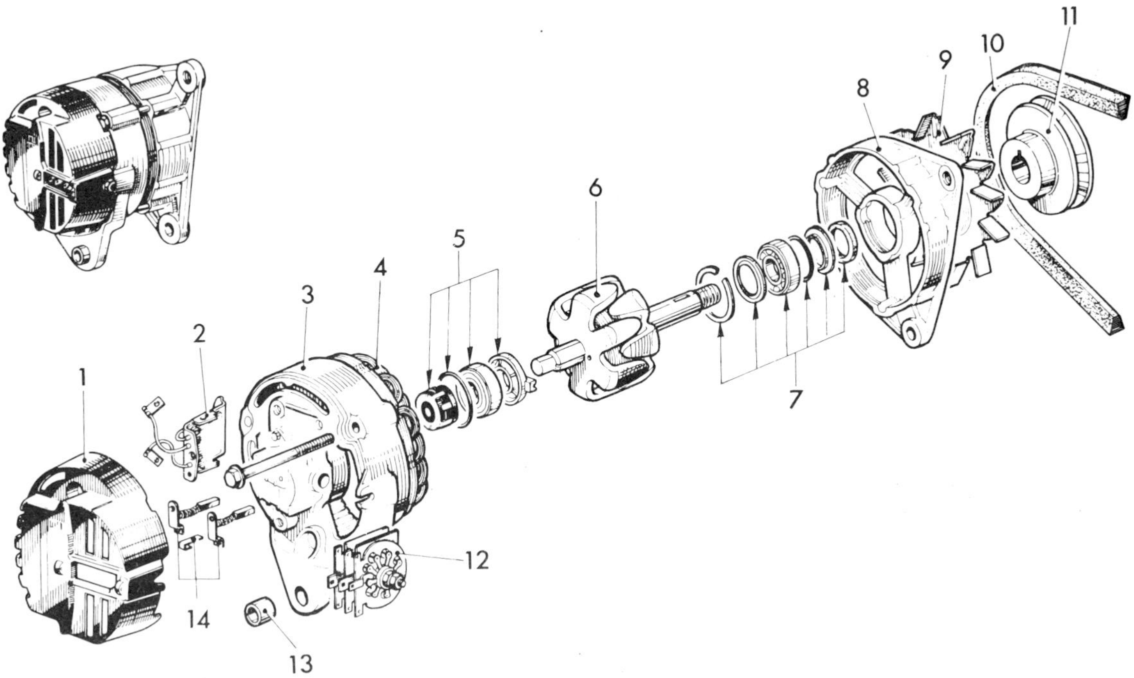

FIG 12:2 Components of 16ACR alternator

Key to Fig 12:2 1 Cover 2 Regulator and heat sink 3 Slipring end bracket 4 Stator 5 Slipring end bearing set 6 Rotor and field winding assembly 7 Drive end bearing set 8 Drive end bracket 9 Fan 10 Driving belt 11 Pulley 12 Rectifier 13 Bush 14 Brush set

12:4 Checking alternator output

1 To check the alternator without removing it from the car, first examine the driving belt for tension and condition. To avoid misleading results the test procedures must be carried out with the alternator as near as possible to its normal working temperature.

Alternator output with regulator inoperative:

2 Uncouple the alternator harness connector, take out two screws and withdraw the moulded cover.
3 Refer to **FIG 12:1** and link together the regulator terminal 'F' and the (—) negative terminal.
4 Connect an external test circuit as illustrated within the broken-lined square and take great care not to reverse connections of polarity. The variable resistor 13 must not be left connected longer than necessary to carry out the test.
5 Start the engine and run it at 800 rev/min (1500 rev/min: alternator), the test circuit bulb should now be extinguished.
6 Increase engine speed to 3200 rev/min (6000 rev/min: alternator), adjust the variable resistance until the voltmeter reads 14 volts. The ammeter reading should be approximately equal to the rated output (34 amps: hot).
7 Any appreciable deviation from these readings will prove the unserviceability of the alternator and it should be removed for further examination, preferably by a Lucas service agency as failure of one or more of the diodes is a probable cause. In some instances a defect such as this will be synonomous with alternator high temperature and noise level.

Regulator test:

8 Assuming the previous test was satisfactory continue with a regulator test.
9 Disconnect the variable resistor 13 and remove the bridge link between terminal F and (—) negative. Leave the rest of the test circuit as it is.
10 Start the engine and run it at 3200 rev/min (6000 rev/min: alternator) until the ammeter reads an approximate 10 amps (on the minus side). The voltmeter should be showing a reading between 14 and 14.4 volts. Any appreciable deviation will mean the regulator is not functioning correctly.

Charging circuit test:

11 If the foregoing tests are satisfactory continue by completely disconnecting the test circuit and replacing the harness connector.
12 Connect a low-range voltmeter between the positive terminals of the battery and the alternator. Switch on the headlights and run the engine to 3200 rev/min. Make a note of the voltmeter reading.
13 Now connect the voltmeter to the negative battery terminal and to the frame of the alternator. Again, make a note of the voltmeter reading.

FIG 12:3 Position of the oil lubrication hole in the generator end plate

14 If the reading exceeds .50 volt on the positive side OR exceeds .25 volt on the negative side there is a high resistance in the charging circuit which must be traced and rectified.

12:5 Removing alternator

1 Release the radiator filler cap to depressurize the system. This is to prevent a water leak when the timing cover strap bolt is released.
2 Release the tension on the drive belt and remove the belt.
3 Take off the nuts, washers and bolts securing the alternator and take care not to lose the distance bush from the slip ring end bracket. Lift the alternator away.

Dismantling:

Dismantling the alternator is not recommended, the unit is so sensitive that serious damage can be caused without the operator realizing it, particularly when unsoldering and resoldering the diode pins to the stator cables. Either get the alternator tested at a Lucas service depot or renew it through the Chrysler service stores on an exchange basis.

12:6 Generator

The generator is a shunt wound, two pole machine, Lucas type C.40. It is mounted on a bracket to the left of the engine and is V-belt driven from the crankshaft with the fan. Armature speed is 1.5 times the crankshaft speed though, with automatic transmission, this is increased to 1.8 times crankshaft speed to compensate for the lower average engine speeds achieved.

The only maintenance required is to check the belt tension at regular intervals and to inject a few drops of Shell X100.30 engine oil into the hole marked OIL in the end of the commutator housing once every 6 months or at 6000 mile intervals. This oil will be absorbed by the felt ring within (see **FIG 12:3**). Brushgear and commutator will not need attention until the routine overhaul at 30,000 miles or after three years in service.

To remove the generator from the engine compartment, first disconnect the battery earth, then pull off the clip connections to the generator terminals D and F. Note which lead goes to each terminal. Slacken the three securing bolts and tilt the generator towards the engine, then remove the fan belt. Loosen the securing bolts and detach the generator.

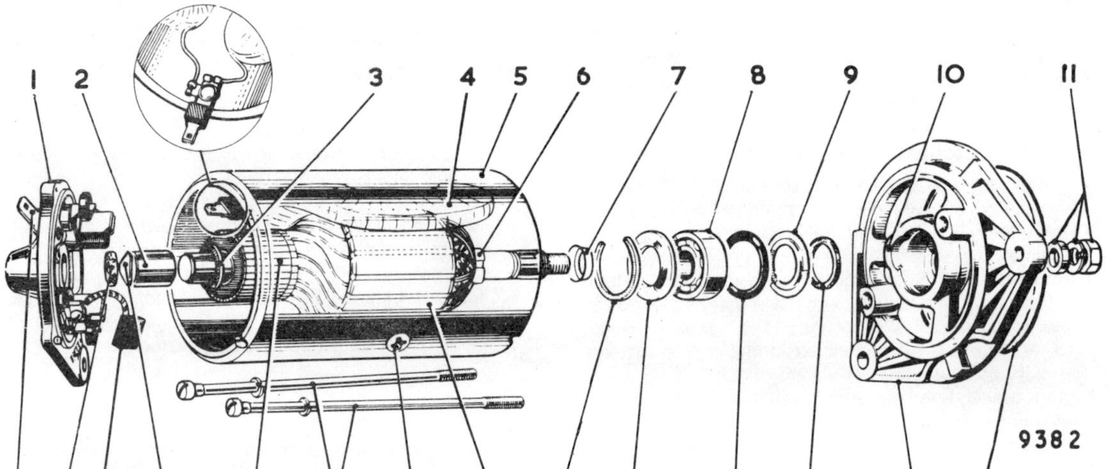

FIG 12:4 Exploded view of generator, type C.40L

Key to Fig 12:4 1 Commutator end bracket 2 Bearing bush 3 Washer 4 Field winding 5 Yoke 6 Shaft 7 Retaining cup 8 Drive end bearing 9 Pressure ring plate 10 Extractor notch 11 Nut and washers 12 Terminal 13 Felt ring 14 Carbon brush 15 Felt ring retainer 16 Commutator 17 Through-bolts 18 Pole shoe screw 19 Armature 20 Circlip 21 Bearing retainer plate 22 Pressure ring 23 Felt ring 24 Drive end bracket 25 Pulley

The alternative generator for use with the 40 amp/hr battery is the Lucas C.40L. Externally, this is identical in appearance with the C.40, the differences being in the winding specifications.

12:7 Generator overhaul

To dismantle at the bench, remove the pulley and shaft key, then unscrew and withdraw the through-bolts 17 (see **FIG 12:4**). Raise the brushes free of the commutator and support in the brushboxes by allowing the spring to bear on the sides of the brush (see **FIG 12:5A**). Withdraw the commutator end bracket 1 (see **FIG 12:4**) from the yoke 5, then extract the drive end bracket 24, from the opposite end, complete with armature and bearing assembly.

Unless the bearing 8 has failed, no further dismantling of the assembly is necessary. However, examine the state of the commutator periphery and field polepieces for signs of rubbing, usually indicative of bearing failure at one end or the other. If such wear is present, examine the state of the bronze bush at the commutator end 2 and, if this appears to be in good order, push out the armature from the bearing inner ring and remove the retaining plate 21. This releases the bearing from the end bracket housing. (On the C.40L this may be secured by a circlip.)

Brush the interior free from dirt and carbon deposits and remove any traces of oil or grease that may be present Clean the surface of the commutator with a petrol-damp rag and examine it for condition and colour. It should be smooth, free from ridging and of a dark brown colour. Should the edges of any of the bars show signs of burning, an open circuit in the winding or at the soldered junction to the bar is indicated. Check with a continuity tester between adjacent bars around the periphery and note if there is any change in the note from the buzzer or even a complete break of sound. The latter is an indication of a faulty joint at the commutator bar; the former usually an indication of a break in one of the windings.

If the commutator surface is slightly ridged but the armature is otherwise satisfactory, the surface may be cleaned by applying the finest grade glasspaper (not emerypaper) to it while being rotated in the chuck of a drill, finishing off with blue-black paper to give a smooth finish. Wipe clean with a petrol-damp rag.

Winding faults in an armature cannot be rectified by the average owner/mechanic. The only thing to do is to return the generator to the manufacture in exchange for a new or reconditioned one.

Remove the brushes from the brushboxes, clean the boxes and check that the springs are in good condition. If the brushes are badly ridged, or the length has been reduced to around $\frac{1}{4}$ inch, replace by the special grade carbon (H100) type specified for the C.40 generators. This grade is marked on the side of the brush. **Ordinary grade B brushes are not suitable.**

Reassemble the brushes in the holders and secure in the raised position as before. Reassemble the generator and fit and secure the through-bolts. Check that there is no end-play in the armature and that it revolves freely in the bearings. During assembly, repack the ballbearing with suitable grease and, should the bronze bush need replacement, extract the old one and install a new. The bush should be allowed to stand in engine oil, completely immersed, for 24 hours before installation to allow the

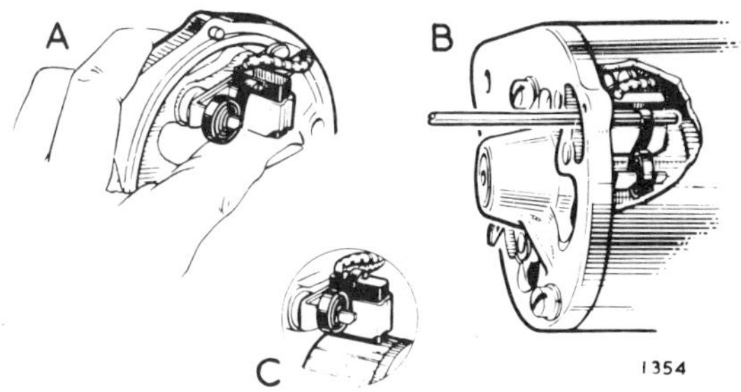

FIG 12:5 Details of brushgear on the C.40 and C.40L generator

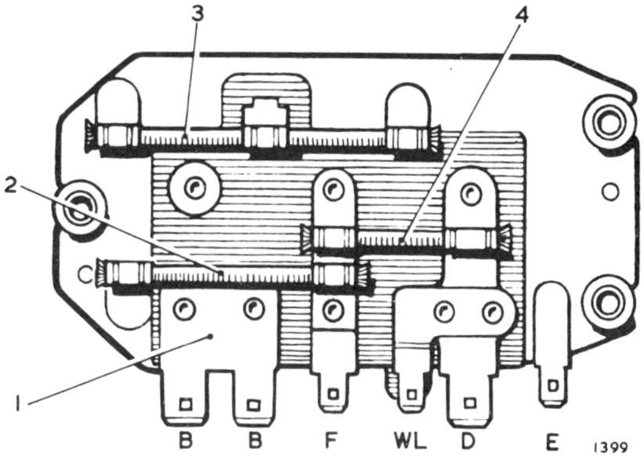

1 TERMINAL PLATE B-B
2 FIELD PARALLEL RESISTOR (WHEN FITTED)
3 SWAMP RESISTOR
4 FIELD SERIES RESISTOR

FIG 12:6 Underside of regulator showing the marked terminal tags and position of resistors

pores to absorb the right amount of lubricant. **The inner bore of the bush must not be reamed or scored as this will impair its porosity.** When fitting, use a mandrel with a highly polished pilot end for pressing the bush into place in the housing.

With the generator assembled, the final stage is to lower the brushes on to the commutator and to reinstall the pulley and key. The unit is then ready for reinstallation on the engine.

No instruction for skimming the commutator has been given. Though it is possible to re-skim the commutator, experience shows that where such work is necessary, it is better to leave it to the makers and to refit a new generator.

On a new generator, the residual field necessary for the generation of the first flow of current through the shunt field coils may be of the wrong polarity. In these circumstances the generated voltage will build up in the reverse direction. It is this characteristic which enables the same generator to be installed on positive or negative earth installations. Initial polarization is, therefore, essential. This is effected by leaving the D and F connections loose while the engine is run up to speed. Then, with a length of wire connected at one end to the live (positive) terminal of the battery, flick the F terminal with the other end a few times to polarize the field. The engine can then

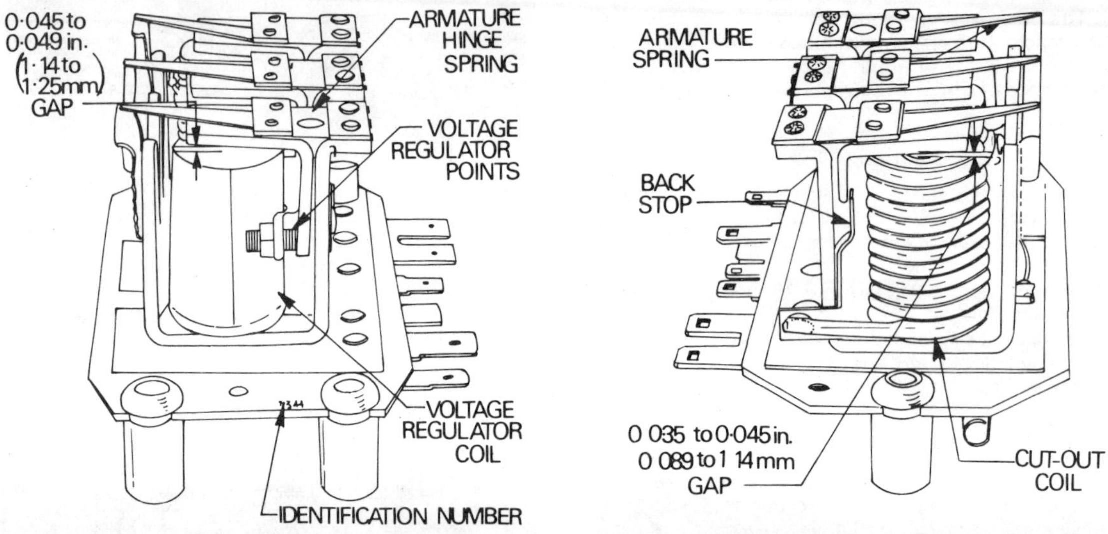

FIG 12:7 Views of the voltage and current regulator with cover removed. The cut-out element is on the right and the dimensions are as set by the manufacturer

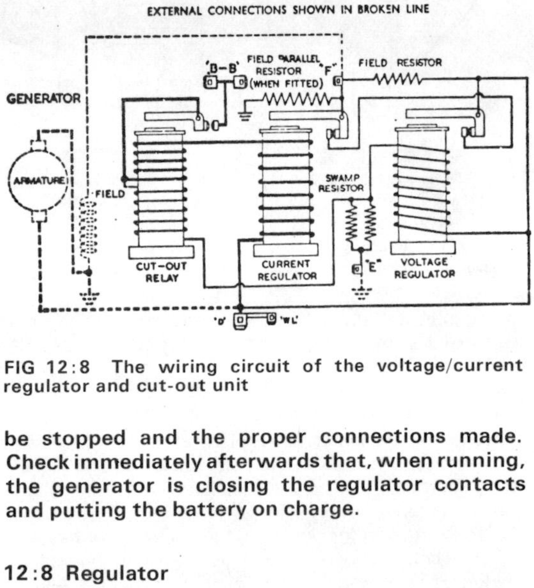

FIG 12:8 The wiring circuit of the voltage/current regulator and cut-out unit

be stopped and the proper connections made. Check immediately afterwards that, when running, the generator is closing the regulator contacts and putting the battery on charge.

12:8 Regulator

The regulator is supplied as a sealed unit ready set to suit the combination of generator and battery. The seals must not be broken during the warranty period and, should trouble be experienced later, it is better to fit a replacement unit rather than to attempt to readjust the regulator yourself. Where replacement is necessary, check that the number on the base of the new unit is identical with that on the old one.

With the cover removed, the three regulators are exposed to view (see **FIG 12:7**). The terminal tags are marked E, D, WL, F and B. WL is a cut-in voltage test point and is not used as an installation connection. The cable colours for the corresponding terminals are black to E (earth), brown and yellow to D (generator positive), brown and green to F (generator field) and brown to B (output). Viewed from the terminal side, the coil to the right is the cut-out, that to the left is the voltage regulator and the centre unit is the current regulator. The internal connections are shown in **FIG 12:8**.

The contacts of the current and voltage regulators are connected in series with the generator field winding and serve to open a shortcircuiting path across the series resistor which forms the solid link in the field winding circuit. With both contacts closed, the full armature voltage is applied across the shunt winding and maximum excitation results. With either contact open, the extra resistance is inserted in the field circuit and excitation is reduced.

In each case the change in output voltage is reflected back to the voltage regulator winding, the armature of which rises and falls cyclically so that the effective excitation current is something between full and that possible with the resistor in circuit. That is to say, the excitation at any instant is related to the proportion of a cycle during which the contacts are closed and this varies with load.

Control of the system is, therefore, effected by the voltage regulator on normal or no-load and by the current regulator on overload. Under fault conditions, the current regulator armature is held over for as long as the fault persists, keeping the voltage down and limiting the current to a safe value.

Initially, the contacts of the third element, the cut-out, are open, isolating the generator from the battery, external appliances and instruments. When the generator is running, the voltage applied to the current and potential windings rises until, at a voltage slightly above system volts, the pull on the armature is sufficient to overcome that of the hold-off spring and the contacts close, putting the generator on line.

When the speed of the generator falls, the voltage also falls to a point at which the regulators become inoperative and the pull of the potential winding on the cut-out is reduced. When it falls below system nominal volts, the

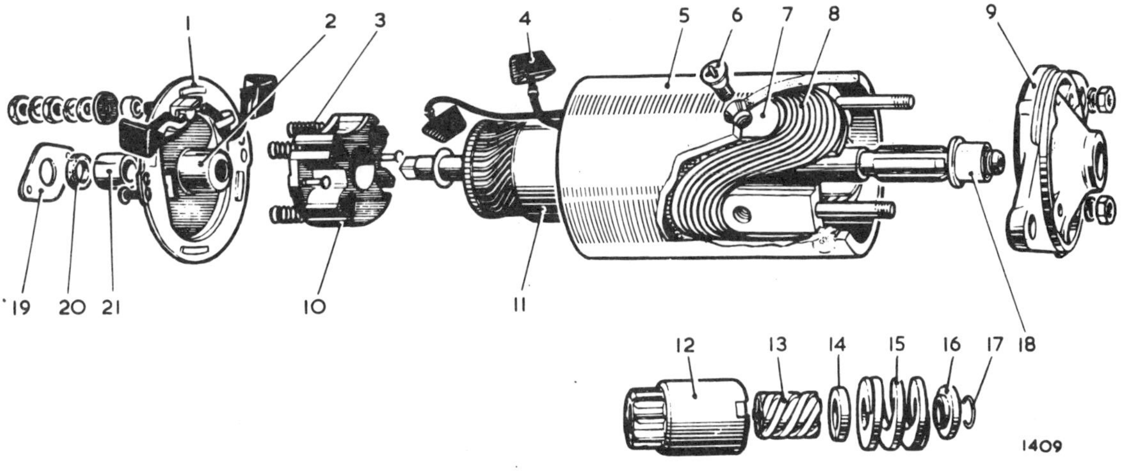

FIG 12:9 Exploded view of inertia type starter motor

Key to Fig 12:9 1 Commutator end bracket 2/3 Brush housing and springs 4 Brushes 5 Yoke 6 Pole screw 7 Pole shoe 8 Field coils 9 Drive end bracket 10 Brush box 11 Armature 12 Bendix pinion 13 Four-start sleeve 14 Buffer washer 15 Main spring 16 Cup spring 17 Circlip 18 Bush 19 Bush cover 20 Felt washer 21 Bush

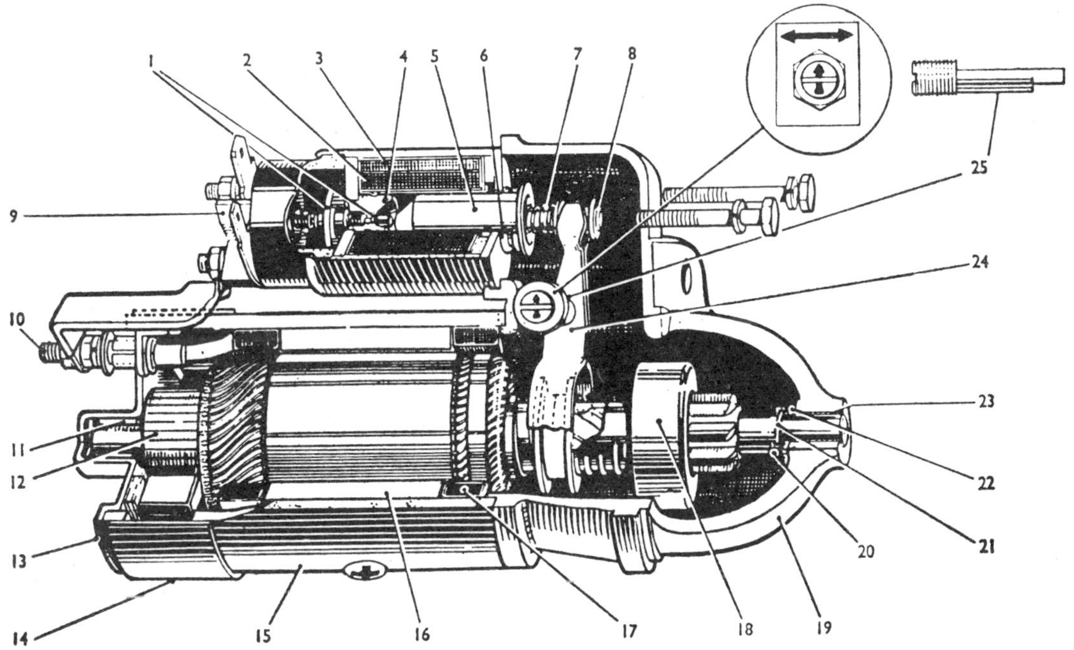

FIG 12:10 Section through pre-engaged starter

Key to Fig 12:10 1 Contact shaft 2/3 Solenoid windings 4 Armature 5 Plunger 6 Plunger return spring 7/8 Spring and collar 9 Solenoid housing 10 Heavy current terminal 11 Bush 12 Commutator 13 End cap 14 Commutator cover 15 Body 16 Polepieces 17 Field coils 18 Roller clutch 19 Drive end housing 20 Thrust collar 21/22/23 Ring, collar and bush 24 Engagement lever 25 Pivot pin

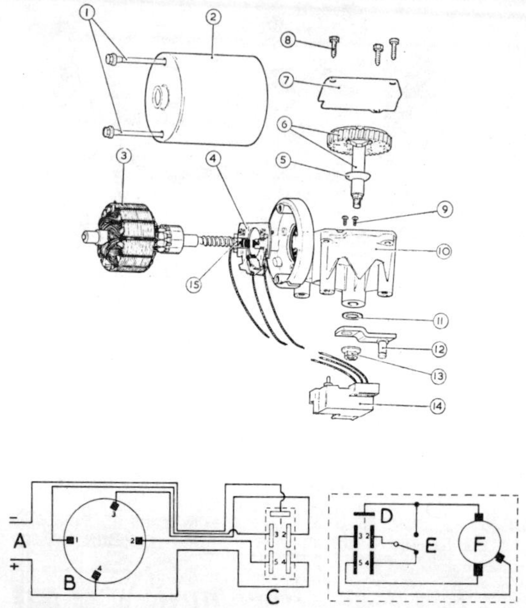

FIG 12:11 Exploded view of windscreen wiper with, below, the control circuit

Key to Fig 12:11 1 Through-bolts 2 Body 3 Armature 4 Brush holders 5/6 Washer, shaft and gear 7 Coverplate 8 Screws 9 Limit switch screws 10 Gear body 11/12/13 Crank assembly 14 Limit switch and connector socket **A** Battery input **B** Twospeed switch **C** Connector plug **D** Connector socket **E** Limit switch **F** Motor armature

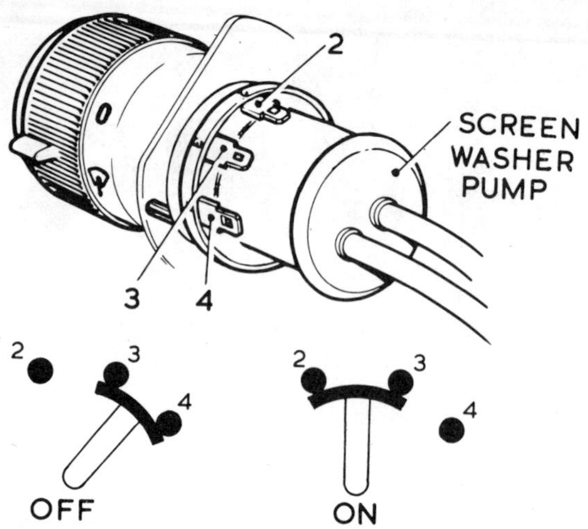

FIG 12:13 Screen washer pump and contact positions

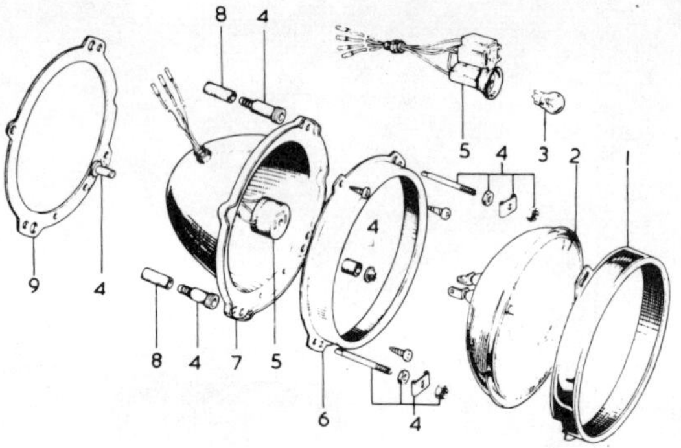

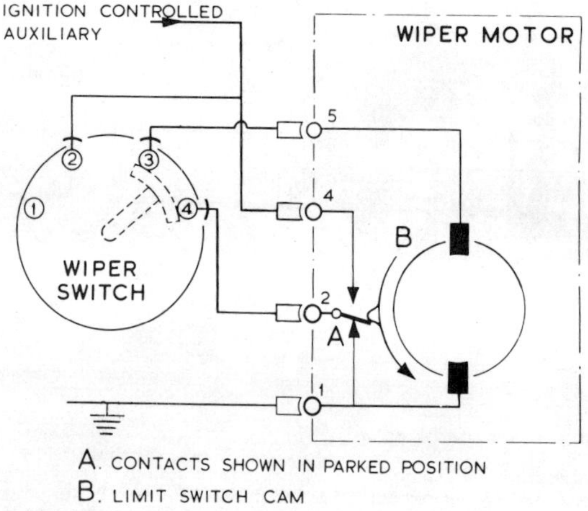

FIG 12:12 Wiring diagram for single speed wiper

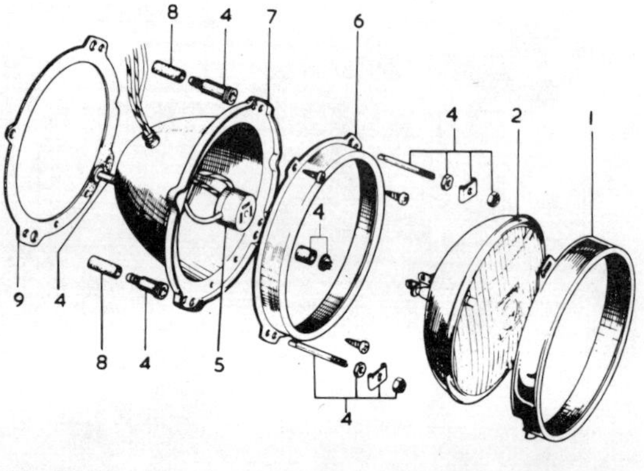

FIG 12:14 Circular headlamp (twin set) equipped with sealed beams

Key to Fig 12:14 1 Rim 2 Light unit 3 Pilot (side) bulb 4 Beam alignment set 5 Adaptor 6 Inner rim 7 Body 8 Sealing sleeve 9 Gasket

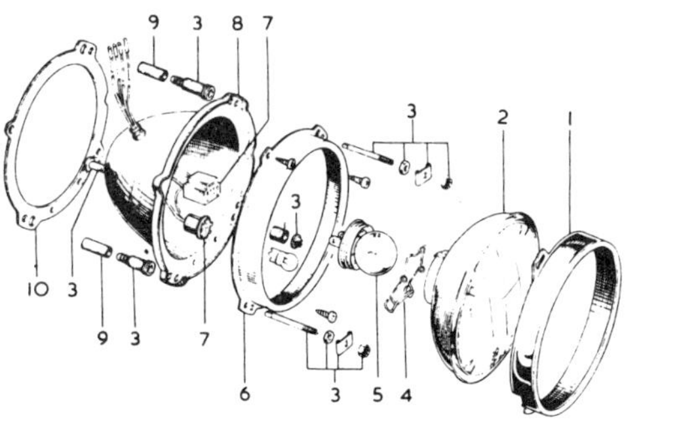

FIG 12:15 Circular headlamp (twin set), detachable bulb type

Key to Fig 12:15 1 Rim 2 Light unit 3 Beam alignment set 4 Spring to retain bulb 5 Bulb 6 Inner rim 7 Adaptor 8 Body 9 Sealing sleeve 10 Gasket

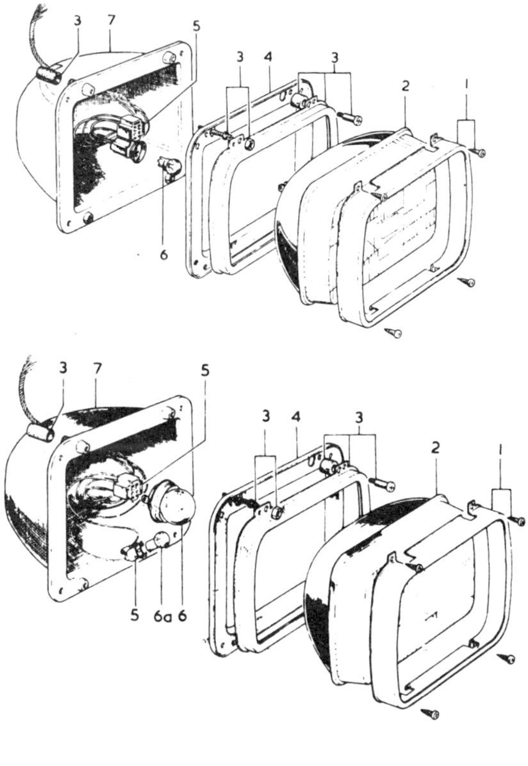

FIG 12:16 Rectangular headlamp (single). Sealed beam and detachable bulb type

Key to Fig 12:16 1 Rim 2 Light unit 3 Rim (unit assembly and alignment) 4 Mounting plate 5 Adaptor 6 Bulb 6a Pilot (side) bulb 7 Body

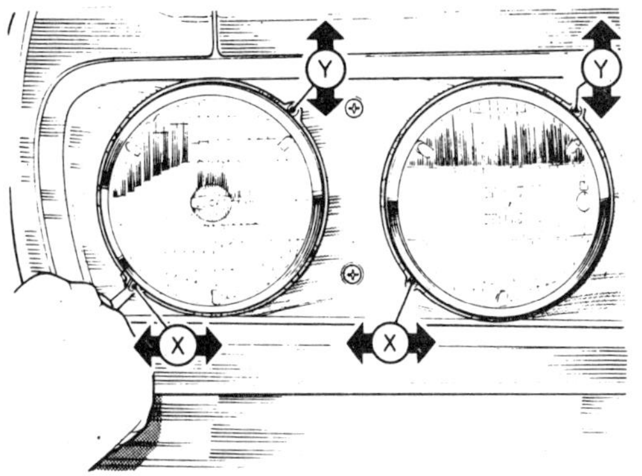

'X' – HORIZONTAL ADJUSTMENT SCREW
'Y' – VERTICAL ADJUSTMENT SCREW

FIG 12:17 Twin beam alignment screws

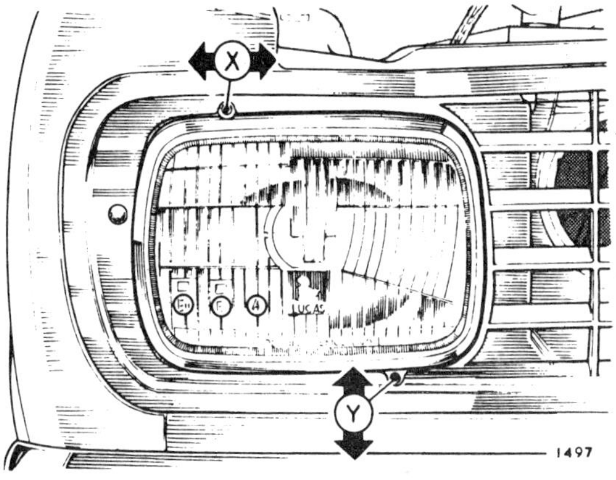

'X' – HORIZONTAL ADJUSTMENT SCREW
'Y' – VERTICAL ADJUSTMENT SCREW

FIG 12:18 Rectangular type alignment screws

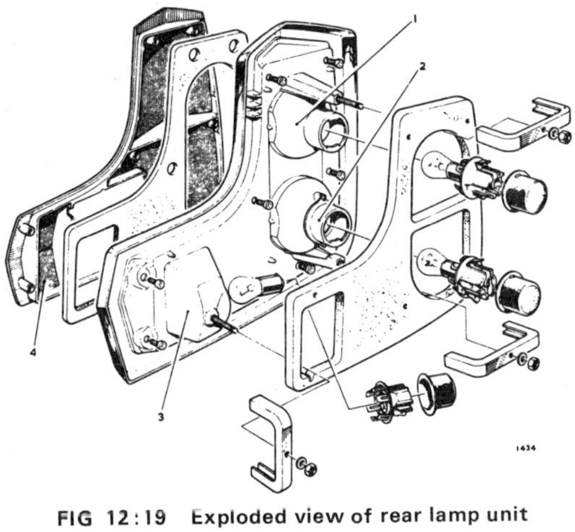

FIG 12:19 Exploded view of rear lamp unit

Key to Fig 12:19 1 Direction indicator bulb 2 Stop/tail dual filament bulb 3 Reversing light 4 Lens and reflector assembly battery starts to pump current back into the generator, reversing the flow in the current winding. Immediately the two pulls cancel out, the armature is released and the hold-off spring opens the contacts isolating the battery from the generator.

In no circumstances should the cut-out contacts be closed by hand with the generator not running. The reverse flow of current from the battery is then sufficient to hold the contacts of the cut-out closed and the current flow back through the generator may be high enough to cause serious damage, even a complete burn-out.

12:9 Starter motor

On all home models, the inertia type starter motor Lucas M35.J is fitted. This has the conventional Bendix type of engagement in which the pinion is driven into engagement with the flywheel ring gear by rotation of the starter motor armature and is disengaged by overdrive when the engine starts. The motor is energized by a solenoid switch operated from the ignition key or manually by a rubber covered plunger cap on the solenoid switch. **To prevent manual operation of the solenoid on cars with automatic transmission, some vehicles are fitted with a metal cap over the plunger.**

On certain export models a pre-engaged starter motor, is fitted. In this, the pinion is mechanically engaged with the flywheel ring gear before current is switched on, a roller clutch drive in the pinion assembly enabling the pinion to freewheel on overdrive when the engine starts. The solenoid switch and mechanical engagement are mounted on the motor yoke and cannot be engaged manually or energized apart from the ignition switch.

Inertia type motor:

This is a series parallel four-pole machine with four brushes, an exploded view of which is shown in **FIG 12:9**. It is a robust and reliable machine which will give long trouble-free service with the minimum of maintenance. The only trouble likely to be experienced is failure of the pinion to mesh with the ring wheel through gumming up of the pinion on the four-start sleeve 13, or, as a result of wear in the pinion or ringwheel, jamming of one of the other at starting.

To clear the first, disconnect the battery negative, break the heavy duty cable connection at the motor, loosen and remove the two bolts securing the motor to the cylinder block flange and extract the motor. Wash the Bendix assembly with paraffin and lubricate with light machine oil, checking the condition of the pinion teeth and ringwheel teeth at the same time.

If the starter jams, engage the gear in top and, with the ignition switched off, rock the car backwards until the engine is free. If this fails, fit a spanner to the squared end of the shaft and turn in a clockwise direction to draw the pinion free of the ringwheel. **Check tightness of the motor fixing bolts.**

If the pinion teeth are worn or there is any other trouble with the starter motor, exchange it for a new or reconditioned one from the agents.

Pre-engaged type motor:

A part section through the pre-engaged motor is shown in **FIG 12:10**. The motor itself is identical with that of the inertia type starter, a different drive end bracket and solenoid/lever assembly being secured to the drive end. Energizing the solenoid, pulls the lever 24, over to engage the pinion 18, with the ringwheel before the motor switch contacts are closed. Adjustment of the lever travel to ensure full engagement of the pinion with the ring gear is by the eccentric pivot pin 25. To set, with the heavy duty connection cable removed from terminal 10 and the solenoid energized, press the pinion lightly back against the armature to take up slack motion, and turn the pivot adjustment until the gap between the pinion face and thrust washer 20, is .01 inch. Tighten the locking bolt. **The arrow head on the bolt must point upwards to the double arrow head as in the inset.**

12:10 Horn and horn control

The horns fitted are factory set and should not be interfered with. The volume of sound can be adjusted by the slotted screws at the rear and, when twin horns are installed, one should be disconnected while the other is adjusted. Failure of the horns to sound can be due to a wiring fault, blown fuse or failure of the horn button contact. These are easy to check. If the fault is still there when current is available at the horn terminal, replace the horn.

The 'horn button' is not a button as such but a pair of contacts in the Lucas steering column control unit. These are operated by pressing the end of the control lever inwards towards the steering column.

12:11 Windscreen wiper and washer

The windscreen wiper is the Lucas 15W, a single or twospeed model driven from a permanent magnet motor with a limit switch controlling the parking cycle when the motor is switched off. The choice of speeds is by a simple switching arrangement selecting one of two commutator brushes with the third as the common. An exploded view is shown in **FIG 12:11** with the wiring diagram to and from the five-pin plug and socket connector. The single speed: self-parking wiper wiring diagram is shown in **FIG 12:12**.

The screen washer is manually operated by pressing in the wiper switch, see **FIG 12:13**. Some later models are equipped with a foot operated screen washer.

12:12 Lamps and lighting

Headlamps:

The sealed beam units, either twin circular or single rectangular have non-detachable main beam bulbs. The front lens and reflector are a sealed unit, and no attempt should be made to separate them, the pilot bulb (parking) however can be removed for renewal, if fitted, although some pilot bulbs are combined with the front flasher lamp.

Certain export territories have models fitted with detachable bulb light units.

Exploded views of the different types of headlamps are shown in **FIGS 12:14, 12:15** and **12:16**.

Beam setting:

Beam setting, although a simple adjusting operation in itself, is better left to the local service garages which have the special alignment gauges and screens that conform to the lighting regulations of the country or state. One of the most dangerous hazards when driving at night is meeting oncoming cars with misaligned beams, particularly during wet weather.

When renewing bulbs avoid tampering with the beam setting screws shown in **FIGS 12:17** and **12:18**.

Front side and flasher lamps:

The front side and flasher lamp housings each contain a pair of single filament bulbs, the flasher rated at 21-watt and the side at 6-watt, behind a dual colour lens, the portion over the flasher bulb being tinted amber and that over the side bulb left clear. Replacement of the bulbs is by removal of the front visor. On some export models the parking bulb is incorporated in the front flasher lamp unit.

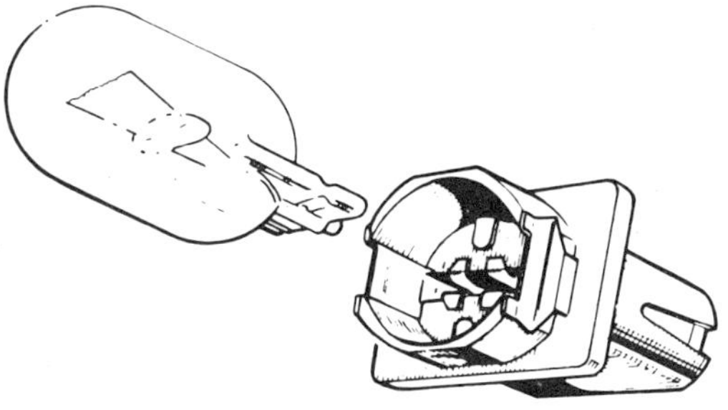

FIG 12:20 Capless bulb as fitted to the instrument panel assembly

Stop, tail and flasher lamps:

The rear stop, tail and flasher lamps are mounted in mirror pairs of Lucas fitting L380/382 with a two-piece lens, the flasher section being separate to meet local

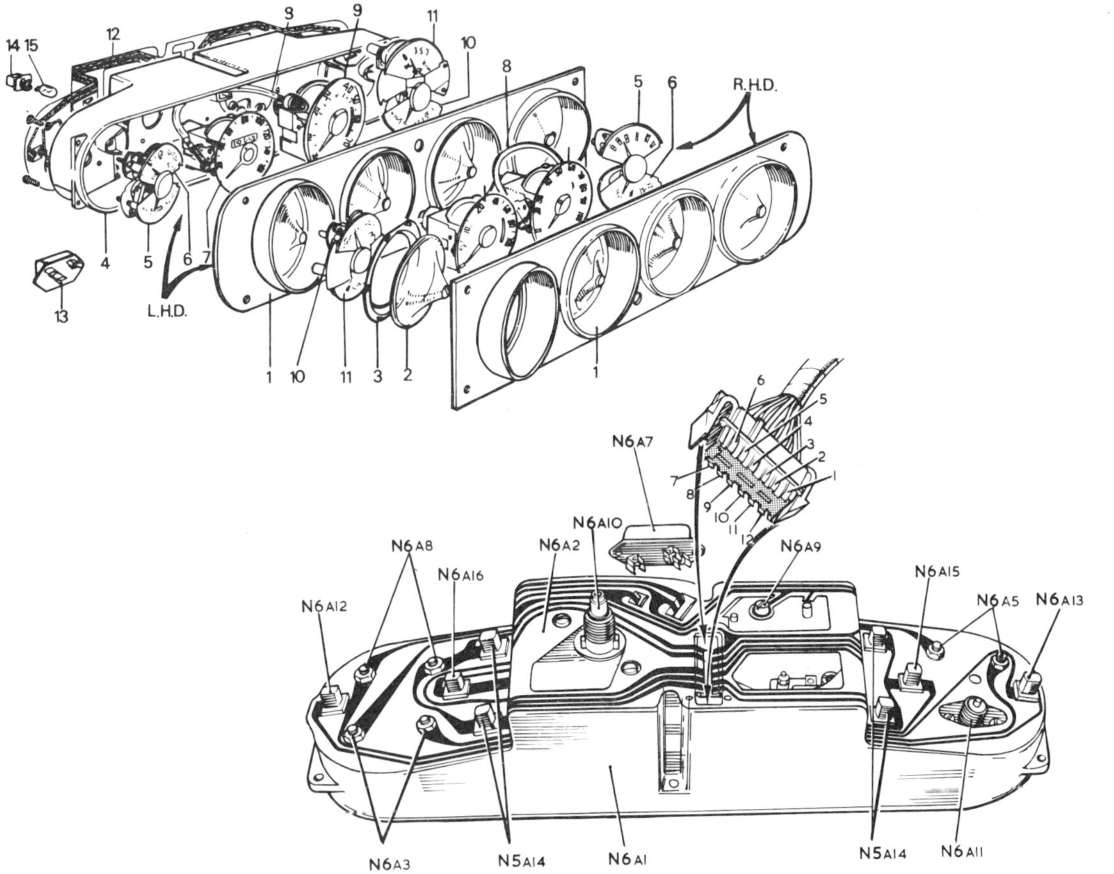

FIG 12:21 Exploded view of binnacle lamp and instrument assembly for circular instruments on righthand drive and lefthand drive cars. Below is the printed circuit at rear of binnacle

Key to Fig 12:21 1 Facia 2 Glass 3 Mask 4 Case 5 Charge indicator (voltmeter) 6 Fuel gauge 7 Speedometer 8 Odometer reset 9 Tachometer 10 Water temperature gauge 11 Oil pressure gauge 12 Printed circuit 13 Stabilizer 14 Bulb holder 15 Capless bulb The references on the printed circuit diagram refer to the wiring diagrams in the Appendix requirements as to flasher colour. In the UK this flasher lens is amber and the stop lens, red.

The exploded view shows (see **FIG 12:19**) the positions of the double filament 21/6-watt stop and tail light bulb and the single filament 21-watt flasher lamp. The bayonet cap bulbs are replaced by unscrewing the lens screws and removing the appropriate section of lens.

Reversing lamp:

The reversing lamp at the rear of the car, switched on automatically by engagement of reverse gear, is rated at 21-watt.

12:13 Direction indicator switch and hazard warning

The direction indicator switch on the steering column is the Lucas pattern 119SA and, in addition to providing the self-centring control of the flasher lamps by movement of the lever at right angles to the column, parallel with the face of the steering wheel, it also provides control of main and dipped beam by vertical movement away from the wheel to select main beam, returning it to centre for dipped beam. The lever stays in either position until reset and the direction flasher movement operates in both positions.

The same lever, raised upwards towards the steering wheel will switch on the main beam for signal flashing,

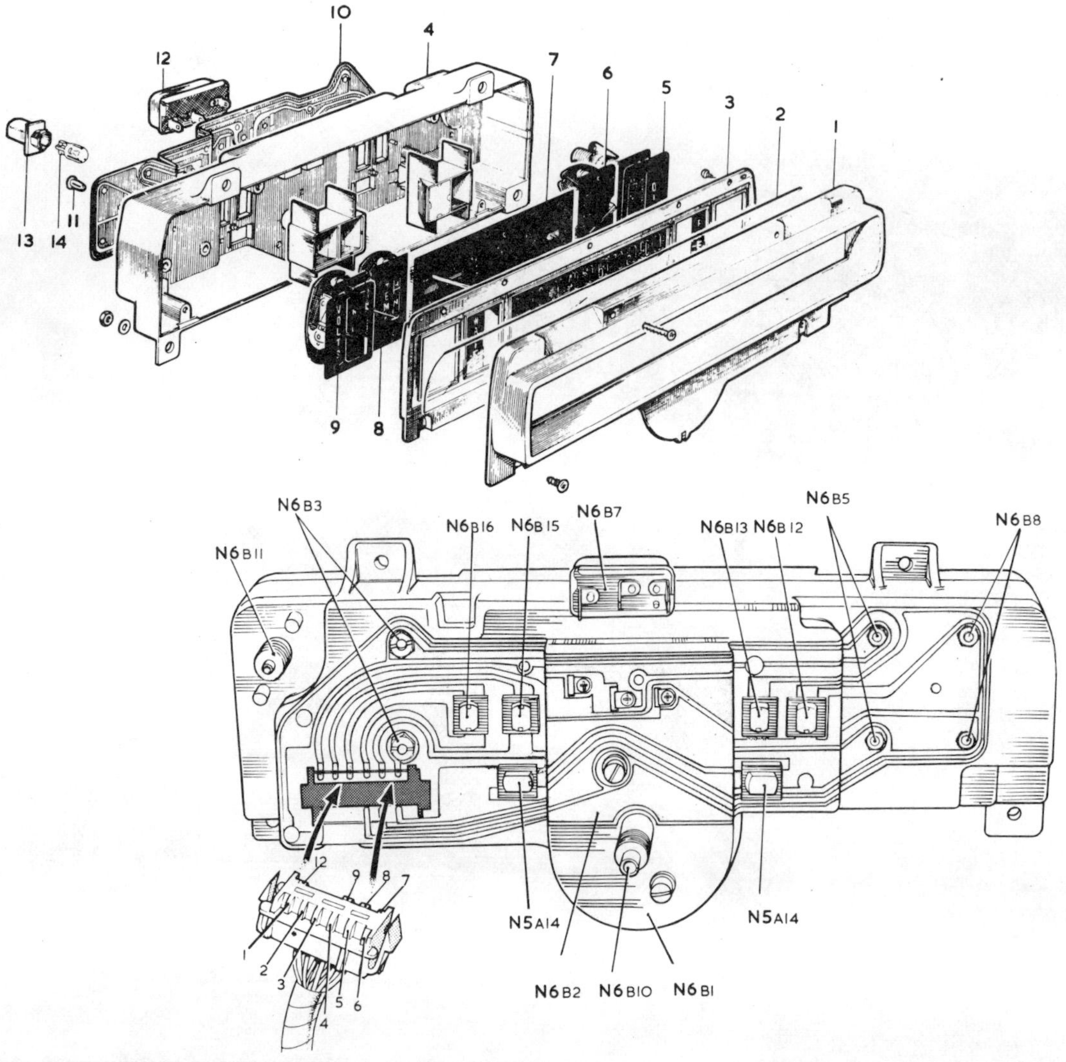

FIG 12:22 Exploded view of binnacle lamp and instrument panel assembly for rectangular instruments on righthand drive and lefthand drive cars with, below, the printed circuit at rear of the binnacle

Key to Fig 12:22 1 Front moulding 2 Window 3 Mask 4 Case 5 Oil pressure gauge 6 Fuel gauge 7 Speedometer 8 Water temperature gauge 9 Charge indicator (voltmeter) 10 Printed circuit 11 Rivet 12 Stabilizer 13/14 Bulb and holder

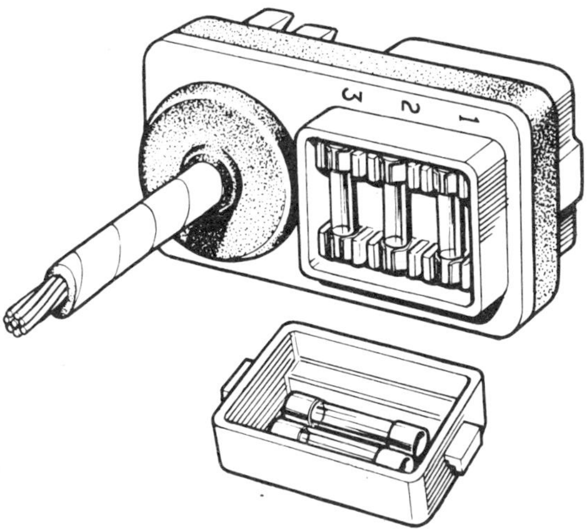

FIG 12:23 Fuse unit with spare fuses in cover

returning to the central position when it is released. This flashing, unlike the main beam and dipped positions, operates with the panel lighting switch off. The wiring of the switch may differ slightly from model to model and can be followed by reference to the individual diagrams in the Appendix.

On overseas models with hazard warning lights installed, these are of the capless pattern (see **FIG 12:20**) with separate flasher unit controlled from a hazard switch on the instrument panel which incorporates its own warning lamp.

12:14 Instruments

All the instruments fitted to this range of cars are of conventional standard pattern and require virtually no maintenance. Apart from the speedometer and oil gauge which are mechanical devices, the rest operate from the electrical system via a voltage stabilizer. Tachometers are of the impulse type while temperature and fuel gauges are of the bi-metal pattern. The instruments are mounted in one of two binnacle assemblies with rear printed circuit connections. One assembly (see **FIG 12:21**) accommodates circular pattern instruments; the other (see **FIG 12:22**) embodies rectangular pattern instruments. An unusual feature is the incorporation of a voltmeter on some models as a battery charging indicator in place of the more usual ammeter.

Replacement of the illuminating bulb, where these are not part of general panel illumination, is from the rear and, in some cases, necessitate removal of the facia panel to gain access.

12:15 Fuseboard

The Lucas 8FJ fuse unit secured to the vehicle bulkhead houses five fuses, two of which are spares. All are rated at 35-amp (see **FIG 12:23**).

For fuse connections, refer to the wiring diagrams in the Appendix.

12:16 Fault diagnosis

(a) Battery discharged

1 Internal cell fault—replace battery
2 External wiring fault—check circuits
3 Alternator not charging
4 Ignition left on overnight

(b) Battery will not start engine

1 Faulty battery
2 Discharged battery
3 Starter jammed (inertia type only)

(c) Ignition light fails to go out

1 Loose or broken belt
2 Faulty regulator
3 Loose connection in charging circuit

(d) Lamps will not light

1 Fuse blown
2 Lamp burnt out
3 Faulty earth connection
4 Loose connection in wiring

(e) Horn will not work

1 Faulty wiring
2 Bad earth at horn
3 Fuse blown

(f) Instruments inoperative

1 Fuse blown
2 Loose connection
3 Voltage stabilizer fault

(g) Windscreen wiper inoperative

1 Fuse blown
2 Loose connection

(h) Direction indicator not working

1 Fuse blown
2 Loose connection
3 Flasher unit failed
4 Broken wire in cable loom

Always check fuses before attempting to locate a suspected fault and then check the efficiency of the earth connection.

NOTES

CHAPTER 13

THE BODYWORK

13:1 Body maintenance

The body structure is made up from a series of pressed steel sections jointed together by welding. Damage to any section too great to permit of local rectification can be dealt with by replacing the section and welding it into position. As this is a process entailing, in many cases, realignment of the chassis or its assembly in a special jig, the work should not be attempted by the owner/mechanic but placed with a Chrysler repair agent who is in possession of the necessary jigs and tools. The front wings however are secured by eleven spire bolts which makes the replacement of the wing a fairly straightforward operation.

The enamel finish is of a durable nature and will last many years if kept reasonably clean by regular washing and polishing. **Do not attempt to wipe road dust from the body with a dry cloth or its high finish will be impaired by fine scratches.** Always wash the dirt and dust away by copious flushing with water from a jet or hose. If very dirty, sponge over with a shampoo in warm, not hot, water until all is loose and rinse off with a hose before finally drying off with a chamois leather and polishing with a soft cloth.

The surfaces should be protected by a film of wax from time to time. There are two good indications of surface deterioration. The first is when water sprayed on to it tends to wet it all over. Water should run off or, at least, stand in globules on the surface if the protective film is in good condition. The second is the 'feel' of the surface when polishing after drying. If the clean duster slips easily over the surface with no effort, the film is present. If there is the slightest feel of drag, either the film has deteriorated and you are down to the base enamel, or the film present is contaminated by ingrained dirt and must be removed.

Renovation is then in two stages, the removal of the old film with its ingrained dirt and the replacement by a new wax surface. Many excellent proprietary cleaners and waxes are available and can be used with safety so long as the instructions are followed. The separate compounds are to be favoured, but the polishing can be a long and arduous task which, however, pays good dividends in appearance and extended protection. Combined cleaners and polishers are an acceptable second best.

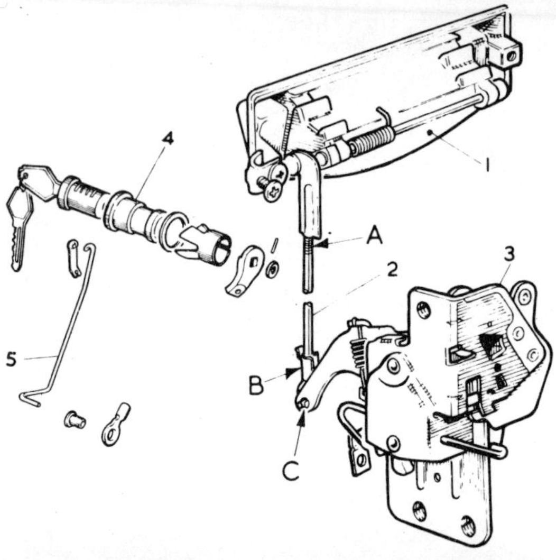

FIG 13:1 Diagrammatic view of front lock and key cylinder showing component parts

Key to Fig 13:1 1 Door handle 2 Handle connecting rod 3 Door lock 4 Barrel lock 5 Locking rod For references to **A**, **B** and **C**, see text

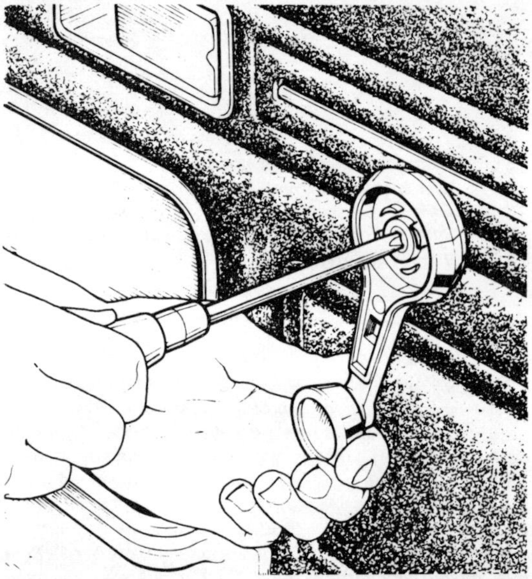

FIG 13:2 Removing window raising gear handle from door

Most products today are based on silicone waxes and should not be allowed to contaminate the windscreen. The water-repellant film left behind by the smallest trace of silicone makes the use of the windscreen wiper inefficient in preserving a clear view when light rain is falling. The film is difficult to remove and, in any case, prevention is better than cure. To remove, try non-abrasive scouring powders with plenty of water or metal polish.

It is not generally known that chrome plating is porous and, despite its high finish, water can penetrate through it to the metal beneath, causing pitting, bubbling and even stripping over large areas. The longer life of some pre-war chrome plating was due to a heavy undercoat of non-porous copper plating and the more extensive use of brass in place of the present day die-casting alloys. The pores, however, can be closed by application of body wax and it is good practice to go over all plated parts with the polish whenever the body is being done. Then clean off the surface wax and what is left behind will give good protection for many years despite the use of chrome polishes.

Tar can be removed by the use of a little butter on a soft cloth, finishing off with an application of body wax. Bird droppings must be removed as soon as possible. Wipe off with a rotary motion using a very wet cloth and minimum pressure until all is clear. Rinse, dry and renew the wax. Most bird droppings have constituents which eat through the wax and affect the colour of the enamel beneath, leaving a lighter colour area.

Scratches and abrasions of the paintwork can be rectified by rubbing down and spraying over with a cellulose base paint. The fact that the original enamel is acrylic based is not important. Tins of spray paint in pressurized containers are quite suitable for small areas but care must be taken in matching the colour. When spraying, use many coats of thinly applied paint rather than a single coating heavily applied. For large areas, it is better to put the work in hand with a professional paint sprayer who will be able to match the existing colour more efficiently. All paint surfaces change in colour over the years and repainted areas, though they may match at the time of application, tend to become more noticeable with time.

13:2 Upholstery and trim

Clean the plastic covered panels, seats and roof linings with a wet cloth and soap or soap liquid. Proprietary detergents (Handy Andy, Flash, etc.) can also be used but not those which contain ammonia in any form. **Do not use spirit cleaners or soda.**

Brush out the interior and the upholstery at frequent intervals using a vacuum cleaner, if possible, to extract the dirt from crevices otherwise out of reach. The upholstery is waterproof and can be sat on immediately after cleaning.

13:3 Locks and hinges

Locks and hinges must be kept in good condition and oiled regularly. Be sparing with the oil however, as any excess will work its way into positions where it can dirty the hands or clothes of the occupants.

The two front doors are secured by rotary, or latch type, locks operated by a button set in the door adjacent to the handle on the outside and by a lever on the inside. The rear doors are also secured by a rotary lock operated on the inside by a lever and on the outside by a button. The front door lock incorporates a cylinder pattern key lock in the button while the rear locks embody a child-proof safety locking feature.

FIG 13:1 shows an exploded diagrammatic representation of the front door lock with the key-cylinder button. To remove the door locks, first wind the window to the fully closed position and then remove the regulator handle, interior door handle, arm-rest, plastic covers and screws from the door pocket and the door trim. The window regulator handle is secured by a cross-head screw immediately below the plastic insert in the handle (see **FIG 13:2**). The arm-rest is secured by two cross-head screws while the screws securing the lock handle are located behind the handle in the housing and are revealed when the handle is pulled out to operate the lock. The trim pad is held in position by the normal method of clips and can be eased clear by inserting a screwdriver between trim and door metal adjacent to each clip (see **FIG 13:3**).

Disconnect the connecting rod between the button and locking mechanism and then the rod between the door handle and lock. Disconnect the internal lever at the lock end and remove the the two screws from the door which secure the lower glass run channel. Extract the channel through the aperture in the door and then release the lock by extracting the three screws securing it to the door jamb. The lock, complete with internal locking lever connecting rod, can then be extracted. Reinstallation, naturally, is a reversal of this procedure.

The exterior handle operates the lock by enabling the rotary locking wheel to turn freely, so disengaging it from the latch plate when the door is pulled open. Adjustment to this end is by setting the length of the connecting rod 2 (see **FIG 13:1**) after releasing it from the clip B, and screwing it in or out of the handle ferrule at A.

13:4 Window raising gear

The window raising gear is of the normal lever pattern, the glass being supported on a channel section. On those cars with a quarterlight fitted to the door, this must first be removed before it is possible to either extract the main glass section or to extract the raising and lowering mechanism. In each case, front or rear, extraction of the quarterlight involves the removal of pop rivets. It is not necessary to replace these by similar pop rivets on reassembly; self-tapping screws of the appropriate size can be used quite effectively.

13:5 Windscreen and backlight glazing

The windscreen glass is secured by rubber weatherstrip sealed in place by Silastic SR51 compound. The weatherstrip has a metallized rubber finishing strip insert on the outside. To remove, after taking down the windscreen wiper, visors and rear mirror, ease the glass free from the old sealant by working a screwdriver round the edge to ease the rubber away from the glass. Remove the strip insert and then, with a second person supporting the glass from the outside of the car, push firmly from the inside applying the pressure at the edges until glass and weatherstrip come away from the glass.

To reinsert, fit the weatherstrip on to the new screen with a small quantity of sealant and insert a cord around the inner groove with an adequate length of crossover at the lower centre. Fit the windscreen in position from the outside and then pull the cord from the inside of the car to ease the rubber lip of the weatherstrip over the

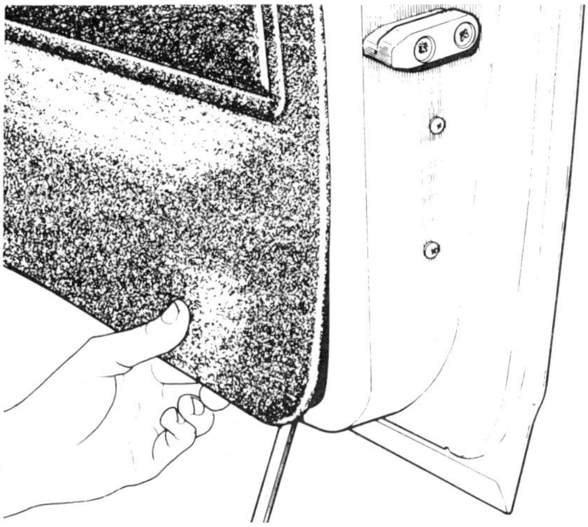

FIG 13:3 Removing door trim

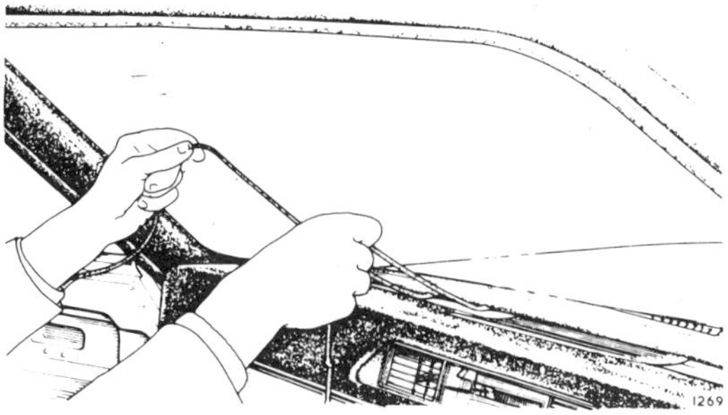

FIG 13:4 Inserting new window glass and weatherstrip for windscreen, showing cord technique

edge of the metalwork aperture (see **FIG 13:4**). Check that the weatherstrip is seating properly all round and then reinsert the finishing strip with an insertion tool (see **FIG 13:5**).

Insert a small quantity of Silastic SR51 between the outer edge of the weatherstrip and the metal with a suitable gun and flat nozzle and press the edge into place. Scrape off any excess of sealant with a wooden spatula and clean the glass where it has been from the last traces with white spirit.

Renewal of the backlight glazing is by a similar process but if a heated backlight is fitted take note of the electrical connections.

If the windscreen has been broken, carefully remove all traces of broken glass from both weatherstrip and surround before attempting to reinstall a new glass panel. Providing that the weatherstrip has not perished or been damaged in the incident, it can quite safely be used again. If a new weatherstrip is installed, before actually fitting in position, check the length of the weatherstrip in the aperture to ensure that the ends meet exactly and neither overlap nor gap at the joint. This is most important if a waterproof seal is to be achieved.

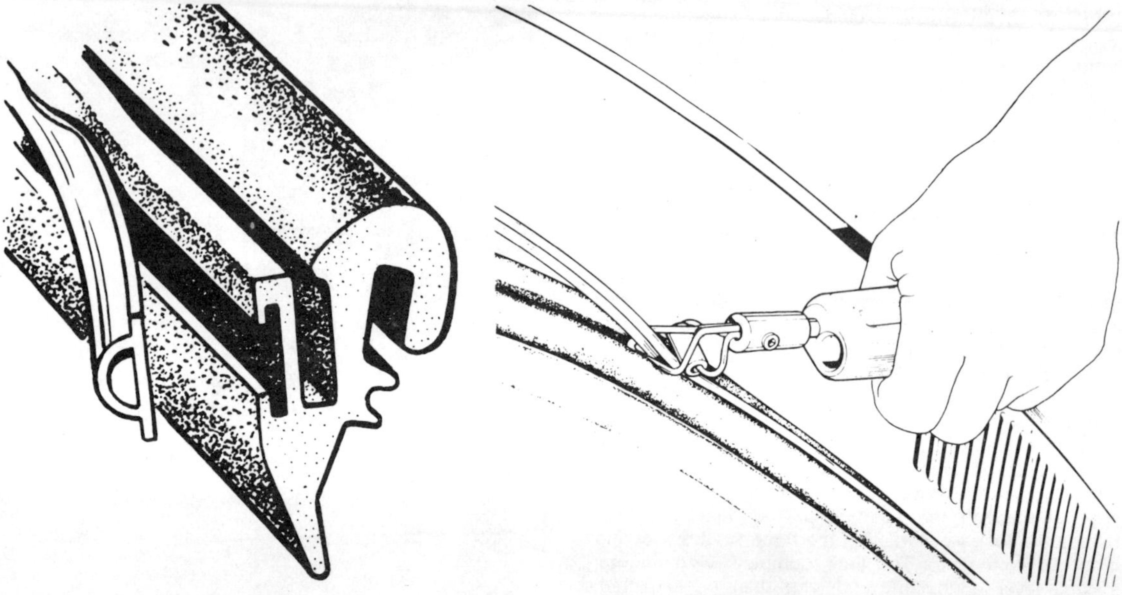

FIG 13:5 Weatherstrip and trim showing use of tool for inserting locking trim into weatherstrip

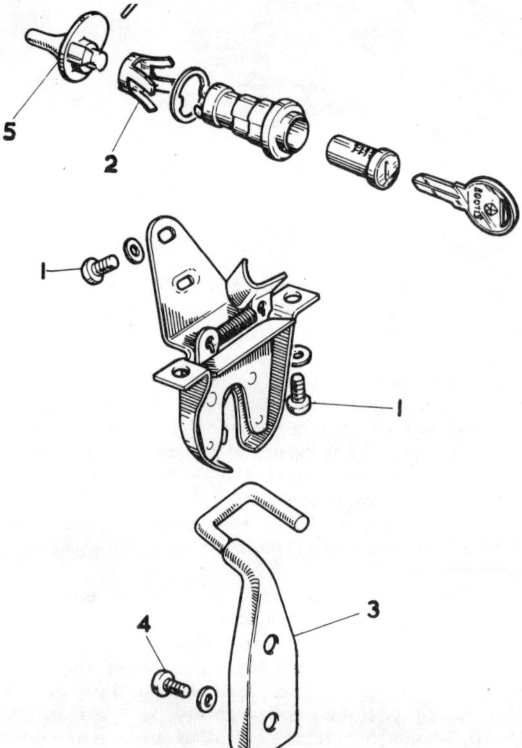

FIG 13:6 Diagrammatic exploded view of boot lock showing component parts

Key to Fig 13:6 1 Bolts and washers 2 Cylinder locking device 3 Latch plate 4 Bolt and washer 5 Rotary cam

13:6 Compartment lids and locks

The boot is supported in the open position by torsion bars which must be unclipped before attempting to remove the hinges. When disengaged from the car body, the torsion bars come away with the compartment lid.

The engine compartment lid, or bonnet, is not supported by springs or torsion bars in the open position but by a strut which is secured within the compartment when the bonnet is down. The hinges incorporate slotted holes for adjustment both in regard to front-to-rear positioning and in vertical height at the hinge end of the compartment lid.

The boot lid lock is secured to the lid by three bolts with the hooked striker plate affixed to the body of the car inside the compartment. An exploded view is shown in **FIG 13:6.** Operation of the release is by a rotary cam plate turned by the cylinder lock barrel when the key is in position. It can only be operated by the key when inserted and is self-locking. To remove the cylinder lock, compress the four spring legs and extract through the front of the assembly.

The bonnet lock is first released from within the car by remote cable control and this gives a limited vertical movement restricted by the external latching device. The lock is secured in position by three bolts and, for removal, the front grille must first be removed to gain access to the remote control cable and disconnecting it from the lock lever. In some cases only an external operated lock is fitted but the mechanism is the same but without the cable release (see **FIG 13:7**).

13:7 Wing replacement

The only part of the general body assembly that is not integral welded is the front wings. These are secured in position by eleven spire bolts and clips located at the positions in **FIG 13:8.** Should a wing become damaged, raise the front of the car on stands and remove the front

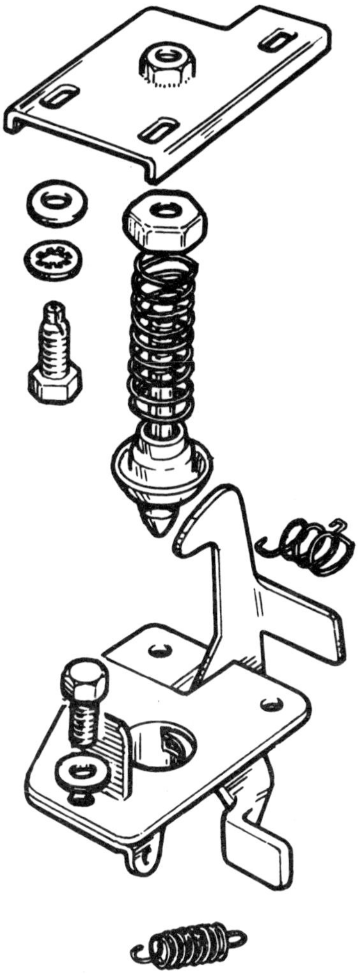

FIG 13:7 Diagrammatic view of bonnet lock showing component parts

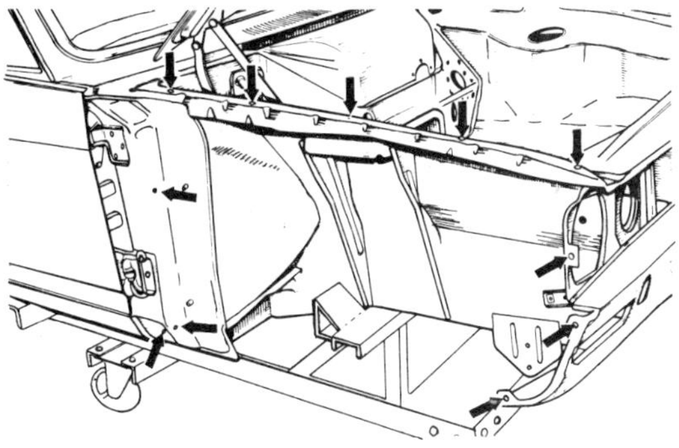

FIG 13:8 Location of the eleven spire bolts securing the wing panels in position

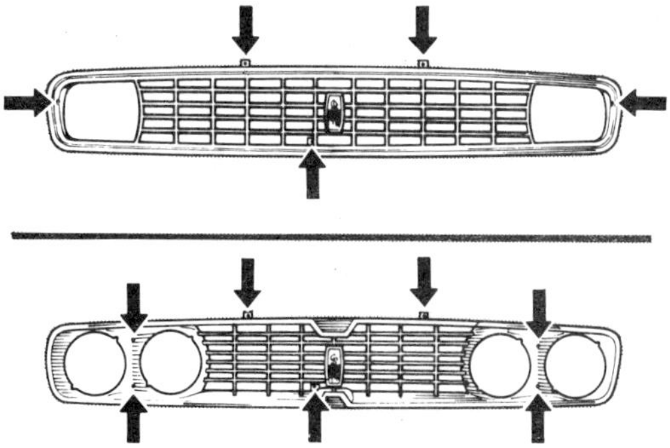

FIG 13:9 Front grille fixing screws

wheel or wheels. Obtain a new wing from the service agent—this will be supplied in a condition ready for spray painting in the desired colour—and check that it is the right shape. Remove the headlamp unit, front grille, direction indicator and sill finisher and unbolt the damaged wing and remove it from the body with the rubber insert between it and the body proper.

Clean the surround on the car and coat both new wing edge and surround with Glasticon grade 16, 279 compound, obtainable from the Chrysler agent, set in position and insert the spire bolts. Before finally tightening down ensure that the panel is flush with the surrounding metal of the body. Replace all parts removed from the car or, should they too have been damaged, their replacements.

13:8 Safety belts

Lap diagonal safety belts are fitted to the front seats of all models intended for home domestic use where their installation is mandatory. The belts are of nylon webbing and must be tested at regular intervals for signs of chaffing or twisting. To renew the belts, prise the hooked end of the plastic retainer clear of the attachment bolt and unhook. When fitting the new belt, be sure that it is installed in exactly the same way as the one it has replaced. The belts may be cleaned with soap and water and, since nylon does not absorb moisture, it will dry quickly. It is not necessary to saturate the webbing.

13:9 Weatherproofing and undersealing

Though the body structure is given a fair degree of resistance to rust and corrosion during manufacture, the benefits of undersealing in prolonging the life of the car are undeniable. Undersealing is a process which must be carried out by a properly equipped garage and, for maximum protection, should be done within the first few weeks from delivery. The cost is well worth the extra life it gives and, in comparison with the capital cost of the car, it is small.

At all times a careful watch must be kept on the general condition of the bodywork and any signs of rust or corrosion dealt with out of hand. In particular, make a regular inspection of the joints in the wheel arches and at similar points open to the dust, mud and water thrown up from the road. Another point to watch is the lower inner sills of the door panels. Wherever water can accumulate, rust can rapidly eat into the metal, despite production rust-proofing processes.

Deal with corrosion areas by drying them out, brushing clear any dirt or dried mud and then remove the rust with a wire brush and emerypaper. Coat with a zinc base compound and cover with a bitumastic base compound or other suitable water repellant proprietary paint. Remember that prevention is better than cure and early notice followed by prompt attention can save a very expensive repair bill at a later date.

13:10 The front grilles

Referring to **FIG 13:9** the grilles can be detached by removing all the retaining screws (arrowed).

APPENDIX

NOTES

TECHNICAL DATA

Dimensions in inches unless otherwise stated

ENGINE

Number of cylinders	4
Firing order	1–3–4–2
Position of No. 1	Front of vehicle
Bore and stroke, nominal:	
1250 cc	78.60 x 64.3 mm
1500 cc SC and TC	86.12 x 64.3 mm
Bore:	
Diameter, 1250 cc Grade A	78.60 to 78.61 mm
Grade B	78.61 to 78.61 mm
Grade C	78.62 to 78.63 mm
Grade D	78.63 to 78.64 mm
Diameter, 1500 cc Grade A	86.12 to 86.13 mm
(SC and TC) Grade B	86.13 to 86.14 mm
Grade C	86.14 to 86.15 mm
Grade D	86.15 to 86.16 mm
Displacement (actual):	
1250 cc	1248 cc
1500 cc	1498 cc
Compression ratio:	
1250 cc	9.2:1
1500 cc High compression, SC and TC	9.2:1
Low compression, SC	8.0:1
Fuel octane rating:	
High compression engines	97 (4-star)
Low compression engines	90 (2-star)
Brake horsepower, maximum (testbed):	
1250 cc	53 at 5000 rev/min
1500 cc, HC:SC	63 at 5000 rev/min
1500 cc LC:SC	57 at 5000 rev/min
1500 cc TC	75 at 5400 rev/min
Torque, maximum (testbed):	
1250 cc	66 lb ft at 3000 rev/min
1500 cc HC:SC	80 lb ft at 3000 rev/min
1500 cc LC:SC	74 lb ft at 3000 rev/min
1500 cc TC	81 lb ft at 3750 rev/min
Cylinder block:	
Material	Cast iron
Maximum oversize bore 1250 cc	.76 mm
1500 cc	.76 mm
Cylinder liner, o.d. 1250 cc	82.32 to 82.34 mm
1500 cc	89.83 to 89.86 mm
Cylinder liner, interference fit	.050 to .101 mm
Cylinder head:	
Material	Cast iron (1500 TC: 'S' cast on face)
Gasket marking 1250 cc	SB
1500 cc SC and TC	LB
Combustion chamber volume	13.7 to 16.2 cc
Valves:	
Position	Overhead
Operated by	Pushrods
Clearance: Inlet valve (hot or cold)	.008 (.010 on 1500 cc twin carburetter engine)
Exhaust valve (hot or cold)	.016

Timing: 1250 cc	Inlet opens	38 deg. BTDC
	Inlet closes	66 deg. ABDC
	Exhaust opens	72 deg. BBDC
	Exhaust closes	20 deg. ATDC
SC, 1500 cc	Inlet opens	35 deg. BTDC
	Inlet closes	69 deg. ABDC
	Exhaust opens	69 deg. BBDC
	Exhaust closes	23 deg. ATDC
TC, 1500 cc	Inlet opens	44 deg. BTDC
	Inlet closes	78 deg. ABDC
	Exhaust opens	69 deg. BBDC
	Exhaust closes	23 deg. ATDC
Stem identification No.:		
1250 and 1500 cc SC	Inlet, standard	71244380
	Inlet, oversize +.003, +.015, +.030	71244381, 2 and 3
	Exhaust, standard	71244386
	Exhaust, oversize +.003, +.015, +.030	71244387, 8 and 9
1500 cc TC	Inlet, standard	71244361
	Inlet, oversize +.003, +.015, +.030	71244362, 3 and 4
	Exhaust, standard	As 1250 cc
	Exhaust, oversize	As 1250 cc
Head diameter	Inlet, 1250 also 1500 SC	1.418 to 1.422
	Exhaust, 1250 also 1500 SC	1.198 to 1.202
	Inlet, 1500 TC	1.468 to 1.472
	Exhaust, 1500 TC	As 1250
Valve seat angle		45 deg.
Valve guide bore	Standard, all models	.3125 to .3135
	Oversize	.015 and .030
Stem diameter	Standard inlet, all models	.3110 to .3115
	+3	.3140 to .3145
	+15	.3260 to .3265
	+30	.3410 to .3415
	Standard exhaust, all models	.3095 to .3100
	+3	.3125 to .3130
	+15	.3245 to .3250
	+30	.3395 to .3400
Springs	Type 1250 and 1500 SC	Single (1500 TC: twin)
	Length, fitted	1.505 (Inner 1.0, Outer 1.34)
	Load, fitted	70 lb (Inner 17.3 lb, Outer 52.7 lb)

Camshaft (all models):

Number of bearings		3
Bearing material		Aluminium tin
Journal diameter	Front	1.9345 to 1.9352
	Centre	1.7470 to 1.7477
	Rear	1.5595 to 1.5602
End float		.004 to .009

Crankshaft (all models):

Number of bearings		5
Type of bearing		Steel, aluminium tin lined
Throw		1.264 to 1.266
Main journal diameter:	A	2.1245 to 2.1252
	B	2.1145 to 2.1152
Crankpin diameter:	A	1.9995 to 2.0000
	B	1.9895 to 1.9900
End float		.002 to .008

Main bearing clearance	.0005 to .0025
Big-end bearing clearance	.0009 to .0024

Connecting rod (all models):

Material	Alloy steel
Section	H
Distance between centres: 1250	4.964 to 4.966
1500	4.964 to 4.966
Big-end bearings	Steel, aluminium tin lined
Big-end bore, less shells	2.1460 to 2.1465
Float	.007 to .012

Gudgeon pin (all models):

Type	Floating
Material	Steel
Located by	Circlips
Length	2.621 to 2.625
Diameter: Blue	.9377 to .9378
White	.9376 to .9377
Green	.9375 to .9376
Yellow	.9374 to .9375
Fit	Thumb push at 68°F

Piston:

Type	Slotted upper skirt
Material	Aluminium alloy, tin plated
Height	2.98
Diameter: 1250 Grade A	3.0926 to 3.0930
Grade B	3.0930 to 3.0934
Grade C	3.0934 to 3.0938
Grade D	3.0938 to 3.0942
1500 SC Grade A	3.3887 to 3.3891
Grade B	3.3891 to 3.3895
Grade C	3.3895 to 3.3899
Grade D	3.3899 to 3.3903
1500 TC Grade A	3.3873 to 3.3877
Grade B	3.3877 to 3.3881
Grade C	3.3881 to 3.3885
Grade D	3.3885 to 3.3889
Grade E for service only, 1250	3.0942 to 3.0946
1500 SC	3.3903 to 3.3907
1500 TC	3.3889 to 3.3893
Oversize available, Grade B bore only	+.030 (all models)
Rings	2 compression 1 scraper
Ring gap: Top ring	.014 to .018
Second and scraper	.010 to .014

Lubrication:

Pump type	Eccentric lobe
Drive	Skew gear from camshaft
Oil pressure, hot	50 to 60 lb/sq inch
Filter	Fullflow, disposable

Tightening torques:

Cylinder head bolts	60 lb ft
Cylinder head nuts	60 lb ft
Cylinder head studs in block	14 lb ft
Rocker pedestal bolts	17 lb ft
Manifold bolts and nuts	16 lb ft
Manifold studs in head	10 lb ft
Connecting rod nuts	29 lb ft
Main bearing cap bolts	52 lb ft

Flywheel bolts	40 lb ft
Crankshaft pulley bolt	52 lb ft
Crankshaft sprocket bolt	34 lb ft
Mounting bracket bolts	17 lb ft

FUEL SYSTEM

Pump:	
Type	Mechanical diaphragm
Carburetter:	
Type	Stromberg 150 CDS
Slow running speed: Single carburetter	700 to 750 rev/min
Twin carburetter	950 rev/min
Automatic	600 to 650 rev/min
Needle: 1250	5BB (6AL*)
1500—Single carburetter	6AG (6AK*)
Twin carburetter	6BC

**To comply with certain European emission regulations*

Spring—Single carburetter	Red
Twin carburetter	Blue
Type	Stromberg 150 CDSE (E.E.C.)
Slow running speed: Manual	800 rev/min
Automatic	600 rev/min
Needle	B5BD
Spring	Red
Tightening torques:	
Carburetter to manifold	12 lb ft
Fuel pump	10 lb ft

IGNITION SYSTEM

Sparking plugs:	
Type	Champion N.9.Y; N.7.Y on twin carburetter engine
Gap setting	.025
Coil	Lucas 11C12
Distributor	Lucas 25D4
Rotation	Counterclockwise
Contact breaker gap	.015
Dwell	60 deg. ± 3 deg.
Service No. 1250 cc	41302
1500 cc HC, SC or TC	41304
LC	41303
LC, with EEC	41301
Static ignition timing:	
1250	6 to 8 deg. BTDC
1500 HC and LC	6 to 8 deg. BTDC
1500 TC	7 to 9 deg. BTDC
1500 with EEC	7 deg. BTDC

COOLING SYSTEM

Type	Centrifugal pump, fan, pressurized
Capacity	13 pints including heater
Radiator cap relief pressure	9 lb/sq inch
Thermostat:	
Type	Wax pellet
Opening at	82°C
Fully open at	95°C

CLUTCH

Type	Diaphragm, single dry plate
Driven plate diameter:	
1250 cc	7.25
1500 cc SC and TC	7.50
Number of springs	4
Operation	Cable
Tightening torques:	
Cover assembly screws	16 lb ft
Adjuster locknut	3 lb ft

GEARBOX, MANUAL

Type	4-speed synchromesh
Gear ratios:	
Top	1.000:1
Third	1.366:1
Second	2.029:1
Bottom	3.317:1
Reverse	3.450:1
Final drive:	
1250 cc	4.375:1
1500 cc	3.889:1
Oil capacity	3 pints
Tightening torques:	
Front cover nuts	6 lb ft
Top cover	4 lb ft
Reverse plunger	5 lb ft
Speedometer drive	4 lb ft
Rear cover to casing	14 lb ft
Plunger coverplate	4 lb ft
Reverse fulcrum pivot	25 lb ft
Mainshaft front nut	70 lb ft
Mainshaft rear nut	69 lb ft
Clutch bellhousing	30 lb ft
Mount to crossmember	26 lb ft
Propeller shaft flange nuts	17 lb ft
Drain and filler plug	34 lb ft
Mounting to crossmember	26 lb ft
Crossmember to body	12 lb ft

GEARBOX, AUTOMATIC

Type	Borg-Warner Model 35
Gear ratios:	
Top	1:1
Second	1.450:1
Bottom	2.393:1
Reverse	2.094:1
Tightening torques:	
Crankshaft to drive disc bolts	30 lb ft
Drive disc to converter bolts	30 lb ft
Transmission case to converter housing	9 lb ft
Extension housing to transmission case	9 lb ft
Oil pan to transmission case	9 lb ft
Front servo to transmission case	9 lb ft
Pump adapter to front pump body—No. 10 bolt	2 lb ft
$\frac{5}{16}$ bolt	20 lb ft

Pump adapter to transmission case	12 lb ft
Centre support to transmission case	12 lb ft
Lever to manual valve shift	6 lb ft
Oil pan drain plug	12 lb ft
Oil tube collector to lower body	2 lb ft
Governor line plate to lower body	2 lb ft
Lower body end plate	2 lb ft
Upper body end plate	2 lb ft
Upper body to lower body	2 lb ft
Body assembly to transmission case	5 lb ft
Front servo lever adjustment nut	17 lb ft
Rear servo adjustment locking nut	27 lb ft
Starter inhibitor switch locknut	5 lb ft
Filler tube to connector sleeve nut	17 lb ft
Downshift cable adapter to transmission	9 lb ft

FRONT SUSPENSION

Type	Independent, Macpherson strut, anti-roll bar
Springs:	
Type	Coil
Inside diameter	4.50
Free length: Righthand standard	14.40
Righthand heavy duty	13.29
Lefthand standard	13.30
Lefthand heavy duty	12.32
No. of coils: Righthand standard	7.88
Righthand heavy duty	7.54
Lefthand standard	7.28
Lefthand heavy duty	7.03
Toe-in	$\frac{1}{32}$ to $\frac{1}{8}$
Camber	1 deg. positive + 45′
Castor	1 deg. + 30′
Shock absorber	Integral Armstrong telescopic

REAR SUSPENSION

Type	Coil springs with links. Panhard rod on Estate versions
Springs:	
Inside diameter: Standard	3.517
Heavy duty	3.517
Number of coils: Standard	8.09
Heavy duty	8.49 (one stripe of orange paint)
Shock absorbers	Direct acting twin tube, telescopic

STEERING

Type	Rack and pinion
Overall ratio	17.65:1
Turning circle	31 ft 6 inch
Steering wheel diameter	15.75
No. of turns, lock to lock	3.66

BRAKING SYSTEM

Type	Girling hydraulic
Front wheels:	
Disc diameter	9.5
Pad material SC models (TC models)	Mintex M108GH (Ferodo 2430F)
Area per wheel SC models (TC models)	7.82 sq inch (8.70 sq inch)
Rear wheels:	
Drum diameter	8.00
Show linings	Don 202 GG
Area per wheel	23.0 sq inch
Master cylinder diameter SC models (TC models)	.625 (.750)
Front brake cylinder diameter (caliper)	1.893
Rear brake cylinder diameter, SC models (TC models)	.700 (.625)
Servo	Girling, Type 28

ELECTRICAL EQUIPMENT

Battery	Lucas D/7 or D/9
Volts	12
Nominal capacity	38 amp/hr
Weight: D9	31 lb
D7	26 lb
Length	9.375
Width	5.375
Height	8.00
Generator:	
Type	Lucas C40-I or C40-L
Regulator	RB340
Alternator:	
Type	Lucas 16 ACR
No. of poles	12
Phases	3
Connection	Star
Rectification	Silicone diodes
Excitation	Self, half-wave rectifier
Regulated voltage	14.00 to 14.4
Maximum speed	12,500 rev/min
Nominal output	34 amp
Starter:	
Pre-engaged	Lucas M35J
Drive	Roller clutch
No-load current	65 amps
Inertia	Lucas M35J/1
Drive	Bendix type
No-load current	50 amps
Fuse unit:	
Type	Lucas 8FJ
No. of fuses	3
Spares	2
Fuse cartridge rating	35 amp
Lamps and lighting:	
Twin headlamp	Lucas F575
Single headlamp	Lucas 4FR (sealed beam) or Lucas 410

For replacement lamp bulbs, see Section 12:11

TORQUE WRENCH SETTINGS

Front suspension:	*lb ft*
Strut upper swivel fixing	15
Strut to upper swivel bearing using P5026	31
Steering arm to lower strut	58
Lower swivel ball joint to steering arm	44
Track control arm to crossmember	28
Crossmember to body	54
Drag strut bracket to body	28
Drag strut to bracket	40
Drag strut to track control arm	36
Stabilizer bar bracket to body	28
Stabiliser bar drop link (both ends) from face of washer to end of link adjustment	$\frac{9}{16}$ to $\frac{5}{8}$ in
Strut gland nut	48
Rear suspension:	
Suspension link pivot nuts and bolts	44
Shock absorber spindle to top bracket	13
Top bracket to body	10
Shock absorber lower fitting	12
Steering:	
Track rod end to steering arm	32
Track rod locknut	30
Steering rack to crossmember	18
Steering wheel to column	32
Intermediate shaft to column	15
Flexible coupling to intermediate shaft	15
Flexible coupling to pinion flange	15
Pinion flange pinch bolt	10 to 15
Yoke coverbolts	6 to 8
Pinion coverplate bolts, Burman	6 to 8
Cam gears	12 to 15
Brakes:	
Disc to hub	33
Caliper to stub axle carrier	60
Backplate to axle casing	18
Bleed screws	9
Hydraulic pipes	8

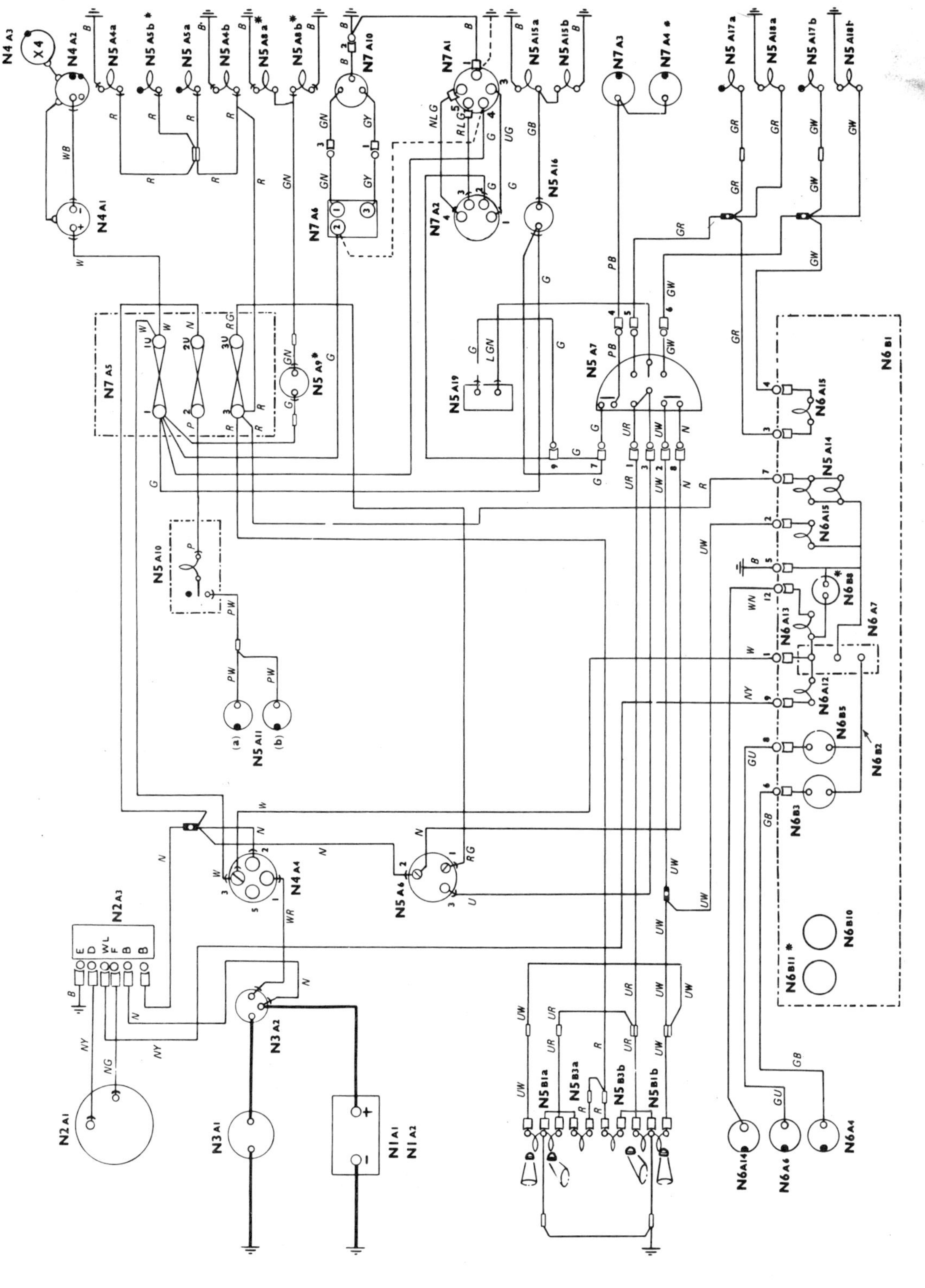

FIG 14:1 Avenger De Luxe, Avenger Super, Sunbeam 1250/1500, Sunbeam 1250/1500 De Luxe

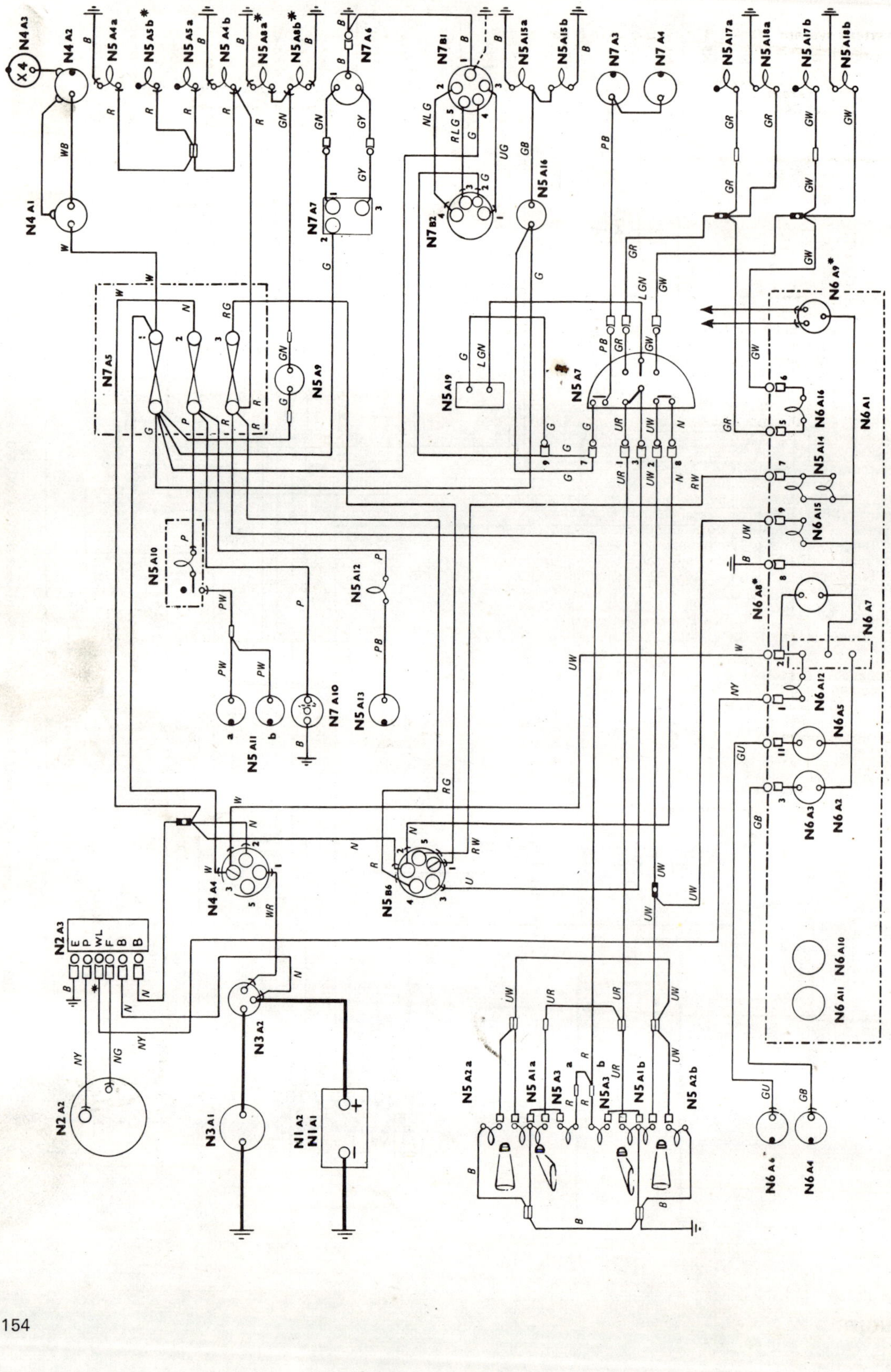

FIG 14:2 Avenger Grand Luxe, Sunbeam 1500 Super

Key to Figs 14:1 and 14:2

N1 Battery system N1A1 Battery, D7 N1A2 Battery, D9

N2 Charging system N2A1 Generator, C40-I N2A2 Generator, C40-L N2A3 Regulator

N3 Starting system N3A1 Starter motor N3A2 Starter solenoid

N4 Ignition system N4A1 Ignition coil N4A2 Distributor N4A3 Sparking plug N4A4 Ignition switch

N5 Lighting system N5A1 Headlamp, circular outer N5B1 Headlamp, rectangular twin N5A2 Headlamp, circular inner N5A3 Sidelamp N5B3 Sidelamp N5A4 Tail lamp N5A5 Number plate lamp N5A6 Light switch N5B6 Light switch with dimmer N5A7 Steering column switch N5A8 Reversing lamp N5A9 Reversing lamp switch N5A10 Interior lamp N5A11 Door jamb switch N5A12 Glove box lamp N5A13 Glove box lamp switch N5A14 Panel lamp N5A15 Stop lamp N5A16 Stop lamp switch N5A17 Direction indicator, front N5A18 Direction indicator, rear N5A19 Flasher unit

N6 Instrument system N6A1 Binnacle, circular instruments N6B1 Binnacle, rectangular instruments N6A2 Printed circuit for N6A1 N6B2 Printed circuit for N6B1 N6A3 Fuel gauge, circular N6B3 Fuel gauge, rectangular N6A4 Fuel gauge transmitter N6A5 Temperature gauge, circular N6B5 Temperature gauge, rectangular N6A6 Temperature sensing bulb N6A7 Voltage stabilizer N6A8 Voltmeter N6A9 Tachometer N6A10 Speedometer, circular N6B10 Speedometer, rectangular N6A11 Oil gauge, circular N6B11 Oil gauge, rectangular N6A12 Battery charging indicator N6A13 Low oil pressure warning N6A14 Transducer for N6A13 N6A15 Main beam indicator

N7 Accessory system N7A1 Screenwiper, 1-speed N7B1 Screenwiper, 2-speed N7A2 Screenwiper switch for N7A1 N7B2 Screenwiper switch for N7B2 N7A3 Horn, high tone N7A4 Horn, low tone N7A5 Fusebox N7A6 Heater blower N7A7 Switch for N7A6 N7A10 Cigar lighter

Colour code **R** Red **Y** Yellow **G** Green **U** Blue **N** Brown **P** Purple **W** White **B** Black

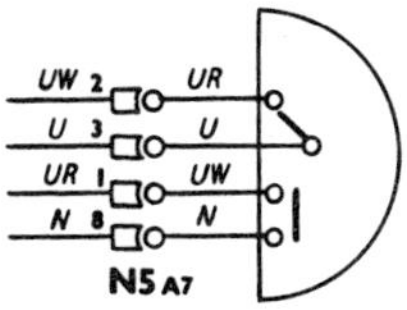

Connections to N5A7

Key to symbols

Lucar connector

Snap connector

Plug and socket

Earth through cable

Earth through unit

In-line connector

When fitted

Alternative wiring for L.H.D. vehicles

Main beam

Dipped beam

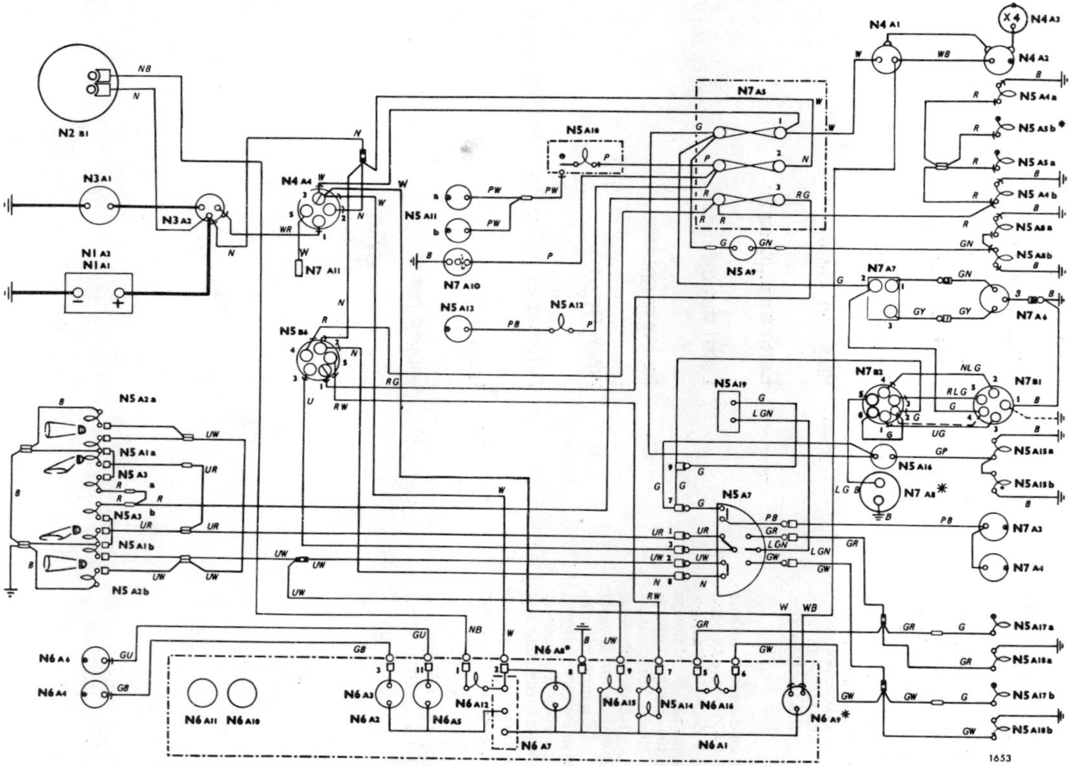

FIG 14:3 Wiring diagram for for Avenger/Sunbeam GT and Avenger Grand Luxe

Key to Fig 14:3 **N1/N1A1/N1A2** **Battery** **N2** **Charging system** **N2B1** Alternator **N3** **Starting system** **N3A1** Starting motor (intertia engaged) **N3A2** Starter solenoid **N4** **Ignition system** **N4A1** Coil **N4A2** Distributor **N4A3** Sparking plug **N4A4** Ignition switch **N5** **Lighting system** **N5A1** Headlamp (circular outer) **N5A2** Headlamp (circular inner) **N5A3** Sidelamp **N5A4** Tail lamp **N5A5** Number plate lamp **N5B6** Light switch **N5A7** Column switch **N5A8** Reverse lamp **N5A9** Reverse lamp switch **N5A10** Interior light and switch **N5A11** Courtesy light switch **N5A12** Glove box light **N5A13** Glove box light switch **N5A14** Panel light **N5A15** Stop lamp **N5A16** Stop lamp switch **N5A17** Direction indicator (front) **N5A18** Direction indicator (rear) **N5A19** Flasher unit (a) Lefthand (b) Righthand **N6** **Instrumentation** **N6A1** Binnacle **N6A2** Printed circuit **N6A3** Fuel gauge **N6A4** Fuel gauge tank unit **N6A5** Temperature gauge **N6A6** Temperature gauge bulb unit **N6A7** Voltage stabilizer **N6A8** Voltmeter **N6A9** Tachometer **N6A10** Speedometer **N6A11** Oil gauge **N6A12** No-charge indicator **N6A15** Main beam warning light **N6A16** Direction indicator warning light **N7** **Ancillaries** **N7A3** Horn **N7A4** Horn **N7A5** Fuse unit **N7A6** Heater blower motor **N7A7** Blower motor switch **N7A8** Screen washer pump motor **N7A10** Cigarette lighter **N7A11** Radio pickup **N7B1** Screen wiper **N7B2** Screenwiper/washer switch

Key to Cable Colour Code **R** Red **Y** Yellow **G** Green **U** Blue **N** Brown **P** Purple **W** White **B** Black

Lucar connector* Snap connector* Plug and socket* Earth through cable* Earth through unit* In-line connector* Lucar connector* When fitted* Snap connector* Alternative wiring for Lefthand Plug and drive vehicles* Main beam* Dipped beam* Connections for flash on dip beam*

*See Key to **FIGS 14:1** and **14:2** for symbols

Inches	Decimals	Milli-metres	Inches to Millimetres Inches	mm	Millimetres to Inches mm	Inches
1/64	.015625	.3969	.001	.0254	.01	.00039
1/32	.03125	.7937	.002	.0508	.02	.00079
3/64	.046875	1.1906	.003	.0762	.03	.00118
1/16	.0625	1.5875	.004	.1016	.04	.00157
5/64	.078125	1.9844	.005	.1270	.05	.00197
3/32	.09375	2.3812	.006	.1524	.06	.00236
7/64	.109375	2.7781	.007	.1778	.07	.00276
1/8	.125	3.1750	.008	.2032	.08	.00315
9/64	.140625	3.5719	.009	.2286	.09	.00354
5/32	.15625	3.9687	.01	.254	.1	.00394
11/64	.171875	4.3656	.02	.508	.2	.00787
3/16	.1875	4.7625	.03	.762	.3	.01181
13/64	.203125	5.1594	.04	1.016	.4	.01575
7/32	.21875	5.5562	.05	1.270	.5	.01969
15/64	.234375	5.9531	.06	1.524	.6	.02362
1/4	.25	6.3500	.07	1.778	.7	.02756
17/64	.265625	6.7469	.08	2.032	.8	.03150
9/32	.28125	7.1437	.09	2.286	.9	.03543
19/64	.296875	7.5406	.1	2.54	1	.03937
5/16	.3125	7.9375	.2	5.08	2	.07874
21/64	.328125	8.3344	.3	7.62	3	.11811
11/32	.34375	8.7312	.4	10.16	4	.15748
23/64	.359375	9.1281	.5	12.70	5	.19685
3/8	.375	9.5250	.6	15.24	6	.23622
25/64	.390625	9.9219	.7	17.78	7	.27559
13/32	.40625	10.3187	.8	20.32	8	.31496
27/64	.421875	10.7156	.9	22.86	9	.35433
7/16	.4375	11.1125	1	25.4	10	.39370
29/64	.453125	11.5094	2	50.8	11	.43307
15/32	.46875	11.9062	3	76.2	12	.47244
31/64	.484375	12.3031	4	101.6	13	.51181
1/2	.5	12.7000	5	127.0	14	.55118
33/64	.515625	13.0969	6	152.4	15	.59055
17/32	.53125	13.4937	7	177.8	16	.62992
35/64	.546875	13.8906	8	203.2	17	.66929
9/16	.5625	14.2875	9	228.6	18	.70866
37/64	.578125	14.6844	10	254.0	19	.74803
19/32	.59375	15.0812	11	279.4	20	.78740
39/64	.609375	15.4781	12	304.8	21	.82677
5/8	.625	15.8750	13	330.2	22	.86614
41/64	.640625	16.2719	14	355.6	23	.90551
21/32	.65625	16.6687	15	381.0	24	.94488
43/64	.671875	17.0656	16	406.4	25	.98425
11/16	.6875	17.4625	17	431.8	26	1.02362
45/64	.703125	17.8594	18	457.2	27	1.06299
23/32	.71875	18.2562	19	482.6	28	1.10236
47/64	.734375	18.6531	20	508.0	29	1.14173
3/4	.75	19.0500	21	533.4	30	1.18110
49/64	.765625	19.4469	22	558.8	31	1.22047
25/32	.78125	19.8437	23	584.2	32	1.25984
51/64	.796875	20.2406	24	609.6	33	1.29921
13/16	.8125	20.6375	25	635.0	34	1.33858
53/64	.828125	21.0344	26	660.4	35	1.37795
27/32	.84375	21.4312	27	685.8	36	1.41732
55/64	.859375	21.8281	28	711.2	37	1.4567
7/8	.875	22.2250	29	736.6	38	1.4961
57/64	.890625	22.6219	30	762.0	39	1.5354
29/32	.90625	23.0187	31	787.4	40	1.5748
59/64	.921875	23.4156	32	812.8	41	1.6142
15/16	.9375	23.8125	33	838.2	42	1.6535
61/64	.953125	24.2094	34	863.6	43	1.6929
31/32	.96875	24.6062	35	889.0	44	1.7323
63/64	.984375	25.0031	36	914.4	45	1.7717

UNITS	Pints to Litres	Gallons to Litres	Litres to Pints	Litres to Gallons	Miles to Kilometres	Kilometres to Miles	Lbs. per sq. In. to Kg. per sq. Cm.	Kg. per sq. Cm. to Lbs. per sq. In.
1	.57	4.55	1.76	.22	1.61	.62	.07	14.22
2	1.14	9.09	3.52	.44	3.22	1.24	.14	28.50
3	1.70	13.64	5.28	.66	4.83	1.86	.21	42.67
4	2.27	18.18	7.04	.88	6.44	2.49	.28	56.89
5	2.84	22.73	8.80	1.10	8.05	3.11	.35	71.12
6	3.41	27.28	10.56	1.32	9.66	3.73	.42	85.34
7	3.98	31.82	12.32	1.54	11.27	4.35	.49	99.56
8	4.55	36.37	14.08	1.76	12.88	4.97	.56	113.79
9		40.91	15.84	1.98	14.48	5.59	.63	128.00
10		45.46	17.60	2.20	16.09	6.21	.70	142.23
20				4.40	32.19	12.43	1.41	284.47
30				6.60	48.28	18.64	2.11	426.70
40				8.80	64.37	24.85		
50					80.47	31.07		
60					96.56	37.28		
70					112.65	43.50		
80					128.75	49.71		
90					144.84	55.92		
100					160.93	62.14		

UNITS	Lb ft to kgm	Kgm to lb ft	UNITS	Lb ft to kgm	Kgm to lb ft
1	.138	7.233	7	.967	50.631
2	.276	14.466	8	1.106	57.864
3	.414	21.699	9	1.244	65.097
4	.553	28.932	10	1.382	72.330
5	.691	36.165	20	2.765	144.660
6	.829	43.398	30	4.147	216.990

NOTES

HINTS ON MAINTENANCE AND OVERHAUL

There are few things more rewarding than the restoration of a vehicle's original peak of efficiency and smooth performance.

The following notes are intended to help the owner to reach that state of perfection. Providing that he possesses the basic manual skills he should have no difficulty in performing most of the operations detailed in this manual. It must be stressed, however, that where recommended in the manual, highly-skilled operations ought to be entrusted to experts, who have the necessary equipment, to carry out the work satisfactorily.

Quality of workmanship:

The hazardous driving conditions on the roads to-day demand that vehicles should be as nearly perfect, mechanically, as possible. It is therefore most important that amateur work be carried out with care, bearing in mind the often inadequate working conditions, and also the inferior tools which may have to be used. It is easy to counsel perfection in all things, and we recognize that it may be setting an impossibly high standard. We do, however, suggest that every care should be taken to ensure that a vehicle is as safe to take on the road as it is humanly possible to make it.

Safe working conditions:

Even though a vehicle may be stationary, it is still potentially dangerous if certain sensible precautions are not taken when working on it while it is supported on jacks or blocks. It is indeed preferable not to use jacks alone, but to supplement them with carefully placed blocks, so that there will be plenty of support if the car rolls off the jacks during a strenuous manoeuvre. Axle stands are an excellent way of providing a rigid base which is not readily disturbed. Piles of bricks are a dangerous substitute. Be careful not to get under heavy loads on lifting tackle, the load could fall. It is preferable not to work alone when lifting an engine, or when working underneath a vehicle which is supported well off the ground. To be trapped, particularly under the vehicle, may have unpleasant results if help is not quickly forthcoming. Make some provision, however humble, to deal with fires. Always disconnect a battery if there is a likelihood of electrical shorts. These may start a fire if there is leaking fuel about. This applies particularly to leads which can carry a heavy current, like those in the starter circuit. While on the subject of electricity, we must also stress the danger of using equipment which is run off the mains and which has no earth or has faulty wiring or connections. So many workshops have damp floors, and electrical shocks are of such a nature that it is sometimes impossible to let go of a live lead or piece of equipment due to the muscular spasms which take place.

Work demanding special care:

This involves the servicing of braking, steering and suspension systems. On the road, failure of the braking system may be disastrous. Make quite sure that there can be no possibility of failure through the bursting of rusty brake pipes or rotten hoses, nor to a sudden loss of pressure due to defective seals or valves.

Problems:

The chief problems which may face an operator are:

1 External dirt.
2 Difficulty in undoing tight fixings
3 Dismantling unfamiliar mechanisms.
4 Deciding in what respect parts are defective.
5 Confusion about the correct order for reassembly.
6 Adjusting running clearances.
7 Road testing.
8 Final tuning.

Practical suggestion to solve the problems:

1 Preliminary cleaning of large parts—engines, transmissions, steering, suspensions, etc.,—should be carried out before removal from the car. Where road dirt and mud alone are present, wash clean with a high-pressure water jet, brushing to remove stubborn adhesions, and allow to drain and dry. Where oil or grease is also present, wash down with a proprietary compound (Gunk, Teepol etc.,) applying with a stiff brush—an old paint brush is suitable—into all crevices. Cover the distributor and ignition coils with a polythene bag and then apply a strong water jet to clear the loosened deposits. Allow to drain and dry. The assemblies will then be sufficiently clean to remove and transfer to the bench for the next stage.

On the bench, further cleaning can be carried out, first wiping the parts as free as possible from grease with old newspaper. Avoid using rag or cotton waste which can leave clogging fibres behind. Any remaining grease can be removed with a brush dipped in paraffin. If necessary, traces of paraffin can be removed by carbon tetrachloride. Avoid using paraffin or petrol in large quantities for cleaning in enclosed areas, such as garages, on account of the high fire risk.

When all exteriors have been cleaned, and not before, dismantling can be commenced. This ensures that dirt will not enter into interiors and orifices revealed by dismantling. In the next phases, where components have to be cleaned, use carbon tetrachloride in preference to petrol and keep the containers covered except when in use. After the components have been cleaned, plug small holes with tapered hard wood plugs cut to size and blank off larger orifices with grease-proof paper and masking tape. Do not use soft wood plugs or matchsticks as they may break.

2 It is not advisable to hammer on the end of a screw thread, but if it must be done, first screw on a nut to protect the thread, and use a lead hammer. This applies particularly to the removal of tapered cotters. Nuts and bolts seem to 'grow' together, especially in exhaust systems. If penetrating oil does not work, try the judicious application of heat, but be careful of starting a fire. Asbestos sheet or cloth is useful to isolate heat.

Tight bushes or pieces of tail-pipe rusted into a silencer can be removed by splitting them with an open-ended hacksaw. Tight screws can sometimes be started by a tap from a hammer on the end of a suitable screwdriver. Many tight fittings will yield to the judicious use of a hammer, but it must be a soft-faced hammer if damage is to be avoided, use a heavy block on the opposite side to absorb shock. Any parts of the steering system which have been damaged should be renewed, as attempts to repair them may lead to cracking and subsequent failure, and steering ball joints should be disconnected using a recommended tool to prevent damage.

3 If often happens that an owner is baffled when trying to dismantle an unfamiliar piece of equipment. So many modern devices are pressed together or assembled by spinning-over flanges, that they must be sawn apart. The intention is that the whole assembly must be renewed. However, parts which appear to be in one piece to the naked eye, may reveal close-fitting joint lines when inspected with a magnifying glass, and, this may provide the necessary clue to dismantling. Left-handed screw threads are used where rotational forces would tend to unscrew a right handed screw thread.

Be very careful when dismantling mechanisms which may come apart suddenly. Work in an enclosed space where the parts will be contained, and drape a piece of cloth over the device if springs are likely to fly in all directions. Mark everything which might be reassembled in the wrong position, scratched symbols may be used on unstressed parts, or a sequence of tiny dots from a centre punch can be useful. Stressed parts should never be scratched or centre-popped as this may lead to cracking under working conditions. Store parts which look alike in the correct order for reassembly. Never rely upon memory to assist in the assembly of complicated mechanisms, especially when they will be dismantled for a long time, but make notes, and drawings to supplement the diagrams in the manual, and put labels on detached wires. Rust stains may indicate unlubricated wear. This can sometimes be seen round the outside edge of a bearing cup in a universal joint. Look for bright rubbing marks on parts which normally should not make heavy contact. These might prove that something is bent or running out of truth. For example, there might be bright marks on one side of a piston, at the top near the ring grooves, and others at the bottom of the skirt on the other side. This could well be the clue to a bent connecting rod. Suspected cracks can be proved by heating the component in a light oil to approximately 100°C, removing, drying off, and dusting with french chalk, if a crack is present the oil retained in the crack will stain the french chalk.

4 In determining wear, and the degree, against the permissible limits set in the manual, accurate measurement can only be achieved by the use of a micrometer. In many cases, the wear is given to the fourth place of decimals; that is in ten-thousandths of an inch. This can be read by the vernier scale on the barrel of a good micrometer. Bore diameters are more difficult to determine. If, however, the matching shaft is accurately measured, the degree of play in the bore can be felt as a guide to its suitability. In other cases, the shank of a twist drill of known diameter is a handy check.

Many methods have been devised for determining the clearance between bearing surfaces. To-day the best and simplest is by the use of Plastigage, obtainable from most garages. A thin plastic thread is laid between the two surfaces and the bearing is tightened, flattening the thread. On removal, the width of the thread is compared with a scale supplied with the thread and the clearance is read off directly. Sometimes joint faces leak persistently, even after gasket renewal. The fault will then be traceable to distortion, dirt or burrs. Studs which are screwed into soft metal frequently raise burrs at the point of entry. A quick cure for this is to chamfer the edge of the hole in the part which fits over the stud.

5 **Always check a replacement part with the original one before it is fitted.**

If parts are not marked, and the order for reassembly is not known, a little detective work will help. Look for marks which are due to wear to see if they can be mated. Joint faces may not be identical due to manufacturing errors, and parts which overlap may be stained, giving a clue to the correct position. Most fixings leave identifying marks especially if they were painted over on assembly. It is then easier to decide whether a nut, for instance, has a plain, a spring, or a shakeproof washer under it. All running surfaces become 'bedded' together after long spells of work and tiny imperfections on one part will be found to have left corresponding marks on the other. This is particularly true of shafts and bearings and even a score on a cylinder wall will show on the piston.

6 Checking end float or rocker clearances by feeler gauge may not always give accurate results because of wear. For instance, the rocker tip which bears on a valve stem may be deeply pitted, in which case the feeler will simply be bridging a depression. Thrust washers may also wear depressions in opposing faces to make accurate measurement difficult. End float is then easier to check by using a dial gauge. It is common practice to adjust end play in bearing assemblies, like front hubs with taper rollers, by doing up the axle nut until the hub becomes stiff to turn and then backing it off a little. Do not use this method with ballbearing hubs as the assembly is often preloaded by tightening the axle nut to its fullest extent. If the splitpin hole will not line up, file the base of the nut a little.

Steering assemblies often wear in the straight-ahead position. If any part is adjusted, make sure that it remains free when moved from lock to lock. Do not be surprised if an assembly like a steering gearbox, which is known to be carefully adjusted outside the car, becomes stiff when it is bolted in place. This will be due to distortion of the case by the pull of the mounting bolts, particularly if the mounting points are not all touching together. This problem may be met in other equipment and is cured by careful attention to the alignment of mounting points.

When a spanner is stamped with a size and A/F it means that the dimension is the width between the jaws and has no connection with ANF, which is the designation for the American National Fine thread. Coarse threads like Whitworth are rarely used on cars to-day except for studs which screw into soft aluminium or cast iron. For this reason it might be found that the top end of a cylinder head stud has a fine thread and the lower end a coarse thread to screw into the cylinder block. If the car has mainly UNF threads then it is likely that any coarse threads will be UNC, which are not the same as Whitworth. Small sizes have the same number of threads in Whitworth and UNC, but in the $\frac{1}{2}$ inch size for example, there are twelve threads to the inch in the former and thirteen in the latter.

7 After a major overhaul, particularly if a great deal of work has been done on the braking, steering and suspension systems, it is advisable to approach the problem of testing with care. If the braking system has been overhauled, apply heavy pressure to the brake pedal and get a second operator to check every possible source of leakage. The brakes may work extremely well, but a leak could cause complete failure after a few miles.

Do not fit the hub caps until every wheel nut has been checked for tightness, and make sure the tyre pressures are correct. Check the levels of coolant, lubricants and hydraulic fluids. Being satisfied that all is well, take the car on the road and test the brakes at once. Check the steering and the action of the handbrake. Do all this at moderate speeds on quiet roads, and make sure there is no other vehicle behind you when you try a rapid stop.

Finally, remember that many parts settle down after a time, so check for tightness of all fixings after the car has been on the road for a hundred miles or so.

8 It is useless to tune an engine which has not reached its normal running temperature. In the same way, the tune of an engine which is stiff after a rebore will be different when the engine is again running free. Remember too, that rocker clearances on pushrod operated valve gear will change when the cylinder head nuts are tightened after an initial period of running with a new head gasket.

Trouble may not always be due to what seems the obvious cause. Ignition, carburation and mechanical condition are interdependent and spitting back through the carburetter, which might be attributed to a weak mixture, can be caused by a sticking inlet valve.

For one final hint on tuning, never adjust more than one thing at a time or it will be impossible to tell which adjustment produced the desired result.

NOTES

GLOSSARY OF TERMS

Allen key Cranked wrench of hexagonal section for use with socket head screws.

Alternator Electrical generator producing alternating current. Rectified to direct current for battery charging.

Ambient temperature Surrounding atmospheric temperature.

Annulus Used in engineering to indicate the outer ring gear of an epicyclic gear train.

Armature The shaft carrying the windings, which rotates in the magnetic field of a generator or starter motor. That part of a solenoid or relay which is activated by the magnetic field.

Axial In line with, or pertaining to, an axis.

Backlash Play in meshing gears.

Balance lever A bar where force applied at the centre is equally divided between connections at the ends.

Banjo axle Axle casing with large diameter housing for the crownwheel and differential.

Bendix pinion A self-engaging and self-disengaging drive on a starter motor shaft.

Bevel pinion A conical shaped gearwheel, designed to mesh with a similar gear with an axis usually at 90 deg. to its own.

bhp Brake horse power, measured on a dynamometer.

bmep Brake mean effective pressure. Average pressure on a piston during the working stroke.

Brake cylinder Cylinder with hydraulically operated piston(s) acting on brake shoes or pad(s).

Brake regulator Control valve fitted in hydraulic braking system which limits brake pressure to rear brakes during heavy braking to prevent rear wheel locking.

Camber Angle at which a wheel is tilted from the vertical.

Capacitor Modern term for an electrical condenser. Part of distributor assembly, connected across contact breaker points, acts as an interference suppressor.

Castellated Top face of a nut, slotted across the flats, to take a locking splitpin.

Castor Angle at which the kingpin or swivel pin is tilted when viewed from the side.

cc Cubic centimetres. Engine capacity is arrived at by multiplying the area of the bore in sq cm by the stroke in cm by the number of cylinders.

Clevis U-shaped forked connector used with a clevis pin, usually at handbrake connections.

Collet A type of collar, usually split and located in a groove in a shaft, and held in place by a retainer. The arrangement used to retain the spring(s) on a valve stem in most cases.

Commutator Rotating segmented current distributor between armature windings and brushes in generator or motor.

Compression ratio The ratio, or quantitative relation, of the total volume (piston at bottom of stroke) to the unswept volume (piston at top of stroke) in an engine cylinder.

Condenser See capacitor.

Core plug Plug for blanking off a manufacturing hole in a casting.

Crownwheel Large bevel gear in rear axle, driven by a bevel pinion attached to the propeller shaft. Sometimes called a 'ring gear'.

'C'-spanner Like a 'C' with a handle. For use on screwed collars without flats, but with slots or holes.

Damper Modern term for shock-absorber, used in vehicle suspension systems to damp out spring oscillations.

Depression The lowering of atmospheric pressure as in the inlet manifold and carburetter.

Dowel Close tolerance pin, peg, tube, or bolt, which accurately locates mating parts.

Drag link Rod connecting steering box drop arm (pitman arm) to nearest front wheel steering arm in certain types of steering systems.

Dry liner Thinwall tube pressed into cylinder bore

Dry sump Lubrication system where all oil is scavenged from the sump, and returned to a separate tank.

Dynamo See Generator.

Electrode Terminal, part of an electrical component, such as the points or 'Electrodes' of a sparking plug.

Electrolyte In lead-acid car batteries a solution of sulphuric acid and distilled water.

End float The axial movement between associated parts, end play.

EP Extreme pressure. In lubricants, special grades for heavily loaded bearing surfaces, such as gear teeth in a gearbox, or crownwheel and pinion in a rear axle.

Fade Of brakes. Reduced efficiency due to overheating.

Field coils Windings on the polepieces of motors and generators.

Fillets Narrow finishing strips usually applied to interior bodywork.

First motion shaft Input shaft from clutch to gearbox.

Fullflow filter Filters in which all the oil is pumped to the engine. If the element becomes clogged, a bypass valve operates to pass unfiltered oil to the engine.

FWD Front wheel drive.

Gear pump Two meshing gears in a close fitting casing. Oil is carried from the inlet round the outside of both gears in the spaces between the gear teeth and casing to the outlet, the meshing gear teeth prevent oil passing back to the inlet, and the oil is forced through the outlet port.

Generator Modern term for 'Dynamo'. When rotated produces electrical current.

Grommet A ring of protective or sealing material. Can be used to protect pipes or leads passing through bulkheads.

Grubscrew Fully threaded headless screw with screwdriver slot. Used for locking, or alignment purposes.

Gudgeon pin Shaft which connects a piston to its connecting rod. Sometimes called 'wrist pin', or 'piston pin'.

Halfshaft One of a pair transmitting drive from the differential.

Helical In spiral form. The teeth of helical gears are cut at a spiral angle to the side faces of the gearwheel.

Hot spot Hot area that assists vapourisation of fuel on its way to cylinders. Often provided by close contact between inlet and exhaust manifolds.

HT High Tension. Applied to electrical current produced by the ignition coil for the sparking plugs.

Hydrometer A device for checking specific gravity of liquids. Used to check specific gravity of electrolyte.

Hypoid bevel gears A form of bevel gear used in the rear axle drive gears. The bevel pinion meshes below the centre line of the crownwheel, giving a lower propeller shaft line.

Idler A device for passing on movement. A free running gear between driving and driven gears. A lever transmitting track rod movement to a side rod in steering gear.

Impeller A centrifugal pumping element. Used in water pumps to stimulate flow.

Journals Those parts of a shaft that are in contact with the bearings.

Kingpin The main vertical pin which carries the front wheel spindle, and permits steering movement. May be called 'steering pin' or 'swivel pin'.

Layshaft The shaft which carries the laygear in the gearbox. The laygear is driven by the first motion shaft and drives the third motion shaft according to the gear selected. Sometimes called the 'countershaft' or 'second motion shaft.'

lb ft A measure of twist or torque. A pull of 10 lb at a radius of 1 ft is a torque of 10 lb ft.

lb/sq in Pounds per square inch.

Little-end The small, or piston end of a connecting rod. Sometimes called the 'small-end'.

LT Low Tension. The current output from the battery.

Mandrel Accurately manufactured bar or rod used for test or centring purposes.

Manifold A pipe, duct, or chamber, with several branches.

Needle rollers Bearing rollers with a length many times their diameter.

Oil bath Reservoir which lubricates parts by immersion. In air filters, a separate oil supply for wetting a wire mesh element to hold the dust.

Oil wetted In air filters, a wire mesh element lightly oiled to trap and hold airborne dust.

Overlap Period during which inlet and exhaust valves are open together.

Panhard rod Bar connected between fixed point on chassis and another on axle to control sideways movement.

Pawl Pivoted catch which engages in the teeth of a ratchet to permit movement in one direction only.

Peg spanner Tool with pegs, or pins, to engage in holes or slots in the part to be turned.

Pendant pedals Pedals with levers that are pivoted at the top end.

Phillips screwdriver A cross-point screwdriver for use with the cross-slotted heads of Phillips screws.

Pinion A small gear, usually in relation to another gear.

Piston-type damper Shock absorber in which damping is controlled by a piston working in a closed oil-filled cylinder.

Preloading Preset static pressure on ball or roller bearings not due to working loads.

Radial Radiating from a centre, like the spokes of a wheel.

Radius rod Pivoted arm confining movement of a part to an arc of fixed radius.

Ratchet Toothed wheel or rack which can move in one direction only, movement in the other being prevented by a pawl.

Ring gear A gear tooth ring attached to outer periphery of flywheel. Starter pinion engages with it during starting.

Runout Amount by which rotating part is out of true.

Semi-floating axle Outer end of rear axle halfshaft is carried on bearing inside axle casing. Wheel hub is secured to end of shaft.

Servo A hydraulic or pneumatic system for assisting, or, augmenting a physical effort. See 'Vacuum Servo'.

Setscrew One which is threaded for the full length of the shank.

Shackle A coupling link, used in the form of two parallel pins connected by side plates to secure the end of the master suspension spring and absorb the effects of deflection.

Shell bearing Thinwalled steel shell lined with antifriction metal. Usually semi-circular and used in pairs for main and big-end bearings.

Shock absorber See 'Damper'.

Silentbloc Rubber bush bonded to inner and outer metal sleeves.

Socket-head screw Screw with hexagonal socket for an Allen key.

Solenoid A coil of wire creating a magnetic field when electric current passes through it. Used with a soft iron core to operate contacts or a mechanical device.

Spur gear A gear with teeth cut axially across the periphery.

Stub axle Short axle fixed at one end only.

Tachometer An instrument for accurate measurement of rotating speed. Usually indicates in revolutions per minute.

TDC Top Dead Centre. The highest point reached by a piston in a cylinder, with the crank and connecting rod in line.

Thermostat Automatic device for regulating temperature. Used in vehicle coolant systems to open a valve which restricts circulation at low temperature.

Third motion shaft Output shaft of gearbox.

Threequarter floating axle Outer end of rear axle halfshaft flanged and bolted to wheel hub, which runs on bearing mounted on outside of axle casing. Vehicle weight is not carried by the axle shaft.

Thrust bearing or washer Used to reduce friction in rotating parts subject to axial loads.

Torque Turning or twisting effort. See 'lb ft'.

Track rod The bar(s) across the vehicle which connect the steering arms and maintain the front wheels in their correct alignment.

UJ Universal joint. A coupling between shafts which permits angular movement.

UNF Unified National Fine screw thread.

Vacuum servo Device used in brake system, using difference between atmospheric pressure and inlet manifold depression to operate a piston which acts to augment brake pressure as required. See 'Servo'.

Venturi A restriction or 'choke' in a tube, as in a carburetter, used to increase velocity to obtain a reduction in pressure.

Vernier A sliding scale for obtaining fractional readings of the graduations of an adjacent scale.

Welch plug A domed thin metal disc which is partially flattened to lock in a recess. Used to plug core holes in castings.

Wet liner Removable cylinder barrel, sealed against coolant leakage, where the coolant is in direct contact with the outer surface.

Wet sump A reservoir attached to the crankcase to hold the lubricating oil.

NOTES

air filter CA 2631

INDEX